Chamberlain and the Lost Peace

A GREAT MEDIATOR

John Bull: 'I've known many Prime Ministers in my time, Sir, but never one who worked so hard for security in the face of such terrible odds.'

5 October 1938.

Chamberlain
and the Lost Peace

JOHN CHARMLEY

Ivan R. Dee, Publisher
CHICAGO

The paperback edition of this book carries the following ISBN:
1-56663-247-1

CHAMBERLAIN AND THE LOST PEACE. Copyright © 1989
by John Charmley. All rights reserved, including the right to reproduce
this book or portions thereof in any form. For information, address:
Ivan R. Dee, Inc., 1332 North Halsted Street, Chicago 60622. First
American edition 1990. Manufactured in the United States of America
and printed on acid-free paper.

Library of Congress Cataloging-in-Publication Data:
Charmley, John, 1955–
    Chamberlain and the lost peace / John Charmley
      p.   cm.
    Includes bibliographical references (p.).

    1. Chamberlain, Neville, 1869–1940. 2. Great Britain—Politics
and government—1936–1945. 3. Great Britain—Foreign relations—1936–1945. 4. Great Britain—Foreign Relations—Germany.
5. Germany—Foreign relations—Great Britain. 6. World War,
1939–1945—Causes. I. Title.
DA565.C4C48 1990
941.084—dc20   90-32618

CONTENTS

LIST OF ILLUSTRATIONS

All the illustrations are taken from *Punch*, 1937–9.

Maps

ACKNOWLEDGMENTS

The first acknowledgment any historian working in this heavily ploughed field has is to his fellow historians – the length of the bibliography bears witness to the nature of this debt. Alastair Parker of Queen's College, Oxford, first got me interested in this period, and I should like to thank him, and Professor P. M. Kennedy of Yale, for much stimulating conversation – even if neither of them will agree with what follows.

I am grateful to my publisher, John Curtis, who first suggested this topic to me and who has been its good friend and mentor ever since. My agent, Felicity Bryan, has been her normal fund of cheerful good humour and aid. Professor J. R. Jones has, once again, taken time off from his labours to comment on the result of mine – and the final version of the book is much the better for his comments; I am deeply grateful for his efforts to make it even better.

I would also like to thank Dr B. Z. Benedikz of Birmingham University for much stimulating and informative conversation about the Chamberlains, and for permission to cite extracts from the Chamberlain papers. I would like to extend thanks for similar permission to the Keeper of the Public Records (Documents in the Public Record Office); to Bill Barnett and Liz Bennett of Churchill College, Cambridge, for access to collections housed there; and to John Harvey, the Rt Hon. Julian Amery and the Rt Hon. Paul Channon for permission to quote extracts from the diaries of their respective fathers.

I must thank the Research Grants Committee of the School of English and American Studies for providing funds to pursue research on this book, and the Study Leave Committee for helping provide conditions in which serious research can still be carried on. I should also like to thank the students of my special subject classes on Churchill for their contribution to sharpening my wits; I owe a particular debt to Mary Palmer, who bore with my views with exemplary patience and forced me to re-examine some of them.

I also owe a debt of gratitude to my former research student, Dr Louise Atherton, who not only helped garner some of the research materials at an early stage of this project, but also discussed the ideas which informed it. In a book of this sort it is, perhaps, particularly necessary for the author to say that the final result is entirely due to his own idiosyncracies.

All married historians are wise to put in a passage of thanks to their wives, and I am grateful to Dorothea for suffering yet another of my excursions into the realms of Cockayne. My sons, Gervase and Gerard, have used the discarded versions of the manuscript to good effect.

John Charmley
Adam & Eve House
Little Hautbois
Norfolk

INTRODUCTION

In December 1918 Arthur Neville Chamberlain entered the House of Commons as MP for the new Birmingham seat of Ladywood. His background in business and local government well-fitted him to participate in building that land 'fit for heroes' which would recompense the people of Britain for the sufferings of the Great War which had just ended, and for eighteen years his career followed this chosen path; that his name is now inextricably linked to the outbreak of the next great conflict was, in part, the result of what others did during the year following his own entry into Parliament.

For, as Chamberlain found his feet in national politics, it fell to his Prime Minister, David Lloyd George, to take part in the peace conference in Paris, which sought to create an international system to ensure that there would be no repetition of the blood-letting of the previous five years. With Germany's navy safe beneath the waves at Scapa Flow and her colonies in Allied hands, the British had already achieved their major objectives, but the same could not be said of the French. The views of the Americans also had to be taken into account. Prolonged and often bitter discussion gave birth to the Versailles Settlement, which consisted of three main parts: Versailles, itself, which settled only the affairs of Germany; St Germain and Trianon, which dealt with those of Central and Eastern Europe; and Sèvres, which applied to the Ottoman Empire.

It was hardly to be expected that any group of men would possess both the omniscience and the omnipotence to create and maintain a peace settlement that would satisfy everyone; the defeated were, naturally, beyond the reach of that emotion, but even the architects of the settlement had mixed feelings about their work. It was beyond the power of man to satisfy all the victors. The French, ever conscious of the narrowness of the margin of victory, as well as of its cost, sought a peace of Carthaginian proportions that would render the enemy impotent; the British, with their war aims already largely met, were less inclined to harshness; the Italians over-valued their services and over-priced their reward accordingly; whilst the American President, Woodrow Wilson, brought both Olympian detachment and liberal prejudice to design the Procrustean bed upon which to reshape the frontiers of Europe: 'open covenants of peace openly arrived at' and the triumph of the principle of nationalism were to be the basis of the new system.

In the West, Versailles shaped an order which the Germans themselves were willing to ratify in 1925, with the signing of the Locarno Treaties. They could not have expected to keep the plunder of the victory of 1871, and Alsace and Lorraine were, accordingly, returned to France. The loss of the Saarland was a blow, but it was given to France for only fifteen years, as some recompense for the destruction which the Germans had wreaked in her north-eastern provinces; a plebiscite at the end of that time would most probably result in its restoration to Germany. The demilitarisation of the Rhineland was a blow, but as the alternative to the French desire to break up the Reich, it was bearable. If neither Teuton, Frank nor Anglo-Saxon was entirely satisfied, then at least no one was left with a festering grievance.

This was not true of the results of the Treaties of St Germain and Trianon, which sought to re-order relations between the old Teutonic and Magyar master races and their Slav former subjects. Here the peacemakers were confronted by a chaos which would have baffled the diplomatic resources of an omniscient angel. In place of the Habsburg Empire was a scramble of 'successor states', whose propagandists furnished claims to whatever territory arms could grab. The ancient Romanov Empire had fallen into the tumult of a bloody civil war, where the communist Lenin attempted to establish a new Jerusalem on the bones of his enemies. Autocratic order had yielded to frightful anarchy, and out of the mists of debate and war emerged a new order, sanctioned, but not wholly created, at Trianon.

In order that Poland should once again join the concert of nations, it was necessary to dispossess the Powers which had thrice partitioned her: the Austrians were in no position to complain; the Russians fought a bitter war until 1923 over the final disposition of frontiers; and the Germans, in the aftermath of defeat, suffered the humiliation of losing the unitary structure of their state to the requirements of the reborn nation. The areas of Posen and western Pomerania were allotted to the Poles, thus dividing East Prussia from the rest of Germany, whilst Danzig, an indisputably German city, was made a free port, to the benefit of Polish commerce. When Gustav Stresemann ratified the western frontiers of Germany in 1925, he did not follow it up with an Eastern Locarno, nor did any of his successors as Foreign Minister in the Weimar Republic.

Had Versailles and Trianon wrought nothing more, they would have done enough to fill the hearts of patriotic Germans with the desire for revenge and restitution, but their sins of omission were, in the eyes of the defeated, almost as great as those of commission. 'National self-determination', the parrot-cry of the American President, was denied in the case of Austria, where the demand

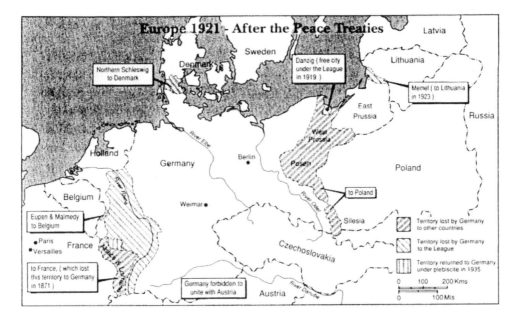

for a plebiscite on the question of the *Anschluss*, or union with Germany, was refused. It would hardly have done to have let Germany emerge from the war larger than she had entered it. Those German-speaking peoples in the mountain regions of Bohemia, the so-called Sudetenland, were united with the polyglot, multi-racial state of Czechoslovakia in order to give it a defensible frontier. From being privileged subjects of the Habsburgs, these German speakers were now a minority; like the other master race of the Habsburg Empire, the Magyars, they adapted badly to the reversal of roles.

The third of the treaties made in Paris, that of Sèvres, was the first to fall. The regime of Kemal Ataturk successfully challenged it by force of arms, securing a new treaty at Lausanne in 1923. It did not take genius to predict that if ever Germany recovered her strength, she too would seek to challenge the work of the conquerors. With the coming to power of Adolf Hitler in 1933, this moment arrived. The next three years saw the Saarland pass under German rule (thus did the Versailles settlement provide Hitler's first triumph), an unsuccessful coup in Austria, which raised the spectre of *Anschluss*, and, more daringly, in 1936 the reoccupation of the Rhineland. The lack of concerted respose from the Versailles Powers revealed what was already apparent, that where the threat of defeat had brought unity, the reality of peace had engendered disunion. The Americans had drawn back into isolation, refusing even to join Wilson's brainchild, the League of Nations. The shortcomings of that organisation had been exposed by the Italian dictator, Benito Mussolini, who successfully defied its strictures in 1935–6 to mount a brutal and successful conquest of Abyssinia.

In this he was merely aping an equally successful act of brigandage in 1931 by the Japanese in Manchuria.

As Hitler proceeded on his way, he made offers of mutual disarmament to the other Powers: was this merely the smile on the face of the tiger? Was Hitler the portent of a new war, or merely a sign that the work of Versailles needed recasting? Chamberlain saw no gains for Britain in another war, and, despite the pious assumptions of British historians, it is by no means clear that the results of the Second World War were commensurate with the sacrifices it entailed. The old balance between the fascist and communist Powers on the continent was tipped decidedly in favour of the latter, whilst the economic and diplomatic foundations of the British Empire received a mortal blow; nor was the lot of the Poles, on whose behalf war was declared, improved. The world was handed over to a Manichean struggle between America and Russia; was this whither a thousand years of British history were tending? The following pages delineate Chamberlain's struggle to avert the inevitable consequences of war.

Prologue

It is given to few men to read their own obituaries, but politicians, when they resign, suffer something close to this experience. For the man whose name featured prominently in the morning papers on 4 October 1940 for this reason, his reaction to what he read was shadowed by the knowledge that his actual death could not be far distant. Neville Chamberlain had already suffered under the surgeon's knife and gained little relief, which was why he had resigned – and why he could gain the bitter foretaste of what the obituarists would write.

The press comments were 'short, cold, for the most part deprecatory' about Chamberlain's part in 'the international politics of the last few years'. Not one of them, he noted in his diary, 'shows the slightest sign of sympathy for the man or even any comprehension that there may be a human tragedy somewhere in the background'; but then he had expected no more.[1] It was a bleak prospect which lay before him: death, and death in the knowledge that where the crowd had once shouted 'Hosanna', they now cried 'crucify him'; the vicissitudes of politics are, indeed, endless.

Winston Churchill, the greatest opponent of Chamberlain's foreign policy, ruled in his stead in Downing Street, and his inheritance seemed, at best, a precarious one, with Europe divided between the Nazis and the communists. All the things that Chamberlain had stood for lay in ruins. Instead of leaving a political legacy which would further enhance the name of Chamberlain in the history books, the ailing former Premier knew that he was leaving a blasted reputation – and that he was the end of a tradition, which was perhaps the bitterest blow of all.

The road of excess leads to the palace of wisdom
WILLIAM BLAKE

The Prime Minister
and the Ambassador

The cold October morning which saw the bitter end of so many hopes was divided by only forty months from May 1937, when at the age of sixty-eight the least of the Chamberlains became Prime Minister, but in mood it was an age away.

Coming as he did from a close-knit and loving family, it was natural that Neville's thoughts at that time should have dwelt upon the strange fate that had brought him to a position which might have been held by his half-brother, Austen, or by his father, Joseph. In this there was something of an excess of filial piety. 'Brummagem Joe', the erstwhile Radical turned Imperialist, had certainly been the founder of a political dynasty and the most dynamic politician of his day, but although Birmingham worshipped him, Westminister distrusted him. Austen, as though to make up for this, 'always played the game and always lost it', and remains the only leader of the Conservative Party never to have become Prime Minister. Now the post had come to Neville: 'without my raising a finger to obtain it, perhaps because there is no-one else and perhaps because I have not made enemies by looking after myself rather than the common cause'.[1]

Born in 1869, the only son of his father's second marriage, Neville was destined to follow the business side of his father's career, just as Austen was to go into politics. He did not enter the House of Commons until 1918, almost twenty-five years after Austen, but if he started late, he gained ground rapidly. A backbencher at the age of fifty, he was in the Cabinet within two years and one of the leading figures in the Conservative hierarchy within five years. By 1929 he was, along with Churchill, one of the obvious successors to Stanley Baldwin; and with Churchill's eclipse after 1930, he became the heir-apparent.[2]

Such a meteoric rise owed something to chance – if the Conservative Party had not split in 1922 Chamberlain, like his leader Baldwin, would not have had the opportunity of displaying his talents in high office so swiftly – but he possessed the ability to capitalise upon what luck threw his way. His formidable capacity for work and his powers as a Minister were shown to great effect during his period as Baldwin's Minister of Health in the 1920s; and as Chancellor of the Exchequer in the National Government after 1931, he was the power behind the increasingly senile Ramsay MacDonald and somnolent Baldwin. Thus it was that his accession to the premiership did, indeed, seem the most natural of events. On 31 May 1937 at a meeting at Caxton Hall, Lord Derby formally moved the motion nominating Chamberlain as leader of the Conservative and Unionist Party, ably seconded by Churchill.[3]

If, as one observer noted, there was a touch of 'bitterness' in Churchill's oration, that was hardly to be wondered at.[4] After all, he had entered the Commons a full eighteen years before his new leader and had been a Cabinet Minister when Chamberlain had been a local businessman. But Churchill's various attempts to overthrow Baldwin after the election defeat of 1929 had failed, and his long campaign to deny India greater self-government had succeeded only in isolating him on the right wing of the party.[5] Now, at the age of sixty-two, and omitted from the new Cabinet as he had been from the old, Churchill seemed to have nothing left before him save literature and the role of elder statesman.

The new Prime Minister, on the other hand, having decided upon the composition of his Cabinet, had more than enough to keep him occupied. All his 'legislating Ministers' were ordered to 'prepare a two-year programme', which, in the autumn, he would 'collate' into a 'provisional Government programme for two years'; after that would probably come a general election.[6] The one potential weak spot in Chamberlain's armour was the fact that the parliamentary majority which supported him had been won by Baldwin, sheltering under the 'National Government' label, in 1935; but two years would give the Prime Minister enough time to achieve a legislative programme which ought to enable him to gain his own majority in 1939. His formidable powers of executive government were in sharp contrast to Baldwin's increasingly evident lack of grip, and within a few weeks of his accession the press, noting that the Government now seemed to know where it was going, ascribed the change to the 'firm grip' of the new Prime Minister.[7]

This was particularly true in the field of foreign policy. Baldwin's reaction to the rise of German power under Hitler's leadership was to preside over a review of Britain's defence capabilities and to look to his Foreign Secretary, the young Anthony Eden, to relieve the diplomatic pressure. Chamberlain, who had played a vital part in that defence review, had no intention of letting things drift on aimlessly. Although it had been Austen who had been Foreign Secretary, Neville was not without views on foreign affairs.

As Chancellor his opinions had carried great weight when the reports of the Defence Requirements Committee had been debated in 1934 and 1935. Chamberlain saw no need for a large army, having imbibed the views of the controversial military historian, Basil Liddell-Hart, that the army of the future would be a small, professional, mechanised affair, and that the 'British way in warfare' demanded spending on an air force and a navy. By 1936 the Chancellor had successfully defeated attempts by the Minister of War, Duff Cooper, to procure financial support for a 'continental-sized' army.[8]

Of necessity, Chamberlain's actions in this area had been known only within a narrow compass, but his major intervention in foreign affairs in 1936 had created a public sensation. Mussolini's invasion of Abyssinia had outraged 'world opinion', but the sanctions imposed upon Italy by the League of Nations had little effect – save to alienate the Italians. In these circumstances Chamberlain concluded that to continue sanctions was 'the very midsummer of madness', and he gave vent to this opinion in a speech on 10 June which shocked 'liberal' sentiment. The Chancellor was unrepentant, feeling that he had given the lead which 'the Party and the country needed'.[9] Although no diplomatist, Chamberlain felt that there were times when such a 'blazing indiscretion' could be useful in foreign policy; this was a lesson which he passed on to the man chosen to be the new British Ambassador in Berlin, Sir Nevile Henderson.[10]

On 1 June, four days after Chamberlain became Prime Minister, Henderson took advantage of the 'licence' which he felt he had been given to make an appeal for better Anglo-German relations, declaring that 'peaceful goodwill and mutual co-operation' would resolve all questions at issue. There was considerable criticism of Henderson in the British press; some even spoke of 'our Nazi Ambassador in Berlin'.[11] Lord Derby, one of the grandees of the Conservative Party, under whom Henderson had served in Paris, wrote to Chamberlain on 10 June defending him by saying that the speech 'was just the one that we wanted'; he deplored what he saw as Eden's repudiation of the message Henderson was purveying. The Prime Minister, who was not displeased with the speech, replied that neither he nor Eden took the view that the Ambassador 'had been snubbed', it was simply that the wording was 'somewhat embarrassing for the Government'; Chamberlain added that Derby could 'rest assured that I have every confidence in Henderson'.[12]

Others, far from sharing that confidence, later used it to cast doubts upon the Prime Minister's judgment and intentions. Sir Lewis Namier called Henderson 'the Beau Brummel of diplomacy', who prided himself on 'his social savoir-faire, and attached the utmost importance to intercourse with the great, but was hardly happy even in his diplomatic contacts. Self-conscious, irritable, and vain, he oscillated between the wish to please and the urge to instruct.'[13] Namier's verdict was concurred in by others: the British journalist, Ian Colvin, described him as 'an emotional man. Tall, lean, fastidiously dressed, he had the outward points of a British diplomat without any inner strength';[14] whilst Eden, widening the indictment, called it 'an international misfortune that we should have been represented in Berlin at this time by a man who, so far from warning the Nazis, was constantly making excuses for them, often in their company'.[15]

As early as July 1937, the Permanent Under-Secretary at the Foreign Office, Sir Robert Vansittart, was moved by an indiscreet letter from the Ambassador to minute that it was 'an act of folly and completely improper for Sir N. Henderson to have written it ... In 35 years' experience I cannot recall such a series of incidents created by an Ambassador.'[16] Within three months of his appointment, Henderson was regarded in some quarters as *plus allemand que les allemands*. That Henderson's views were not those which held dominion within the Foreign Office is plain; the marginalia upon his despatches bear witness to it. But that these views deserve the almost universal and dismissive condemnation which they received is by no means self-evident; nor were they so dismissed elsewhere in Whitehall.

What did for Henderson was the verdict of history, especially when it was written by those who had opposed him at the time. The Second World War and the 'anti-appeasers' combined to damn the Ambassador whose mission failed. The hero of the piece was Vansittart:

> Six foot one, a strongly jawed face with a twinkle of humour in his eye, he seemed alert, comprehending and straightforward in an occupation tending to the devious and the obscure. He was, besides, a versatile man, with a brilliant past, and a great swell even among contemporaries who were used to wealth and fastidious living. He was an eccentric, a poet and a dramatist, and withal a successful senior civil servant.[17]

He was the one strong man who had warned, prophetically, of the 'old Adam' of German aggression: 'a great public servant, whose masters were unequal to the high precepts to which he had earnestly sought their adherence'.[18]

Not everyone was as admiring as Colvin. Eden remembered Vansittart as 'seldom an official giving cool and disinterested advice based on study and experience. He was himself a sincere, almost fanatical crusader, and much more a Secretary of State in mentality than a permanent official.'[19] But this did not serve to lessen the influence of his message, as it partook of the shared but 'unspoken assumptions' which the Foreign Office entertained about Germany. Vansittart's long experience of diplomacy took him back to the days before the Great War and the *'morbus Germanicus'*, which had then infected the Foreign Office, was carried by him into the post-war era, and reinforced by the bitter memories of the conflict and the 'war-guilt' clause in the Treaty of Versailles, by which Germany acknowledged her responsibility for the war.

The publication by the British Government of documents on the origins of the Great War provided, in volume three, a *locus classicus* for the views of the Germanophobes in the form of a memorandum by Eyre Crowe. Crowe had argued in 1907 that Germany represented the latest in a line going back through Napoleon and Louis XIV to Philip II of challenges to the traditional British policy of maintaining the balance of power in Europe.[20] 'Van' was the latter-day successor to this prophet.

Famous as it became, the 'Crowe memorandum' was, in fact, no more than a statement of a case, and it did not go unchallenged; but the Great War, by seeming to vindicate its author, threw into the shade the argument of Lord Sanderson, who had been Lord Salisbury's Permanent Under-Secretary, that Anglo-German rivalry had not been a predominant theme of British diplomacy in the years under review.[21] For 'Van', as for other diplomatists of his generation, the 'German menace' was axiomatic and it was no accident that former diplomats such as Duff Cooper, Harold Nicolson and Paul Emrys Evans were, as politicians, prominent in warning against the rise of Germany. For these men, the system created at Versailles, and a strong France with allies in Eastern Europe, were the essential barriers against the recrudescence of German power.

It was, therefore, only natural that Vansittart should have been less than pleased to find an Ambassador referring disparagingly to the 'out of date theory' that Britain's role was to maintain the balance of power in Europe; and when the peccant diplomat was based in Berlin, this was proof that he was either 'naif' or pro-German.[22] Such fears were easily aroused, especially when, as in a despatch on 5 July, he argued that, 'The aim of German policy is . . . to induce Great Britain to dissociate herself, not from France, but from the French system of alliances in Central and Eastern Europe.'[23] When he compounded this heresy by stating that Germany's ambitions lay to the east, 'where she feels that her future lies by means of the realisation of aspirations which are in her opinion vital to her well-being, legitimate and not in conflict with any direct British interest',[24] he was treated to the Foreign Office equivalent of burning at the stake. At the end of a long series of critical minutes, Vansittart commented: 'It is a curiously naif document and had better be consigned to oblivion, for it hardly enhances its author's reputation for insight.'[25]

Henderson responded to cautionary notes from London with a letter to Sir Orme (Moley) Sargent written on 20 July containing a memorandum dated 10 May which expressed his views.[26] These are of interest not merely because they were held by the Ambassador in Berlin, but because, although they ran counter

THE DILEMMA
10 February 1937.

to the doctrines of Vansittart, they reveal why Chamberlain had 'confidence' in Henderson.

The Ambassador doubted whether the Germans had 'any precise idea as to what they themselves want. German unity, German expansion, a German place in the sun, are vague terms' – and no one could be sure where their pursuit would lead Hitler. Henderson did not argue for a policy of isolation from Europe, which would be impracticable, but warned that Britain should 'never identify herself too closely with any single or group of Powers'. In this plea against the policy which had led to war in 1914, Henderson did not ignore the fact that 'Germany must be regarded as the most formidable menace of all at the present moment', but, 'provided she does not ruthlessly disregard the vital principles of the League of Nations or revert to a policy of naval and overseas rivalry or of a renewed push to the West, or deliberately threaten us by air', he did not see 'why – ruthless and troublesome though she is bound to be – she should perpetually constitute a danger of war for us . . . Germany . . . impinges on no British possession.'

All of this was as little to Vansittart's taste as the arguments of Sanderson had been to Crowe, especially when Henderson went on to argue that, 'British friendship with Germany could and would serve British national policy by restraining both Russian intrigues and ambitions, either in Asia or possibly once more at Constantinople, as well as Italian aspirations in the Mediterranean.'

Drawing upon the valedictory despatch of his predecessor, Sir Eric Phipps, Henderson summarised German aims as: 'The absorption of Austria and other Germanic peoples (e.g. the German fringes of Czechoslovakia)'; expansion 'in the East'; and the 'recovery of Colonies'. None of these, Henderson argued, 'injure purely British national interests': an *Anschluss* 'when – but only when – Austria herself spontaneously desires it'; the recognition in principle of Germany's 'right to own colonies and an eventual arrangement whereby some part of say West Africa is allotted to her'; and an assurance that the British had 'in principle no jealous objection to German economic and even political predominance' in Eastern Europe; these, Henderson argued, might form the basis of an Anglo-German agreement.

Vansittart damned the whole despatch, but the last point in particular made his hackles rise: 'What does that mean – *exactly?*' he minuted crossly. But the Ambassador had made perfectly plain what he thought it meant. Given that Hitler could and would never accept the restrictions of Versailles, there would have to be modifications in the international order and, as Germany was blocked by Locarno 'from any Western adventure . . . have we the right to oppose German *peaceful* expansion and evolution in the East?' He encapsulated perfectly the dilemma facing those who made British policy:

> We have at long last realised ourselves that the League of Nations, collective security and Treaty arrangements constitutes no reliable substitute for a Navy and Air Force capable both of defending Great Britain from invasion or attack and of making her due influence felt in the world. Would it not be equally wise to admit at once, without further delay, that Germany is now too powerful to be persuaded or compelled to enter into an Eastern Pact, that a certain German predominance eastward is inevitable, and that peace in the West must not be sacrificed to a theoretically laudable but practically mistaken idealism in the East – mistaken in the sense that the Treaty of Versailles was fallible and hence an unjust basis on which to build up a permanent settlement of Eastern Europe.

Putting it 'quite bluntly', Henderson declared that Eastern Europe was 'neither definitely settled for all time nor is it a vital British interest'.

Such ideas ran counter to Vansittart's, but they were by no means as heretical as they were made to appear after 1939. In 1925 Sir Austen Chamberlain had written that 'no British Government ever will or ever can risk the bones of a British grenadier' for the defence of the Polish corridor,[27] and in so doing he was enunciating a platitude of British diplomacy. Although British Foreign Secretaries in the nineteenth century had many occasions upon which to complain of the behaviour of the autocratic powers in Eastern Europe, that area had lain outside those in which they were willing to contract obligations which carried a casus belli. Not until March 1939 was this doctrine overturned and then only in peculiar circumstances. Henderson's prescription, or something like it, offered a basis upon which a peaceful revision of Versailles might be made; it might be that Germany did not want that, but to proceed upon this assumption was to make war inevitable – as it was certain that only a successful war could reassert the terms of a settlement made when Germany had been defeated in war.

In his memoirs, written towards the end of his life, under the shadow of the failure of his mission and of the cruel disease that was killing him, Henderson gave an immediate hostage to fortune when he wrote that such an unexpected posting 'could only mean that I had been specially selected by Providence for the definite mission of, as I trust, helping to preserve the peace of the world'.[28] Such sentiments attracted the scorn of historians who wondered at how such an appointment could have been made. But although Chamberlain concurred in many of Henderson's assumptions, it was not the new Prime Minister who had sent him to Berlin; it was Vansittart and Eden, both of whom were to win golden opinions for their opposition to appeasement.

The primary responsibility for the appointment lay with Eden himself, but Vansittart, who thought that 'Sir Nevile has done his stint in South America. He shall have his reward', played his part.[29] Almost at once both men began to regret their choice. At dinner at Windsor on 22 April Eden was 'rather aghast at the nonsense he [Henderson] was talking about what he was going to do in Germany' and asked Vansittart to have a word of warning with the Ambassador before he left for Berlin.[30] Cautionary despatches, such as the warning in early November 1937 that it was 'of the greatest importance' that the Germans should be given 'no encouragement whatever' for believing that the British 'would contemplate any settlement at the expense of the political independence of the nations of Eastern and Central Europe',[31] brought not the swift and easy response of acquiescence, but rather one which Vansittart found 'a little disquieting'.[32]

Henderson's reply, dated 8 November, reiterated his view that some changes were inevitable and that it was, therefore, 'extremely unwise to refuse even to consider at all the possibility of the Germans living in solid blocks outside the Reich gravitating of their own free will and in due course to Germany and demanding under the principle of self-determination their right to join the Reich'. The peacemakers at Versailles had invoked the liberal shibboleth of 'self-determination' to sanctify their work, but had, perforce, to deny Germany its benefits. If a revived Germany now demanded them, then Henderson thought that the 'minimum we shall have to concede so far as Central and

Eastern Europe' was concerned would be the possibility of *Anschluss* and recognition of the claims of the *Sudetendeutsche* of Czechoslovakia to join the Reich.

Such views were 'a very considerable departure from the policy hitherto followed by HMG'. In the eyes of the Foreign Office Britain was committed to Austrian independence and the status quo in Eastern and Central Europe. The main reason for this was that Europe was in 'a tense and politically unstable condition' and (in the British version at least) the only thing keeping it from collapse was 'the closeness of the Anglo-French connexion', the 'published programme of British rearmament' and a 'lingering doubt in the minds of some Government[s] whether, in fact, Great Britain would refrain from armed intervention' if trouble arose.[33] That Hitler could never acquiesce in that status quo, that the 'tension' this created could be dissipated only by war or concession was a point of view foreign to the thinking of those who could see only the 'German menace'; Henderson's espousal of it was taken as evidence not of an acute understanding of the problem, but rather as proof of his inadequacy.

But if Henderson's views found little support in the Foreign Office, the same was not true elsewhere in Whitehall, which was why the diplomats went to the trouble of drawing up a memorandum refuting the ambassadorial heresies. This was sent to the Lord President of the Council, Viscount Halifax, who, much to the dismay of the Foreign Office, was about to depart for Berlin.

In October 1937 Halifax had received an invitation to an exhibition to be held in Berlin by the German Hunting Association.[34] Attracted by the novel idea that foxes might be shot rather than hunted in a more orthodox way, the Lord President decided to take up the offer. The Prime Minister was entirely in favour of the visit and was 'horrified' when he heard that Vansittart had tried to dissuade Halifax, seeing, as he told his sisters, 'another opportunity to be thrown away'. Chamberlain, who saw in Halifax's visit the possibility of making some headway in improving Anglo-German relations, was profoundly irritated with Vansittart's pessimism: 'But really that FO! I am only waiting for my opportunity to stir it up with a long pole.'[35] This did not, however, necessarily mean that he had decided that Eden was to be dispensed with.

The demonology constructed after 1939 saw this affair as the beginning of a series of events through which Chamberlain was to remove Eden from the Foreign Office as the prelude to implementing his own foreign policy; the reality was more prosaic and complicated. The doubts which Eden purported to have expressed about the Halifax visit are more noticeable in his memoirs than they were at the time, when, according to Chamberlain, he seemed 'quite happy'.[36] Eden's objections, if such there were, pertained to the fact of Chamberlain's interference rather than to its occasion.

Robert Anthony Eden had come to the Foreign Office in December 1935 at a younger age (thirty-eight) than any man since 1807; the circumstances in which he had arrived there had made his appointment essential. His predecessor, Sir Samuel Hoare, had been driven from office by the force of outraged public opinion. Arriving at the Foreign Office in October 1935, Sir Samuel, an effective if rather unattractive politician (Lord Birkenhead once said of him that he looked as though he came from a long line of maiden aunts), had won cheap and easy applause at the League of Nations by seeming to imply that Britain intended to do something about the Italian aggression against Abyssinia. The revelation in December that this actually meant coming to an arrangement with the French, in the Hoare-Laval pact, to partition the country in Mussolini's favour caused a public outcry.

In the circumstances, Baldwin decided that it was his patriotic duty to sacrifice his Foreign Secretary in order to save his administration. This gesture, along with an implication that Sir Austen Chamberlain might be appointed in Hoare's place, served to placate parliamentary critics and, having achieved that objective, Baldwin calmed the public storm by actually appointing young Eden; he then settled down to hide behind the reputation which the new Foreign Secretary had built up in the early 1930s as a champion of the League of Nations.[37] It was the sort of manœuvre which made Baldwin's enemies gnash their teeth, but it did land the Government with a Foreign Secretary who was the envy of those colleagues who felt unable to patronise him because of his youth.

The new Foreign Secretary was undoubtedly a 'prima donna'. An immensely ambitious and hard-working man, Eden lived on his nerves even more than most politicians. His 'antennae' were sensitively attuned to the nuances of diplomacy, but he was apt to take the tactical rather than the strategic view. Those who knew him slightly were inclined to think that he had inherited his mother's good looks and his father's notoriously unreliable temper; those who knew him better wondered whether perhaps the looks and the air of effortless superiority might not have derived from George Wyndham whom he closely resembled and whom his mother, so rumour had it, knew rather better than she should have done; but then, as Lord Melbourne once remarked, 'maternity is a matter of fact, paternity is a matter of opinion'.[38]

Whatever the facts about Eden's paternity, one thing which cannot be doubted is the swiftness of his rise up the political ladder. In this there were disadvantages. His elders were apt to think they could do a better job than him, especially those who had held the Foreign Office before him (MacDonald and Sir John Simon before 1937, Hoare and Simon thereafter); whilst his contemporaries were prone to regard his promotion with envy. Eden's failure to cultivate any great parliamentary following gave him a narrow political base from which to operate; given the nature of his inheritance this was unwise of him.

Britain had followed her victory in 1918 by pursuing a diplomatic course that would, it was hoped, make it safe for her to reduce her spending on armaments to a low level. Successive British Governments, acting on the assumption that their diplomacy had succeeded, proceeded to cut defence spending. Particularly active in this sphere was Churchill, Baldwin's Chancellor in the 1920s, who, operating upon the assumption that there would not be a major European war for ten more years, proved to be the last great Gladstonian financier at No. 11 Downing Street as he pared the defence estimates ruthlessly.

However, as the rise of Hitler after 1933 cast doubt on the correctness of the assumption that diplomacy had brought lasting peace, the Government was faced with a series of dilemmas which might be summed up thus: could Britain afford to rearm and, if so, how many foes should she prepare to fight? By the time Britain got round to doing anything about rearmament in 1935, she found herself facing not merely threats from Germany and Japan, but also from Italy. The Abyssinian war had led to an Anglo-Italian estrangement, which the outbreak of the Spanish Civil War did nothing to heal. The structure created at Versailles to contain Germany was breaking down and Britain was not strong enough to repair it alone – British foreign policy amounted to an exercise in making bricks with insufficient straw.

This was young Eden's inheritance. At the time he was apt to complain that Baldwin, having appointed him, assumed that he need trouble himself no further about foreign policy. Far from regarding Chamberlain's advent to the premiership with any sort of dread, Eden looked forward to it, writing later that he and the new Prime Minister had been 'closer to each other than to any other member of the Government'.[39] Chamberlain had told him in March that he 'intended to give him more support at the FO than he had hitherto'. Eden thought that 'Chamberlain had the makings of a really great Prime Minister if only his health held out . . . he has a grip of affairs which Stanley Baldwin never had.'[40]

The question of whether Halifax should visit Germany exposed the differences which existed between the Foreign Office and 10 Downing Street on the German question. Henderson wanted the Lord President to visit Hitler at Berchtesgaden, a prospect which Eden's Private Secretary, Oliver Harvey, likened to another 'Canossa'.[41] There is a surreal quality about the idea of the tall, aristocratic Halifax as a barefoot penitent seeking absolution from Hitler, but it was one which concerned the Foreign Office and which prompted Eden to make Halifax promise that he would 'listen and confine himself to warning comment on Austria and Czechoslovakia'. Chamberlain, however, was equally keen that Halifax should see Hitler, despite the Foreign Office dislike of 'cadging for an invitation',[42] and he made it clear to Eden's Parliamentary Under-Secretary, Lord Cranborne, on 10 November that such an encounter should take place.[43]

The Foreign Office was not disposed to surrender so lightly. In order to ward off any evil effects which might come from Halifax having been exposed to Henderson's memorandum of 10 May, the Foreign Office sent the Lord President an eloquent counter-blast to the heresiarch's views. On 16 November, even though it meant rising prematurely from his sick-bed, Eden made a final attempt to prevent 'Canossa'; it was not a success. Although Chamberlain agreed to 'damp down' the enthusiasm of the press, he 'insisted on the value of Halifax's visit' and, 'at the end of some exchanges which became rather sharp, the Prime Minister adjured me to go home and take an asprin'.[44] Heedless of this good advice, Eden went away and wrote a letter in which he stressed the importance of not over-emphasising the significance of the visit.

The visit went ahead, and it did so because Chamberlain saw in it an opportunity for making contact with the Nazi leader at a high level. What he had seen of the Foreign Office 'mind' worried him; the diplomats seemed unable to 'keep the major objects of foreign policy in mind'.[45] Halifax, on the other hand, was more in tune with his own way of thinking, and Chamberlain was confident that he 'won't spoil the effect of his visit by any ruthlessness when he comes to talk with Hitler. I am quite sure the country thoroughly approves of what I am doing.'[46]

Where the Foreign Office seemed as unwilling to open talks with Hitler as it was to envisage changes in the Versailles settlement, Chamberlain saw the visit as a golden opportunity for 'creating an atmosphere in which it was possible to discuss with Germany the practical questions involved in a Eur[opean] settlement'. It was too early to formulate or discuss any precise plans, but what Chamberlain wanted was 'to convince Hitler of our sincerity and to ascertain what objectives he had in mind'.[47]

Nor was this the naive foolishness which critics later alleged. When Halifax wrote to Chamberlain on 6 November about the 'desirability of our recognising, and perhaps bringing greater sympathy to, [the German] point of view', he was recognising, as did Henderson and Chamberlain, that 'Nationalism and Racialism is a powerful explosion, but I can't feel that it is either unnatural or immoral.'[48] Prophecies of war tend to be self-fulfilling; talking with the Nazis offered a way of avoiding this happening.

Holy Fox and the Gamekeeper

In the art of talking to fanatics, few were more skilled than Edward Lindley Wood, first Baron Irwin of Kirby Underdale and third Viscount Halifax, known to Lord Beaverbrook as 'Holy Fox'. To his admirers he was 'the highest kind of Englishman now in politics', one whose 'life and doctrine were in complete harmony with a very lofty moral principle, but who has no harsh judgement for men who err and go astray'.[1] As Viceroy of India he had incurred Churchill's wrath for his dealings with that 'half-naked fakir', Gandhi, but Irwin could talk to the Indian as mystic to mystic. Born in 1881 the sixth child and fourth son of Charles, second Viscount Halifax, Edward had inherited his father's devotion to the Anglo-Catholic cause in the Anglican Church even as, after the deaths of his brothers, he was to inherit the family title.[2]

If Edward Halifax attracted the malice of men like Beaverbrook, it was because all of life's good things seemed to come to him effortlessly; this was not quite so. Although his intellectual career at Oxford had not appeared distinguished, he had topped it with a prize fellowship at All Souls; and if he seemed to graduate into politics in a spirit of noblesse oblige, he insisted on serving at the front in the Great War despite a withered left arm. Beneath the languid exterior there was Yorkshire granite.

Wood's post-war political career seemed, to the envious, a prime example of 'how much more paying it is to be blameless than to be brilliant'.[3] But from the start he was the exemplar of liberal conservatism. *The Great Opportunity*, which he wrote with a fellow Unionist MP, George Lloyd, at the end of the war, became 'a bible to many of the young men of the immediate post-war era';[4] but it was not until April 1921 that Wood received preferment as Under-Secretary of State for the Colonies. His Minister, Churchill, responded by refusing to see him. It was a mark of Wood's qualities that he marched into Churchill's office and told him that 'he had no more wished to be his Under-Secretary than

Churchill had desired his appointment, but that since he was there he claimed the right to be treated like a gentleman'.[5] After that the two men co-operated well.

Like Chamberlain and Baldwin, Wood's political career had prospered dramatically after the downfall of the Lloyd George coalition in 1922; he shared with them a legacy of mistrust of the 'Welsh Wizard', whom he was inclined to regard as a 'good argument for the doctrine of purgatory; he is not fit for the society of the elect, but not quite bad enough to burn permanently!'[6] Wood was firmly at home with Baldwin's 'honest to the point of simplicity' Conservatism, and, chosen by his leader as Viceroy of India in 1925, he proved to be an enlightened and liberal ruler.

Irwin's co-operation with the Labour Government of 1929–31, in particular his declaration in October 1930 that the eventual object of British rule in India was 'Dominion Status' for the country, brought him bitter hostility on the right wing of the Conservative Party. Beaverbrook, who scornfully called him 'a sort of Jesus in long boots', an 'earnest and honest fellow' who 'brought up with a silver spoon in his mouth . . . has never had to face up to the realities of the world', spoke for many in his misjudgment.[7]

Irwin's personal religious faith was apt to mislead contemporaries who did not share it, even as it has done with historians. High Anglicanism did not exclude realism, and, as he wrote to a friend in March 1938, 'we go badly wrong if we allow our judgement of practical steps to be taken, to be perpetually deflected by our moral reactions against wrong that we can in no circumstances immediately redress'.[8] He recognised in India that the 'demands of the Indian politicians' were not wholly reconcilable with the 'responsibilities' of Empire, and tried to follow a middle path between repression and concession.[9]

If something as prosaic as Baldwinian Conservatism could have a *beau sabreur*, then Halifax (as he became in 1934) was it. Upon his return from India Baldwin had pressed him to take office as Foreign Secretary, an offer which he declined; but in 1932 he agreed to take on his old post of President of the Board of Education, moving on, briefly, to the War Office in 1935 before becoming Lord Privy Seal in Baldwin's third administration in November 1935. By this stage of his career Halifax was the quintessential Conservative grandee:

> Halifax was long and thin . . . the loftiness of the face as a whole could not cause one quite to forget an ever-present, questioning look in the eyes; and beneath a long upper lip the line of the mouth itself was expressive less of wit or irony than of a controlled and philosophical melancholy, innate and instinctive rather than acquired. Yet his was by no means the neglected body of a dreamer. His back and legs were magnificently straight and he looked his best astride a horse . . . [his] clothes were well-cut, well-cared for (it is

tempting to say well-preserved for his black office coat in war-time . . . had a greenish tint in sunlight) and even when they were new they were slightly dated, as for some reason befits an Englishman who is fond of horses. Although his suits were sober he was not above brightening them discreetly with a spotted handkerchief half falling from the pocket.[10]

Yorkshire squire, Colonel of Yeomanry and Conservative worthy, Halifax was a man upon whom political office sat loosely. As Lord Privy Seal he took a special interest in foreign policy, though 'it would scarcely have occurred to him, in or out of office, to claim any special aptitude for foreign affairs'. It was Halifax who had insisted upon Hoare's resignation at the time of the Abyssinian crisis,[11] despite the fact that he could, himself, see much to recommend the Hoare-Laval pact.[12] During the course of 1936 he had been increasingly active in British foreign policy, acting almost as Eden's deputy.

In the diplomatic activity which had followed the Nazi reoccupation of the Rhineland in 1936, it had been Halifax who had declared in March that: 'We want no encirclement of Germany. We want no exclusive alliances. We want to build a partnership in European society in which Germany can freely join with us and play the part of a good European for European peace.'[13] In a further speech on 8 April, Halifax made it clear that the announcement that the British Government stood by its obligations under the Locarno treaties to defend the French and Belgian frontiers did not mean that they had 'disinterested ourselves from all events and issues arising outside what perhaps I may call the Locarno area . . . such an attitude would be quite impossible . . . because peace is indivisible'.[14] At the same time he held out to Hitler the prospect of having Germany's claims to 'equality' recognised in return for his convincing Europe of his sincerity.

With Baldwin's retirement Halifax lost his closest political friend and patron, but Chamberlain, who respected and admired him, made him Lord President of the Council, which allowed him to continue in his role as Eden's alter ego. It also made him the ideal figure to send to Berlin on an exploratory trip. Although conscious that he and Hitler were not 'speaking the same language', Halifax felt that the visit was worthwhile.[15]

Henderson had primed the Lord President with the hope that 'the Prime Minister will go as far as he possibly can':

> I believe that, if we are not too niggardly, Germany will keep her word, at any rate for a foreseeable period. One cannot legislate for more. And particularly so, if we take it for granted that she *will* keep her word. The surest way of getting her to break it is to doubt. That is elementary.[16]

Halifax recognised the 'necessity of this country going as far as we possibly can to secure a general all-round settlement'.[17] Unlike Vansittart he saw that some modification in the Versailles settlement was essential if Germany was to become a satisfied power; he did not rule out the possibility that Germany might not be interested in a peaceful revision of the treaty, but nor did he assume that this was, of necessity, the case.

The Lord President arrived in Berlin on 17 November to be met by Henderson's remark that the 'most important thing' was to 'make it plain that whether we were able to accept it or not, we did appreciate the German point of view – and were honestly out to make friends'.[18] This was followed by luncheon with the German Foreign Minister, Baron Constantin von Neurath, and his family, which he found 'all very cheery and lighthearted'; the same could not be said of his conversation with Hitler at Berchtesgaden on 19 November.

There was, however, a moment at the start of their encounter when a '*bêtise* of classical proportions' seemed on the cards as Halifax almost handed his hat to the Führer, mistaking him for a footman until von Neurath muttered 'Der Führer' into his ear;[19] it would have been a moment to have treasured.

Having established that the nondescript figure facing him was, indeed, the object of his visit, Halifax, through the medium of an interpreter, began his conversation. He told Hitler that he hoped that their meeting 'might be the means of creating better understanding between our two countries – on such understanding it seemed to me that the future not only of our two nations but of civilization might well depend'.[20] It was easy enough for Halifax's biographer to comment that nothing in his upbringing had 'equipped him with the instinct to fathom the true wickedness' of such men,[21] but it is difficult to deny the truth of the Lord President's comment.

The dictator was not very forthcoming about the chances of such an agreement and launched into what Halifax described as a 'subdued tirade' about the difficulties of dealing with democracies. Halifax's response was firm: 'If we were to wait for any advance until Great Britain had ceased to maintain a democratic system, then clearly I had wasted my time coming to Berchtes-gaden.' He told Hitler that his 'disarmament and other offers had failed . . . because . . . other nations did not feel satisfied as to the measure of security that they in fact afforded'.

If Eden was happy with such comments, he was less so with those which Halifax made about 'possible alterations in the European order'.[22] Mentioning Danzig, Austria and Czechoslovakia, Halifax said that Britain did not necess-arily 'stand for the status quo as today, but we were concerned to avoid such treatment of them as would be likely to cause trouble'; but if 'reasonable settlements could be reached with the free assent and goodwill of those

'The time had come,' Herr HITLER said,
  'To talk of many things,
Of might and right and swastikas
  And triangles and rings,
And why the world is boiling hot,
  And whether Peace has wings.'
Lord HALIFAX. 'But not about Colonies.'
Herr HITLER. 'Hush!'

primarily concerned we certainly had no desire to block them'.[23] The conversation, which then moved on to the question of colonial compensation for Germany and the possibility of linking this to a general settlement, reflected the views held in Downing Street rather than in the Foreign Office.

Halifax was not disposed to rate the 'political value' of the talk very highly, gathering the distinct impression that 'apart from Colonies there was little or nothing he wanted from us and that he felt time was on his side as regards European problems'; still, it was useful to have 'made contact'.[24] He thought that Hitler felt that,

> whilst he had attained power only after a hard struggle with present-day realities, the British Government was still living comfortably in a world of its own making, a make-believe land of strange, if respectable, illusions. It had lost touch with realities and clung to shibboleths – 'collective security', 'general settlement', 'disarmament', 'non-aggression pacts', which offered no practical prospect of a solution of Europe's difficulties.[25]

Such grim reflections were banished on the morrow when Halifax had met Field Marshal Goering, who was clad in

> brown breeches and boots all in one, with green leather jerkin and fur-collared short coat on top – the green jerkin surmounted with a green leather belt, to which was hung a dagger in a red leather sheath – altogether a very picturesque and arresting figure, completed by a green hat with a large chamois tuft![26]

He found the Field Marshal an entertaining and 'attractive' mixture of 'film star, great landowner, interested in his estates, property manager, head gamekeeper at Chatsworth'. But the Gamekeeper had not gulled the Fox.

Halifax gave the Cabinet a full account of the visit on 24 November.[27] His general impression was that 'the Germans had no policy of immediate adventure' and he thought that the 'basis of an understanding might not be too difficult as regards Central and Eastern Europe'. His satisfaction was shared by the Prime Minister, who wrote to his sister on 26 November describing the visit as a 'great success' as it had achieved its objective of 'creating an atmosphere in which it was possible to discuss with Germany the practical questions involved in a European settlement'. Chamberlain was convinced that, at least in the short term, Hitler had no intention of resorting to war, and he was clear-eyed about Nazi objectives:

> Of course they want to dominate Eastern Europe; they want as close a union with Austria as they can get without incorporating her in the Reich and they want much the same things for the *Sudetendeutsche* as we did for the Uitlanders in the Transvaal.

Such an analogy was perhaps natural for a son of Joseph Chamberlain. He was well aware of German colonial ambitions and was willing to see them partially satisfied. Although all these points 'bristle[d] with difficulties', he did not see why 'we shouldn't say to Germany, give us satisfactory assurances that you won't use force to deal with the Austrians and Czecho-Slovakians and we will give you similar assurances that we won't use force to prevent the changes you want if you can get them by peaceful means'. Such were 'the lines' on which Chamberlain aimed to progress – and he thought that the 'obstacles don't look insuperable', provided 'the press and the House will abstain from badgering us to reveal exactly how far we have got or what we are proposing to do next'.[28] Thus did Chamberlain plan to take that grip upon foreign affairs which had been so lacking in Baldwin's day.

But the Prime Minister's satisfaction with Halifax's visit was not shared by his Foreign Secretary, who, whilst Chamberlain was writing to his sister, was composing a memorandum in which he argued that it 'would be a mistake to try to detach any one member of the German-Italian-Japanese bloc by offers of support or acquiescence in the fulfilment of their aims'.[29] The debate over whether Halifax should go to Berlin had revealed differences between Downing Street and the Foreign Office over Germany; the aftermath of the visit showed that these were strategic rather than tactical.

Eden and Chamberlain

At the very start of his period as Foreign Secretary, Eden had arrived at the conclusion that Hitler's aim was the 'destruction of the peace settlement and re-establishment of Germany as the dominant power in Europe'.[1] This, however, did not preclude the possibility of 'some modus vivendi – to put it no higher – which would be both honourable and safe for this country' and which would, simultaneously, lessen the increasing tension in Europe. In 1936 both he and Vansittart were willing to entertain some form of 'colonial restitution' in order to sweeten negotiations with Germany.[2] Even after the reoccupation of the Rhineland, when the outlook was hardly 'rosy', Eden told the Cabinet that it would make no difference 'to our intention to probe and explore Herr Hitler's offers and to construct, if possible, something reliable out of them'.[3] He told the Commons on 18 June that he aimed at 'nothing less than a European settlement and appeasement'.[4]

Eden's line on Italy was, however, a good deal tougher – as behoved the Foreign Secretary who had come to power on the wave of opposition to the Hoare-Laval pact. Vansittart, more realistically, wanted to avoid alienating both Hitler and Mussolini:

> Compromise is always disagreeable, but our condition necessitates it in the case of *both* Dictators if possible. We shall, however, certainly have to compromise with Mussolini, for we can never compromise or even live safely with 'Dictator Major' if we are at lasting loggerheads with 'Dictator Minor'.[5]

With that feline malice which characterises his treatment of Chamberlain in his memoirs, Eden retells the story of a dinner-party at 11 Downing Street during which Austen Chamberlain said to his brother: ' "Neville, you must remember you don't know anything about foreign affairs." '[6] We are assured by Neville's son that he did not mind the remark, which was, so we are told, meant humorously.[7] In the context in which Eden places it, the anecdote clearly reinforces a view then prevalent of Chamberlain as a provincial businessman who, in Lloyd George's immortal phrase, 'looked at international affairs through the wrong end of a municipal drainpipe'. But where Eden seems to have imagined that Britain could afford to deal with both dictators on the merits of their cases, Chamberlain had long realised the necessity of tailoring British foreign policy to the requirements of her defence policy.

As early as August 1935 Chamberlain had urged Baldwin to take 'the bold course of appealing to the country on a defence programme',[8] something the Prime Minister was reluctant to do as it would have been (in his words to a deputation led by Churchill and Lord Salisbury in July 1936) 'an extremely difficult thing in a free country to have started rearming freely in 1934'; the nature of the danger? – 'You might have lost the election when it came.'[9] For all Churchill's later allegations that Baldwin had been guilty of 'putting party before country',[10] the National Government had begun to take action about the state of Britain's defences, and Chamberlain had played a major part in the process. Writing to his sisters about the first report of the Defence Requirements sub-Committee as it emerged from the Cabinet in July 1934, Chamberlain commented with immodest truthfulness:

> I have really won all along the line . . . what does not satisfy me is that we do not shape our foreign policy accordingly. It may be true as the FO say (and I think it is) that the menace from Germany has perceptibly receded, but it does not seem to me to have disappeared so completely as to warrant our disregarding her altogether. And if we are to take the necessary measures of defence against her we certainly can't afford at the same time to rebuild our battle-fleet. Therefore we ought to be making eyes at Japan.[11]

Chamberlain's reading of the theories of Liddell-Hart and others convinced him that 'the next war, if it ever comes' would not 'be like the last one', and over the next three years he laboured to produce a defence policy which would equip Britain with 'an air force of such striking power that no-one will care to run risks with it'.[12] He did not believe in inflating the defence estimates to provide against another war like the last one; Britain's main concern must be with the defence of her own islands, and if she did have to take part in a continental war then she would contribute her air and naval forces. The problem of how to 'shape our foreign policy accordingly' remained.

A defence policy of 'limited liability' implied a foreign policy which took the same line, but, given the worldwide nature of Britain's commitments, this was not easily achieved. By April 1936, having concluded that 'collective security' had failed, Chamberlain wanted to 'reform the League and develop a series of regional pacts';[13] his idea was that 'we should enter such as directly concern our interests, e.g. Locarno or Far East, but should leave Eastern Europe to others'.[14] These were the ideas which he brought with him to 10 Downing Street.

The failure of the Foreign Office to secure any improvement in Anglo-German relations irked Chamberlain, who, throughout the months before he became Prime Minister, had urged the utility of colonial concessions as a way of getting talks started. He did not believe that 'we could purchase peace by handing over Tanganyika', but took the view that if that were possible 'I would not hesitate for a moment to do so. It would be of no more value to them than it is to us.'[15] The Halifax visit was, in Chamberlain's view, a good way of breaking the ice, finding out what Germany wanted and seeing what could be done about it. It was also in tune with the policy which Chamberlain was already trying to follow with regard to Italy.

The cancellation in July 1937 of a proposed visit to Britain by von Neurath had left Chamberlain with little alternative save to begin his foreign policy initiative by seeking better relations with Italy.[16] At a meeting of the Committee of Imperial Defence on 5 July, the Prime Minister successfully opposed suggestions from the Chiefs of Staff that Italy 'must now be regarded as a potential enemy'. Even on his assumption that 'we ought so to direct our foreign policy that we did not quarrel with Germany', Chamberlain thought that she remained 'our greatest potential danger' and that 'we should give first priority to 'defensive preparations' against her.[17]

Chamberlain moved swiftly to improve relations with Mussolini, sending him a letter at the end of July expressing his willingness to 'enter upon conversations with a view to clarifying the whole situation and removing all causes of suspicion or misunderstanding'.[18]

Much has been made of Chamberlain's later comment in his diary that, 'I did not show my letter to the Foreign Secretary, for I had the feeling he would object to it,'[19] but Eden had been aware of the idea of sending a letter to Mussolini since Halifax had suggested it in early July – he had even considered writing one himself;[20] any pique was retrospective and, one suspects, influenced by the events of February 1938. Oliver Harvey, who whilst being Eden's Private Secretary seems to have seen himself as a mixture of his master's conscience and *chef de cabinet*, warned him that a letter from Chamberlain might 'revive the legend that you alone are intransigent', but even he acknowledged that the day was coming when they would have to recognise the Italian conquest of Abyssinia. But, like Eden, he thought that 'here, as in Germany, time is on our side' and that 'we must seek to gain time by riding the dictators on the snaffle. If we bring them up short we might get away with it, but it would be a great and unjustified risk.'[21]

THE SEA OF OBLIVION
The Anglo-Italian Rapprochement, 11 August 1937.

It was, therefore, only in a tactical sense that the Foreign Office concurred with Chamberlain's plans. The very different spirit which animated the Prime Minister can be gauged from the optimistic tone of a letter which he sent to his sisters on 1 August:

> I believe that the double policy of rearmament and better relations with Germany and Italy will carry us safely through the danger period if only the FO will play up. I see indications that they are inclined to be jealous, but though it is natural that they should be annoyed at Press headlines about the

'Chamberlain touch' instead of the 'Eden touch' there is no desire on my part to take credit away from the FS and I shall now try to put him in the foreground again.[22]

As the dictators were 'men of moods', Chamberlain thought that it was important to seize the momentum created by Mussolini's favourable reply to his letter.[23] He was quite willing to grant de jure recognition to the Italian position in Abyssinia whilst 'we can get something substantial for it'.[24] With Halifax at the Foreign Office in August during Eden's absence, the time seemed propitious, and Chamberlain reported on 8 August that the 'FO is coming along nicely though I can see that if left to themselves there would be a danger of their letting pass the critical moment'. Exultant in the feeling that he, although an amateur, had the professionals beaten at their own game, Chamberlain boasted:

> I can look back with great satisfaction at the extraordinary relaxation of tension in Europe since I first saw Grandi [the Italian Ambassador in London]. Grandi himself says that it is 90% due to me and it gives one a sense of the wonderful power that the Premiership gives you.[25]

The Prime Minister's mood of exaltation was heightened by reports from the British Ambassador in Rome, Lord Perth, that his letter had produced 'an enormous impression in Italy' and

> He at least believes that if we can follow it up, we can to a great extent, if not entirely, restore Anglo-Italian relations to what they were before the Abyssinian adventure. If so, we shall have made a most important step towards European appeasement.[26]

Eden, who tried to 'put a brake' on the optimism evinced by the press, deprecated what he saw as a 'scrambling hurry to offer incense on a dictator's altar', and naval incidents off the Spanish coast in early September involving British and Italian ships encouraged him in his policy of *festine lente*.[27] On 8 September he and the Prime Minister publicly disagreed in Cabinet and the latter urged him to 'do everything we possibly could to recover the better atmosphere of the early summer'.[28]

The persistence of the Foreign Office in seeing 'Musso only as a sort of Machiavelli putting on a false mask of friendship in order to further nefarious ambitions', seemed to Chamberlain another indication that the department had 'no imagination and no courage'; he was 'terribly afraid lest we should let the Anglo-Italian situation slip back to where it was before I intervened'. The price of Eden's policy would be 'appallingly costly defences in the Mediterranean'.[29]

Eden appeared quite willing to pay such a price. His success in mid-September at the Nyon conference in establishing, with French assistance, an effective naval patrol of the Mediterranean increased the Foreign Secretary's confidence. Instead of 'continually' retreating before the dictator powers, a 'counter-attack . . . against the weakest member of the three in overwhelming force' was, Eden thought, the policy to pursue.[30]

If Chamberlain thought that the Foreign Office had 'no imagination and no courage',[31] Eden responded by believing that the Prime Minister '*au fond* had a certain fondness for dictators whose efficiency appealed to him'.[32] The Foreign Secretary was encouraged in this line of thinking by Harvey, who suspected Chamberlain of wanting to 'deal with foreign affairs himself and keep A.E.[den] out of the picture'.[33]

Nor was he the only one of those close to the Foreign Secretary who did nothing to calm him down; indeed, there are indications that by this time Eden's entourage was developing the characteristics which mark any group of secretaries: along with the belief that they were right and everyone else was wrong, went the conviction that every man's hand was against them. An unclubbable man, and one who, moreover, was going through the traumas which mark the disintegration of any marriage, Eden harboured, in the words of a later Private Secretary, 'a strong affection for a far narrower circle of friends' than most men.[34] He commanded immense admiration and affection from this narrow circle and leant upon these friends for support, but this, in turn, made it easy for all of them to develop a sectarian mentality. His coterie (to call it a 'group' would be portentous and unduly flattering) consisted of his Parliamentary Private Secretary, Jim Thomas, his Parliamentary Under-Secretary, Lord Cranborne, and his Private Secretary at the Foreign Office, Oliver Harvey.

Harvey's diaries reveal the growth of the sectarian frame of mind – although it might, of course, be that they merely reflect Harvey's own mental processes. It may also be the case that he exaggerates, unconsciously perhaps, his own influence; he certainly bombarded Eden with advice and, self-consciously a man of the left, he sought to guide Eden's feet along a path which would take him to the leadership of a National Government led from a left of centre position; but to give advice is not always to have influence. Certainly both men shared a common distrust of the dictators, a dislike of running after them and a mistrust of what Chamberlain might be up to. Harvey's caustic assessment of the other members of the Cabinet can only have increased Eden's feeling that he was the 'coming man':

> The worst ones are Hoare and Swinton: the first is consumed with ambition to be PM . . . Simon is slippery and evasive, a moral coward . . . Hailsham has had a stroke and should have been dropped . . . Kingsley Wood is a severe critic of A.E. . . . De La Warr, Malcolm MacD[onald] . . . Ormsby-Gore, Elliot, Stanley are all lightweights, though on A.E.'s side. Duff Cooper is bone-idle, Halifax is idle and pernickity.[35]

Of the three men closest to him, Jim Thomas was the most recent in terms of acquaintanceship. The two men had hardly met before Thomas became Eden's Parliamentary Private Secretary. Soon after this appointment Thomas was invited to tea with Chamberlain's Industrial Adviser, Sir Horace Wilson, and the Head of the Civil Service, Sir Warren Fisher. They made it clear that they were 'thoroughly dissatisfied with the Foreign Office and especially with Vansittart' and that they were relying upon Thomas to counter his influence and thus 'build a bridge between 10 Downing St and the Foreign Office'.[36] Thomas scorned to play such an ignoble role and became, instead, one of Eden's inner circle.

If Thomas was a young man of relatively modest antecedents, recessive influence and subordinate position, the same could hardly be said of Lord Cranborne. The heir to the Salisbury marquessate and its millions, the inheritor of the Cecilian High Tory tradition, Cranborne was born to a role of influence. The career of his intellectually undistinguished father bore witness to what could be done with no more than these assets, but in Cranborne an acute intellect was allied to an elevated character. Like most Cecils he suffered from hypochondria, as well as its political counterpart – a propensity to resign on points of principle invisible to less cultivated sensibilities.[37] He admired Eden but was capable of viewing him dispassionately, recognising that 'if he wants to be regarded as a leader, he must act like one'.[38] Whether a remark made in 1947 reflects a wisdom acquired by the experience of watching Eden during the previous decade, or whether it illustrates an enduring tendency to brace him up is unclear, as both Eden's papers and those of Cranborne are unavailable for research, but, given their relative performances in February 1938, it is reasonable to conclude that Cranborne provided his friend with fire and firmness; if influence is to be attributed to any of Eden's entourage, Cranborne is the most likely candidate.

By November Harvey and Thomas felt that Eden 'must sooner or later have a frank explanation with the PM; he must either support A.E. or A.E. must resign and the Government would then fall. The Cabinet cannot use A.E.'s popularity and sabotage his foreign policy.'[39] Harvey told Eden on 7 November that he was 'the only Foreign Secretary in sight' and that the Government, who were 'living on your popularity and reputation', would 'fall' if he resigned; the conclusion to be drawn from this was that 'you are not only entitled to but you are able to impose your terms'.[40]

A more absurd misreading of the political situation is difficult to imagine, and on this showing Harvey was right not to have followed the path into politics beaten by some of his former diplomatic colleagues. But it certainly encouraged Eden in his general line, and when he saw Chamberlain the following day he pressed for an increase in the rearmament programme. He was unimpressed by the Prime Minister's anxieties about Britain's 'financial situation', maintaining that a 'good financial position would be small consolation if London were laid flat because our Air Force had been insufficient'. This Chamberlain dismissed as 'too alarmist a view. Despite darkening international outlook, which he admitted, he did not think anybody was going to attack us for the next two years. It was necessary to follow a very cautious foreign policy.'[41]

Where Chamberlain was trying to bring British foreign policy into line with the defence policy which he felt Britain could afford, Eden, whose natural propensity to take an exaggeratedly moral line in foreign policy was encouraged by the vapourings of his coterie, seems to have imagined that some sort of 'firm line' could be taken with 'the dictators'. To make this effective 'rearmament must go faster', and 'we should buy abroad if necessary',[42] but this was to beg the questions of where the money was to come from and what was to be bought with it. If the money was to be spent upon the defence policy which the Cabinet was following, then this would not increase Britain's ability to intervene in a continental quarrel.

Chamberlain's thinking on defence was moulded by his experiences as Chancellor, when his chief task had been to rescue the economy from the debacle of the 1931 economic crisis. His officials there had warned in January 1937 that unless defence spending was brought under control the country was headed for another economic crisis and, as Prime Minister, Chamberlain was determined to prevent this. A repeat of 1931 would not discourage Hitler and Mussolini.[43]

Bringing defence spending under control meant determining the priorities of the Service Departments; this, in turn, required a clear-cut view of the defence requirements of a worldwide Empire. Empires cost money to defend, and it was not easy to persuade a mass electorate that guns rather than butter should have priority. When, in his last budget, Chamberlain had sought to introduce a tax on business profits, euphemistically called a 'National Defence Contribution', the City, the Stock Market and the boys on the backbenches all had combined to ensure its still-birth.

Chamberlain regretted this and saw trouble ahead, with inflation, caused by increased defence spending, leading to 'a series of crippling strikes', which would spoil the rearmament programme; and a sharp rise in costs, 'due to wage increases, leading to the loss of our export trade': in short, 'a feverish and artificial boom, followed by a disastrous slump'. This would lead to 'the defeat of the Government and the advent of an ignorant, unpurposed and hurriedly pledged Opposition' to handle 'a crisis as severe as that of 1931'.[44] None of this would help efforts to restrain the dictators.

The defence policy bequeathed by Baldwin contained ambiguities, largely due to his reluctance to face up to the quarrels that any attempt to impose priorities on the Service Departments would cause. Chamberlain grasped the nettle. Britain could not afford a two-Power standard for the navy, an expeditionary force for the army and a large RAF. Britain could not take on Germany, Italy and Japan. With the aid of his Chancellor, Sir John Simon, and the Minister for the Co-ordination of Defence, Sir Thomas Inskip, Chamberlain instigated a thorough-going defence review.[45]

The Chiefs of Staff reported in November 1937 that 'we could not hope to confront satisfactorily Germany, Italy and Japan simultaneously' and that, with little prospect of help from other Powers, it was vitally important for diplomacy to 'reduce the number of our potential enemies'.[46]

Chamberlain's course in foreign policy was designed to meet these various demands. Better relations with either Italy or Germany would enable him to reduce the crippling burden of armaments spending – nothing else would. It was all very well for Eden to assert that it would be 'a mistake to try to detach any one member of the German-Italian-Japanese bloc by offers of support or acquiescence in the fulfilment of their aims' and, if necessary, 'acquiesce perforce in more than one fait accompli', but this would accomplish nothing.[47] The dictators would get what they wanted, Britain would continue to rearm and then there would be war – unless the dictators backed off – which was a gamble, the loss of which would exact a terrible cost.

But the high diplomatic thought of the Foreign Office disdained such considerations. It was better and nobler to take the moral line. Eden does not seem to have appreciated the connection between Chamberlain's foreign policy and his defence policy, and he raised the theme of greater spending on rearmament when he saw the Prime Minister on 16 November to protest about Halifax's visit to Germany. Chamberlain adjured him to 'take an aspirin', but instead of taking this advice he sent him a letter reiterating his arguments; he was infuriated to receive a reply which attributed his 'feverish concern' to his illness.[48]

Nor was Eden's fury diminished by reports from Thomas that his immediate predecessors at the Foreign Office, Simon and Hoare, were spreading rumours that Eden's flu was 'the beginning of the end' and that the 'strain was too great and he would soon go', perhaps to be replaced by Hoare. Assurances from Horace Wilson that Chamberlain was 'devoted to A.E. and regarded him as first man in his Cabinet' counted for little in Harvey's mind compared with the fact that the Prime Minister seemed to think that 'his own policy of using every opportunity of getting together with the dictators was right and that he was determined to go on with it', thus 'saving A.E. from himself'.[49]

Where, in Chamberlain's eyes, overtures to Mussolini and Halifax's visit to Germany were steps towards bringing British foreign policy into line with her economic requirements and her defence policy, to Eden and his secretaries, these things were tantamount to supping with the devil with an insufficiently long spoon – and impure intentions.

Chamberlain and Co.

Because Eden resigned in February 1938 and because his later reputation depended to a great extent upon his having been an 'anti-appeaser', it is both easy and tempting to see his relationship with the Prime Minister during the period after Halifax's visit to Germany as the prelude to a resignation; but that would be to foreshorten the perspective and to mistake myth for reality.

When the French Premier, Camille Chautemps, and his Foreign Minister, Yves Delbos, visited London in late November, there was no sign of any difference between the British Prime Minister and his Foreign Secretary. The French were reassured that a bilateral Anglo-German agreement was not in prospect, and Eden did not dissent from Chamberlain's comment that:

> There was a strong feeling that we ought not to be entangled in a war on account of Czechoslovakia, which was a long way off and with which we had not a great deal in common. But the public would welcome anything that could be done about a settlement in Central and Eastern Europe.[1]

Eden thought that 'if we could tell the Germans what the Czechs were prepared to do for the *Sudetendeutsche* our hopes would be strengthened in getting what we wanted as regards Czechoslovakia'.[2]

Nor was there any dissent from him when Chamberlain said that 'our policy ought to be to make [German expansion] . . . more difficult or even to postpone it until it might become unrealisable'. The Prime Minister thought that he might 'be ready to say that they were ready to discuss the colonial question if they were satisfied that Germany was ready to discuss the things that His Majesty's Government wanted in return': 'disarmament, the League, Western Pact, Central and Eastern Europe'.[3] On Italy too, Chamberlain and Eden sang much the same tune, both agreeing that Mussolini must demonstrate his bona fides by stopping anti-British propaganda before talks were opened.

CLOCKING IN
Chamberlain and Co.: (l to r) Sir Samuel Hoare, Oliver Stanley, 'Shakes' Morrison and Hore Belisha, 27 October 1937.

After the French visit Harvey wrote of Chamberlain and Eden as being 'together again', whilst the Foreign Secretary talked of himself and the Prime Minister as holding the same 'minority' position within the Cabinet.[4] Although there were still musings about resignation, Eden felt able to send Chamberlain a letter on New Year's Eve thanking him for 'your unvarying kindness and help to me this year'.[5]

There is a strand of writing which purports to discern in Chamberlain's actions during this period a ruthless determination to rid himself of heretics, within and without the Cabinet: first Vansittart goes, then Eden and, finally, Duff Cooper.[6] This is another myth. Of the three, only Vansittart was 'pushed' – and that was very much the result of another example of Foreign Secretary and Prime Minister acting together.

Whatever confidence Chamberlain may have possessed in Vansittart had been destroyed by his behaviour over the Halifax visit to Germany.[7] He had long felt that the 'support and guidance' which Eden needed was 'not forthcoming from the FO', and it seemed to him that Vansittart had 'the effect of multiplying the extent of Anthony's natural vibrations'.[8] In this opinion he was joined by Sir Warren Fisher, who had even been willing to take a cut in salary to become Permanent Under-Secretary at the Foreign Office in order to 'reform' that department and save its Minister.[9] Eden might have disagreed with these sentiments, had he known of them, but he was certainly willing to rid himself of his turbulent servant when Chamberlain told him in early December that he was 'quite determined' to remove Vansittart.[10]

'Van's' overbearing behaviour, his refusal to take the Paris Embassy the previous year, and his long tenure of his office all made him a vulnerable figure. His acceptance of the 'new' post of Chief Diplomatic Adviser, offered by Chamberlain, may be taken either as evidence of his vanity, or else of a naive unawareness that he was to be the great panjandrum with the button on the top and nothing to do. For the Prime Minister, who had managed to do in 'three days' what Baldwin had wasted months in failing to achieve, his action was a cause of deep satisfaction. He had removed a man whose 'instincts were all against my policy', and replaced him by the steady figure of Sir Alexander Cadogan, who could act as a good influence upon Eden's taut nerves.[11]

Chamberlain had no intention of 'isolating' Eden; in any case, the Foreign Secretary had very effectively done that all by himself. Those who purport to have discerned the existence of a plot by Chamberlain to remove Eden from the Foreign office are also apt to see the Prime Minister as out to create a Cabinet in his own image and under his own control. But when Chamberlain boasted of the excellence of his Ministerial team,[12] he was nearer the truth than was Harvey in his carpings about the weakness of Eden's colleagues; if the latter did not support Anthony, that was because there were good reasons for not doing so, not because they were lick-spittles and lackeys.

Halifax was a figure of great weight in the Conservative Party and certainly no one's puppet, and the other leading figures in the Government, Sir Samuel Hoare, Sir John Simon and Sir Thomas Inskip, were all men of long experience in office and would have been senior figures in anyone else's Cabinet. But, like Chamberlain himself, their historical reputation has suffered from their association with 'appeasement' – and the fact that they did not possess personalities which are easily warmed to.

Beaverbrook, who was one of the select group of Hoare's political friends, and who, after 1938, paid him a retainer and received from him political gossip, described him as having 'all the materials which go to making up the leader of the Conservative Party'; he was 'not stupid, but is very dull', was 'not eloquent' but 'talks well', and 'was not honest (politically), but is most evangelical' and 'a great leader in the Church of England'.[13] His fall over the pact with Laval and his supersession by Eden had not warmed his feelings towards the latter, and, following his reinstatement by Baldwin at the Admiralty in 1936, he seems to have harboured delusions that he might succeed the Prime Minister; this was correctly dismissed as absurd by Chamberlain, who knew that 'our people would not have him'.[14] As one of his Parliamentary Private Secretaries wrote of him: 'His powers of application were phenomenal, but – and it was a large but – he had no instinctive compassion and no red blood in his veins.'[15]

Simon had been a prominent political figure in the days when the Liberals had existed as a party of government and he had proved to be more buoyant. Ensconced once more on the Treasury front bench in the 1931 National Government as Foreign Secretary, he proved himself possessed of the sticking power of a barnacle. When the Samuelite Liberals took themselves and their free-trade principles into the political wilderness in 1932, the Simonite Liberals found no obstacle to retaining their offices. One of the leading K Cs of the day, he impressed juries more than political colleagues. Beaverbrook said of him that, if his character had equalled his cleverness, 'he would be bigger than God';[16] but it did not. Widely perceived to have been a failure as Foreign Secretary, he became Deputy Leader of the House in 1935, but Chamberlain, who suspected him too of nurturing leadership ambitions, knew that he 'never need be jealous of him because I know now that he lacks certain qualities essential to a leader ... The fact is the House detests him; he hasn't a friend, even in his own Party, and the reason is that, quite wrongly, they distrust his sincerity.'[17]

But if neither man was, in the eyes of the heir-apparent in 1935, fit to be leader, both were obvious figures for high office in the view of the Prime Minister of 1937. Simon was a man who could ably summarise the pros and cons of a case, but who was 'temperamentally unable to make up his mind to action when a difficult situation arose'.[18] However, there was nothing in this to prevent his becoming Chancellor of the Exchequer, and if, as it turned out, he had difficulty in mastering his brief,[19] Chamberlain was confident that his own expertise would compensate for any shortcomings.

Simon's twin in the defence review, Inskip, had been appointed Minister for the Co-ordination of Defence by Baldwin in March 1936. Professor Lindemann's remark to Lord Lloyd that it was 'the most cynical thing that has been done since Caligula appointed his horse a consul',[20] was amusing, but reflected the bitterness felt in Churchillian circles rather than anything else. Another lawyer, Inskip had entered politics in 1910 as a Conservative and, despite siding with Austen Chamberlain and the Coalitionists in 1922, he too, like Baldwin, Chamberlain, Halifax and Hoare, had profited from the peasants' revolt which carried Andrew Bonar Law to power. A stout (in both senses) evangelical Protestant, Inskip had to his credit a noble and successful stand in 1927 against Archbishop Davidson's attempt to mutilate the Book of Common Prayer; but, although a man of weight, he was no expert on defence.[21]

Despite the jibes of his opponents, Inskip proved to be an effective chairman of the Chiefs of Staff Committee; 'his lawyer's mind saw clearly to the heart of the problem and . . . he expressed his views with admirable clarity and unusual brevity'.[22] Chamberlain did not believe that it was necessary for the Minister of Co-ordination to be a strategist, it was enough that he should ensure that 'strategical problems are fairly and thoroughly worked out by the strategists';[23] in other words, he was a man to prick the bubble of the inflated demands which all Service chiefs make as part of their job.

From the defence review came a policy which would keep expenditure under control and provide the naval and air strength that the defence of the British Isles and her imperial trade routes necessitated. The new Minister of War, Leslie Hore-Belisha, endorsed Chamberlain's view that the army's future lay outside the domain of continental warfare; what now remained was for diplomacy to play its part in reducing Britain's potential enemies.

When the Cabinet discussed Inskip's report on defence expenditure on 22 December, Halifax emphasised that it brought out clearly 'how the limitation imposed on defence by finance threw a heavy burden on diplomacy', and that they had arrived at that 'position which above all we had wished to avoid . . . in which we were faced with the possibility of three enemies at once'. His own conclusion, which he 'had no doubt' Eden would share, was 'that this threw an immensely heavy burden on diplomacy and that we ought to make every possible effort to get on good terms with Germany'.[24]

But Eden was torn between the dictates of the situation in which Britain found herself and the dictates of morality, and he was not disposed, as were Halifax and the Prime Minister, to move swiftly. Before there could be any agreement with Germany over the restitution of colonies, he wanted a 'general settlement' that would include a disarmament agreement and a Western pact.[25]

On Italy Eden's moral indignation came into play even more strongly. He told Harvey in late December that he 'must be particularly careful to prevent his personal prejudices from colouring his attitude too much', but as he regarded Mussolini as 'anti-Christ' this was rather difficult, especially as Harvey 'did too'.[26] This was the spirit which animated a letter to Chamberlain on New Year's Day 1938 in which, after mentioning the possibility of striking a bargain with Italy in return for granting de jure recognition of her rule in Abyssinia, he discarded it: 'first, because we have so repeatedly . . . said we would not do so', and secondly, because 'I feel we would be putting ourselves in a somewhat invidious position by appearing to withhold de jure recognition until and unless we were offered our price'.[27] Rather than strike such a 'sordid' 'bargain', Eden preferred to grant recognition and then announce that they were ready for conversations.

As this meant 'giving away our best card for nothing', Chamberlain was less than impressed by this example of Eden's moral diplomacy. He thought they 'should approach the matter from the angle of obtaining general appeasement to which each must make its contribution and justify de jure on that ground';[28] Mussolini could be told, through the medium of a private letter, that he could have de jure recognition as part of a general agreement.[29]

In Eden's book this showed the Prime Minister's hankering after a 'sordid' bargain, even if he 'would not admit the word'.[30] His response, on 9 January, showed how much harder he was on the Italian than on the German issue, as he thought 'an agreement with the latter might have a chance of a reasonable life, especially if Hitler's own position were engaged, whereas Mussolini is, I fear, the complete gangster and his pledged word means nothing'.[31] Mussolini was, in his view, secondary to the 'big issues of this year', which were 'Anglo-American co-operation', the 'chances of effectively asserting white race authority in the Far East and relations with Germany'.

Chamberlain was not disposed to argue that the Far East and Germany were issues of the first importance, but so too was Italy – and for the same reason as the others: success in any one sphere would enable him to slow down 'the mad armaments race, which if allowed to continue must involve us all in ruin'.[32] The deterioration in relations between the Western Powers and Japan in the Far East was, in his eyes, further evidence of the need to come to agreements with Germany and Italy.[33] Where Eden was apt to think that a correct moral stance on Italy would, in some way, secure American co-operation in the Far East, Chamberlain was less sanguine.

When fighting between Japan and China flared up again in July 1937, it had been natural that the Foreign Office should have looked towards America for co-operation. In October President Roosevelt had made a speech in Chicago during which, with a characteristic mixture of vague rhetoric and moral uplift, he had denounced the 'epidemic' of international lawlessness and spoken of putting the infected states in 'quarantine'. These were sentiments which spoke to Eden's own instincts and aroused optimism, but Chamberlain had been around rather longer and was less inclined to throw his hat in the air: 'In the present states of European affairs . . . we simply cannot afford to quarrel with Japan and I very much fear, therefore, that after a lot of ballyhoo the Americans will somehow fade out and leave us to carry all the blame and the odium.'[34]

Chamberlain's opinion that it was 'always best and safest to count on nothing from the Americans but words',[35] has often been quoted as though it was his final word on the matter; in fact, what it does show is the danger of selective quotation. Writing just after a Japanese attack on an American ship in the Yangtze, Chamberlain was, in fact, hopeful that this might actually rouse the Americans: 'It seems to me a Heaven sent opportunity and you can bet your bottom dollar I am making the most of it. It is always best and safest to count on *nothing* from the Americans except words but at this moment they are nearer to "doing something" than I have ever known them and I can't altogether repress hopes.'[36]

A real American commitment in the Pacific would greatly ease the burden resting on the shoulders of the 'weary titan' of the British Empire. When Roosevelt sent a representative, Captain Ingersoll, to London, Eden postponed his planned holiday, seeing in the visit 'the most important thing which had happened and that he had been working for for years'.[37] It was, Harvey thought, too important a thing to be left to the Prime Minister, who was 'heavy-handed and has no touch for dealing with delicate situations', and who might 'easily upset the Americans for good'. Better to leave it to Eden, with his 'natural "flair", which enables him to say and do exactly what is needed'.[38]

However, it transpired that there was not very much that even natural 'flair' could accomplish when Captain Ingersoll arrived in London. He had no 'definite plans or proposals to submit for moving American ships to the Far East',[39] or for anything else. Chamberlain had been willing to consider sending 'a fleet of eight or nine capital ships to the Far East' if the Americans would follow suit,[40] and his exasperation with Ingersoll's 'mission' was considerable. Writing on 9 January to his sister, he let his feelings show: 'I do wish the Japs would beat up an American or two! But of course the little d-v-ls are too cunning for that'; he feared that 'we may eventually have to act alone & hope the Yanks will follow before it's too late'.[41] In the end Chamberlain decided not to act alone – that would only expose Britain's weakness and do nothing to help negotiations with Italy.[42]

But, with relations with Germany still awaiting some follow-up to Halifax's visit, and the situation in the Far East becoming dangerous, it was imperative that something was done about Anglo-Italian relations. Britain's foreign policy had to be tailored to her economic and defence capabilities; if that meant supping with Eden's 'anti-Christ' then it was time to bring out the long spoon. Inskip and Simon's review of defence expenditure would incline them in the Prime Minister's direction, and the latter, like Hoare, had worked with Eden on foreign policy and mistrusted his ideological approach to a pragmatic subject. Halifax's thinking on these matters followed the same lines – and it remained to be seen whether, as Harvey and company alleged, Eden was so indispensable that all these men would, at the end of the day, abdicate their reasoning to his moral imperatives.

The Extrusion of Eden

But, even as Chamberlain was preparing to pursue his policy of 'general appeasement', on 13 January the British Ambassador in Washington passed on a proposal from Roosevelt to convene a general conference to discuss all outstanding issues on the international scene.[1]

Since 1941 Britain has been wedded to an American alliance of one kind or another and, from the perspective that this has created, the idea of securing that alliance in 1938 seems like a great opportunity lost. In his memoirs Eden made a big song and dance about this episode, as did Churchill, who called Roosevelt's proposal 'a formidable and measureless step' and stigmatised its rejection as 'the loss of the last frail chance to save the world from tyranny otherwise than by war'.[2] This is an absurd overestimation of the significance of Roosevelt's proposal, even in the context of Churchill's sustained attempt to denigrate his predecessor. If either Churchill or Eden believed in 1938 what they claim retrospectively to have believed, then both of them were showing signs of the lack of judgment which was to mar the career of the one and ruin that of the other.

With the example of Roosevelt's 'quarantine' speech in mind, Chamberlain entertained little hope of such a vague and 'fantastic' plan; indeed, by exciting the 'derision of Germany and Italy' and giving rise to suspicions that the 'democratic bloc' was trying to put them 'in the wrong', British adherence to the proposals might even result in a postponement of the opening of talks.[3] Cadogan, who was sceptical about the chances of the scheme's success, nevertheless felt that Roosevelt ought not to be discouraged, and Sir Ronald Lindsay, the British Ambassador in Washington, felt that they ought to accept it.[4] But, with Eden on holiday, it fell to Chamberlain to make the decision and he, like Sir Horace Wilson, took the view that rather than become entangled in

WILL HE COME RIGHT OUT?
13 October 1937.

what looked like one of Roosevelt's bright, unthought-out ideas, the British should get on with positive appeasement.[5]

Without consulting Eden, Chamberlain replied that whilst appreciating 'most highly the mark of confidence which the President has shown in consulting me', he thought that his own diplomacy might enable them all to 'look forward to some improvement' in the international situation. Taking the President into his confidence, Chamberlain told him about recent Italian inquiries 'as to when conversations could be opened with His Majesty's

Government', adding that Eden was going to discuss with the French 'the possibility of making a fresh approach towards a reconciliation with Italy that might bring appeasement to the Mediterranean region at least'. In view of all this, Roosevelt was asked if he would 'consider holding his hand'.[6]

Harvey, who was horrified both at the nature of the reply and at its being despatched without Eden being consulted, urged his chief to take firm action, begging him not to underestimate either his 'influence in the Cabinet' or his 'importance in the Government! You can afford to take a *very* strong line – they couldn't let you go on this.'[7] It was without surprise that he learnt that Eden thought 'we must accept. He regarded the PM's reply as much too chilling.'[8] Without consulting Chamberlain, the Foreign Secretary 'sent a fresh wire to . . . Washington saying [as the PM put it] I had not exactly meant what I had said'.[9]

Conversations with Churchill and Lloyd George whilst on holiday had fortified Eden in his determination not to grant de jure recognition to the Italian position in Abyssinia.[10] The fact that the Prime Minister, without consulting him, had turned down Roosevelt's offer in pursuit of such a goal, was more than either Eden's amour-propre, or his concern for the American connection, could bear. Indeed, following up the initiative would provide a cast-iron argument for postponing conversations with Mussolini. Thus, with Harvey's words about his indispensability ringing in his ears, Eden prepared to take a stand.

On Sunday 16 January Eden went down to Chequers to lunch with Chamberlain. In his memoirs, which present the whole episode as the prelude to his resignation, Eden described their conversation as 'profoundly unsatisfactory', commenting that 'for the first time our relations were seriously at odds'.[11] But, at the time, he commented to Cadogan that he had had 'a fairly satisfactory day', whilst even the zealous Harvey, who was busy pouring petrol on to the embers, recorded that Chamberlain had been 'personally friendly'.[12]

It was somewhat disingenuous of Eden to write to Chamberlain on the morrow that acceptance of Roosevelt's proposal 'need not necessarily injure the attempts which we are making to improve relations with Germany' nor even have 'any repercussions on the conversations which you are so anxious to start with Italy'; if he really believed this, it casts almost as much doubt over his judgment as his remarkable statement that it was 'almost impossible to overestimate the effect which an indication of American interest in European affairs might produce'.[13] He told Lindsay to tell the Americans that he hoped 'nobody would be tempted to chuck their hand in, because if they returned to the charge, we should, I was sure, be able to help'.[14] Roosevelt's reply to Chamberlain on 18 January was all Eden could have wished. Whilst expressing disappointment, the President evidently regarded the door as still being open and warned against de jure recognition on the grounds of its possible effect on the attitude of the Japanese in China.[15]

Eden's friends, taking the view that the Prime Minister's 'vanity' and Americanophobia had led him into a colossal blunder, thought they discerned a 'fundamental difference' between their hero and Chamberlain, and that Eden should now take advantage of his position to insist on getting his way.

There was indeed a 'fundamental difference' between the two men, but it was not the one which Harvey thought he discerned. Eden shared Lindsay's opinion that, 'What brings America closer to us is the identity of American aims, desires and policies with our views.'[16] This was not vastly different from Chamberlain's view that Britain and America wanted the 'same fundamental things in the world': peace, liberty, order, 'respect for international obligations' and 'freedom for every country to devote all its resources to the improvement of the conditions of its own people, instead of being forced to pile armaments on its back 'till it comes near to breaking'.[17] Where they differed was in their estimate of the possibility of Roosevelt actually doing anything save talk.

Lindsay did allow himself to be mildly troubled by the fact that a 'first glance' at the American political scene seemed to reveal 'practically nothing but rampant isolationism, except in some limited circles, and in Congress, it is very bad'. Trying to 'avoid wishful thinking', Lindsay proceeded to indulge in it, believing 'that it is really not quite as bad as it seems' because 'a large part of the press is very sensible, and there is widespread genuine friendliness towards us and universal dislike of totalitarian systems'.[18] This rosy-tinted Americano-philia ignored the Neutrality Acts and equated, absurdly, 'genuine friendliness' with a hostile Congress as factors in the American political equation. Chamberlain did not make this mistake.

Unlike Churchill and Eden (and many British Prime Ministers after them), Chamberlain realised that 'public opinion in a good part of the States still believes it possible for America to stand outside Europe and watch it disintegrate, without being materially affected herself'. American 'goodwill' was not lacking, but when it came to translating that commodity into action, 'disappointment' was all that could be expected. Chamberlain did not doubt that the Anglo-American 'combination' was 'the greatest instrument in the world for the preservation of peace', but he was too much of a 'realist' to expect action – save on American terms. In the meantime, it behoved the 'realist' to 'adjust our foreign policy to our circumstances' until 'our armaments are completed'.[19] Thus, for Chamberlain the first priority remained moving ahead with negotiations with Mussolini and Hitler.

Eden, however, perceiving a good wicket when he saw one pressed his point home, telling Chamberlain that they 'must decide to drop . . . *de jure* recognition in deference to Roosevelt' and 'tell him that we would back his initiative in the fullest possible measure'.[20] To improve relations with Mussolini at the cost of America withdrawing into isolation would, he alleged, be 'the greatest possible disaster to the peace of the world'. So much for his earlier view that Roosevelt and Mussolini were compatible.[21]

When a meeting between the two men on 18 January failed to convince either of them of the merits of the view which the other took, the matter passed to the Foreign Policy Committee of the Cabinet on 19 January, where most Ministers were on Chamberlain's side. Eden noticed that Inskip had a piece of paper in front of him which read: 'Eden's policy to line up with the USA, GB and France – result war.'[22]

In despair, the Foreign Secretary's friends appear to have contemplated 'leaking' the news of the American initiative to the press. Thomas was told by Wilson that, if they did, he 'would use the full power of the Government machine in an attack on A.E.'s past record with regard to the dictators and the shameful obstruction by the FO of the PM's attempt to solve the peace of the world'.[23] Eden's official biographer, whilst respecting his subject's 'integrity and decency' in not 'leaking', has regretted that these qualities stopped him 'exploding' the 'political hand grenade' which Roosevelt's telegram represented.[24] Certainly, in view of the apocalyptic tone of Eden's language, with 'nothing less than' world peace at stake, his reticence does appear surprising, but it was not mere pusillanimity which dictated his course.

When the Foreign Policy Committee met on 20 January, Eden found Chamberlain 'no longer so sure of his case, although he still argued fiercely', whilst his colleagues were 'noticeably less stiff'. Although Chamberlain later noted that the meeting resulted in a 'compromise reply [to Roosevelt] in which we had elucidated our position and made it clear that de jure was only to be given as part of a factor in general appeasement',[25] this was putting a brave face upon defeat. Perhaps, as Eden surmised, the threat of his resignation effected his colleagues' resistance, but, for whatever reason, they agreed to support Roosevelt's initiative; only the fact that it had been a piece of Rooseveltian moonshine prevented it causing further complications.[26]

Feelings in the Eden camp were mixed. The Foreign Secretary had won his point, but, as Harvey noted, it might have been better for Eden to have gone on the issue, thus tackling head-on the 'fundamental difference' which existed between him and the Prime Minister.[27] The episode was, in fact, more important for Eden's future than for Anglo-American relations. Roosevelt seems not to have minded Chamberlain's reaction,[28] but both Prime Minister and Foreign Secretary were left feeling dissatisfied. Eden had not quite lived up.

to the expectations of his friends, whilst Chamberlain had failed to assert his grip. Both would do better next time.

Still, from Chamberlain's point of view, the road was now open for his approaches to Italy and Germany. For some time he had thought that 'any satisfactory settlement would involve the handing over of Tanganyika', but it was only after conversations with the Secretary-General of the League of Nations, M. Avenol, on 8 January that he had formulated a 'definite plan'.[29] He put this to the Foreign Policy Committee on 24 January, where it was 'accepted promptly and even enthusiastically'.[30] Only Eden raised any objection. It was a sign either of his inattention, or of the extent to which he believed his own picture of Chamberlain as a man who was out to do a deal with the dictators at any cost, that he 'observed that the Prime Minister has not expressly mentioned the relation of any colonial settlement to the general settlement with Germany', when it was with just such a statement that Chamberlain had prefaced the discussion.[31]

The plan was worthy of Joe Chamberlain's son and involved the 'opening of an entirely new chapter in the history of African colonial development', including the creation of a new zone in Central Africa under international control in which the Germans might find a place in the sun. Chamberlain told his colleagues that he could see 'no reason why Germany should reject such a scheme . . . it met the German desiderata and gave them what they so strongly insisted upon, namely equality of opportunity and treatment'. Henderson was informed of this decision, asked for comments and told that he would be required in London for further discussion.[32]

Eden's terms for any Anglo-German agreement remained tough. Germany would be required to make concessions in five areas: 'the conclusion of a Western pact of non-aggression' or a 'new Locarno'; a disarmament agreement; a return to the League; a 'settlement' of the Austrian situation; and finally, but more speculatively, guarantees would have to be given about Czechoslovakia in return for Czech concessions on the *Sudetendeutsche*.[33] Vansittart, smarting under the rejection of his proposal that 'any major paper' should pass to the Foreign Secretary over his desk, pointed out the ambiguity in the passages concerned with Central Europe, stressing that 'unless we are really satisfied [there] . . . it would be incredibly rash & dangerous to restore colonies on any large scale to Germany'.[34] Wilson, in a note passed to Chamberlain along with Eden's paper, commented: 'I do not think the FO have yet worked out . . . the possible "picture" on the assumption that we really *do* want to get an agreement if we can.'[35]

Despite the fact that Henderson was less than encouraging about the chances of the scheme, stressing that Germany would want 'full sovereignty' over any colonies, Chamberlain determined to push ahead with it; but he did not ignore Henderson's view that Italy offered better prospects of a quick success.[36] In this he was encouraged greatly by letters from his sister-in-law, Lady Ivy Chamberlain, Austen's widow. An admirer of Il Duce, she wrote from Rome that he would respond to the right sort of approach. She also fed Neville's growing doubts about Eden's influence by reporting the 'strong dislike and distrust' with which he was regarded.[37]

Hitler's actions in early February, replacing von Neurath with the more servile Joachim von Ribbentrop and purging the army's High Command, seemed to put back the prospects of any movement on that front.[38] Chamberlain was not without fears that his ultimate objective might be unattainable. When Eden went to see him on 30 January, he found him 'much less optimistic of prospects of agreement with Germany, having just read *The House that Hitler Built* [an anti-Nazi tract by an Australian author, Stephen Roberts]'; the Prime Minister even suggested 'that if we couldn't reach agreement, we should have to go in for encirclement and perhaps an arrangement with Russia'. Eden was baffled by what he took to be a sudden rush to 'realism', whilst Harvey was exasperated by what he took to be a change of mind.[39] Both men mistook a passing mood for their own settled conviction, for, as Chamberlain told his sisters, 'If I accepted the author's conclusions I should despair, but I don't and won't';[40] nor did he.

The events in Germany only made Chamberlain more determined to make a move on the Italian front, where he felt that Lady Ivy's activities in Rome had helped 'materially to create the atmosphere ... necessary for the opening of conversations.'[41] But this brought him right up against the moralising tendencies of his Foreign Secretary.

The fact that Eden took a harder line on Italy than on Germany has already been noted; Roosevelt's evident abhorrence of the idea of granting de jure recognition of the Italian position in Abyssinia strengthened the Foreign Secretary's reluctance to take the final plunge, as did Cranborne's reports from the League at Geneva.[42] Given that Eden had agreed to the principle of opening talks, even the patient Cadogan found this shying at the fence 'silly'.[43] He preferred to reiterate his line that the moment was inopportune – and to complain about Lady Ivy's activities because they gave Mussolini the impression that he could 'divide' the democracies, and because they derogated from his authority.[44]

Matters came to a head following Hitler's actions on 11 February in putting pressure on the Austrian Chancellor, which led to the declaration of the *Anschluss*. As it was Germany which was involved, Eden did not mount his white steed; indeed, he forbore to act, not wanting to get himself into a position of 'suggesting a resistance which he could not in fact furnish'.[45] Chamberlain thought it vital to push ahead as quickly as possible with the conversations which Count Grandi, the Italian Ambassador, had already indicated his Government was willing to undertake. He hoped that Germany's action in Austria might have loosened the bond between the two dictators and that, if he struck whilst the iron was hot, he might get an agreement.[46] On 17 February Eden concurred that talks should open.[47]

Second thoughts came quickly. After embarrassing Cadogan, who did not feel 'as passionately' about Italy,[48] by asking him to give Chamberlain reasons for postponing talks, Eden did the job himself that evening in a memorandum which argued that the Italians must first show signs of their good faith by withdrawing their 'volunteers' from helping Franco in Spain. He felt that to open talks in the current climate would be seen by Hitler as a clumsy attempt to break the Rome–Berlin axis.[49]

In retrospect the Prime Minister regarded the receipt of this extraordinary missive as the moment at which he decided that 'the issue between us must be faced and faced at once'. He feared that Eden's policy would mean a strengthening of the Axis and the end of Austrian, and possibly Czech, independence. He told Wilson on the morning of 18 February that he was 'determined to stand firm even if it means losing my Foreign Secretary'.[50]

So too would Eden. Jim Thomas, who had attended a meeting of the Conservative Foreign Affairs Group on the evening of 17 February, returned the following morning 'breathing fire' and assured Eden that its members, including Churchill, were right behind him.[51] Harvey stoked the flames of his master's indignation with a note telling him that the 'country loathes Musso' and looked to the Foreign Secretary to stand for 'principle against mere expediency'. 'You must insist', he added, 'on getting your own way in foreign affairs or you cannot continue in the Government.'[52] But if Eden and his coterie thought that such threats would work a second time they were mistaken.

Grandi, acting upon instructions from his Foreign Minister, Count Ciano, avoided Eden's requests to see him alone for conversations.[53] He was aware, through the intermediacy of 'Chamberlain's confidential agent', Sir Joseph Ball, that the Prime Minister was willing to see him and open negotiations.[54] Ball, a former MI5 officer, had joined Conservative Central Office in the 1920s and ran 'a little intelligence service';[55] through this medium Chamberlain circumvented Foreign Office vacillations.[56] Eden, however, insisted upon being present when Grandi saw the Prime Minister on the morning of 18 February – and the meeting brought to the surface the underlying difference between the pragmatist and the moralist.[57]

Grandi, who was aware of these things, played his part to perfection. His

HONOURABLE INTENTIONS?
Peace. 'Lor! Mister Mussolini, How You Do Startle One!'
27 October 1937.

replies to Chamberlain's questions about the Italian attitude towards events in Austria and Mussolini's willingness to open talks were everything the Prime Minister could have wanted: yes, the Italians were worried about German actions in Austria; no, there was no deal with Germany over Austria; yes, they would like to open negotiations; no, alas, it would not be possible to wait until a decision had been reached on Italian 'volunteers' in Spain since that was a thorny question.

The meeting was adjourned to give Prime Minister and Foreign Secretary a chance to confer in private. According to Eden's account, Chamberlain reacted to his reiteration of his previous position by becoming 'very vehement, more vehement than I had ever seen him', striding up and down the room, saying with great emphasis: 'Anthony, you have missed chance after chance. You simply cannot go on like this.' To Eden's statement that 'your methods are right if you have faith in the man you are negotiating with', Chamberlain responded: 'I have.'[58]

Lunch at the Foreign Office confirmed Eden in his resolve, and when he met Chamberlain and Grandi afterwards he stood his ground. Grandi's account of the scene which followed was, even allowing for Italian hyperbole, dramatic:

> Chamberlain and Eden were not a Prime Minister and a Foreign Minister discussing with the Ambassador of a foreign power a delicate situation of international character. They were – and revealed themselves as such to me in defiance of all established convention – two enemies confronting each other, like two cocks in true fighting posture.

Grandi's assertion that they were fighting for 'the high stakes of their future destiny in the Cabinet and in the Conservative Party' was no more than the truth.[59]

It might be, as critics have alleged, that Chamberlain's actions at the meeting with Grandi demonstrated a determination to get rid of his Foreign Secretary, but it should be remembered that it was Eden who had insisted on attending the meeting against Chamberlain's wishes, and it was his line, despite the pressing reasons there adduced for opening talks, which precipitated a crisis. There are also signs that the Prime Minister wished to avoid what was bound to be a damaging confrontation by giving Eden a bridge over which to retreat if he wished so to do. Sir John Simon, who went round to see Eden at the Foreign Office after the meeting with Grandi, button-holed Thomas and, in what the latter called 'an extraordinary interview', said that as it was clear that Eden was 'both physically and mentally ill' he should have 'six months rest'. The motive for this intervention was plain: 'resignation would be fatal to the Government, nay the country, nay the peace of the whole world'.[60]

But Eden and his coterie were in no mood to compromise. Cranborne, Harvey and Thomas all encouraged him to stand and fight, with the latter recording that Eden was 'very bitter at the way his colleagues treat him and feels he cannot go on. We all feel he is right.'[61] The Foreign Secretary was preparing for martyrdom.

Chamberlain did his best to deny Eden the fulfilment of this wish at a Cabinet meeting on 19 February, but as the Foreign Secretary would brook no compromise and the Prime Minister was convinced of the importance of haste, the question came down to the balance of power within the Cabinet – and as Duff Cooper, no friend of Chamberlain's, recorded: 'I feel that anyone who had not already made up his mind must have been convinced by the Prime Minister.' It came as a great shock to him, and to other Ministers, when, at the end of the discussion, Eden said he would have to resign.[62] Chamberlain agreed that, in view of the seriousness of the situation, they should all sleep on the matter.

Suggestions for compromise were showered upon Eden by those outside his own circle of devotees, but he would not even accept Cadogan's sensible idea that, although an official announcement could be made that talks were to open, nothing further should be done until the situation in Spain had been cleared up.[63] Thus, when he saw Chamberlain just after noon, 'we were able to agree that the difference between us was vital and unbridgeable and that the only way out was resignation'.[64] But far from the Prime Minister seeking to bring the Cabinet meeting on the afternoon of 20 February swiftly to this point, he agreed to let a 'committee of mediators' try to see if Eden would agree to a compromise along the lines of the one that Cadogan had suggested. But even though the Cabinet adjourned and reconvened in the evening, it was to no avail – Eden was determined to get his way or resign. As he lacked the support to force Chamberlain to back down, resignation was the inevitable conclusion.[65]

In his memoirs Eden waxed indignant that Chamberlain's letter accepting his resignation said that 'such differences as have arisen between us in no way concern our ultimate aim or the fundamentals of our policy', but that was not far wrong. Chamberlain, writing to his sisters on 27 February, commented that it was not until 18 February that he knew that the time had come when 'I must make my final stand and that Anthony must yield or go'.[66] In retrospect it appeared to him that 'Anthony was always against negotiations with dictators' and that he had, therefore, been 'right to go'.[67] But it had been more complex than that.

Halifax got closest to the truth when he discerned that Eden was 'as perhaps most of us are' a 'dual personality': the Foreign Secretary 'impressed by the dangers of the present situation and anxious to relieve them' was countered by the public 'Anthony Eden, generous, idealist, intolerant of baseness and anything that was unworthy', who hated dictators with 'every fibre in his body'. The consequence was that 'when the Foreign Secretary came to the point where he was perhaps going to ease tensions, Anthony Eden stepped in and told him it was quite too beastly for words'; so nothing happened.[68] In the end Chamberlain confronted him with a choice – and 'Anthony Eden', with a little help from his friends, triumphed over the 'Foreign Secretary'.

Despite the later legends, it appears unlikely that Chamberlain wanted to lose his Foreign Secretary; it was 'Anthony Eden' who had become an intolerable obstacle in the way of progress, and the Prime Minister had no regrets about standing his ground: 'I have never felt a doubt that it was now or never and must be now if we were to avoid another Great War.'[69] With Eden departing to play the role of the 'king over the water', Chamberlain selected the tall, aristocratic and pragmatic figure of Edward, Viscount Halifax, to take his place at the Foreign Office. It had taken time, perhaps too much time, but at last the Prime Minister could push ahead with trying to make Britain's foreign policy harmonise with her economic circumstances and the defence policy which that seemed to dictate; universal approbation for such a step was unlikely to be forthcoming.

The Cave of Adullam

When David fled from the wrath of King Saul he took refuge in the cave of Adullam, where he was soon joined by 'everyone who was in distress, and everyone who was in debt, and everyone who was discontented'; in this way he gathered a following of about four hundred. Something similar befell Eden when he fled from Chamberlain's Cabinet to the backbenches, although he failed to gather even a tithe of the four hundred supporters who rallied to King David. But even had Eden been able to replicate, in some gentler fashion, David's feat of collecting the foreskins of two hundred Philistines as a dowry, he would still only have been hailed by a few latter-day Adullamites.

Foremost among these was one who was certainly in 'distress . . . debt' and 'discontented' – Winston Churchill, who wrote urging him not to let 'feelings of friendship' for his late colleagues prevent him from 'doing full justice to your case'.[1] The deliverer of an 'enthusiastic eulogy of Anthony' at the Foreign Affairs Group on 17 February, Churchill had, along with Lloyd George, encouraged Eden to stand firm when they had met him on holiday in January.[2] These 'two pirates', as Chamberlain once called them,[3] were the two senior malcontents – but they were hardly the best company for a respectable, recently resigned, young ex-Foreign Secretary.

When he had been Prime Minister, Lloyd George had appointed Chamberlain as Director-General of National Service; not much given to confessions of error, Lloyd George freely admitted that this had been one. From the start he disliked Chamberlain because his 'forehead was too narrow or his skull the wrong shape',[4] and he soon sacked him, dismissing him as 'a retail mind in a wholesale business'.[5] Thanks to the way the political chips fell after 1922, Chamberlain had a chance to show that the dislike was mutual. Indeed, Chamberlain's feelings went deeper than that, as he found the ex-Premier 'impossible to work with', so 'sly, so treacherous and unscrupulous' was his nature; he 'never had the rudiments of the instincts of a gentleman'.[6]

If Chamberlain detested Lloyd George, whom he and Baldwin kept out of office after 1922, his feelings towards Churchill, with whom he had worked from 1924–9, were more ambivalent. He recognised that he was a 'brilliant' and 'mercurial' figure, but thought that there was 'somehow a great gulf fixed between us which I don't think I shall ever cross'.[7] The better he got to know Churchill, the more he could not help 'liking and admiring him'; but this was 'accompanied by a diminution of my intellectual respect for him'.[8] He found Churchill 'lacking in judgement' and possessing Lloyd George's amoral attitude to politics.[9]

From that point in 1929 when Churchill and Chamberlain had been the two leading figures in the Conservative Party after Baldwin, their careers had diverged. Chamberlain's steadiness and quiet efficiency had carried him to the premiership, but Churchill had taken a different route. During the period 1929–31 when Baldwin's fortunes had been at their lowest ebb, Churchill had taken up the cause of the 'die-hards' on India and had come close to defeating his leader, who favoured granting the sub-continent a greater measure of self-government. But he had not succeeded, and the formation of the National Government in August 1931 had left him in the political wilderness; those who take pot-shots at Santa Claus need not, as Beaverbrook once commented, expect any presents if they miss.[10]

But it had been against Baldwin that Churchill's oratorical projectiles had been hurled, and his feelings towards the new Prime Minister were such that he was willing, as we have seen, to second Lord Derby in proposing Chamberlain as the new leader of the Conservative Party. Even when, as over Eden's resignation, Churchill pushed himself to the forefront of the Government's critics, he remained 'as friendly as you please' to Chamberlain in the lobby of the Commons, and the Prime Minister did not think his 'enmity' was 'personal to me; it is just his restless ambition that keeps him incessantly criticising any administration of which he is not a member'.[11]

Chamberlain's view was a common one, and both Churchill and Lloyd George were widely regarded as politically embittered ageing adventurers whose venom had lost the power to kill, even if it could still wound; they were not 'sound' men, but rather dwellers in the nethermost part of the cave. To those National MPs who nursed ambition, but little love for the Prime Minister's foreign policy, Eden was a god-send; as Harold Nicolson, the National Labour MP for Leicester West, wrote to his wife on 2 March, 'I am not going to become one of the Winston brigade. My leaders are Anthony and Malcolm [MacDonald].'[12]

But the reaction to the resignation speeches given by Eden and Cranborne on 21 February did not indicate that, literary dilettantes and ageing adventurers apart, there were many who dwelt in this modern cave of Adullam. Nicolson noted that apart from himself and a few others, only the Labour Party cheered Eden: 'the rest kept silent. Those who have toadied and grovelled to Anthony all these years just kept silent.'[13] Of course they did. Eden was about to learn what other young politicians with a meteoric career behind them have learnt, namely that when the divinity that doth hedge Office is removed, the wind is seldom tempered to the poor shorn lamb.

That Eden's resignation speech should have fallen flat was not surprising, for his position was a difficult one. Having risen so far so fast he did not want to burn any boats, and when his resignation letter expressed the customary 'deep regret' at having to part from such splendid colleagues and the hope that nothing would impair his 'friendship' with Chamberlain, he was, according to the unspoken custom of his kind, making obeisance towards a political future.[14] To criticise severely a Government of which he had so recently been a member would have been not only to incur that most deadly of charges in the Conservative lexicon, 'disloyalty', but also to invite questions about why it was he had not resigned before.

Eden thus began his career as a 'caveman' in the way he was to continue – lingering on the threshold, casting many a backwards glance at the Promised Land. It was Cranborne's speech which bore the sting of bitter reproach; but the Cecils were notoriously masters of 'gibes and jeers and flouts' – and the future Marquess of Salisbury could not expect the premiership.[15] Eden, on the other hand, followed up his mild speech in the Commons with one to his constituents that was so innocuous that it brought forth from the Prime Minister a congratulatory letter.[16]

One historian has commented that upon closer examination, 'Conservative opposition to appeasement is rather like a mirage; the more it is studied the less substantial it appears; but in this case, it never vanishes completely.'[17] But in the days after Chamberlain's destruction, the numbers of dissidents, like Falstaff's men in buckram, grew every time the tale was retold. Yet, not only were the numbers of dissentients in the 1930s small, but theirs was a house divided. Emrys Evans, one of the select few, later recalled that Eden's 'group' would have nothing to do with Churchill, partly because 'he would have dominated our proceedings and would associate us with causes we did not want to follow', but also because it was feared that he 'would bring in Bob Boothby who, it was felt, wasn't to be trusted. Winston greatly resented his exclusion . . . and has never forgotten it.'[18]

Churchill's displeasure at the spurning of his overtures was not surprising.

Six years of opposing the National Government on almost any issue which presented itself had got him nowhere; or, to be more precise, it had got him into places where few respectable Conservatives were likely to follow.

Since early 1936 Churchill had been associated with a shadowy group calling itself 'The Focus'. On the surface it seemed an innocent enough 'All-Party group opposed to Nazism',[19] but not only were there suspiciously few Conservatives in it, its members and policies were not such as were likely to attract many Tories. Its ancestry can be traced to the 'Anti-Nazi Council', which Churchill misnamed 'the Anti-Nazi League'; he was more accurate when he described it as originating in 'Jewish resentment at their abominable persecution'.[20] Its organiser, Eugen Spier, a German-Jewish refugee, claimed that he had provided the running capital, but £9,600 would not have gone very far even in 1936.[21] The great bulk of its finance came from rich British Jews such as Sir Robert Mond (a director of several chemical firms) and Sir Robert Waley-Cohen, the managing director of Shell, the latter contributing £50,000.[22] That British Jews should have wished to help their co-religionists in Germany was understandable, but it inevitably aroused in others a feeling of 'why should Britain fight for the Jews?' – especially at a time when Jewish activities in Palestine were causing the Government a great deal of trouble.

Anti-Semitism, an emotion not unknown in British Society, was not the only reason why The Focus failed to pull in Conservative recruits. The President of the Anti-Nazi Council was the trades union leader, Walter Citrine, and Vice-Presidents included Norman Angell, a noted pacifist and left-wing polemicist; Sylvia Pankhurst, the feminist and socialist; and Eleanor Rathbone, an 'Independent' MP with pacifist leanings and socialist sympathies. For Churchill to align himself with such people and declare, after a decade of unremitting hostility to 'Bolshevism', that 'Russia can for the present be looked upon as an asset to the cause of peace',[23] was reason enough to doubt both his judgment and his motives. But when, in October 1936, he declared his support for The Focus policy of adherence to 'the Covenant of the League of Nations; that is our rock',[24] it seemed proof positive of these things. The League, which had never been wildly popular amongst Conservatives, had just failed to deal with the Abyssinian crisis, and its supporters came predominantly from the left of the political spectrum (Austen Chamberlain described them as 'some of the worse cranks I have ever known');[25] Churchill's espousal of such causes in such company was enough to warn any Conservative MP away.

The idea that Churchill was not fussy what tools he used to attack the Government was not far from the truth. He was, he told his son Randolph in November 1936, quite prepared to offer the 'left-wing intelligencia [*sic*]' 'protection' for 'their ideas' in 'return for their aid in the rearmament of Britain'.[26] It was, however, all very well for the *New Statesman* to declare that 'the logic of present politics is surely the formation of a Centre Front with Winston Churchill as the effective leader, if not as the potential Prime Minister',[27] but neither that, nor the company he kept, attracted many supporters.

In so far as Churchill had any followers, they were not such as to bring to his door orthodox young MPs who were worried about Chamberlain's foreign policy. The flamboyant MP for Buchan, Robert Boothby, who had been Churchill's Private Secretary, although often labelled a 'follower' was not cut out for the role of disciple.[28] When Churchill managed to squander the political capital which his speeches on rearmament had built up by supporting Edward VIII during the abdication crisis, Boothby scolded him for his lack of political judgment, lamenting that 'for ten years, as one of your most devoted followers, I have fought a losing battle against the influence of the die-hards, the Press Lords and Brendan [Bracken]';[29] warnings against such associates were well-directed, but many would have added Boothby's own name to the list.

Boothby's raffishness and his air of contrived eccentricity, combined with some odd political views, made him exactly the sort of character whom staider souls would associate with someone like Churchill. His views on foreign policy veered from the sound to the alarming. In his memoirs he wrote that Chamberlain could have chosen either Russia or Germany as an ally, and that for his part he preferred the former 'because socialism was still their proclaimed goal; because in socialism there was at least some hope, and because Litvinov [the Soviet Foreign Minister] had espoused the cause of collective security'.[30] But letters written to Chamberlain in the late 1930s hardly suggest that his opposition to the Prime Minister's policy was that fundamental.[31]

In 1930 Boothby had written to Sir Oswald Mosley warning him that the reaction of the great British public to a 'combination' of themselves, the Press Lords and one or two others from the political margins was likely to be: 'By God, now all the shits have climbed into the same basket, so we know where we are';[32] the same could have been said if Churchill's name was substituted for Mosley's.

Of those included in Boothby's interdict, the 'die-hards' were already becoming estranged from Churchill by the company he was beginning to keep; of the Press Lords, Beaverbrook and Rothermere, the former thought him a 'busted flush',[33] whilst the latter disagreed with him on Germany;[34] only Brendan Bracken remained close – and he was 'the best friend and the worst counsellor in the world'.[35]

A garrulous, red-haired Irishman whose background was, deliberately, shrouded in mystery, Bracken once said that 'Winston is very credulous, he has always been easily taken in'; his own presence at the centre of Churchill's entourage was proof of that.[36] He had first attached himself to Churchill in the early 1920s and, during the 1930s, became a fixture at Chartwell – Winston's 'faithful chela'. That such an odd character should so quickly have gained intimacy with Churchill fostered rumours (which Bracken was not averse to encouraging) that he was Churchill's illegitimate son.[37] Where Boothby was neither politically nor personally unconditionally loyal to Churchill, Bracken could at least claim to be the latter. But on foreign policy, his views were closer to Beaverbrook's than they were to Churchill's, as he believed that 'we could not afford to take a strong line in foreign policy at all. We would not take the risk of war, so it was wrong to give advice and then politely bow ourselves out.'[38] Thus it was that, when it came to The Focus and foreign policy, not even the exiguous support usually accorded to Churchill actually existed.

Underneath his newly acquired League of Nations credentials, Churchill was an old-fashioned balance-of-power man with a traditional understanding of Britain's role in Europe. As he was writing a biography of his great ancestor, Marlborough, he naturally adopted the 'Whig' view that Britain's role in foreign policy was to prevent any one power dominating Europe, and that 'in all the struggles of four centuries England has always marched with the mass of opinion of the world and has stood for the general interest of all nations to dwell in peace and toleration with one another'.[39] What he saw in the covenant of the League was a way of getting a Balkan pact, an Anglo-French alliance and an encirclement of Germany to ensure that she behaved herself – and of ensuring that Labour and trades union opinion backed him.

Churchill had also cultivated Eden, corresponding with him about foreign policy and inviting him to a Focus luncheon in late 1937.[40] But now Eden was out of the Government, he followed the advice of Baldwin, who warned him to steer clear of Churchill, association with whom would do him no good.[41] Eden would probably have done so even without such advice, for he was aware, as 'Rab' Butler put it, that he 'would become a new focus for a political movement among the younger and more sentimental members of the House' – a respectable 'alternative to the "old gang"'.[42] Since Sir Austen Chamberlain's death in 1937 there had been a vacancy in this quarter, and Eden intended to fill it; as he told Nicolson in early April, he would not rejoin the Cabinet but would, instead, make 'a few big speeches' on such topics as 'Democracy and Young England' by which means he would 'clearly indicate that he stands for post-war England against the old men'.[43]

If Eden wanted to keep clear of Churchill, then that old Adullamite's attitude was not as clear-cut as the hyperbolic comments in his memoirs, about the 'vision of death' which came to him when Eden resigned, might suggest.

Churchill's was the fourth signature on a 'round robin' expressing confidence in the Prime Minister's policy, which was circulated around the Conservative benches a few days after Eden's resignation.[44] Eden returned the compliment in early March by being absent from the Commons when Churchill made a powerful speech against Hitler's annexation of Austria; and neither of them bothered to protest about the Anglo-Italian Agreement when it was signed in April.[45]

Churchill, firmly stuck in the cave, took the view that parliamentary action would be totally ineffective and looked to 'events' and strange combinations to bring him to power;[46] but, essentially a parliamentarian, he waited upon circumstances to aid his cause. There were some in Labour circles who were equally catholic in their tastes and, in the immediate aftermath of the *Anschluss*, Dr Hugh Dalton recorded that, 'The idea of a new coalition Government', with Churchill as Prime Minister, Eden as Foreign Secretary and with Labour and Liberal Ministers, 'was much in the air';[47] but that was where it remained.

For all its lack of heroism Eden's strategy (if such it can be called) was more sensible than Churchill's; but then it could afford to be. Worried by what he saw as the polarising effects of disagreement over foreign policy, Eden came to see himself in the role of mediator.[48] It was to him that the discontented rallied. But even when an 'Eden group' was formed after Munich, its members 'decided that we should not advertise ourselves as a group or even call ourselves a group'.[49] It is not by such means that a Government with a majority of three hundred is overthrown; but as it is difficult to work out any means of accomplishing such a feat, discretion was the better part of valour.

Even so, only something like twenty MPs ever gathered to the banner which Eden so decorously raised.[50] The list sent by Emrys Evans to Leo Amery in 1954 contains one member, Nicolson, who was not a Conservative and, of the remainder, Duff Cooper did not join until after Munich; the rest, Eden and Cranborne excepted, were an odd assortment of rebellious backbenchers and nonentities. Harold Macmillan, for all his future fame, was a notorious rebel who had actually resigned the Party Whip over Abyssinia; Lord Wolmer was a 'die-hard' over India; Sidney Herbert was a distinguished backbencher in poor health and with close connections to Cranborne; and Richard Law, son of the former Prime Minister, Bonar Law, was inclined to blame Women's Conservative Associations for phenomena like Neville Chamberlain.[51] The rest were even less distinguished: General Spears (a former National Liberal, well-known Francophile and businessman), Anthony Crossley, Michael Tree, Michael Patrick, Herbert Bower, Herbert Duggan and Derrick Gunston were not names to conjure with when making Cabinets. Ronald Cartland, brother of the novelist, was furious with Chamberlain whom he described as the

Conservative Party's very own 'Führer', but he had to acknowledge, as did Churchill, that the Prime Minister had a tight hold on the Party.[52]

Just as Cartland was fulminating, Chamberlain was writing happily to his sisters that the Party Chairman, Sir Douglas Hacking, had assured him that

> he'd never known the Party so united, but on the other hand that my outspokenness and precision had probably frightened the weak-kneed Liberals who felt safe with S.B. I expect that is true . . . I can't change my nature and must hope to make up for Liberal defections by greater enthusiasm in our own Party.[53]

The fact that neither the *Anschluss* nor the events of the summer and autumn of 1938 were to break the ranks of the Conservative Party was testimony not merely to the accuracy of Chamberlain's prediction, but also to the political acumen which he showed in bringing Halifax to the Foreign Office; he could provide the Baldwinians with reassurance that all was well and that Eden's departure was not a disaster.

The Traditions
of British Foreign Policy

One German newspaper, reporting the arrival of Halifax and his Under-Secretary, Rab Butler, at the Foreign Office, wrote of the 'citadel' being successfully 'stormed'.[1] Historians, who have tended to see in the new regime pliant replacements for the extruded Eden, with the Prime Minister now exercising control of foreign policy, have not subjected it to any great analysis. Halifax was never the Prime Minister's tool, not even in the early days before he had mastered his new job, and if he and Butler held similar views to those of Chamberlain, that was the result of a genuine congruence of opinion rather than a sign of sycophancy.

Those 'weak-kneed Liberals who felt safe with S.B.', and others who felt that Chamberlain's style of leadership was 'leading us back to Party politics' with the risk that many who 'for washy reasons have supported us before, will not do so in the future',[2] found in the new order a source of reassurance. Where Churchill had taken the 'die-hard' line over India, Halifax had been the Viceroy who had talked to Gandhi, and Butler had been Hoare's Under-Secretary at the India Office and had fought the cause of the India Bill with great skill and success.

But if both men could reassure the 'National' element in the Government's support, they could also appeal to the middle ground of the Conservative Party. Indeed, Halifax's credentials as a Conservative were better than Chamberlain's, whose radical and municipal antecedents allowed enemies to sneer at him as a 'middle-class businessman with no scrap of imagination'.[3] Halifax was the quintessential English gentleman, and his Baldwinian affiliations, viceregal experience and personal gravitas brought great political weight to a rather shaken Government. It also brought a new style to the conduct of diplomacy.

Eden, despite his diplomatic 'flair', had been almost a 'Foreign Office official' in his attitudes towards the dictators.[4] He had brought with him to his office the intense atmosphere created by someone who relied upon his 'anten-

THE OLD-FASHIONED CUSTOMER
'I wonder if you've got a song I remember about not wanting to fight, but if we
do ... something, something, something ... we've got the money too?'
23 March 1938.

nae' and lived on his nerves. Halifax came as a soothing breeze, detached and
sensible where Eden had been committed and sensitive. He felt 'very clearly'
that 'we go badly wrong if we allow our judgement of practical steps to be taken,
to be perpetually deflected by our moral reactions against wrong that we can in
no circumstances immediately redress'.[5] Although he liked Eden, Halifax had
always mistrusted his revulsion from dictators as being 'too strong ... inasmuch
as you have got to live with the devils whether you like them or not'.[6] He thought
that 'perhaps the greatest difficulty in the conduct of foreign affairs, and the one

least appreciated by those not actually engaged in it, is the fact that the ideal policy is scarcely ever practicable'. Everyone wanted to see 'peace established, injustice righted' and 'law respected', but when it came to the 'practical working out of what we want to see done we find ourselves faced with harsh and obstinate realities which often turn the ideal into the Utopian'.[7]

Butler was the ideal collaborator for such a man. The Butler stock mixed Indian administration with academic success, and Rab shone in both spheres. After a short period as a Cambridge don, he had entered the Commons as MP for Saffron Walden in 1924. Having married into the Courtauld family, he had little need to worry about money and, where other contemporaries like Macmillan made their mark through rebellion, Rab chose the less glamorous and (seemingly) more rewarding course of conformity; not for him the stance of *Athanasius contra mundum*. When Macmillan wrote bitterly to *The Times* in 1930 about the need to 'change the rules' of the parliamentary game, Butler and like-minded colleagues in the so-called 'Boys' Brigade' responded that 'when a player starts complaining "that it is hardly worth while bothering to play" the game at all it is usually the player, and not the game, who is at fault'.[8] But Macmillan did not take their advice and find 'a new field for his recreation and a pastime more suited to his talents'; had he done so Butler's career would have been rather different.

Butler's loyalty, and his talents, had been rewarded after 1932 with the junior post at the India Office, where he had won plaudits for his handling of the formidable Churchill; the junior post at the Foreign Office was a fitting, if belated, promotion. He had had little contact with his new chief, but the two men worked well together. Butler found Halifax 'charming' and 'efficient', if a little remote. His feline nature appreciated Halifax's quiddities: his tendency to adorn his speeches with metaphors from the hunting-field, and his meanness: 'One day a messenger brought in four biscuits and two cups of tea. Halifax pushed away the biscuits and said, "Mr Butler does not want these. Nor do I. Do not charge me."'[9]

Meanness was one of the few charges that could not be levelled against the one exotic in the new team, Butler's Parliamentary Private Secretary, Henry 'Chips' Channon. He threw himself into the embrace of British High Society with the zest of the American intent on forgetting his country of origin. Wealth and marriage into the Guinness clan provided his passport to the salons of England, and his political views, right-wing, anti-Semitic and pro-German, were not such as would mark him out for expulsion from the paradise he had entered. His description of himself as 'able but trivial' was unduly flattering, at least as far as the first adjective was concerned,[10] but his worldliness, love of gossip and sociability provided contacts into parts of the Conservative

Party which neither Halifax's saintliness nor Butler's rectitude could reach.

Channon's appointment symbolised the end of the Eden regime with a vengeance. As Butler had expected, it 'caused a good many ripples in the press' and made 'Harold Nicolson and others who are critical of us quite angry'. But it served to 'break the old FO team where PPSs, Ministers and officials had all got O[ld] E[tonian] ties and called each other by their Christian names and had exactly the same type of brains'.[11] The new order would be different.

With this more congenial team Chamberlain looked forward to successful negotiations with Mussolini. Despite being 'abused like a pickpocket' by 'foolish people who either will not or cannot see what I am doing', the Prime Minister was unaffected by either qualms or 'self-doubts'.[12] He announced that negotiations had opened with Italy for a settlement of all 'outstanding questions'.[13] But hopes that closer co-operation with Italy might yet save the 'last shreds of Austrian independence'[14] were not to be realised.

In fact the new order at the Foreign Office had the roughest start possible. First of all, on 3 March, came the news that Henderson's offer to Hitler of colonial concessions in return for contributions 'towards restoration of tranquillity and confidence in Europe' had been greeted with 'passionate invective' about the lot of the ten million Germans living outside the Reich. Then, on 11 March, whilst Ribbentrop was having his farewell luncheon at Chequers, came the news that Hitler had announced the *Anschluss* and that German troops were in Vienna.[15]

Halifax had warned Ribbentrop only the previous day about the dangers of precipitate action in Central Europe, telling him that although Britain desired neither to deny legitimate German demands in Central Europe, nor to resort to war, 'the experience of all history went to show that the pressure of facts was sometimes more powerful than the wills of men: and if once war should start in Central Europe, it was quite impossible to say where it might not end and who might not get involved.'[16] The problem facing the new Foreign Secretary was what to do now.

Chamberlain found it 'all very disheartening and discouraging' and concluded that 'force is the only language which Germany understands';[17] but was it feasible to use force in this instance? Westminster attempted to read the runes: some said that dissident Ministers were going to resign; others that Baldwin had been seeing Eden and that he would return as tutelary deity in a Churchill Government with Eden restored to the Foreign Office.[18] No one did resign, but although all Ministers denied the rumours, Chamberlain thought it worth telling Hore-Belisha that he trusted 'my colleagues to tell me first if they disagreed with me'.[19] By the evening of 16 March Chamberlain 'felt as if it was going to be too much for me': the rumours of wars; the intrigues; and, most of all, 'the state of Europe and the problem of what our reaction should be'.[20]

One of Butler's old friends and fellow-members of the old 'Boys' Brigade', Michael Beaumont, begged him, 'For God's sake do what you can to stop the country being stampeded by hysteria . . . [from] entering into any more foreign commitments, particularly with regard to Czecho-Slovakia'; Butler assured him that 'we are the last to be stampeded by hysteria'.[21]

Beaumont's fears were prompted, at least in part, by the suggestion which Churchill had put forward on 14 March: the policy of the 'Grand Alliance' – 'a number of states assembled around Great Britain and France' in a pact for mutual defence based upon the Covenant of the League of Nations and 'sustained by the moral sense of the world'.[22] Historians, who have often favoured such a policy, have condemned Chamberlain harshly for not following it, some even alleging that he unduly influenced the Chiefs of Staff's assessment of the situation, others that he did not seek the advice of the Foreign Office.[23] Such views, based as they are upon an unflattering estimate of Chamberlain's diplomatic virility, hardly correspond with the Prime Minister's reaction at the time.

The idea of the 'Grand Alliance' had also occurred to Chamberlain, and he was 'much attracted by it'. But as, unlike Churchill, he had to take responsibility for whatever was done, he decided to examine the proposal 'much more thoroughly and in particular get military advice on it'.[24] Once this was done it was plain that 'there is almost everything to be said for it until you come to examine its practicability. From that moment its attraction vanishes. You only have to look at the map to see that nothing that we or France could do could possibly save Czechoslovakia from being overrun by the Germans if they wanted to do it.'[25] Military and diplomatic advice both pointed in this direction.

There was far from being a 'Foreign Office' view on how to react to the possibility of future German action in Central Europe, as the three papers, which Cadogan considered on 16 March before advising the Prime Minister, showed.[26] Sir Orme Sargent, a senior Under-Secretary who shared Vansittart's views, took a modified Churchillian line, arguing for staff talks with the French and the Belgians, and better relations with Poland, Russia and America. Gladwyn Jebb, Cadogan's Private Secretary, argued that an Anglo-French guarantee to Czechoslovakia was tantamount to 'suicide', so there was no use trying to stop Hitler that way; he preferred cultivating Mussolini and getting back to the situation of 1934, when he had kept a 'watch on the Brenner pass'. The third paper, from the head of the Central Department, William Strang, shared their assumption that Czechoslovakia would be Hitler's next target, but his advice was closer to Jebb's.

The British Minister in Prague, Basil Newton, argued that nothing was to be gained from offering the Czechs a guarantee; it might stop them making reforms in the way they treated the Sudeten German minority, and, in so doing, make war more likely; if war came, 'nothing that we or France could do would save Czechoslovakia from being overrun'. The most that could be done would be 'to restore after a lengthy struggle a status quo which had already proved unacceptable and which, even if restored, would probably again prove unworkable'; 'Czechoslovakia's present political position' was, Newton advised, 'not permanently tenable'.[27]

These assumptions informed Strang's paper, which argued against extending a guarantee to Czechoslovakia, maintaining instead that as British public opinion would never go to war to deny self-determination to the Sudetens it would be better to try to resolve their grievances by means of an international commission of inquiry. As for the 'Grand Alliance',[28] Strang reminded Cadogan that such an arrangement was not to be had overnight and that, in the meantime, Germany might well feel obliged to strike by force. As for the idea, advanced by Sargent, that Britain should guarantee to help France if she became involved in a war as a result of her obligations to Czechoslovakia, this would mean that the final decision for war or peace would be taken out of the hands of the British Government. He recommended that Britain should make no new commitments, but should try to persuade the Czechs and the French that the way forward was for the former to make the best terms they could with Hitler; at the same time Chamberlain's policy of trying to detach Italy from the Axis should be pursued. To those who argued that the risks of war were worth taking because Germany would be even stronger in two years' time, Strang's reply was laconic: 'This is not a good argument for risking disaster now.' In view of what did happen in the summer of 1940 this is not to be taken lightly.

This was an argument which, however unpalatable to some historians, was accepted by Chamberlain because it coincided with the assumptions behind his foreign and defence policies, as well as with the reports of the Chiefs of Staff. Advocates of the 'Grand Alliance' who argue that Britain would have had the help of the Russians, Poles and Czechs if war had broken out in 1938 have been quick to dismiss the Chiefs of Staff report as unduly pessimistic; but perhaps they are unduly optimistic.

Even if Britain and France had possessed a concerted plan of attack on Germany in the event of a crisis arising over the situation in Czechoslovakia, and even had their armed forces been ready to put it into effect, it is still doubtful whether the advantages alleged to have been available for a war in 1938 would have materialised. When Chamberlain briefed the Chiefs of Staff and advised them to leave Russia out of the equation, he was being realistic, not pessimistic;

the recently purged Red Army was, at best, a dubious asset, even on the assumption that Stalin would enter a war between the capitalists and the fascists. The Poles had their own territorial ambitions on Czechoslovakia and would hardly have co-operated with the Russians against Germany, whilst the other Powers in the region, Romania and Bulgaria, were also unlikely to risk choosing between either of the major Powers. It may well be, as some historians argue, that the Czech army would have fought well, but given the unlikelihood of all the other Powers actually coming to Czechoslovakia's aid, her most probable fate would have been to anticipate by a year what befell the Poles.[29]

Behind the 'Grand Alliance' strategy lay Churchill's 'Whiggish' vision of the traditions of British foreign policy which was shared by former diplomats like Duff Cooper and Paul Emrys Evans, who were apt to claim that they had 'studied foreign policy'; Butler took the view that they had, in fact, 'been reared in Edwardian politics' and were so imbued with the Eyre Crowe view of the balance of power and the German menace that they failed to appreciate 'the facts of life'.[30] Butler did not believe that a worldwide Empire had ever had 'a simple traditional policy': British interests, 'and the world itself, are too complicated to enable us to follow any one high road'.[31]

Halifax, who took the view that 'the world is a strangely mixed grill of good and evil' and that 'for good or ill we have got to do our best to live in it and not withdraw from it into the desert because of the evil, like the ancient anchorites',[32] thought that no British policy 'short of war' could have prevented the *Anschluss* and doubted whether other members of the League would have stood by Britain on the issue. He was still 'perfectly willing to recognise the special interest of the German Government' in Austria, and even saw no objection to Germany 'having economic hegemony in Central Europe', not supposing that the status quo could be 'maintained for all time'; what he did not like were Hitler's methods. Those who spoke of the League as the answer to all things and yet opposed the spending of vast sums of money on rearmament now had to bow in the face of the 'extremely ugly truth that neither treaty texts nor international law have any influence when dealing with power politics' where 'force and force alone decides'.[33] Thomas Hobbes put it more succinctly: 'Covenants without swords are but mere words.'

Halifax put forward his views at the Foreign Policy Committee of the Cabinet on 18 March; like Chamberlain's they were influenced by Strang's paper.[34] When Halifax rejected the idea of the 'Grand Alliance', it was almost in the *ipissima verba* that Strang had used: 'the long and difficult negotiations which would be necessary . . . would afford both a provocation and an opportunity to Germany to dispose of Czechoslovakia before the Grand Alliance had been organised'. As for the idea of giving a guarantee to Czechoslovakia, Halifax referred to Newton's opinion and said that they were 'entitled to decline the risk of involving Great Britain in a fresh war in order to shore up the present position if it is one which seems to us fundamentally untenable'. When Chamberlain asked whether it would not be possible to arrive at some settlement of the Czechoslovak problem that would be 'more acceptable' to Germany, he was basing himself not upon some craven desire to grovel to Hitler, but upon advice coming from the very Foreign Office which he is supposed to have ignored.

Churchill regarded France and Russia as solid blocks upon which to build a policy, but Halifax and Chamberlain were less sanguine. Halifax reminded the Foreign Policy Committee that the more closely they associated themselves with France and Russia, 'the more we produced in German minds the impression that we were plotting to encircle Germany and the more difficult it would be to make any real settlement with Germany'. This echoed the idea that one of the causes of the Great War had been such a German fear, and it would have been folly to have made the same mistake as Sir Edward Grey with his talk about a 'Triple Entente'.

Chamberlain, like many Conservatives, was not disposed to regard the France of the Third Republic as a solid bastion behind which to shelter, and he saw in Russia a dictatorship as evil as Hitler's and a country which was 'stealthily and cunningly pulling all the strings behind the scenes to get us involved in a war with Germany': 'our secret service doesn't spend all its time looking out of windows'. A positive response to Russian requests for talks would be the prelude to war, whilst a guarantee to Czechoslovakia would 'simply be a pretext' for that war: this he was unwilling to undertake 'unless we had a reasonable prospect of being able to beat [Germany] to her knees in a reasonable time and of that I see no chance'.[35]

It may be that, as Churchill and company sometimes alleged, a commitment to the 'Grand Alliance' would have deterred Hitler from fighting; but then perhaps it would not have done so – and Britain would have had her bluff called and have had to fight a war which her military could not prosecute for a cause which her diplomats pronounced indefensible. A war in defence of the terms of the Treaty of Trianon might have appealed to Churchill's sense of what a thousand years of British history and the necessities of the balance of power demanded, but it made no appeal to Chamberlain's sense of what the realities of Britain's situation could afford.

The first public sign of the way in which the Government intended to react to the *Anschluss* came on 18 March when the Under-Secretary at the Ministry of Labour, Alan Lennox-Boyd, made a speech in his Bedford constituency, in which he declared that he did not think that 'we should tie ourselves in advance by giving undertakings to go to the aid of European countries if they were invaded unless their security was a vital concern to us'; whilst implying no guarantee for Czechoslovakia, his words left open the question of whether France would be helped if she became involved in a war because of her treaty obligations to the Czechs.[36]

This was strikingly similar to Halifax's recommendations to the Foreign Policy Committee on the same day that:

> We should try to persuade France and Czechoslovakia that the best course would be for the latter to make the best terms she could with Germany while there was yet time and that we would use any influence we might have with Germany to induce her to take up a reasonable attitude. If in the result a satisfactory solution of the Sudeten problem was reached we might offer in that event to join Germany in guaranteeing Czechoslovakia's independence.[37]

Having agreed upon a policy, it took another meeting of the Foreign Policy Committee on 21 March to finalise details of what statement the Government should make.[38] But not everyone was happy when the results of the deliberations went before the Cabinet on 22 March.[39]

The First Lord of the Admiralty, Duff Cooper, got up from his sick-bed to attend the meeting, so agitated was he by the terms of the proposed statement to the French and the Commons. He 'fought hard . . . not quite in favour of giving the guarantee to Czechoslovakia, but for making a more friendly gesture to France', on the grounds that 'when France fought Germany, we should have to fight too, whether we liked it or not'. Only the Minister of Labour, Oliver Stanley, who had argued at the Foreign Policy Committee in favour of a guarantee to Czechoslovakia, and Buck de la Warr supported Cooper's line. It was decided 'that the two statements should be redrafted but that the policy should remain'.[40]

The statements made by Chamberlain in the Commons and Halifax in the Lords on 24 March represented a successful affirmation of the bases of the foreign policy for which both men had contended during the crisis; that policy remained in operation for the rest of the year.[41] By maintaining a deliberate ambiguity about the exact British response to any further aggression, it was hoped at once to 'bluff' the Germans whilst keeping the French from acting rashly. Britain's existing commitments involving a casus belli were reiterated: the Locarno agreements, which bound her to defend France or Belgium if they were victims of unprovoked aggression; bilateral treaties to the same effect with Portugal, Iraq and Egypt; and the obligations arising out of the Covenant of the League; the last of these being covered by Eden's statement at Leamington Spa in 1936, which limited a casus belli to instances where vital British interests were threatened. These were Britain's *legal* obligations, but whilst refraining from adding Czechoslovakian independence to them, or commenting about what would happen if France became involved in a war over Czechoslovakia, Chamberlain was careful to state that:

> Where peace and war are concerned, legal obligations are not alone involved, and, if war broke out, it would be unlikely to be confined to those who have assumed such obligations. It would be quite impossible to say where it might end and what Governments might become involved. The inexorable pressure of facts might well prove more powerful than formal pronouncements . . .

At the same time he announced a major increase in spending on armaments, further emphasising that British policy remained: 'By reason if possible – by force if not.'

For the moment Chamberlain's anxieties subsided. His statement had an '*éclatant* success' and he confessed himself unable to remember a speech by a 'British Minister at a critical time which has won such universal approval in Europe'; so much, he thought, for 'weak-kneed colleagues' like Stanley and de la Warr. Having weathered the storm, the Prime Minister could, in tranquillity, forget the anxieties he had felt and claim that he had refused to bow to hysteria; he had merely weighed up the situation and 'decided quite definitely what was the right course and to my great satisfaction I found Halifax had come independently to the same conclusion'. Once that had been done, 'the public' gradually 'settled down on the same side, whereupon our colleagues, as well as the clever young men in the Party, all came to the conclusion that our plan, if not perfect, was near enough theirs to be accepted'.

Churchill was given a private interview with the Prime Minister, who impressed upon him the reasons why the 'Grand Alliance' strategy had been rejected; he assured Chamberlain that 'he would not intrigue against me' and that his attitude towards the Government 'even though critical would be "avuncular"'. Chamberlain assured his sisters that, whilst 'everyone in the House enjoys listening to him and is ready to laugh at his sallies', he had 'no following of any importance'. As for the 'dissentients' in the Cabinet, Chamberlain was confident that 'there is no wish to have any other leader'.[42]

If Chamberlain had emerged from the crisis caused by the *Anschluss* in a dominant position it was not because the Conservative Party was peopled by 'yes men' and the Cabinet by spineless worms, but because the only alternative to his policy was Churchill's 'Grand Alliance'. However, as that amounted to standing four-square behind the Versailles system, which no longer existed, it was not an option many found attractive. Speaking in the Lords on 29 March Halifax rejected 'any short cuts, by threats or by exhortation, by resting on the theory of the balance of power or isolation or collective security . . . to reach the place where we seek to be'; in order to 'induce reason in others, we must be reasonable ourselves'.[43]

The new order at the Foreign Office had survived its first major test and had managed to formulate a policy which would serve for the future. If the crisis had resulted in the Foreign Office being 'cemented with No. 10', it was not because Halifax was subservient, but because his 'lack of "heresy-hunting"' chimed with Chamberlain's instincts. Both men were willing to face the need for 'readjustment in Europe' without being 'perpetually inspired by a fear of the "German menace"'. This did not mean that they were 'simple or naive', but rather that war would be a last, rather than a first, resort.[44]

Towards a Commitment

The refusal of Chamberlain and Halifax to commit themselves to guarantee the independence and integrity of Czechoslovakia, containing as it did the seed of the policy which blossomed at Munich, has incurred the censure of historians who deprecate the results of that conference. One convicts the Prime Minister and Foreign Secretary of blindness to the 'simple and obvious truth about German intentions' since 'it does not seem to have occurred to them that the German grievances [in the Sudetenland] were simply a pretext . . . a tactical gambit in a struggle for Europe';[1] another dismisses Chamberlain's assertion that he had originally favoured the 'Grand Alliance' option as 'clearly disingenuous';[2] whilst a third, driven even further to distraction by what he can glean from the archives, records sternly that 'less than a week after the *Anschluss* . . . without seeking military advice . . . in opposition to the Foreign Office [and] in almost complete ignorance of Soviet attitudes', the Foreign Policy Committee 'accepted Chamberlain's policy and abandoned any attempt to resist further German aggression against Czechoslovakia'.[3] As a picture of the process described in the previous chapter, this is a caricature.

The 'truth' about Hitler's intentions is so 'simple and obvious' that it has spawned a scholarly industry. Chamberlain was not blind to the possibility that Hitler might be aiming at something wider than self-determination for the Sudetens, but that seemed insufficient reason to refuse this demand. The Chiefs of Staff report was certainly pessimistic, but Chamberlain did consult them, as he did the Foreign Office; it is, therefore, a trifle harsh to condemn him on the one hand for not consulting expert opinion and then, on the other, to condemn him for not disregarding their views. Nor had Chamberlain abandoned the Czechs; they had not asked for British help and he had not offered it. His statement on 24 March was not a carte-blanche to Germany and his policy over the next six months does not suggest otherwise.

Those who persist in believing that Chamberlain was an obstinate old gentleman who knew nothing about Europe or diplomacy ignore a few 'truths' which, whilst neither 'simple' nor 'obvious', are applicable to the foreign policy he and Halifax pursued. It was not a 'personal' policy, but one which took account of professional diplomatic and military advice; it also took note of economic and political considerations. None of these things suggested that a British guarantee to Czechoslovakia would be a useful way of deterring Hitler (it might, in passing, be noted that if Hitler was really determined on war, there is no reason to suppose that he would have been deterred). Moreover, such an action would have cut across the main thrust of Chamberlain's policy, which was to secure a lessening of the tension in Europe. As he told an audience in Birmingham in April 1938:

> An ancient historian once wrote of the Greeks that they had made gentle the life of the world. I do not know whether in these modern days it is possible for any nation to emulate the example of the Greeks, but I can imagine no nobler ambition for an English statesman than to win the same tribute for his own country.[4]

The editors of the British documents on Foreign Policy for this period have a lot to answer for. Beginning the third series, dealing with the period from March 1938 to the outbreak of the war, as they did, they unwittingly gave a handle to those who would see British policy as being improvised in the aftermath of the *Anschluss*. From the beginning of 1937 the British had been urging upon the Czechs and their French allies the need to make concessions to improve the lot of the Sudetens. Recognising that Hitler might really have designs on Czechoslovakia's independence, the Foreign Office saw that as no excuse for 'not trying to remove a major pretext and at least gain time'.[5]

The idea of giving the Czechs a guarantee in return for the concession of autonomy to the Sudetens had been considered and rejected in November 1937. The diplomats had feared that British opinion would not accept 'a new and extremely important commitment in Central Europe', a feeling which Eden shared, although he acknowledged that 'we shall have to be associated in some form with any settlement reached, indeed none can be reached without our active participation'.[6] Chamberlain's policy followed these lines and was informed by Cadogan's view that 'it would be a very difficult decision to choose any course of action that might plunge Europe into war now to avert what may be a worse war later on', as well as by Newton's advice that the 'least favourable place' to resist the '*Drang Nach Osten*' was Czechoslovakia, 'which is at Germany's very doors, surrounded by potential enemies, completely inaccessible to any force that Great Britain could possibly put into the field, and exposed, in any case, to economic strangulation'.[7]

Given the priorities which Chamberlain was following in bringing defence spending under control, Newton's warning was well-merited; moreover, as Simon reminded the Cabinet on 14 March: 'At the present moment we are in the position of a runner in a race who wants to reserve his sprint for the right time, but does not know where the finishing tape is. The danger is that we might knock our finances to pieces prematurely.'[8] The British rearmament programme would not peak until 1939–40, and even then it would not equip the country for a war on the Continent.[9] If war did not break out by then, Chamberlain would be faced with a dilemma. The British economy could scarcely afford the cost of the current rearmament plan, indeed in March 1938 £70 million was cut from the War Office budget; by 1940–41 it would be necessary to restrict arms spending still further. In the meantime, bringing on an economic crisis by increasing current expenditure was unlikely to add weight to British diplomacy.

Nor could Britain have relied upon much help if Churchill's policy had prevailed. Although the French had an alliance with the Czechs, they had no plans to help them in the event of their being attacked by Germany; indeed, they had frightened themselves with nightmares about the Siegfried Line and could see no way of helping the Czechs.[10] As for Churchill's much-vaunted Russians, the British Military Attaché in Moscow reported that the recent purges in the Red Army had 'had a disastrous effect' on its 'morale and efficiency'; with sixty-five per cent of its officers gone, it was 'not capable of carrying the war into the enemy's territory with any hope of ultimate success'.[11] Even had this not been the case, and even had the Czechs requested their help, it is far from clear how Russian aid could have been made effective as neither the Poles nor the Romanians were likely to let Soviet troops on to their soil.[12]

It has been pointed out that the German Chiefs of Staff were as pessimistic about their capacity to wage a successful war as their British counterparts, and that the balance of forces was not as unfavourable as the British thought.[13] This is true, but it ignores not only all the reasons already outlined for not gambling on the chance of a war in 1938, but also the fact that Chamberlain, unlike Hitler, objected to gambling with human lives. He would not do that, as he told an audience on 8 April, unless he was 'absolutely convinced that in no other way could we preserve our liberties'.[14]

It was by no means as apparent to contemporary diplomats as it seems to be to modern historians that peace was a doomed cause. Although the *Anschluss* made Henderson lament that 'all the work of the last eleven months has crashed to the ground', he wrote to Halifax on 7 April that it was 'defeatism' to say that 'war sooner or later between Great Britain and Germany is inevitable'. Peace could still be preserved, he believed, 'only if Germany is allowed to become one of the satisfied angels'.[15] Cadogan concurred with the spirit of this approach, wondering if it was, 'even now, too late to treat the Germans as human beings?' He recognised, as did Henderson, the risk that 'perhaps they wouldn't respond to such treatment', but thought it might be worth taking: 'We should ask them whether they won't let us try our hand at helping to remedy the grievances which they make so much of but which they don't make very clear.'[16]

Henderson had a definite view of what the Nazis might want if they were to become 'satisfied angels', warning Halifax at the beginning of April that, after the *Anschluss*, Hitler would aim at the Sudetenland then 'Danzig, and settlement of Poland and Memel'.[17] Whilst prepared, as any 'wise man' ought to be, for 'any exhibition of German power-politics', Halifax did not feel it necessary to assume that 'Hitler's racial ambitions are necessarily likely to expand into international power lust'. This, he recognised, was the crucial point. Churchill and company seemed to be arguing that,

> when Germany has done this that and the other in Central Europe, she will in overwhelming might proceed to destroy France and ourselves. That is a conclusion which I do not believe myself to be necessarily well-founded and, if you do not necessarily believe this, it makes you look jealously at the remedies that are immediately proposed to forestall it.[18]

The Sudeten Germans undoubtedly had grievances against the Prague Government, and a desire to rectify these was not necessarily a sign of 'international power lust'. Although not blind to the possibility that the Sudetens might be a stalking horse for wider ambitions, Halifax was not willing to start a war on the off-chance, preferring, instead, to urge upon the French the necessity of persuading the Czechs to 'face the realities of the situation' and to 'make the best bargain' they could with Hitler 'before the twelfth hour strikes'.[19]

Chamberlain, however, wanted to pursue a more active line, by asking Hitler to 'tell us exactly what you want for your Sudeten Deutsch'; if his demands were 'reasonable, we will urge the Czechs to accept it and if they do you must give assurances that you will let them alone in future'. Under these circumstances Chamberlain was even prepared to consider joining 'in some guarantee *with* Germany of Czech independence'.[20] There was no intention here of letting the whole of Czechoslovakia fall into Hitler's lap; and if it did, then he would have failed the acid test.

But, as in the previous November, the Foreign Office favoured a less bold line; the furthest they were willing to go was to impress upon the Czech President, Eduard Beneš, 'the need for making a considerable effort'. Later they '*might* find an opportunity of putting a word in Berlin in favour of Beneš'

G.R.P.
Chamberlain and Daladier prepare to damp down the Czechoslovak crisis,
1 June 1938.

proposals', but Cadogan was wary of taking on anything which looked like an
obligation to support the Czechs. Such a line of policy might get the Germans to
spell out their aims: 'My experience is that German demands, like mushrooms,
grow in the dark.'[21]

For all the accusations of dictatorial behaviour on the part of the Prime
Minister, it was Cadogan's policy which prevailed and Beneš was pressed to

'make a really satisfactory arrangement with the Sudeten Germans'.[22] This exercise was to continue until September. Beneš, who was no dictator, had problems with his own political parties, and this gave him plenty of room to finesse. It also allowed the Sudeten leader, Konrad Henlein, to put forward (with Berlin's connivance) his Carlsbad programme on 24 April; this amounted not only to a demand for autonomy, but also for a veto on the direction of Czech foreign policy.[23] Rumours that Hitler intended to act in the near future to resolve the problem prompted the new French Premier, Edouard Daladier, and his Foreign Minister, Georges Bonnet, to come to London at the end of April.

At the first meeting with Chamberlain and Halifax on 28 April, it was Daladier who put forward the pure milk of the Vansittart doctrine, saying that the 'ambitions of Napoleon were far inferior to the present German Reich.'[24] He argued that Britain and France ought to extend a guarantee to Czechoslovakia, even if they thought they might not be able to fulfil it: 'the military situation was really determined by the political situation'.[25] This came perilously close to 'bluff'. Whilst Chamberlain had 'asked himself' if it might not one day be necessary 'to put down one's foot and take all risks to prevent a further deterioration in the situation',[26] Daladier's policy meant 'casting the die and deciding that, in our view, this was, from the military point of view, the opportune moment to declare war on Germany with the object of bringing about her defeat'; but the Chiefs of Staff report said that this was not the case. Chamberlain reminded the Frenchman that 'whatever the odds might be in favour of peace or war, it was not money but men with which we were gambling'; the Prime Minister was unwilling to thus 'lightly enter into a conflict which might mean such frightful results for innumerable families, men, women, children, of our own race'.[27]

There was a paradox at the centre of the French position. They were afraid that, if they deserted their eastern allies, they would sink to the rank of a second-class power, but they were intermittently aware that, if they could not help those allies without British aid, nor yet make their own decisions on policy, they might already have arrived at that position.[28] On this occasion they settled easily enough for what Chamberlain was offering – Staff talks with Britain and advice to Prague to make concessions to Henlein.[29]

Chamberlain was pleased with the result of the talks, but conscious of the problems created by France's network of Eastern European alliances.[30] On the one hand was the danger of Britain being dragged into war because of these French commitments, on the other lay the possibility that a France unwilling to meet those commitments might be grateful to have in the British a scapegoat for her failure.

Chamberlain hoped to use France's connection with Czechoslovakia in order to help defuse the Sudeten problem and remove the temptations which its existence offered to Hitler, but Henderson feared that this might lead to Britain becoming entangled in France's eastern web of alliances. He told Halifax on 3 May that he loved 'my country more than Czechoslovakia or *Sudetendeutsche*, or Austrians or Poles or even Frenchmen', and that he thought the Foreign Office was throwing away 'our opportunities for the sake of international mirages'. Henderson favoured getting Mussolini to act as an intermediary, and telling the Germans that Britain had 'no intention of trying to hamper' her '*legitimate* economic freedom of action in Central or Eastern Europe'. This seemed to him no more than realism: 'the French dog-in-the-manger attitude in this respect is not only futile but silly . . . it is, I submit, a mistake to give the impression that, since we cannot hem her in territorially (*vide* Austria), we must hem her in economically'; personally, Henderson was 'only too glad to wish that she should look eastwards instead of westwards'.

As Chamberlain and Halifax were considering whether it would be possible to combat German expansionism through economic means, Henderson's warning went unheeded.[31] There were other matters to worry about – including the Ambassador himself.

Most worrying of all was the fact that the quick progress towards a removal of the Sudeten problem, which seemed to be promised in early May, did not materialise. The Czech Minister in London, Jan Masaryk, whose father, Tomas, had been the founder of Czechoslovakia, told Halifax on 1 May that he favoured a 'Swiss solution' to the Sudeten problem.[32] This idea, of Czechoslovakia as a 'state of nationalities' rather than a nation state, was the formula which the British pressed on Prague;[33] but progress was so slow as to cause anxiety in London.[34]

British policy depended, for its success, upon the Germans not knowing exactly what the British were up to in Prague, for fear that they would raise the stakes; it was enough that they should be told that the British were 'using their good offices' to persuade Beneš and Henlein to negotiate.[35] But it was feared that Henderson, in his anxiety to convince the Germans of Britain's sincerity, might have let slip something of the British plan.[36] So, in Cadogan's graphic phrase, he was given 'a gentle jab in the mouth'[37] and reminded of the necessity of drawing 'a clear distinction between the language we use in Prague and the language we use in Berlin'; in Prague 'the weakness of the military situation' was to be emphasised, but Berlin should be made to 'think long before doing anything likely to break the peace'.[38] For all Chamberlain's dislike of bluff, there were times when it was necessary.

A 'peaceful solution of the Czech problem'[39] would have given a harassed Prime Minister a useful fillip. Although, by the middle of May, 'foreign affairs' were 'a bit easier',[40] Chamberlain was badly in need of a parliamentary triumph. The Anglo-Italian Agreement had been signed on 16 April, but his hopes that it would give a 'nasty jar' to the Rome–Berlin Axis had not been realised because of a delay in bringing it into effect.[41] His enemies accused him of sympathy with fascism,[42] and his policy and style created a feeling in some quarters that he was losing 'the floating vote'.[43] Even the King complained (to Butler) that the Government's policy 'was without morality', and suggested that 'the Prime Minister tended to break the basis of National Government by being rude to the Opposition'.[44] Staunch Conservatives, who did not mind that sort of thing, were also out of sorts with the Prime Minister because of his agreement with Eamon de Valera over the control of southern Irish naval bases.

In such a climate the rumours bred rapidly, and during May Westminster was 'redolent of speculations' of the usual sort. Some said Eden was to be Prime Minister, others that Churchill was to become Minister of Supply, and there were the usual speculations that Baldwin would undergo political resurrection to give his blessing (and some respectability) to this enterprise.[45] Far-fetched though such tales were, there was a little fire behind the smoke as Halifax, although the most loyal of colleagues, was already evincing a concern that was to grow over the months that the Government's basis was 'too narrow', and speculating that Eden might be brought back into the Cabinet.[46]

In this atmosphere an incompetent performance by Lord Winterton during a debate over a motion critical of the Government's rearmament programme for the RAF created a minor parliamentary crisis. It was clear to Chamberlain that both he and his senior partner, the efficient but abrasive Lord Swinton, would have to go.[47] This entailed an obvious loss of face and the necessity of finding a new Air Minister, but an unfortunate concatenation of circumstances complicated matters for the Prime Minister. Lord Harlech and the Duke of Devonshire had recently died and their eldest sons, both in the Government, were called up to the Lords; as the new Lord Harlech, William Ormsby-Gore, was Dominions Secretary, this meant that the Government now had more peers in it than was constitutionally permissible. Chamberlain was, therefore, forced to make a major reconstruction of the Cabinet at a time when he would much rather not have done so.[48]

As always at such times, hopes of preferment rise in unexpected breasts, but Chamberlain, as on future occasions, made no concessions to his opponents. Harold Nicolson was incredulous at the nature of the reshuffle:

> Nobody understands why Euan Wallace is sent to the Treasury. Nobody understands why on earth Stanley (who is aimiable but stone-deaf) is given the Dominions. Nobody understands anything. There is a real impression that the whole show is going to crack up.[49]

Realistic critics knew that the Government was not going to 'crack up',[50] but the rumours and their persistence reflected a feeling which Chamberlain himself could not entirely ignore. He did not think that socialist propaganda branding him 'a Fascist, an enemy of the League of Nations and a materialist' would have too much effect 'because the country wants peace and appreciates the fact that this Government is delivering the goods'.[51] But what would happen if the goods were not delivered after all?

For a moment in late May it looked as though the Government might not deliver the expected fruits of its foreign policy. One of the things which the British feared might hamper their efforts to get the Czechs and Sudetens talking, apart from Beneš' procrastination and Henlein's obstinacy, was the occurrence of an 'incident' in the troubled Sudetenland. One such happened in late May, when it was reported that two Sudetens had been shot by Czechs. On 20 May Henderson warned that the tone of the German press had grown 'sharper' and that there was talk of armed intervention.[52] A day later Newton, in Prague, telegraphed that the Czechs had had reports of 'abnormal' German troop movements in the border region and that they might mobilise their army.[53]

The feeling that Europe might be on the verge of war was increased by the report of the conversation which Henderson had with Ribbentrop on 21 May, which inspired Cadogan's Private Secretary to send for him urgently.[54] In a 'highly excited and pugnacious mood', Ribbentrop had said that the 'Czechs ... were mad and if they persisted in their present attitude they would be destroyed'; the situation was, Henderson reported, 'extremely critical'.[55]

Chamberlain, who had just managed to get away to Scotland for the weekend, was literally fetched from the trout stream by an urgent message summoning him to London. He was, understandably, furious: 'The fact is that the Germans who are bullies by nature are too conscious of their strength and our weakness and until we are as strong as they are we shall always be kept in this chronic state of anxiety.'[56] The 'May crisis' cut straight across his efforts in Prague, with the Germans claiming insolently that all they had done was to inspire the Czechs to kill Germans.[57] All the information available in London on 21 May made it 'look certain that Germany intends either to confront Beneš with an ultimatum or to march in – in any case that Czechoslovakia is for it'.[58] But Chamberlain had faith in his 'steady and unruffled Foreign Secretary',[59] who had already decided 'we must *not* go to war'.[60]

Historians have endlessly debated whether Hitler did or did not mean to go to war and whether or not the 'May crisis' made him more determined to 'smash' Czechoslovakia in the near future. Whilst not wishing to deny both the pleasure and the utility of such speculation, it might be worth pointing out that the crisis marked a step towards a British commitment to Central Europe.

There had already been the sort of creeping encroachment upon Britain's role as 'honest-broker' that Henderson had foreseen, with the French 'want[ing] HMG to put as much pressure as possible on Beneš to reach a settlement . . . in order to save France from the cruel dilemma of dishonouring her Agreements or being involved in war'.[61] The 'May crisis' pushed British involvement a stage further. Stern public and private warnings were given to the Germans, and the Czechs were also exhorted to patience. The inevitable consequence was, as Strang reported after visiting Berlin and Prague in late May, that 'we are, naturally, regarded as having committed ourselves morally at any rate to intervene if there is a European war, and nothing that we are likely to say will remove that impression'. The warning to the Germans might have been couched in the very terms of Chamberlain's statement of 24 March, but it had made 'a much deeper impression'; whatever the British had intended, 'we are certainly regarded as being now more deeply committed in the Czech affair than before'.[62]

In fact, at least in its own eyes, the Cabinet was still continuing the tightrope walk. Determined not to go to war, indeed 'anti-Czech',[63] its messages to Berlin emphasised the pressure which was being put upon the Czechs, warning that 'only the Communists' would benefit from a war.[64] But the French were cautioned not to 'read more into those warnings than is justified'. Britain would help France if she was the victim of unprovoked German aggression, but to 'assume that HMG would at once take joint military action with them to preserve Czechoslovakia against German aggression' was to go too far.[65]

But, even whilst the British were still trying to pretend they were walking their tightrope, they were being inexorably drawn into the vacuum left by the collapse of French morale. They were being drawn there too by the fact that German resentment was focused upon them, which made it even more essential to get some concessions from Prague.[66] At the end of May suggestions were floated that an Anglo-French commission of inquiry might be sent to Czecho-slovakia.[67] Halifax still stressed that 'we do not wish to be manœuvred into the position of arbitrator',[68] but they were already close to it.

The crisis had also lessened faith in German assurances that they would be a 'saturated power' when the Sudeten question was resolved.[69] Henderson had always maintained that Hitler's ambition was a united 'Greater Germany' and that only 'a successful war will prevent or delay the realisation of this aim'.[70] His view that 'a war for the Sudetens would be the most senseless of undertakings'[71] was endorsed by most Ministers, who recognised German policy as 'opportunist'.[72] But Chamberlain, who regarded Czechoslovakia as an acid test of Hitler's intentions, now stigmatised the Germans as 'bullies by nature'[73] and was convinced that only his warning had prevented a German coup.[74] The whole affair had shown how 'utterly untrustworthy and dishonest' the German Government was.[75] This mood did not settle on him, or his Government, permanently, but it made them warier. It did not signify any unwillingness to negotiate, but it did erode faith in German goodwill.

It was, as yet, only part of a steady erosion, but what if, as the British were drawn, despite themselves, into a prominent role in Central Europe, that stock of patience was to dwindle further? Would its possessors be able to avoid being drawn into a commitment there when they felt themselves stronger? This was the real significance of the attempts to negotiate by proxy and of the 'May crisis'.

Chamberlain and Halifax

The new regime at the Foreign Office had survived its hectic introduction to the art of diplomacy, and those who perceived a new element of firmness in British policy tended to attribute it, however unfairly, to Halifax. Indeed, the Foreign Secretary was seen by some as the most probable successor to Chamberlain, should one be needed.[1] He certainly represented a reaffirmation of the 'national' character of the Government, which was being eroded by the 'unbelievable . . . personal dislike' which Chamberlain 'engendered . . . among his opponents'. His opponents found his 'cold intellect was too much for them, he beat them up in argument and debunked their catch phrases'; this, and his 'sarcastic' manner, rendered him both feared and disliked.[2] Butler thought that 'people with nervous temperaments' found his manner 'difficult to survive', likening Chamberlain's approach to problems to 'a ton of bricks' falling on the unwary.[3] Halifax was the natural beneficiary of these perceptions of the Prime Minister's shortcomings.

Chamberlain was aware of the effect he had on his opponents, but he was inclined to revel in his unpopularity amongst them, seeing it as the natural result of his aggressive leadership after the drift of the Baldwin years. He took great comfort from remarks such as those made to him by the Chief Whip, David Margesson, after he had routed Labour in a debate on foreign policy on 5 April: 'he had never known such enthusiasm over the lead the Party is getting'.[4] Appearances were, he knew, against him, and the sight of himself on film prompted him to remark that he seemed 'pompous, insufferably slow in "diction" and unspeakably repellent in "person" '![5] However, his efficiency, 'realism', and the confidence which these qualities inspired, made Chamberlain a considerable political force; but they did stir longing in some quarters for a return to the good old days of Baldwin and a 'broader Government with more idealism and less brutal clarity'.[6] Halifax was the beneficiary of these feelings too, but this did not mean that he had stiffened Chamberlain's foreign policy.

Margesson commented that Chamberlain's foreign policy was 'far simpler than those who love to discover recondite motives would suppose', being the 'logical outcome of his training and experience'. That training was 'liberal in a period of peace, when to the Liberal mind war between civilised nations was becoming increasingly unthinkable'.[7] Much the same could be said of Halifax. But neither man was unaware of the danger that Hitler might turn out to be unappeasable. However, until such time as the British rearmament effort neared fruition, what could not be cured would have to be endured. If Hitler's attitude towards Czechoslovakia proved that he wanted more than German unification then, within the year, British rearmament would have reached a level at which threats of force would no longer be bluff. The element of steel in British foreign policy could, if necessary, be increased.[8]

Mrs Chamberlain once described her husband as 'a realist as well as an idealist';[9] the same could have been said of Halifax. Speaking to the Council of the League in Geneva on 12 May 1938, Halifax said that when 'the ideal of devotion, unflinching but unpractical, to some high purpose' conflicted with 'the ideal of a practical victory for peace', he could not 'doubt that the stronger claim is that of peace'.[10] Devotion to the 'balance of power' was all very well, but was it worth a war to reinforce the crumbling system of Versailles?

This was the 'new realism'. It naturally held no appeal for those who, in Halifax's phrase, were inclined to think that, 'if only we had Lord Palmerston still with us, we could rapidly and decisively impose British solutions on an acquiescent world'.[11] It was a policy appropriate to an era in which, as Cadogan's Private Secretary, Gladwyn Jebb, remarked: 'The issue is one between losing something of our old magnificence and ceasing to be a great power. We have simply got to throw something to the wolves.'[12] Such a policy entailed neither simplicity nor naiveté. The 'impulsive . . . ill-disciplined . . . deeply appeasement-minded'[13] Henderson actually had few illusions about what the Germans were up to – 'the German attitude is one of blackmail'.[14] But he maintained that, given the geographical and diplomatic facts of the situation, 'a war for the Sudeten would be the most pointless of wars'.[15]

Henderson continued to argue for a policy of non-intervention in Central Europe, doing nothing to hamper Germany's 'legitimate economic freedom of action' in these areas.[16] These views differed but little from those expressed by Churchill in July to the Nazi leader in Danzig, Albert Foerster: 'most [English] people . . . would not resent gradual peaceful increase of German commercial influence in the Danube basin, but that any violent move would almost immediately lead to a world war'.[17]

Not everyone, however, was as sanguine as Churchill and Henderson about German economic domination of Central and South-Eastern Europe, as was shown by a paper circulated on 24 May to the Cabinet by Halifax which underlined the dangers to be apprehended from German economic domination of the region.[18] This reflected the views of some officials who wanted to create a 'Balkan Bloc' to contain Germany's economic expansion.[19] What they omitted to take into account was the problem of creating a diplomatic front out of politically divided and economically weak Balkan states, especially when Britain was in no position to replace Germany as a major market for exports from the region. Chamberlain did not agree with the premise of the memorandum, but, even if Germany did become the dominant economic power in that region, there was not, in his opinion, much that Britain could do about it.[20] The matter was passed on to a Balkan sub-committee.[21]

For Chamberlain it was enough that Hitler had climbed down in May; any attempt to rub his nose in the dirt would have been deliberately provocative.[22] Instead, he preferred to continue with efforts to use the French to persuade Beneš to make concessions whilst, at the same time, using Vansittart's contacts with Henlein to do the same with the Sudetens.[23] However, the prospects on this front were not good, and a period of prolonged crisis would do little for either the peace of Europe or the reputation of a Government which had been praised for its firmness in late May. It was out of this soil that the idea of sending a British 'mediator' to Prague sprang, which eventually bore fruit in the Runciman mission.[24] Thus it was that what began as intervention through the French in Prague designed to 'reduce the risk of a European war'[25] ended, despite an unwillingness 'to be manœuvred into the position of arbitrator',[26] in Britain playing a major role.

The slowness with which Beneš moved in his negotiations led to charges of procrastination by the Henleinists,[27] which were more than half-believed by a Foreign Secretary who suspected the French of not putting sufficient pressure on the Czechs. Exhortations to the British Ambassador in Paris, Sir Eric Phipps, to encourage the French to do more in this direction were accompanied by diplomatic pressure in Prague.[28] The implications of the position into which the British were drifting were brought home in mid-June, when Henderson warned that Czech proposals to introduce a new conscription law would be regarded in Berlin as provocative.[29] The British Minister in Prague, Newton, riposted that if they pressed the Czechs to accept fewer troops than they thought necessary, 'we must inevitably incur heavy moral responsibility of protecting Czech Government from consequences of following our recommendations'.[30] This produced a British rebuke to the Germans about their attitude and a statement that Britain was not 'in present circumstances prepared to undertake the responsibility of pressing the Czech Government further at this stage on the question of military security of which they must be allowed to be the judge'.[31]

Right into July the pressure from London and Paris on the Prague Government continued,[32] with the Czech Premier, Dr Hodza, actually asking the British at the end of June to step up their pressure in order to strengthen his hand in dealing with recalcitrant colleagues.[33] On 26 July Churchill warned the Czechs that they 'owe it to the Western Powers that every concession compatible with the sovereignty and integrity of their State shall be made, and made promptly'.[34] Six days earlier Beneš had received a request from the British to 'invite' a 'mediator' to Prague.[35] As the consequence of refusal would have been the end of British interest in the crisis, he accepted.[36]

The question of who should lead any mission to Prague had been exercising Downing Street since June. The Head of the Civil Service, Sir Horace Wilson, often accused of being Chamberlain's éminence grise, had got out his list of the great and the good, compared their column inches in *Who's Who* and come up with the suggestion of an eminent lawyer, Lord Macmillan. But history was to be deprived of a Macmillan mission, and the great legal mind was to wait until 1939 before entering government service, as the Prime Minister plumped for the second name on Wilson's list, Lord Runciman, 'an ex-Cabinet Minister of wide and varied experience'. A millionaire shipping magnate whose Ministerial career had begun under Asquith, Walter Runciman had been affronted at being left out of Chamberlain's Government in May 1937; now came a chance to soothe the amour-propre of one of the dwindling number of Liberal supporters of the Government. It was true that a man of his 'puzzling demeanour' was 'superficially not a model negotiator', but he was 'capable of a crispness which . . . might turn out to be what was needed'.[37]

Difficult in conception and awkward in its gestation period, a malign fate seemed to hang over the Runciman mission. Runciman himself was less than keen to take what appeared to be an ill-defined post as 'Ambassador at large'. The confusion over the nature of what he was being asked to do was understandable, as even Halifax's definition of the post begged more questions than it gave answers:

> You would be going in your personal capacity as a sort of representative of HMG. You would not therefore receive any official instructions and would not be expected to work on any particular plan. Your position would be that the Czech Government and Sudeten leaders had, on the suggestion of HMG, invited you to help them reach an agreement within the framework of the present Czech State on the points still at issue between them.[38]

Having persuaded Runciman, there was the question of when to play him. By late July lack of progress suggested that the moment should come soon, but the press spoiled the final dénouement by leaking the news in advance of Chamberlain's statement in the Commons on 26 July.

Runciman and his mission were, however, peripheral to the main objective of British policy: an improvement in Anglo-German relations. When Halifax learnt that the German reaction to the Runciman mission was one of reserve, he expressed his disappointment in a letter to Ribbentrop.[39] He had hoped that the Germans would 'encourage and assist' the efforts to solve the Sudeten problem, not merely because that would help clear one obstacle in the way of Anglo-German friendship, but also because the very act of co-operation would be conducive to such a friendship. The straws in the wind, amounting to several bales worth of hay, were far from pointing unanimously in the direction of war.

In early July the Foreign Office received 'mysterious approaches from Germany' indicating that Hitler was anxious to 'send an important personage' to London to 'hold conversations'.[40] Given the odd way in which the Nazis chose to conduct their foreign policy, these leads were followed up. On 18 July Cadogan saw Hitler's ADC, Captain Wiedemann, whose 'serious and straightforward' demeanour made a good impression even on the sceptical Harvey.[41] The 'appeasers' have sometimes been condemned for not perusing *Mein Kampf* with care.[42] Whether they did so or not, Captain Wiedemann was able to remind them that although not everything in that turgid and excruciatingly dull volume was to be taken as gospel, the Führer had there, as always, professed his admiration for England and his desire to secure her friendship. He suggested that Hitler felt that his past overtures had been rebuffed, and proposed that a visit to London by Hermann Goering might carry forward the process initiated by Halifax's visit to Berlin. Equally welcome were assurances that Hitler would not intervene 'by force' in the Czech problem 'unless something occurred such as a massacre of Sudeten'.

Wiedemann's visit, allied as it was with conversations between the new German Ambassador, Herbert von Dirksen, and Chamberlain, led to newspaper comments and questions in the Commons, which gave the Prime Minister the opportunity formally to announce the Runciman mission.[43] What he did not announce was that he was going to follow up Halifax's letter to Ribbentrop with one of his own to Dirksen expressing the hope that he would be able to impress upon Hitler his own benevolent intentions.[44] He did, however, say enough to satisfy his own backbenchers.

Because so much of the Government's policy was, perforce, carried on in secret, Chamberlain had had little with which to offset the disappointment of the summer session. Thanks to Mussolini 'behaving just like a spoiled child', the Anglo-Italian Agreement had still not come into effect.[45] To add to Chamberlain's burdens, Churchill had discovered yet another mare's-nest and made a nuisance of himself over it. His son-in-law and fellow MP, Duncan Sandys, wrote to the Minister of War, Hore-Belisha, in June, announcing that he intended to raise in the House questions relating to supposed deficencies in the country's anti-aircraft defences. Those Cabinet Ministers concerned with defence matters had, for some time, been smarting under what they saw as Churchill's ill-informed but highly public criticisms, and this provided them with an opportunity for hitting back.

The Attorney-General, Sir Donald Somerville, took the view that Sandys could only have obtained his information from someone who had breached the Official Secrets Act and informed him that he could be liable to imprisonment if he failed to reveal his sources. Sandys, outraged, demanded that the matter be referred to the Committee of Privileges which, after finding in his favour, discovered that the facts were not quite as they had been presented.[46] Churchill then became involved in an acrimonious correspondence with Chamberlain and Simon, the latter writing to the former on 14 July that he thought 'Winston and Co. are getting thoroughly sick of this business and would not be sorry to see it dropped, provided, of course, they escape the discredit which may come to them'.[47] Chamberlain was happy to see the affair rebound on its prime mover who, having thought he 'saw an opportunity of giving the Government a good shake', had only increased his own isolation.[48] But the rumours caused by Wiedemann's visit ensured that the session failed to finish on a note of calm.

The socialists made great play of the rumours of wars and 'Air Pacts' of which Wiedemann was supposedly the harbinger, but Margesson and Butler calmed the Government troops. This was not, as Butler told Halifax, too difficult a task given 'the normal disposition of our side and most of the other to prefer the outlook of an unbroken holiday':

> On the whole our party has remained calm except for the 'intellectuals' – Harold Nicholson [*sic*], Louis Spears, etc., who are to the Party what 'Van' is to the Office ... I will watch in the next session that 'Van' whom the intellectual type see and much admire does not unduly unsettle them.

Butler felt that 'people outside, and foreigners in particular, are apt to underestimate the silent and almost undying support that the normal Conservative MP will give to his elected leader and his Chief Whip', which meant that the dissidents got more publicity than they deserved; historians might be added to Butler's list. With Parliament in recess and Runciman adrift in mid-Europe and missing the 'glorious twelfth', Butler intended to catch up on his 'fresh air and early bed': 'I really think you have done all you can in Central Europe and I think a certain calm is possible.'[49] The hopes of the squire of Stanstead Hall were shared by the master of Garrowby and by the temporary laird of Tillypronie, which was where Chamberlain had gone fishing.

HIGH STAKES
Daredevil Runciman (to Messrs. Hodza, Henlein and Hitler): 'Mind if I take a hand, boys?'
10 August 1938.

Less calm was the tone of Henderson's correspondence. Fearing a crisis, he had decided to spend August in Berlin, which he found 'ghastly' and 'almost unendurably hateful'. The heat, the tension, and the preliminary symptoms of the cruel disease which was to kill him, combined to make him feel as if he 'were playing a part in the old Greek tragedies and watching events moving steadily and inexorably towards the final inevitable tragic ending'. Reposing but little hope in Runciman – unless he recommended 'Home Rule' – Henderson could only pray that if the tragedy came, Halifax and Chamberlain would 'keep Great Britain out of it. I cannot bear the thought of losing a single life for either Sudeten or Czech.'[50] The Czechs were, he thought, a 'pig-headed race and Beneš not the least pig-headed among them'.[51] Until the 'folly of Versailles' had been put right, he saw no possibility of 'lasting peace in Central Europe'.[52] He had few illusions about what 'eighty million highly efficient, organised and disciplined Germans' dominating the centre of Europe would mean for the 'liberty and independence of smaller nations', but 'facts must be faced' and what could not be cured had to be endured. He favoured 'the Palmerstonian theory that nothing shall happen in the world without England's consent unless it is something England cannot prevent, in which case the wisest course is to make the best of it'.[53]

The tone emanating from Garrowby, where the Foreign Secretary was now settling into the saddle, was calmer, the conclusions less sombre, but the thinking behind the policy much the same. Taking advantage of a free afternoon on 5 August, Halifax sought to get into closer communion with Henderson by sharing his thoughts with him. He doubted the likelihood of imminent war, saving some 'bloodbath' in the Sudetenland. German policy was characterised by a 'strong element of bluff', although that was not to say that some Nazis were not 'planning the worst'. Everything pointed to the wisdom of continuing the present policy of 'perpetually telling Beneš of what we might *not* do in the event of trouble: and of tactfully reminding the Germans of what we *might* do'. And, in the meantime (and who knew how long that would be?), there was Runciman.[54]

Runciman was the repository of many hopes – most of them of the last-ditch variety. General Ironside, the Governor of Gibraltar, saw the mission as a 'last despairing attempt to arrive at a compromise' by the 'champion compromisers of the world';[55] but those who combined commitment to the Czechs with an unwillingness to compromise and a distrust of Chamberlain's policy, saw in it the possibility that it would commit the British 'up to the hilt'. Halifax, seeing this danger, was determined that Runciman should 'not take any action that would have the effect of committing this country further than it is already committed, to take action in the event of Germany taking military action'.[56] The Germans were indifferent to 'the Lord' (indeed Henlein could not be found for a week or so), and the Czechs, who disliked the mission, looked for nothing good from it. As for poor Henderson:

> I just sit and pray for one thing, namely that Lord Runciman will live up to the role of an impartial British Liberal statesman. I cannot believe that he will allow himself to be influenced by ancient history or even arguments about strategic frontiers and economics in preference to high moral principles.[57]

But how long did Runciman have and what were his prospects of success? Halifax was disposed to think that the odds in both cases were short. If he failed to arrive at a solution he could simply leave; he could, alternatively, leave and blame either the Sudetens or the Czechs for being stubborn. None of these possibilities warmed the spirit, although if it should turn out that Czech obstreperousness had prevented a reasonable solution being found, there would be much less pressure on the British to help them. There was always the possibility of a plebiscite, but Halifax regarded that as the very 'devil' and a final resort.[58] Henderson gave Runciman a month to pull a rabbit out of the hat and, as he knew what that rabbit should be, he was anxious to know 'what lines of thought' his lordship was following.[59]

The 'general idea that in due course' Runciman would produce a scheme, which the parties to the dispute could accept or reject,[60] was exactly what Halifax wished to avoid as it would reinforce the danger that, in the event of the Sudetens being blamed for Runciman's failure, pressure on the British Government to intervene on the side of the Czechs might become intolerable.[61] Halifax, who, in response to Henderson's request to know something of Runciman's thinking, noted that 'we do not know more than he does',[62] hoped that this studied distancing of himself from the mission would avoid the dangers; but Henderson saw further and warned: 'In the latter end the world will hold Britain responsible for whatever recommendations he may make. We may deny it but we shall not be able to get away with it.'[63] It remained to be seen whether, in Leo Amery's words, the appointment of Runciman was 'comic or a stroke of genius', and whether his 'bland invincible ignorance and incapacity even to realise the emotions and aspirations on both sides' would 'help to bring down the temperature and so contribute to a peaceful solution'.[64]

From his arrival in Czechoslovakia in early August until his final departure in September, Runciman (or rather his officials) laboured mightily. He saw everyone of importance, except Hitler – a rather important omission but an essential one if it was to be maintained that the dispute was a Czech one. His aides compiled statistics on everything from the various national groupings inside Czechoslovakia to its imports of fats, and by September Runciman's mission knew more about Czechoslovakia than most Czechs.[65] But the process did not improve Runciman's temper. His nights ruined by insomnia,[66] and his days by interminable ramblings by dim nationalist politicians with unpronounceable names and unrealisable objectives, Runciman did not see Henlein until 18 August, and then it was only to discover what he already knew – that Henlein wanted 'Home Rule' for the Sudetenland, whatever that meant.[67] It was not until the end of the month that there appeared to be any signs that

Runciman's mission was going to produce any results[68] – and they proved illusory.[69]

Vansittart, and those who shared his assumptions, regarded the whole process with distaste. They assumed that war with Germany was inevitable, that France's alliance with Czechoslovakia was thus a source of strength and that a war in Central Europe could be won with Russian help.[70] Moreover, Vansittart had information from the Chairman of the British Council, Lord Lloyd, which suggested that there might not even be a war.

Lloyd's informant was Ian Colvin, whose contacts inside the German army assured him that if Hitler tried to start a war he would be deposed.[71] On 18 August one of his contacts, Ewald von Kleist-Schenzin, came to London to see Churchill, Lloyd and Vansittart to reinforce this message.[72] Chamberlain, mindful of the 'Jacobites at the Court of France in King William's time', was inclined to 'discount a good deal of what he says'.[73] After all, if 'all the Generals' were against war, it was odd that they should need foreign assurances before acting against Hitler – and what guarantee was there that, even if they did act, any new regime would be an improvement?

But Vansittart's were not the only sirens singing songs. Theodor Kordt, a Counsellor at the German Embassy, had approached Butler at the beginning of August to see if 'we would recognise German *lebensraum* in Eastern Europe' if, through 'some concrete act', assurances could be given that this was Germany's last territorial demand.[74]

The key question facing Chamberlain was put by Henderson in a letter to Halifax on 22 August: 'Have we or have we not to fight Germany again?' Behind the arguments of Vansittart, Churchill, Lloyd, Duff Cooper, Bob Boothby, Lord Cranborne and all lay the 'Crowe tradition', which held that war was 'inevitable'. There were, Henderson reminded the Foreign Secretary, German equivalents in Berlin – and down that road lay suicide for Western civilisation. Was war to come in defence of the borders created by Versailles?

> However badly Germany behaves, it does not make the rights of the Sudeten any less justifiable. We are on the worst of wickets . . . Never again are those blocks of Germans on Germany's frontier going to be misgoverned by Czechs as they have been during the last twenty years . . . and we have no earthly or heavenly right to force them to be so.[75]

Henderson did not see why the Sudetenland should lead Britain into war. If Runciman was to anticipate Hitler's demands by declaring that as a 'general principle' he was in favour of 'Home Rule', then it would be difficult for the Führer to take military action without putting himself in a position where Britain and France could declare war on him on the grounds that his ambitions were clearly wider than his current statements suggested.[76]

All three German initiatives – Wiedemann's, von Kleist's and Kordt's – had their effect. The first resulted in a letter from Halifax to Hitler appealing for co-operation and asking him, as a sign of good faith, to 'modify' military measures which he was reported to be about to undertake.[77] The unconciliatory response seemed to support von Kleist's warnings about the imminence of military action; indeed, some sources suggested that this would come sooner than the end of September.[78] Von Kleist's information suggested that time was running short – hence Henderson's anxiety for Runciman to break the deadlock by a declaration. As for Kordt, it was decided that 'the wise course would be to keep the movement alive if the Germans wished that to be the case'.[79]

When, on 25 August, Beneš agreed to make major concessions, Wilson was able to report to Chamberlain that the outlook was 'much more hopeful'. If the crisis was settled, then not only would any risk of war be averted, but the road to a wider Anglo-German agreement might be open, especially if Henlein reported that the British were 'friendly disposed not merely to the *Sudetendeutsche* but to Germany [and] . . . that in his opinion the line which has been worked out is the best one and should be accepted . . . that acceptance could be regarded as the first step'.[80] But such optimism soon faded.

Equivocation disguised as concession by Beneš was matched by Henleinist obduracy.[81] Alarmed at the implications of the situation, the Cabinet met in emergency session on 30 August.[82] The atmosphere was heavy with intimations of crisis. What had begun as a low-key diplomatic manœuvre to ensure that France's alliance with Czechoslovakia did not drag Britain into war had developed into a situation in which the Prime Minister's whole approach to foreign policy was called into question. But even as Runciman's ark seemed to be foundering, there were those who thought that a dove of peace might yet be sent forth into the gathering maelstrom.

The Dove of Peace

The Cabinet met to discuss the situation as it was presented to its members by the Foreign Secretary, the Prime Minister and Sir Nevile Henderson; but although the meeting brought forth most of the points of view which were to dominate debate for the next month, it was not fully informed of the Prime Minister's thinking. This was for prudential, not sinister, reasons. As much of the discussion concerned hypotheses, there seemed little point in airing one scheme which was to become operational only in extreme circumstances; this was probably just as well, as some Ministers were rattled enough without being scared out of what wits they might have possessed.

What should be done in the face of the current state of the Runciman initiative? There were those, Halifax told his colleagues (without naming von Kleist but quoting from a letter from Boothby), who averred that Hitler was bent on war. If this were so, the only deterrent would be a threat to go to war with Germany if she attacked Czechoslovakia. Three difficulties attended this course of action; public opinion at home and in the Empire would be divided; the Czechs, who had shown a genius for prevarication, might be further encouraged; and, if Britain were to go to war, there was nothing anyone could do to 'prevent Czechoslovakia from being overrun by Germany'. In view, however, of the principle involved, that of stopping dictators from obtaining their ends by force, it might be that some would favour fighting now; for his own part he was unsure of the utility of fighting a 'certain war now to forestall a possible war later'. Should, however, the French become involved, then he thought Britain should have to come to her aid – which meant that 'if we were against being involved in war, we should, presumably, try to exercise a restraining influence over France'.

Having given a masterly exposition of one set of possibilites which would follow from the hypothesis that Hitler was bent on war, Halifax moved on to give an even more compelling account of the consequences of taking what, in his eyes, was the more likely view that 'Hitler had not yet made up his mind whether to use force'. In this case there was no need for anything as crude as a threat to resort to force (which avoided the embarrassment of having one's bluff called), merely a continuation of the policy pursued since 24 March: 'We should try to keep Herr Hitler guessing.' He had already urged that Beneš should make known publicly how far he was prepared to go to meet Henlein, and this attempt to 'forward the success of Lord Runciman's mission' would be the second prong of the policy which he thought they should pursue.

These arguments were deployed again and again during September. Following what might be called the 'Kleist line' would lead to the threat of war and, as Chamberlain reminded his colleagues, 'No State, certainly no democratic State, ought to make a threat of war unless it was both ready to carry it out and prepared to do so.' In addition to the difficulties enumerated by the Foreign Secretary, there were other problems attendant upon taking the 'Kleist line'. The strategic situation, with a weak France and an uncertain Italy, was unfavourable; moreover, as Inskip pointed out, 'at the present time we had not reached our maximum preparedness and should not do so for another year or more'. Behind that lay another, and even more serious, problem: British defence policy, with its bias towards the air force and navy, did not provide for a war involving intervention in Central Europe.

These facts all pointed to the wisdom of following the policy Halifax favoured, although there was one Cabinet Minister, Lord Maugham the Lord Chancellor, who was nervous about going so far as to say that France would have to be helped. Only the First Lord of the Admiralty, Duff Cooper, impatiently called for 'strong action' to deter Hitler; but he did not specify what he meant, nor could he deal with the objections tacitly raised by Inskip's remarks. Harvey's comment that the younger Ministers 'favoured a firmer attitude' is too flattering by half: Cooper, Elliot and Stanley all thought it desirable to 'make some move to show that we were envisaging the fact that we might be drawn into hostilities', but all three seem to have taken this line in the belief that Hitler was bluffing.[1]

Much has been written about the Munich crisis and the differences within the Cabinet, but what they amounted to was this: that Cooper and company were prepared to threaten Hitler with war in the hope that von Kleist was correct. If he was not, there would really be war. It would be a war which British defence policy had not foreseen (although Cooper, at least, could argue convincingly that if his policy as Minister of War had been followed, they would have been ready for this sort of war) and for which Britain was ill-equipped. It would have been a war over an area which few Britons could have placed on a map, and which Germany was bound to overrun with some speed. Sir John Simon understated matters when he said that 'any idea of going to war for Czechoslovakia could not be contemplated with equanimity'.

To Chamberlain it was 'positively horrible' to think that 'the fate of hundreds of millions depends on one man' who was 'half-mad'. Racking his brains to 'devise some means of averting the catastrophe', he had come up with an idea 'so unconventional and daring that it rather took Halifax's breath away'.[2] Chamberlain explained his scheme to Henderson after the Cabinet, and Sir Horace Wilson, in a highly secret memorandum drawn up afterwards, recorded that:

> There is in existence a plan, called Plan Z, which is known and must be known only to the Prime Minister, the Chancellor of the Exchequer, the Foreign Secretary, Sir Nevile Henderson and myself. It is to come into operation only in certain circumstances ... The success of the plan if it is to be put into operation depends upon its being a complete surprise, and it is vital that nothing should be said about it.[3]

Not even in his letters to his sisters did Chamberlain do more than hint at what he had in mind: Plan Z would involve the Prime Minister flying to Germany to see Hitler in a last-minute attempt to avert war. It was a plan conceived not in desperation or naiveté, but out of a deep and humane desire to leave no stone unturned to avoid war: it was the conception of a brave man.

But the resources of diplomacy were not yet exhausted. Henderson went back to Berlin on 31 August, warning his hosts that, although the British were not going to make 'idle threats', and whilst they would do all that anyone could to influence Beneš, 'precipitate action' by Germany might well bring in France, in which event it was unlikely that the British would stay out. The Germans, however, remained sceptical, despite Henderson's admonitions to Ribbentrop on 1 September.[4]

Henlein visited Hitler on 1 and 2 September, arriving back in Prague full of expressions of the Führer's peaceful intentions – and with a rejection on 2 September of the Czech proposals to give the Sudetens more autonomy.[5] The Cabinet's policy of 'facilitating' Runciman's task bore fruit in telegrams from Halifax pressing Beneš to, in effect, grant the Carlsbad demands in full – a line of policy which received strong support from Henderson.[6] Beneš' response was to summon the Sudeten leaders to the Hradchany Palace on 4 September and to ask them to write down, with his own pen, exactly what it was they wanted.[7] Had this come a month sooner it might have presented the Sudetens with a real dilemma, but a scuffle between Sudeten deputies and Czech police at the town of Mähsrisch-Ostrau on 7 September gave Henlein an excuse to suspend talks.

With the Nazi Party rally at Nuremberg under way and Hitler due to give a speech on 12 September, minds in London were concentrated on what should be done. Advice was the one thing that was not in short supply.

Plan Z was still a closely guarded secret – and a last resort. Vansittart, whose contacts included not only the German opposition to Hitler but also the British opposition to Chamberlain, wrought himself into a highly nervous state. The Labour spokesman on foreign policy, Hugh Dalton, who saw him on 5 September, found him 'more disturbed than I had often seen him'.[8] He had no faith in any real diplomatic solution of the Sudeten problem and feared that Chamberlain would let Hitler secure the mastery of Central Europe, which would reduce Britain to the rank of 'a second-class power'.[9] He wanted to stiffen the language which Henderson employed at Berlin[10] and, believing that 'the only thing Germany will, or ever does, understand is force',[11] was willing to use the threat of it to force Hitler to back down; something, of course, which his German contacts, and Colvin, had assured him would happen. But again, like Cooper, he had no answer to the problems which would arise if Hitler did not back down – just a belief that the British would win.

Perhaps, like Churchill, he believed in the Russian connection. Probably the most active diplomat in London in late August and early September was the Soviet Ambassador, Ivan Maisky, who busied himself stirring all the opposition forces to Chamberlain: Churchill, Eden, Dalton, Nicolson (and through him Vansittart, de la Warr and anyone else whom he could button-hole), telling them all that Russia would 'fulfil her obligations' to Czechoslovakia.[12] Churchill kept up a steady flow of missives urging Halifax to announce that Britain was consulting with France and Russia about Czechoslovakia – and even urged dragging in the Americans.

Chamberlain and Halifax knew of Churchill's sources of information, and of what the Russians said they were going to do, but they were a good deal more sceptical than the easily convinced Churchill – as was Dalton, who diluted the heady wine of Maisky's optimism with the reflection that the Russians 'have purged their military forces so thoroughly that they are undoubtedly much weakened at the moment'.[13] The geographical and military problems which had led Chamberlain to place Russian help at a discount in March still applied, and the British Ambassador in Moscow, Viscount Chilston, confirmed that, despite brave words, real help from his hosts was unlikely.[14]

It suited Churchill to believe what Maisky told him, and Chamberlain's refusal to follow the advice he was given fitted in well with the picture which Eden and Churchill had already formed of him. Chamberlain was Lord Mayor of Birmingham with 'no conception of world politics' and no inclination to 'welcome advice from those who have';[15] or, as Eden put it to Jan Masaryk when comparing Baldwin and Chamberlain: 'Both thought foreigners "dagoes" –

Baldwin said, "Don't understand them – don't want to have anything to do with them. Anthony, this is your affair." Chamberlain, same attitude, but tries to run his own foreign policy.'[16] It was, after all, 'the day of the uninhibited amateur',[17] when noble and shining diplomats like Vansittart (not that there were *any* others who were even remotely like him) were ignored by the 'Big Four' of Chamberlain, Halifax, Simon and Hoare, with Sir Horace Wilson as éminence grise added for dramatic effect.[18] It is a view which reflects, at once, the bitterness of its proponents at being excluded from power and the vividness of their collective imagination. What it reflects hardly at all is the reality of the situation in Whitehall in 1938.

It is certainly true that the Cabinet as a whole was not consulted again until 12 September, but, as it had approved the main lines of government foreign policy on 30 August, there was no reason to summon its members again. The idea that policy was made up as they went along by the 'Big Four' is risible. Hoare was not brought in on the idea of Plan Z until 10 September and the brunt of the strain was borne by the Prime Minister, the Foreign Secretary and the professional diplomats. Cadogan was intimately involved in every stage of the crisis after arriving back from holiday on 3 September and he fed information to the Prime Minister and Wilson, as did 'Van'. But where 'Van's' information tended to come from disgruntled Germans and his contacts to be disgruntled British politicians, Cadogan's contributions came from the professionals: Henderson in Berlin, Phipps in Paris, Newton in Prague, Howard Kennard in Warsaw and Chilston in Moscow. It may be that they were all wrong, but Chamberlain listened to them; if he had not done so, he would have laid himself open to the charge of acting autocratically; but his enemies already knew that he was autocratic, so they assumed that he was acting without professional advice – when he was merely acting against the advice of the amateurs.

Opinion amongst those who knew of Plan Z was divided upon its merits. Once the negotiations at Prague were suspended on 7 September, Chamberlain's scheme became the object of some debate. Chamberlain's impatience with the policy of keeping Hitler guessing grew, as that, he believed, was precisely what Hitler 'does to us'; but he still hoped to avoid Plan Z.[19] As he told Halifax on 6 September: 'I have a notion it won't come to that.'[20] Halifax, who still hoped for something from Runciman, found himself balanced between the various contending parties; in a graphic phrase he described himself as 'groping in the dark like a blind man trying to find his way across a bog, with everybody shouting from the banks different information as to where the next quagmire is!'[21] Cadogan became increasingly attracted to the idea of sending Hitler a '*private warning*', particularly after Kordt told him on 7 September that Hitler had not been convinced by Henderson's earlier admonitory remarks. He told

Cadogan that Hitler had taken the decision to march on 19 or 20 September. Chamberlain was summoned from his Scottish holiday.[22]

Chamberlain, who arrived in London on 7 September, disliked the idea of yet another warning to Hitler and wanted to implement Plan Z, an opinion with which Cadogan concurred. Characteristically 'Van' was heard to mutter something about 'Canossa'. But, after a compromise plan to issue a statement to the press endorsing the latest Czech proposals rejected by Runciman and Henderson, it was decided to despatch the 'private warning' after all.[23] This expressed British concern at the 'deteriorating atmosphere' at Prague and asked for German co-operation; describing the latest proposals from Runciman as a 'reasonable and hopeful basis for negotiations', the document went on to say that, in the event of France becoming involved in a 'general conflict', the British would not be able to 'stand aside'.[24] So much for the autocratic Chamberlain.

If the atmosphere at Downing Street was, according to Chamberlain, 'enough to send most people off their heads, if their heads were not as well screwed-on as mine',[25] then at Nuremberg, where Henderson was ensconced, it was indescribable. Hoare once described Henderson as 'very intelligent', but 'lacking a very necessary measure of British phlegm'.[26] Coming from the man who, as Ambassador in Madrid in 1940, evinced a marked tendency to 'panic' when the going got tough,[27] and might, therefore, be thought to have qualifications for so pronouncing, this cannot be ignored. Certainly Henderson's letters and despatches have a febrile quality about them at this time.

In part this can be ascribed to being at Nuremberg during the Party rally – a testing time for anyone but a fanatical Nazi. The fact that he was for five days 'cooped up in a diplomatic train, without privacy and practically without means of communication,' failed to help matters. By the latter Henderson was not referring only to complicated things like scrambler telephones and cypher pads, but to ordinary writing paper which he had actually forgotten to take with him and was thus 'obliged to use for the purpose the blank pages torn from some detective stories which I happened to have taken with me'.[28] However, whatever they were written on, his messages showed that this sensitive, highly strung man was now on the verge of breaking down.

Henderson was convinced that Hitler would not swallow another 'May 21',[29] and the secrecy with which the Germans began a 'partial mobilisation' at the beginning of September left the Führer with all his options open.[30] The prospect of delivering 'private warnings' to Hitler at a time when he was preparing himself for his speech to the faithful was not one Henderson relished; not because he was a coward, but because he feared that crying 'wolf' too often, particularly at such a time, might actually have the opposite effect to the one intended.[31] The only alternatives he saw were: 'Either the Karlsbad programme and a State of Nationalities or (a) a Plebiscite or (b) a war after which C.S. [Czechoslovakia] could never be reconstituted as it is today.'[32] With the solicitude of a nurse for the feelings of her patient, Henderson urged the Foreign Office to 'get the . . . Press to write up Hitler as the apostle of Peace', in an attempt to soothe him before his speech.[33]

Henderson was not the only one to be showing signs of frayed nerve-endings. The Daladier Government, which had to deal with a major financial crisis during the summer, was growing increasingly worried not only at the situation in Prague, but also over the British attitude. Halifax's policy of telling Hitler what the British would do in the event of a crisis, and of telling Beneš what they would not do, failed to test Hitler's nerve, but its effect on the French was marked. On 22 August Bonnet told his Ambassador in London, Charles Corbin, to ask for a renewal of something like the warning of 21 May, but received only assurances that British policy remained as defined in Chamberlain's speech of 25 August. Halifax was anxious that the French should do nothing that would give Beneš pause for thought.[34]

The Russians were as active in Paris as they were in London, their Ambassador urging Bonnet to be firm and stirring up those known to be of a 'hawkish' disposition. Sir Eric Phipps, the British Ambassador (and also Vansittart's brother-in-law), had a very British disdain for most French politicians, believing that 'veracity' was not their strongest point.[35] Those British diplomats with 'hawkish' instincts, like Harvey, distrusted Phipps and thought that he worked on 'Bonnet's fears and weakness'; but although Harvey criticised him for giving the 'definite impression that HMG wish to hold France back', he had to admit that this was 'of course true'.[36] Phipps' great sin, like Henderson's, was that he concurred with, and indeed helped mould, Chamberlain's policy; again, like Henderson, but unlike his august relative, he declined to take Russian exhortations at face value. In this he was joined by Bonnet.

Although the French called up their reservists on 31 August and renewed their endeavours to get the British to spell out what they would do in the worst possible case, Bonnet was as eager to be restrained as the British were to restrain him.[37]

Facing the reality of France's commitments to Czechoslovakia and of her reluctance (and perhaps incapacity) to fulfil them, Bonnet looked to the British to provide either a solution – or a scapegoat. On 10 September he told Phipps that if the Germans attacked the Czechs and France said, 'We are going to march, will you march with us?'[38] This question, which was by no means as straightforward as it looked, was hardly of the sort to catch a diplomat with Phipps' experience. Sir Eric made it clear that everything would depend upon the circumstances in which the question ceased being a hypothesis and became a fact; he also 'indicated that the positions of our two countries were not quite similar. France was bound by a definite pact, whereas we were not.' Bonnet retorted that the time had passed for 'legal subtleties' and that it was 'vital for our two countries to act together' in this 'life and death' matter. Histrionics failed to impress Phipps, who concluded, correctly, that 'Bonnet, perhaps more than Daladier, is desperately anxious for a possible way out of this "impasse" without being *obliged* to fight.'

Immersed in the drama of the crisis building up in Prague, eyes fixed on the dénouement of September 1939, it is easy to forget the truth of Henderson's remark that: 'We did not begin our intervention at Prague to be agreeable to the Czechs but to help them out of an intolerable situation and to save Europe from a foolish war.'[39] Chamberlain was fully aware of the risk that if things went 'wrong and the aggression takes place' people would say that if only his Government had had 'the courage to tell Hitler now that if he used force we should at once declare war', all would have been well and that by that time it would be 'impossible to prove the contrary'; but he had rather take the risk of damning his posthumous fame than of allowing the 'most vital decision as to peace or war, to pass out of our hands into those of the ruler of another country and a lunatic at that'.[40] That he was willing to do something perilously close to this within six months is something that the next two chapters attempt to explain.

Henderson's voice was loud in affirmation of Chamberlain's policy. One reason the Prime Minister was against issuing threats was that they might prejudice the chances of Plan Z. Wilson sounded him out about whether the time had now come to put this into operation, but Henderson was adamant that it had not. He scribbled his fly-leaved reply in his carriage on 9 September and begged Wilson 'for Heaven's sake send no more instructions as on May 21st' – that would lead straight to war.[41] The solution still, in his opinion, lay in Prague and in making Beneš correct the errors of Versailles. When a senior Ambassador writes, 'I am acquainted with the views of HMG and being on the spot I feel that they would be well advised to trust me', a Government has to have powerful reason for disregarding his words; when that view coincides with the thinking of the Prime Minister and the head of the diplomatic service, it provides powerful reinforcement for that thinking.

What Henderson disagreed with was Chamberlain's preference for springing Plan Z on Hitler without warning, and this was dropped.[42]

The Government was now treading a thin, thin line. At Henderson's behest Chamberlain decided to hold back the warning which had been despatched on 9 September, but sections of the British press, aware that a messenger had been sent to Nuremberg, decided that an 'ultimatum' had been delivered – something which annoyed Chamberlain and threatened to nullify the effect of holding back the warning.[43]

It was only on the afternoon of 10 September that the 'Big Four' got together to consider Henderson's anguished pleas. They decided that, as he had already delivered the substance of the warning personally to Ribbentrop, he could refrain from passing it on to Hitler. Vansittart was (predictably) infuriated, but even Harvey, who was temperamentally always inclined to follow the Eden view and thus not entirely happy with the decision, saw 'the danger of Hitler going off the deep end if confronted with the risk of a diplomatic defeat which his regime – none too strong – might not survive'.[44]

As the inner Cabinet group (plus Vansittart, Cadogan and Wilson) came out of the room, they encountered Churchill in the hall. He demanded 'an immediate ultimatum to Hitler';[45] the result can be summarised in a phrase of Halifax's from another occasion: 'I pointed out some of the obvious difficulties in the way of this to him and he did not seem violently interested in that side of the subject.'[46] He had to rest satisfied with an announcement that the navy would undertake special manœuvres. As this brought an avowal from the German Naval Attaché that he now, for the first time, realised that the British might enter a war over Czechoslovakia, Chamberlain could feel satisfied that he had made his point without histrionics.[47] There were enough of these at Nuremberg.

Goering, in a vicious speech on 11 September, branded the Czechs as a 'pygmy race' who were threatening the peace of Europe by harassing a 'civilised people'. But, whilst envisaging the possibility of war with England, he did not threaten it, and with negotiations having once more begun in Prague, it remained possible that Runciman might yet pull the rabbit from the hat.[48] And Europe waited to hear what the Führer would say on 12 September.

To ensure that no one could say that he was merely reacting to that speech, Chamberlain called a Cabinet for 11 o'clock on the morning of 12 September.[49]

The Minister who had come under most pressure from the dissentients outside the Government was Halifax. Not only did he have his own Private Secretary, Harvey, and Vansittart to listen to, but he had a visit from Eden on the 11th, a telephone call from Churchill, and then a long and emotional letter from his old friend and fellow Anglo-Catholic, Lord Lloyd: the former urging an ultimatum, whilst acknowledging there was 'some point' in Henderson's advice; Churchill banging his usual drum; and Lloyd, convinced that 'there are worse issues even than war', urging him on the morning of the Cabinet to 'play the man, to face clear-eyed what is coming, confident that we are capable of drinking the cup and that we shall not be left without the power to do so'.[50]

Halifax was apt to say that representations of this sort left his 'withers entirely unwrung', and it is true that, at this time, they had little effect; but it would be untrue to say that they had no effect. Cooper had suggested taking further naval measures which would bring the crews of a destroyer flotilla up to full strength, and Halifax seems to have been inclined to agree with this, but let himself be talked out of it by the argument that this might appear unduly 'offensive' on the day that Hitler was making his speech.[51]

In presenting a résumé of recent events to his colleagues, Halifax commented that 'Hitler was possibly or even probably mad'; this, however, was yet another weight to throw in the balance on the side of Henderson's advice. Both he and the Prime Minister were satisfied that Henderson had made it plain to Ribbentrop and other high-ranking Nazis that Britain might have to take military action and that the Germans knew the risks which they might be running. What had not changed since the end of August was the central nature of the problem: was Hitler intending to use force or not?

The main voice of dissent in the Cabinet was Cooper's; he wanted an ultimatum delivered and was dissatisfied that, on the advice of the 'hysterical Henderson' alone, this had not been done. Like Lloyd and Churchill, Cooper was a man of decided views and firm temper, characteristics which, in many circumstances, must be accounted to virtue, but which, when applied to diplomacy, degenerate into something less. The black and the white exist, but in diplomacy it is seldom that they are unsullied and here, as Chamberlain pointed out, it was not a 'question of never taking the action suggested but only of not taking it now, when Hitler's speech was still in the making, and when it might produce the opposite effect to that desired'.[52] As on future occasions when they clashed in Cabinet, Cooper ended by accepting the Prime Minister's view – but with no good grace, mental reservations and the hope that circumstances would cause his arguments to prevail in future.

To Vansittart, Harvey and others, the 'younger generation' in the Cabinet were the protagonists of virtue against antique defeatism and vice; but there really was pathetically little opposition to the Prime Minister, and not merely because he was a tyrant and they his slaves. Time and again, what sporadic dissent there was yielded to the force of his arguments: no one knew what Hitler would do, so it would be unwise to antagonise him until the necessity arose; no one (with the exception of the Lord Chancellor) was proposing to leave France in the lurch, but the path of statesmanship was to do nothing to encourage the French to act rashly. It was, as Halifax said, 'difficult to go far enough without at the same time going too far'. The military and geographical arguments remained what they had been a fortnight previous, and what they would be a fortnight hence. It was to these realities, as much as to the Prime Minister and the voice of ambition, that the might-be dissentients bowed the knee. Nor did they cabal; indeed, Cooper and Stanley regarded their only other supporters, de la Warr and Winterton, as 'more of liabilities than assets'.[53] It might be that Churchill's sombre ally, 'the march of events', would endow them with cohesiveness, allies and an argument that met the necessities of the situation; but until that day, the tocsin they sounded was both muted and reedy.

Hitler's speech at Nuremberg was, by contrast, strident, vulgar and robust; but it was, by that man's perverse yet cunning standards, diplomatic. It abused Beneš, but then it was always going to do that; it extended the umbrella of protection to the Sudetenland, banged the drum of nationalism and anti-Semitism, and rang the gamut of his standard repertoire which always aroused the faithful. It had not cast the die for war, but nor had it been cast against war.

Reactions to Hitler's speech ran along predictable lines. In the Sudetenland there were riots which the Czechs dealt with firmly, which gave Henlein an excuse to break off negotiations. In Berlin Henderson continued to hope for something from Runciman so that war could be averted.[54] These two hopes were shared by Bonnet in Paris, who had 'completely . . . lost his nerve' and was 'ready for any solution to avoid war'.[55] So anxious was he that, where some Frenchmen jibbed at what they thought was a lukewarm British response to the question of 'If we march, will you?', he welcomed it as a weapon against 'certain bellicose . . . Ministers'.[56] Bellicosity in the Cabinet seemed mainly confined to Cooper, who wanted to mobilise the Fleet but had to confine himself to a violent dislike of the Prime Minister who refused to let him do so.[57] Having decided that, in the face of collapsed negotiations in Prague and deteriorating morale in France, the moment for Plan Z had come, Chamberlain drafted a telegram for Henderson which was telephoned through to Berlin between 11 o'clock and midnight and which he was to give to Ribbentrop for Hitler: 'In view of increasingly critical situation I propose to come over at once to see you with a view to trying to find peaceful solution. I propose to come across by air and am ready to start tomorrow.'[58]

When Chamberlain had broached the plan to Hoare on 10 September, he had been told that he was 'taking a great political risk by personally intervening in a way that was quite likely to fail'.[59] The Prime Minister was aware of this consideration, which is why timing was so important: 'the plan should be tried when things looked blackest' and it 'should be a complete surprise'. He had intended to ask his colleagues for their approval at the Cabinet meeting scheduled for 14 September, but his instincts had told him that 'the moment had come'; then came the waiting.[60]

When the Cabinet met at 11 o'clock on the morning of 14 September, Chamberlain spoke for almost an hour, 'gradually revealing to us his intention of paying a personal visit to Hitler'; 'approval was unanimous and enthusiastic', according to Cooper.[61] That this should have been so was hardly surprising, for the last ditch did, indeed, seem to have been reached; nor was it in the spirit of Canossa that the Prime Minister intended to set out: 'You could say more to a man face to face than you could put in a letter, and . . . doubts as to the British attitude would be better removed by discussion than by any other means.'

Late that afternoon Henderson sent news that the Führer was 'absolutely at the disposal of the Prime Minister'.[62]

Thus it was that, at 8.30 on the morning of 15 September, Chamberlain set off from Heston aerodrome to fly to Munich. It was the first time that he had ever flown anywhere and, as he flew over London and saw thousands of houses spread out below, he thought of the bomber, which would always get through; if his mission failed, it would be war – and war in a given number of days.[63]

Dealing with Hitler

The initiative taken by Chamberlain was to carry him to the summit of popularity – and then blast his fame for two generations. When it was thought that he had saved the peace of Europe, no praise was too lavish to bestow upon him; but once that peace had been destroyed, no abuse was too vile for him. And if, in the period of his prosperity, there were a few Cassandras who dared to say that the sky still darkened and the waves grew higher, there were few to perform the opposite office when his star had set. It is, therefore, pertinent to inquire what Chamberlain hoped to achieve by his journey.

At Heston the Prime Minister's avowed intent was to be the pilgrim of peace, but that begged many questions. Chamberlain later discovered that Hitler professed to be so taken by his initiative that he had thought of flying to London himself, to save 'such an old man such a long journey'.[1] This would not have suited Chamberlain at all. It would not only have deprived his coup of its dramatic force, but would have undercut its main purpose, for Chamberlain had always hoped that, if implemented, Plan Z 'would go far beyond the present crisis and might prove the opportunity for bringing a complete change in the international situation'.[2] Czechoslovakia was the occasion for Chamberlain's visit, not its main purpose: that remained, as always, an Anglo-German entente. Britain had become involved in Czechoslovakia because events˙ there threatened the Prime Minister's objective; now the boil had to be lanced.

Time was when statesmen 'parcelled and allotted'[3] boundaries and peoples with regard only to dynastic convenience. But the triumph of liberalism in nineteenth-century Europe was accompanied by the enthronement of the principle of nationalism as the great deciding force in cartography and, although the peace settlement of 1815 had brought tranquillity to much of Europe for most of the century, its beneficiaries had no good word to say for it: Castlereagh and Metternich stood condemned for their cool disregard of the 'national principle'. The Great War had weakened the Empires of the Habsburgs and Osmanlis to the point where even the most esoteric of nationalisms had been able to raise a voice at the peace conference at Versailles, where the successors of Castlereagh and Metternich, with the help of lectures from an American professor, strove to improve upon the efforts of their predecessors.

But Europe was an old continent, criss-crossed by ancient rivalries and bedevilled by untidy arrangements of borders and linguistic enclaves, which ensured that where one nationality triumphed, another one felt the pang of defeat; nor was it always desirable that the principle of self-determination should prevail in all cases. As Germany had lost the war, so she must lose at the peace settlement: German-speaking areas of the old Habsburg Empire must be allotted to the new state of Czechoslovakia to give her defensible boundaries, regardless of the fact that the boundary thus bestowed was with Germany; German-dominated Danzig and Memel must, also, be taken from her; and even her territorial unity must be sacrificed – all in violation of the national principle, but all for the sake of the balance of power.

But by 1938 the German Government felt strong enough to challenge the balance of power of 1919 with the Wilsonian slogan of national self-determination. Henderson, who lamented that 'in a world of democracies and ideologies' it had become increasingly difficult to 'combine the furtherance of British interests with ... international obligations and the standards of morality',[4] put the 'high moral principle' of national self-determination before 'strategic frontiers and economics'.[5] As even Jan Masaryk was prepared to admit that parts of the Sudetenland should never have been included in Czechoslovakia,[6] it was, indeed, difficult to reconcile the demands of German nationalism with British interests.

It is perhaps natural for historians in an irreligious age to attribute, to politicians of a religious frame of mind, attachment to high moral principles, but Halifax's Whiggish temper had little taste for dramatic confrontations between right and wrong, at least in secular matters. His Anglo-Catholicism did not exclude a good measure of 'the Jesuitical doctrine of the direction of intentions';[7] he would not fall into the error that Eden had committed by allowing his 'judgement of practical steps to be taken to be perpetually deflected by our moral reactions against wrongs that we can in no circumstances immediately redress'.[8]

The 1930s was not, however, an age where the cultivation of such a sensibility conferred advantages upon a diplomatist. As Henderson observed, sadly: 'Right for right's sake doesn't count for anything any more, everything depends on the -ism or the -ology.' As with the religious conflicts of the sixteenth century, zealotry for a cause was the spirit of the age, and, at least in Henderson's view, 'a conflict of philosophies' was 'almost as big a menace to world peace as the ambitions of dictators'.[9] Where dynastic interests had once schooled statesmen in the virtues of moderation, ideology exacted complete obedience, even unto death.

There was, in Chamberlain's nature, a strong streak of the same Romanticism which touched Henderson, but his character had been schooled to appreciate the merits of Halifax's scepticism; both the principle of nationality and the interests of Britain pointed, however, to the same conclusion: Englishmen should not kill Germans in the wastes of the Atlantic because the district of Eger had been given to Czechoslovakia by the Treaty of Trianon. At Cabinet on 14 September the Prime Minister had declared that: 'We were neither pro-Czech nor pro-Sudeten German. Our business was to keep the peace and find a just and equitable settlement.'[10] The authentic voice of liberal optimism could still believe that every problem must have such a solution, but at the heart of the crisis lay the fact that this was not the case.

Chamberlain still endeavoured to hold the ring by warning the Germans (as he did on 11 September) that a 'brief and successful' German campaign in Czechoslovakia could not 'be safely embarked upon without the danger of the subsequent intervention first of France and later of this country'.[11] Chamberlain hoped that Hitler would decide to take the ninety per cent of what he claimed to want, which was on offer through Runciman; if he did not, a resort to force would demonstrate that his objectives were what his enemies alleged and his apologists denied. The so-called 'Fourth Plan', which Runciman had conveyed from Beneš to Henlein on 6 September, 'embodied almost all the requirements of the Karlsbad eight points' and a 'little clarification and extension' might have covered them 'in their entirety'.[12] The Henleinist reaction in the aftermath of Hitler's speech had set back this hope, and Chamberlain's flight to Berchtesgaden was made to resurrect it.

Chamberlain had carefully considered what demands Hitler might make and how to react to them.[13] Suggestions from the French that Runciman might make proposals of his own, or from the Russians for a Four-Power conference, were rejected by Chamberlain because they would drag Britain still further into the morass of Czech-German relations. Hitler might raise the idea of a plebiscite, and it would be difficult 'for a democracy like ourselves to say that we would go to war to prevent it'. But as it was likely to give Hitler nearly everything he wanted, Sir John Simon suggested it might be postponed for a while – which reflected better on his ingenuity than his sense of reality.[14] Finally came the question of how Czechoslovakia could be protected when parts of the Sudetenland joined the Reich. It was only with reluctance that Chamberlain would consider guaranteeing her remaining territory – and then only if Germany, France and Russia would join Britain.

If Hitler did want war, then his reaction to the Prime Minister's visit would show all but the most purblind pacifist that war was necessary and that it had been forced upon Britain. But if, as Hitler claimed, he wanted the friendship of the British, then here was his opportunity to do something to begin to win it. This was the only inducement which the Prime Minister would carry with him to Berchtesgaden. For those of the 'Crowe' school of thought who believed with Cooper that the only real choice facing Britain was 'between war now and a war later', the whole trip was, more or less, worthless. But then Cooper was 'quite confident that if we went to war we should win', whereas, although Chamberlain hoped that 'if we have to fight we should be able to give a good account of ourselves', neither he nor his military advisers 'would feel happy in undertaking to begin hostilities if we were not forced to do so'.[15]

Critics with a taste for historical analogies may have chosen to see Chamberlain's flight as a modern-dress version of Henry IV's barefoot pilgrimage to Hildebrand; the Prime Minister had other ideas. He went not as a supplicant but as the instigator of a dramatic coup, which had not merely taken the initiative away from the Führer but had astonished him with its boldness; Chamberlain was determined to press home his tactical advantage to avert the European war which was, he believed, only days away.[16]

In this belief Chamberlain was mistaken. Hitler's mobilisation plans were laid for late in the month, but the dictator had certainly been taken by surprise and was now threatened by a strategy which might strip away from his policies of aggression those veils of national self-determination which concealed his limitless ambition. He had readily accepted Chamberlain's proposal, even suggesting that Mrs Chamberlain might like to accompany her husband; the Prime Minister's rejection of this has deprived historians of the piquant scene of Annie Chamberlain sipping tea with Eva Braun in one room whilst their menfolk divided the cake of Europe between them in the next.

Those who take the view that Chamberlain was duped by Hitler might see significant symbolism in the fact that the Prime Minister flew into Munich 'blind' through a storm, but Chamberlain preferred to concentrate on the welcome he received from crowds whose enthusiasm not even the rain could dampen. After a three-hour train journey to Berchtesgaden and a quick wash and brush-up, Chamberlain set out for the Brown House for his first meeting with the man whose activities had come to dominate his premiership.

The Prime Minister had thought that a face-to-face meeting might have some impact on the Führer; he seems not to have considered the effect upon himself. In the modern world where national leaders meet with regularity, familiarity breeds boredom, but this was an unprecedented action on the part of a British Prime Minister.

Hitler greeted Chamberlain half-way down the steps of the Brown House; he was, Chamberlain thought, 'entirely undistinguished'. After walking past 'pleasant-faced, smart-looking soldiers', the Prime Minister was ushered into that 'celebrated chamber' with its wall-length window, which, he noted with interest and surprise, was decorated with German and Italian old masters and 'a huge Italian nude!'. Comments on the decor of the room allowed them to break the ice and even gave Chamberlain the opportunity to invite Hitler to London, which prompted the dictator to comment that he would perhaps be 'received with demonstrations of disapproval'. After tea they decided that their conversations would be tête-à-tête.

Chamberlain had thought that they might have a series of talks, beginning with general comments about Anglo-German relations, but it soon became clear to him that 'the situation was much more critical than I had anticipated'. Whilst it is, therefore, certainly correct that, as some historians have claimed, Chamberlain was under a misapprehension as to the timing of German mobilisation, it is more difficult to concur with any wider claim that this led to his being duped.[17] Nothing that Hitler demanded at Berchtesgaden was incompatible with Chamberlain's views on Czechoslovakia. The Prime Minister saw nothing unreasonable in the Führer's demand for the three and a half million Germans in the Sudetenland to be united with the Reich; nor had Henderson, nor yet Runciman. Similarly, the Czech-Soviet alliance was not something for which he was willing to hazard the future of the Empire.

It was only when Hitler went outside the range of Chamberlain's own thoughts by saying, 'I do not care whether there is a world war or not, I am determined to settle it soon,' that Chamberlain grew angry and asked why, in that case, he had been allowed to come all this way. As there was no answer to this which would not have revealed his hand and spoiled his plans, Hitler had no choice but to calm down and ask if the Prime Minister would agree to the cession of the Sudetenland and the negation of the Czech-Soviet alliance. As this was very much what the Cabinet had agreed to before he departed, Chamberlain was on safe ground once again; but he insisted that consultation with his colleagues and the French would be necessary before he could give a firm answer to the question.

Both men were in cheerful spirits afterwards: Chamberlain had obtained a stay of execution, or so he thought, as far as German mobilisation was concerned, whilst Hitler had gained some of the extra time he needed to complete those preparations. They chatted aimiably on their way downstairs, with Hitler asking if Chamberlain had time to stay and see some of the sights.

Chamberlain's satisfaction was increased when he heard from Wilson that the Germans had been tremendously impressed with his dramatic flight and that Hitler thought that he was 'a man'.[18] Having established that 'certain confidence' which had been 'my aim', Chamberlain was confident that Hitler was 'a man who could be relied upon when he had given his word'. It is ironic that this attitude, credulous as it was, has brought Chamberlain so much obloquy, whereas Churchill's declaration to the Cabinet in February 1945 that he had 'every confidence' in Stalin has done little to damage his reputation.[19] In both cases the problem was the same: a British Prime Minister, having committed himself to a summit meeting, needed to bring something away from it; in both cases the dictator's intentions appeared to have some affinity with British policy; and, most fatally of all, both Prime Ministers fell into one of the greatest snares awaiting the 'summiteer' – that of mistaking personal cordiality for a similarity of aim.

Chamberlain, however, met with more opposition to his illusions than did Churchill.

Reaction to the Prime Minister's startling initiative had, generally, followed predictable lines. Churchill, who it might be thought had considerable authority to pronounce so, called it 'the stupidest thing that has ever been done', whilst Leo Amery thought that there was an 'off chance' that his 'courageous action' might have averted war.[20] The Labour Party was suspicious and furious in equal measure and at different times, depending upon whether its members were considering the Prime Minister or their electoral prospects.[21] The 'loyal opposition' found itself in a considerable dilemma; where Churchill could pronounce (at least privately) his anathemas, and the Labour Party could fulminate, those Conservatives who imagined that they had a political future under the Party's current leadership had to take a more circumspect line.

Perhaps this is slightly unfair. Many of them must have shared Harold Nicolson's first reaction upon hearing the news of Chamberlain's flight: 'enormous relief'.[22] Eden was in a cruel dilemma. On the one hand he was in favour of Churchill's policy of 'organising all states who will be against aggression and of so confronting the gangsters with a ring of force',[23] but, having so recently been in power, he was aware that 'he might have done the same' as Halifax had he been in his position. He had no wish to 'lead a revolt or to secure any resignations from the Cabinet'.[24] Nor did anyone else. Oliver Stanley had already told Cooper before Chamberlain went to Berchtesgaden that he was 'most anxious' not to 'form any sort of group of those who shared our opinion'; an opinion with which Cooper agreed.[25]

Chamberlain's dramatic gesture had captured the initiative not only from Hitler but also from his colleagues, emphasising that he was something more than primus inter pares; but if his policy prevailed, it was not because the Prime Minister was an autocrat. This, and the reasons for his success, can be gleaned from the two Cabinet meetings which took place on 17 September upon his return from Germany.[26]

For those Ministers who did not know the details of the meeting, the tension was built up by the way Chamberlain conducted the meeting, having Lord Runciman playing a John the Baptist role. His long account of his mission made one thing quite plain: 'Czechoslovakia could not continue to exist as she was today. Something would have to be done, even if it amounted to no more than cutting off certain fringes.' He also implied that the French were exceedingly unlikely to go to war for the sake of the Czechs. In two moves he had cut away the ground upon which the Prime Minister's few critics in the Cabinet wished to place themselves. Chamberlain's account of his meeting with Hitler completed this process.

That Cooper would rediscover his objections was to be expected, as he had never lost them. But it was not altogether clear what he was objecting to – apart from being obliged to participate in a policy which he found distasteful and for which there was a simple remedy. Moreover, Cooper lacked three things which would have made his objections count: weight, a viable alternative policy and, most important of all, someone who would follow that policy.

Behind the anguished discussions in Cabinet lay a divide between two schools of thought on British foreign policy: the cosmopolitan and the insular. A handsome dividend has always accrued to the Conservative Party from its adoption of the role cast for it by Disraeli as 'the patriotic party', but this has obscured the fact that there is another strand of Conservative thinking on the subject. This school would have agreed with the criticism of Disraeli voiced by his Foreign Secretary from 1874–6, the fifteenth Earl of Derby, that:

> He believes thoroughly in 'prestige' – as all foreigners do, and would think it (and quite sincerely) in the interests of the country to spend 200 millions on a war if the result of it was to make foreign states think more highly of us as a military power.[27]

With his descent from Scottish earls and Hanoverian kings, Cooper was no foreigner, but, like Disraeli, he believed in 'prestige'; or, in a phrase which that Francophile would have appreciated, in '*la gloire*'. He shared General de Gaulle's belief that unless she was 'great', his country was not being true to herself. This attitude, and the Francophilia, was shared by most of the other 'cosmopolitans': Churchill, Lloyd, Eden, Vansittart, Spears and Nicolson. All were men with a highly charged, splendid and romantic view of their country's destiny; all of them knew Europe and placed great reliance upon the French connection; for Britain to behave basely was unthinkable, unpalatable and impossible. With their protests the heart lies; but the difficulty they faced, or rather refused to face, is revealed by Cooper's showing in Cabinet against those Conservatives of a more insular cast of mind.

During the Austro-Prussian war of 1866, the British Foreign Secretary, Lord Stanley (later the fifteenth Earl of Derby), had said that, 'there never was a great European war in which the direct national interests of England were less concerned'; the establishment of a great German Empire in Central Europe caused neither 'injury... menace... [nor] detriment' to British interests.[28] To this school of Conservative thinking belonged, in some measure, the Prime Minister, Halifax and Henderson, but it was represented, in perhaps its most undiluted form, by the Lord Chancellor, Maugham, whose French background had not had upon him the effect it had upon his famous brother, Somerset.

Historians are often foremost amongst those who state that no lessons can be learned from history; this depressing philosophy is not widely shared by laymen, and even less often practised. In 1925 Harold Temperley, Reader in History at the University of Cambridge, published a study of Canning's foreign policy; in September 1938 he sent a copy of his book to Chamberlain, who found its message that 'you should never menace unless you are in a position to carry out your threat' very congenial.[29] Lord Maugham, who had been reading the same book, had also imbibed lessons from it, as he told his colleagues when they gathered at 3 o'clock to continue their discussion. There were, he said, two conditions laid down by Canning and 'approved by Disraeli' which should govern any British intervention abroad: first, that 'British interests were seriously affected; secondly, that we should only intervene with overwhelming force'. Neither of these were, in this instance, applicable: 'except for some possible loss of prestige, British interests were not involved'.

This historical disquisition prompted Cooper, who prided himself upon his erudition and knowledge of diplomatic history, to counter it with one based upon his own, very different, conclusions. He took his stand upon the principle which was at the centre of Crowe's famous memorandum of 1907: 'that it was a primary interest of this country to prevent any single power dominating Europe'; Nazi Germany was, he added, 'the most formidable power that had ever dominated Europe'. From two questionable assertions he drew conclusions which reveal better than any theories of prime ministerial government why Chamberlain's policy prevailed.

Cooper acknowledged the force of Maugham's statements that not only did Britain not possess 'overwhelming force', but also that she had no prospect of doing so, but his heart regarded with detestation the conclusion which intellect placed upon that conclusion. He said that if he thought 'surrender' would bring peace, he would advocate it; however, not only did he not think this, but he was convinced that there could be no peace whilst the Nazis ruled in Berlin. The logic of this policy was that 'defeat' would replace 'surrender' as an unprepared Britain was overwhelmed, but Cooper shied away from this conclusion and, instead, tailed off in the lame fashion which was to ensure that his attitude did not prevail: war being such a terrible thing, he was prepared to postpone it 'in the very faint hope that some internal event would bring about the fall of the Nazi regime'. He would, therefore, be willing to accept a settlement in Czechoslovakia based upon the results of a 'fair' plebiscite. It was not just sycophancy which prompted Inskip to declare that he saw no 'essential difference' between Cooper's conclusion and that reached by the Prime Minister; there was, and remained, a basic difference of attitude between the 'cosmopolitan' and 'insular', but it pointed to no very different policy. As Malcolm MacDonald put it unanswerably: 'the people of this country would be overwhelmingly in favour of a plebiscite rather than a war'.

This was why Chamberlain's views prevailed. No one, as Daladier and Bonnet showed when they came to London on 18 September, was willing to go to war to prevent 'self-determination' on the part of the Sudeteners. The acutest comment on the dilemma of Chamberlain's opponents came from Harold Nicolson, who recorded in his diary:

> Hitler has all the arguments on his side, but essentially they are false arguments. And we, who have right on our side, cannot say that our real right is to resist German hegemony. That is 'imperialistic'. Never have conflicting theories become so charged with illusion.[30]

Liberalism had led to disaster.

The bankruptcy of liberalism in foreign policy is nowhere better revealed than in the fact that its adherents, like the 'cosmopolitans', looked to France for salvation. Ironically, the French were looking towards London for the same boon.

Opinion in Paris was even more divided than in London. Daladier had flashes of spirit and talked as if France would honour her obligations to Czechoslovakia,[31] but he was hampered by fears about what ought to have been three of his main props: the British, Bonnet and the French air force.

British anxiety to do nothing that would make the French unduly bellicose had had the effect of stretching the nerves of some Frenchmen to breaking-point. Whilst Bonnet had been at pains to elicit ambiguous statements which he could use to cool his own 'hawks',[32] those very phrases had alarmed sterner spirits. The Secretary-General at the Quai d'Orsay, Alexis Léger, told Phipps on 11 September that he was 'greatly perturbed', but, despite Halifax's expressed 'surprise' at this, the Frenchman was unsuccessful in trying to extract from the British an unequivocal declaration of unconditional support for any action to help Czechoslovakia.[33]

Bonnet's nerve had, as we have seen, cracked on the eve of Chamberlain's flight and he had been prepared to pay 'any price' to preserve peace.[34] One of the things which had led to this collapse was a report from the American aviator, Charles Lindbergh, that the Luftwaffe was infinitely more powerful than the pitifully weak French air force. This had its effect even on Daladier, who was, on 13 September, a good deal less bellicose than he had been a few days earlier and talked of convening a three-Power conference to settle the affairs of Czechoslovakia.[35]

In an elaborate but easily detected piece of intrigue, Vansittart tried to ensure that Bonnet was not invited to London,[36] but his attempt was frustrated by the actions of his brother-in-law, Phipps, who insisted that he must accompany Daladier.[37] Each man's motive was transparent. Vansittart did not want Bonnet for the same reason that Phipps thought him indispensable: he would weaken Daladier's bold front. 'Van' wanted the Frenchman who took the firmer line, whilst Phipps, fearing that 'Daladier always talks bigger than he acts',[38] was determined that both men should come to London. Indeed, to ensure that Bonnet's views were heard, the Ambassador warned, in a paragraph which spoke volumes about his attitude to his hosts, that the two men should be interrogated separately about the French air force: 'Veracity is not . . . the strongest point of the average French politician, but there is a rather better chance of extracting the truth from him when he is not in the presence of another Frenchman.'[39]

Phipps' mistrust of the French was shared by Halifax, who warned the Cabinet on 17 September of the danger that responsibility for any decision which might seem to abandon Czechoslovakia and cede the Sudetenland would 'be placed on our shoulders, although it was France and not ourselves who had treaty obligations' to the Czechs.[40] It was, he warned, 'important that we should avoid allowing the French to say that they came to London and found that we had decided to give the show away'.[41] Nor was this warning unwarranted. Privately, Daladier had already decided that, 'It is better to resolve the Sudeten affair by a general peace than by a general war',[42] which implied that, like the British, he had made up his mind that the Sudetenland must be ceded; but of this he said nothing at the meeting on 18 September.[43]

Chamberlain began by describing his visit to Berchtesgaden – thus providing what Hoare called 'the sedative of a long narrative' to open a meeting at which the Frenchmen appeared to be visibly under strain: Daladier, 'square and squat', his face 'flushed redder than ever', and Bonnet, 'as white as Daladier was red, sensitive, and apparently on the verge of a *crise de nerfs*'.[43] Daladier was anxious that the British should keep the initiative when it came to deciding what to do next, but Chamberlain was too canny to be caught out like that. It all came down, he said, to whether they accepted 'the principle of self-determination'. That the heirs of the French revolution and the inheritors of Versailles would discard the sacred cause was unthinkable; only the cynical Hoare wondered 'what the nineteenth-century Liberals and President Wilson would have thought of the Frankenstein monster of self-determination that they had so optimistically created . . .'

But the plebiscite, which had seemed so acceptable to the British, met with determined resistance from the French. What Daladier did not tell Chamberlain was that Beneš had already signalled his willingness to sacrifice parts of the Sudetenland – indeed, had provided a map of the areas to be ceded – but was opposed to a plebiscite which was bound to give the Germans more.[44] Daladier declared that France would never abandon her ally, but that was not to say that Czechoslovakian territorial integrity was sacrosanct. In Cadogan's formulation, the question was 'how to (a) avoid war, (b) maintain *independence* (*not* integrity!) of Cz[echoslovakia]'.[45]

Here was where Daladier's bold front led: the Czechs would be strongly advised not to mobilise their forces; Anglo-French 'good offices' would be employed in Prague to persuade the Czechs to give up parts of the Sudetenland; and, for the sake of British 'public opinion', these concessions should appear to be the emanations of Czech goodwill: 'This would dispose of any idea that we were ourselves carving up Czechoslovak territory.' But what of France's vaunted eastern bastions against German revival? The obvious course was to acknowledge that, as Germany had revived, Czechoslovakia was a source of weakness not strength, but this was unthinkable; the precepts of liberal diplomacy left open to them the possibility of guaranteeing what remained of Czechoslovakia – indeed, of inviting Germany to join in such an undertaking.

If anything ran contrary to the traditions of British diplomacy it was, in Hoare's words, 'to undertake guarantees on the Continent that left the final decision of peace or war in hands other than our own'; in the case of a mutilated Czechoslovakia, such a policy also ran counter to common sense. The worldwide nature of Britain's commitments, along with the vagaries of parliamentary democracy , had often furnished the third Marquess of Salisbury with reasons for declining a continental commitment; the existence of the Dominions served the same purpose for Chamberlain on this occasion. But French importunity was not to be denied. Despite his later claims to the contrary, Daladier had not informed Chamberlain before the meeting started that he was willing to concede Czech territory; indeed, on the contrary, he had made a great performance of being forced into that position; his quid pro quo was a British guarantee. Once this had, reluctantly, been granted, they could turn to drafting a telegram for Beneš.[46]

One question remained: what if Beneš should refuse? Over lunch, without revealing the reasons for it, Daladier had expressed his belief that this would not happen.[47] His confidence was left unscathed by the knowledge that the concessions which he was about to urge were much greater than those marked upon the map Beneš had sent to Paris. The British, who did not share this knowledge, feared that it was only too likely, but were unable to get Daladier to confront the possibility. They agreed to telegraph the news of their decisions to Prague and to tell Hitler that Chamberlain would be coming to see him as soon as possible. The initative had passed to Prague and Berlin, but only for the moment.

For the Government the French attitude had provided a lever in Prague and an occasion for telling a few home truths to Churchill;[48] for others it provided a salve to the conscience and an adequate excuse for doing nothing. Of those in the Cabinet who had 'doubts' about the Prime Minister's infallibility, Walter Elliot, 'depressed and bewildered', had no 'very clear view about what is to happen next'[49] and consoled himself with the reflection that, as the Russians would not help and the French were 'as flat as a flat tyre', it was 'simply impossible for Britain to put any weight in the far corner of South-East Europe'.[50] Oliver Stanley, who muttered in Cabinet that he would have 'preferred to have adopted a different policy', was flummoxed when Chamberlain asked him, 'what policy was that?'[51] Lord Winterton, whose interventions were usually counter-productive, spoke about 'fundamental differences of opinion in the Cabinet'. Duff Cooper, who cordially disliked the whole business and suspected that some of his colleagues were 'thinking more of how far we could go in the direction of humiliating surrender', did his best to pour oil on the troubled waters by saying that 'the difference was one of emphasis only'.[52]

Given Cooper's previous debate with the Lord Chancellor over the 'traditions of British foreign policy', it was ironic that he should have found himself defending the proposed guarantee – a clear departure from those principles and one which gave most of the Cabinet an uneasy feeling. Maugham, Hailsham and others felt dubious about such a novel commitment, but there were those sympathetic to Cooper's position, most notably the Minister of War, Hore-Belisha, who disliked it because it would be given to a truncated Czechoslovakia.[53]

If the Cabinet seemed divided and demoralised, it accurately reflected the national mood. The Labour Party, whilst wanting to take a firm line with the dictators, was split on how to do so, and Dalton, who was in clandestine contact with Vansittart, even wondered whether the time had not come to tell the Czechs that they would have to surrender.[54]

Churchill, who, like Dalton, had contacts with Vansittart and with the Czech Government, was in no doubt that no such advice should be tendered to Beneš; the Czechs should fight rather than surrender – and that was bound to change the picture.[55] There were rumours that he and Eden intended to 'take a vigorous line against "giving in"',[56] but whilst Churchill flew off to Paris to see if he could rally his forces there,[57] Eden preferred to take a more genteel approach, writing privately to Halifax to express his 'distress'.[58] There were those such as Nicolson who hoped he 'would come out into the open',[59] but others in his coterie reacted strongly to a proposal that they should attend a meeting with Churchill at Lord Lloyd's house; Anthony Crossley, one of his minor acolytes, told him that his friends had 'decided not to go; that we didn't wish to align ourselves with the Cabal who were notorious for plots against the Government'.[60]

The Government's opponents, as unhappy and divided as the Cabinet itself, were also uneasily aware of the possibility that, if Chamberlain did manage to preserve the peace, there might well be a general election, in which they could scarcely hope to prosper.[61] It was perhaps Elliot's own bewilderment which enabled him to summarise so acutely the national mood:

> The people would like Hitler stopped, but are all for doing it by taking a strong line, or encouraging our Allies but not by actually going out and beginning to fight. That probably means that as the fear of war wears off, they will get angry with the Government.[62]

Under enormous diplomatic pressure, the threat of being left on their own and with many protests, the Czechs capitulated.[63]

Sketch Map¹ based on the Map annexed to the Memorandum handed to the Prime Minister by the Reichschancellor on September 23, 1938.

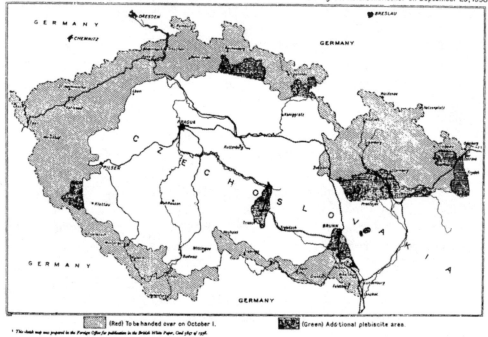

(Red) To be handed over on October 1.   (Green) Additional plebiscite area.

¹ This sketch map was prepared in the Foreign Office for publication in the British White Paper, Cmd 5847 of 1938.

Sketch Map¹ based on the Map annexed to the Agreement signed at Munich on September 29, 1938.

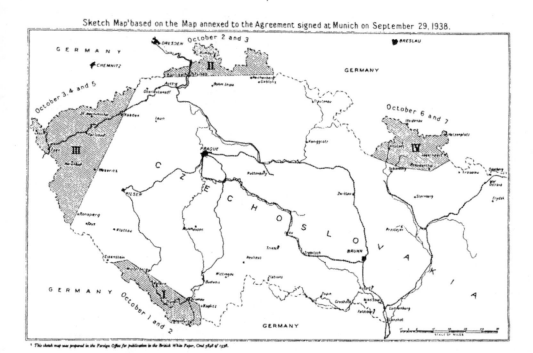

¹ This sketch map was prepared in the Foreign Office for publication in the British White Paper, Cmd 5848 of 1938.

Exercises in Cartography

The proposal made in such deep secrecy by Beneš was based upon a scheme put forward at Versailles by Tomas Masaryk. It envisaged the cession by Czechoslovakia of between four and six thousand square kilometres of territory and a million Sudeten Germans; it would have allowed her to retain her frontier fortifications and lose a third of her Germans.[1] Under Daladier's skilful handling in London, this had become a proposal to cede all areas with eighty per cent German population; in return the Czechs were to receive a guarantee. It was little wonder that with cartographic friends like that, the Czech Government acquiesced only under protest and then resigned.

Even before the Czechs had accepted the terms, details of them were bruited abroad. Jan Masaryk, who had taken to his bed, was voluble in his distress and anxious to rouse British opinion in his country's favour.[2] Vansittart, who had taken to urgent caballing with the Government's opponents, was fertile in news for Dalton and Churchill and, despairing of rousing the Government, thought of resignation.[3] Others, like Harold Nicolson's friend 'Baffy' Dugdale, who vomited three times in one night, showed their appreciation of the Government's policy in more concrete form. Scenting blood, the Labour Party condemned the Government; embracing his policy it did not, to Churchill's disappointment, embrace his tentative overtures. Churchill thus took himself off to Paris declaring that the Government had had to choose between war and shame and that, 'They have chosen shame and they will get war.'[4] This he expressed in more oracular form in a statement for the press, which called for a union of Powers against Germany and the recall of Parliament.[5]

But emotions ran strongly in other directions as news of the Government's cartographic ambitions spread. General Ironside, who sympathised with Churchill's statement, thought it fatally flawed by his lack of realism; it was, he noted, 'All very true, but *we cannot expose ourselves now to a German attack. We simply commit suicide if we do.'* Long depressed by the 'puny' contribution which the British army could make to a continental war, Ironside acquiesced in Chamberlain's 'realism': 'We have not the means of defending ourselves and he knows it.'[6] Hore-Belisha warned Chamberlain that if they sent a British force to oversee the handing over of the Sudetenland, 'we would diminish our capacity to deal with any emergency which may arise, not only in Europe, but in Egypt and Palestine'.[7]

There were, of course, those like the British Minister in Bucharest whose feelings were 'mixed', but were 'dominated by a craven reluctance to see the end of the world'.[8] The prospect of Armageddon may have concentrated the mind and scarified the emotions, but it did not prevent people planning ahead. Butler's friend Michael Beaumont invited him to a shoot in December, but added the caveat 'if we are not all submerged in a holocaust'. He thought that Chamberlain and Halifax had been 'magnificent': 'You must have had a hell of a time. Damn the Czechs!'[9] Beaverbrook spoke for a kindred school of feeling when he said: 'This is no concern of ours, keep out';[10] 'Britain', he wrote in the *Daily Express* on 22 September, 'never gave any pledge to protect the frontiers of Czechoslovakia . . . No moral obligation rests upon us.' With Hoare passing on to him news of Cabinet discussions, Beaverbrook joined *The Times* in praising the Government.[11]

But isolationism could only be had at a price the Government would not pay: the acceptance of German hegemony, the abandonment of France and abdication as a Great Power. As Cadogan wrote on 21 September: '*How* much courage is needed to be a coward!'[12] Aware that Hitler 'may do or ask for anything', he thought it vital to formulate in advance what was and was not acceptable. In the latter category he put Hungarian and Polish territorial demands on Czechoslovakia; and German claims to direct her foreign policy, or to suppress the Communist Party and to persecute Jews. Any call by Hitler to occupy areas of the Sudetenland where the Germans were in a minority should be 'resisted', but the question of the neutralisation of Czechoslovakia would have to be considered:

> I should have thought it was quite clear that we have to go to the limit to try to satisfy what Hitler said were his claims, on the ground that as he put them, they were not entirely unjustifiable. If he goes beyond them, he will have gone beyond our limit, and there will be nothing to be done but to oppose them [*sic*]. Our moral position will be all the stronger for having strained to the utmost to give him satisfaction, and his position before the world . . . will be all the worse.[13]

It was not merely Foreign Office advice which informed the thoughts of Chamberlain as he flew to Bad Godesberg on 22 September. The Cabinet had accepted the idea of a guarantee for Czechoslovakia only as the necessary counter to persuade Beneš to agree to territorial concessions. Meeting on 21 September in an atmosphere made tense by reports that at any moment the situation 'might get out of hand', Ministers had discussed the form of that guarantee and the modus operandi of handing over territory to the Germans.[14]

Everyone agreed that no countenance should be given to the jackal claims of Poland and Hungary; if Hitler raised the matter, Chamberlain was to return to London. On the question of the unwelcome but necessary guarantee, the Prime Minister's suggestion that it must be given jointly, so that the other Powers did not 'run out and leave us to bear the whole burden', met with a warm response, as did the idea that Germany should not become one of the guarantors but rather conclude a non-aggression pact with the truncated Czechoslovakia. The question of who should provide the joint guarantee proved more difficult, mainly because of Halifax dragging in Yugoslavia and Romania. But it was finally agreed that Chamberlain should suggest Britain, France and Russia and that, if the great anti-Bolshevik demurred at the latter, that too would be a matter for reference to the Cabinet.

These were not the only limitations placed upon Chamberlain's freedom to negotiate. He suggested that, as Hitler was bound to demand the withdrawal of Czech police and troops from the areas to be transferred, which would lead to problems over law and order, they might contemplate the occupation of these areas by German troops; other, racially 'mixed' areas might require an international peace-keeping force – which, inevitably, would be mainly British. But this aroused such hostility that Chamberlain had to execute a tactical retreat. Stanley argued for a 'decent interval' before the troops marched in, pointing out that it was essential 'to convince people that German rule did not start before the frontier had been delimited'. Cooper was even more outraged and declared that once German troops entered Czechoslovakia, they would 'end by their overrunning the whole country'; Chamberlain should tell Hitler that if he would not accept international control of the disputed regions pending the report of an International Boundary Commission, 'we should go to war with him' – not over the Sudetenland, but to stop him from 'dominating Europe'. With even the usually complaisant Hoare on Cooper's side,[15] Chamberlain said that he would not put his proposal to the Führer; it was decided that, if the Prime Minister could not get a suitable settlement on the point, it too would have to be referred back to the Cabinet. There was no question here of prime ministerial government.

It was, therefore, with a disagreeable sensation of surprise that Ministers listened to the Prime Minister's description of his conversations with Hitler at Bad Godesberg.

The caveats which the Cabinet had expressed about further concessions had, it soon became clear, been brushed aside.[16] Chamberlain had begun well enough, eschewing self-determination as a general principle in cartography, but accepting it for the Sudetenland; it was suggested that areas with sixty-five per cent German population should be transferred to Germany. Raising the proposal for a guarantee, Chamberlain emphasised that it did 'not necessarily mean that the present Czech frontiers would be guaranteed in perpetuity'. This went somewhat beyond what the Cabinet had decided, but if Chamberlain thought it was preparing the way for a speedy solution to the crisis, he was wrong: Hitler replied that the proposals were not 'acceptable to him'.

Shocked, the Prime Minister listened whilst the Führer raised the question of Polish and Hungarian grievances and described Czechoslovakia as 'an artificial construction . . . established solely on the grounds of political con-siderations'. He demanded the immediate delimitation of a frontier and German occupation of the areas within it; there could be an internationally supervised plebiscite held later to determine 'the final frontier'; he refused to consider a non-aggression pact with Czechoslovakia until Polish and Hungarian claims were settled. This was something very close to the 'worst case scenario' envisioned by the pessimists in the Foreign Office.

Instead of announcing that he must now refer back to London as there was agreement on neither basic principles nor the modus operandi, Chamberlain endeavoured to move Hitler from his position; but his arguments only revealed that the initiative which he had seized at Berchtesgaden had now been snatched back by Hitler. Chamberlain said that he had taken his 'political life into my hands' by negotiating, and that there had been boos as he left Heston. When Hitler replied that only the left booed him, Chamberlain revealed the main source of his anxiety, saying: 'He did not mind what the left thought, but that his serious differences came from the people in his own Party.' Although he did not, he said, believe claims that Hitler wanted to annex Czechoslovakia, he appealed to Hitler to 'help prove to his critics that they were wrong'; British friendship could not be had if Germany resorted to force.

These points were driven home in a letter and a further conversation, which stressed that Britain and France could not agree to an immediate German occupation of disputed areas;[17] but it was to no avail. Chamberlain told his colleagues that he had promised to put the proposals to the Czechs and that, upon reflection, he favoured accepting them.[18] The consternation created by this account was so profound that it took a night for it to break in full force.

The portents that there might be a storm had been apparent even before Chamberlain had returned. On 21 September, Cooper, hypersensitive to any suggestion that Germany might be allowed to occupy parts of the Sudetenland, had taken exception to this idea being raised in a private telegram to Newton, telling Halifax that he 'could never be a party to allowing German troops to march into Czechoslovakia now without the consent of the Czechoslovak Government'; he persuaded Stanley to do the same.[19] Halifax's reply expressed agreement with this point, but denied that such a step was contemplated.[20]

Public opinion, as far as could be assessed, was now highly volatile. The boos for Chamberlain at Heston were not the only signs of disapproval. As Cooper walked home on the evening of 22 September, he saw a 'vast procession' marching down Whitehall crying 'Stand by the Czechs' and 'Chamberlain must go'.[21] Halifax warned Chamberlain that whilst it was likely that a 'mistrustful' public would accept the original plan as an alternative to war, the 'great mass of public opinion seems to be hardening in [the] sense of feeling that we have gone to [the] limit of concession and that it is up to the Chancellor to make some contribution'.[22]

This was much more than an attempt to strengthen Chamberlain's hand in negotiating; it was a sign of Halifax's emergence as an independent political force. The Foreign Secretary was more sensitive to the political climate than Chamberlain. His objective was, Butler wrote, 'to preserve national unity, to keep in play all sections of public opinion and to "get us through", at any rate this present period of crisis, without a war'.[23] This was written in mid-1939, but the phenomenon which Butler remarked had its origins in this period.

As evidence of German intransigence accumulated, so did Halifax's attitude harden. In the light of reported Henleinist incursions into parts of the Sudetenland, he suggested to the French that they should withdraw their advice to the Czechs not to mobilise;[24] on Chamberlain's advice action on this was suspended,[25] but once he heard what was happening at Bad Godesberg, Halifax went ahead with his decision and asked Butler, who was in Geneva at the League, to find out what the Soviet attitude would be if Czechoslovakia became involved in a war with Germany.[26]

Sensitive as he was to the public mood, Halifax was equally susceptible to the Prime Minister's forceful 'realism'. When Chamberlain presented his report to the 'inner Cabinet' at 3.30 p.m. on 24 September, Cadogan was 'completely horrified' at his 'total surrender'. Even worse was the fact that Halifax, who had had lunch with Chamberlain, had, in what his biographer calls 'an extraordinary moment of weakness', fallen in with his views.[27] Nor did the Cabinet meeting at 5 o'clock move him.

Cooper was 'astonished' when Chamberlain finished his rather indignant recital of Hitler's conversation by 'saying that he considered that we should accept those terms and that we should advise the Czechs to do so'. He protested, saying that whereas he had imagined that they were confronted with the alternatives of war or dishonour, he now 'saw a third possibility, namely war with dishonour, by which I meant being kicked into war by the boot of public opinion'.[28] Hore-Belisha was equally unhappy and urged immediate mobil-isation of the British army as the only means of making an impression upon Hitler; in this he was supported by Elliot, Winterton and Stanley.[29] It was agreed to adjourn the discussion to the following morning.

There was much soul-searching and not a few second thoughts that night among members of the Cabinet. Hore-Belisha, who left Cabinet in a 'stiff and bellicose mood', decided that the Godesberg terms amounted to an ultimatum, that they must be refused and that 'we have incurred a moral obligation to the Czechs and . . . are no longer the free agent we were before the matter started'.[30] Elliot, who had been 'flummoxed' by the way in which members of the 'inner Cabinet', who had been firm on 23 September, had come round to Chamberlain's view, was 'intensely disturbed' at the prospect of handing Czech territory over,[31] whilst Cooper, who had been refused permission to begin preparations for protecting the Suez Canal, was furious with Chamberlain and determined not to yield. Hailsham, who had tended to take a pacific line in Cabinet, surprised Cooper by agreeing with him that they would never get Chamberlain's policy through the Commons; his son Quintin was standing at the Oxford by-election and Hailsham had been impressed at the feeling there against a policy of 'surrender'. Stanley, who concurred with Cooper's opinions, promised to act with him on the morrow.[32]

There seemed to be a feeling, going beyond the usual malcontents of Cooper, Elliot, Stanley and Winterton, that Chamberlain had gone 'far beyond his . . . instructions';[33] the problem lay in how to focus the discontent. Hoare and Simon had sounded bellicose when Chamberlain was away, but had now trimmed their sails, which left only Halifax.

Immensely experienced politically as he was, Halifax inclined instinctively to the role of second-in-command and had no taste for dissent. Chamberlain's account had drawn him away from the position he had been tending towards, and Phipps' reports of French opinion had hardened this drift. The Ambassa-dor reported, in strong terms, that only a 'small but noisy and corrupt war group' was really bellicose and that 'All that is best in France is against war, *almost* at any price . . .'[34] Cadogan, who drove Halifax home on the night of 24 September, was horrified at the prospect of endorsing Hitler's proposals and argued against doing so, but, as he recorded in his diary, without success: 'I've never before known him to make up his mind so quickly and firmly on anything.'[35]

Halifax had a bad night. Tormented by his conscience he woke at 1 o'clock and failed to get back to sleep; by the time he arrived at Cabinet at 10.30 a.m., his mind was made up.

Chamberlain asked the Foreign Secretary to lead off. He did so 'in a very low voice and with great emotion'.[36] Not even the dry prose of the Cabinet minutes can quite lose the drama of what he said:

> Yesterday he felt that the difference between ... [Berchtesgaden and Bad Godesberg] did not involve a new acceptance of principle. He was not quite sure, however, that he still held that view ... it might be held that there was a distinction between orderly and disorderly transfer ...

This was not, he said, put forward as a 'final conclusion', but he did not think that they could press the Czechs to accept Hitler's terms. 'This', Cooper recorded, 'came as a great surprise to those who think as I do.'

To Chamberlain it came as a 'horrible blow'. He passed Halifax a note to this effect, adding that should the French say that they were going to help the Czechs 'thereby dragging us in, I do not think I could accept responsibility for the decision'. Halifax replied that he felt 'a brute' but that, after his long night's thoughts, he could do no other.[37] Chamberlain commented that 'night conclusions are seldom taken in right perspective' and argued that no one was saying that the Czechs should be coerced, merely that they should be told that 'we are not coming in unless the French are in it'; Cooper and company wanted, he said, to stiffen the French and Czechs by promising them British assistance: 'That I will not myself consent to.'[38]

It was around this point that the Cabinet discussion revolved, but Halifax's change of front meant that the balance was moving away from the Prime Minister.[39] Only Lords Maugham and Stanhope actually went so far as to advocate recommending the Godesberg terms to the Czechs; the Chamberlain 'loyalists', taking their cue from his attitude and some of Inskip's remarks, took the view that they could not coerce the Czechs, but merely make sure that they were aware of the consequences of rejecting Hitler's terms. There was, amongst these 'loyalists', a grudging acknowledgment that if France became involved in a war they would have to support her but, like Chamberlain, they thought that unambiguous promises of support were likely to increase that possibility.

The usual dissentients, emboldened by Halifax's change of front (even though he had not come as far as Cooper) and strengthened by the adhesion of Lords Hailsham and de la Warr and the vacillation of Malcolm MacDonald and the Secretary of State for Scotland, John Colville, pressed their points home with indignation. They were as careful as the 'loyalists' not to press their case to extremes. No one argued for a declaration of war; the most they wanted on this front was to mobilise the armed forces as a warning. But what they did want was for Chamberlain to make it clear when he saw Masaryk, Daladier and Bonnet that afternoon that, if the Germans attacked Czechoslovakia and France intervened, Britain would march with them.

As the 'loyalists' were saying neither that the Czechs should be coerced nor that France should be abandoned, and as the dissentients were not advocating war, it might have seemed to the dispassionate observer that there was little real ground between the two sides – especially since everyone had already conceded the principle of relinquishing Czech territory. But there were no dispassionate observers on the eve of Armageddon. Chamberlain and company were, in effect, prepared to make further concessions to preserve peace, even to accepting dishonour. In part this was because, as Hoare noted, they had become 'caught up in the toils of a critical negotiation'. Negotiations have a life of their own, and those involved in them become so anxious to see them through to a successful conclusion, so obsessed with the tactics of what they are doing, that they make a concession here and another there until it is no longer clear to them whether the 'substance is being sacrificed to the negotiation'.[40] That Halifax had now reached the conclusion that the answer to this was 'yes' was of immense significance.

The 'toils of negotiation' carried the Cabinet into an unprecedented three meetings that Sunday. Chamberlain's attempt to point out how little divided the two sides failed to bring a consensus. One sign of this was a demand from Cooper and Hore-Belisha that the French Ministers should have the opportunity of seeing some British Ministers who held their point of view.[41] Cooper's private offer of resignation was, however, refused.[42]

By the time the Cabinet reconvened at 11.30 p.m., Chamberlain had seen Daladier and Bonnet; Hoare's summary of the conversations as 'painful in the extreme' accurately summarises their content.[43] Previous to the meeting Halifax had received from Masaryk the official Czech reply to the Godesberg terms: 'The nation of St Wenceslas, John Hus and Tomas Masaryk will not be a nation of slaves'; in rejecting Hitler's demands Czechoslovakia looked to 'the two great Western democracies, whose wishes we have followed much against our own judgement, to stand by us in our hour of trial'.[44] The meeting of the leaders of those two 'great democracies' revealed how embarrassing this request was.

There are times when the presence of a leading K C in the Cabinet is a useful thing, and this was one of them. Sir John Simon cross-examined Daladier in a manner reminiscent of Judge Jeffreys dealing with a peculiarly recalcitrant witness, with feline insinuation replacing brow-beating;[45] the whole thing was conducted in a tone of 'yes, we have heard all the moving oratory about small nations, honour and dishonour, but what are you really going to *do?*' The 'Bull of Vaucluse' was, to change the metaphor, tormented by a particularly skilful picador. In reply to Chamberlain's question as to what would happen if, as Daladier's response indicated, the Godesberg terms were rejected, the Frenchman replied: 'Each of us would have to do his duty'; pressed further as to what would happen if Hitler attacked Czechoslovakia, he stonewalled, saying that he would then 'have brought about a situation in which aggression would have been provoked by him'. This prompted Chamberlain to ask: 'What then?' But Daladier was not being drawn: 'Each of us would do what was incumbent upon him', was all he would say. It was clearly time to let the eminent lawyer loose on this witness.

Daladier fenced skilfully with Simon, emphasising his repugnance for the whole business. He had been, he said, prepared 'like a barbarian' to 'dismember a friendly country bound to France' to avoid war, but he could and would not assent to Godesberg. As well as relieving his feelings, the rhetoric helped avoid a straight answer to Simon's main question: did the French have a war-plan? If so, what was it? Chamberlain chipped in to ask an even more pertinent question: did the French have the capacity to carry out any war-plan – assuming that they had one? Seeing that Daladier's temper was rising under cross-examination, Chamberlain slipped a note to Hoare asking him to intervene, which helped lower the temperature. Daladier then asked Chamberlain about the British position, but the Prime Minister played a straight bat: the question of what to do with Hitler's proposals was one for the Czechs to answer; the question of what France should do if Hitler attacked Czechoslovakia was one for the French to answer. The meeting adjourned twenty minutes before midnight to allow Chamberlain to see the Cabinet; on the morrow General Gamelin, Chief of the French General Staff, would unveil the French war-plan.

Back in the Cabinet room for the third time that Sunday, Ministers were told of the course of the discussions. What he heard increased Cooper's suspicions. It was all very well to say that the French had not said, in so many words, that they were going to fight, but Chamberlain had not pressed them to do so. Making himself 'pretty offensive', Cooper said, in effect, that although Daladier had been evasive, he had been no match for Chamberlain on that score.[46] But the Prime Minister had another card to play even if it was the knave of spades.

Relying upon the relationship which he felt he had established with Hitler, Chamberlain now proposed to send Sir Horace Wilson to Germany with a personal letter for the Führer.[47] In this he would say that the French seemed likely to reject his latest proposals and make one last appeal to preserve peace. He would put to him a variant on a proposal which Hoare had put to the French: that a commission of three consisting of a British, German and Czech representative should consider how to put into effect the proposals accepted at Berchtesgaden in a manner which would not shock 'world opinion'. Chamberlain did not think there was a very good chance that Hitler, who had said that they could 'take or leave' Godesberg, would accept such a proposal, but it was worth trying, if only for the effect it would have on world opinion if war did break out.

Cooper suggested that Hitler be told that, 'if this appeal was rejected, the Czechs would fight and the French would come to their aid, and that we should come in on their side too'; this was refused, but Chamberlain said that he would let Wilson deliver an oral message to this effect to Hitler if he rejected the appeal. Cooper could 'hardly believe his ears'. It appeared to be a 'complete reversal' of the policy Chamberlain had advocated the day before, but, as Stanley remarked acidly, 'we were to tell the Germans that the French would fight although we had just heard that the French themselves refused to say as much'. With Chamberlain looking 'absolutely worn out', the Cabinet adjourned until noon.[48]

Given the late hour at which the Cabinet dispersed, knowledge of the divisions within it took some time to percolate to opponents of the Government's policy. That the Godesberg meeting had gone badly was a matter of common report; so too were stories that Chamberlain intended to yield to something akin to an ultimatum.[49] Amery had written an anguished letter to Halifax on 24 September saying that he did not think that the Commons 'would stand any more surrender to Hitler'.[50] General Spears, who was in close contact with the Czech legation (from which, according to one account, he was receiving a 'retainer'),[51] organised a letter of protest from Conservative MPs expressing 'strong feelings' that the Czechs ought not to be pressed any further.[52]

The opinions of a senior Privy Councillor and backbenchers like Spears, A. P. Herbert, Bob Boothby, Derrick Gunston, Anthony Crossley and Harold Macmillan mattered as far as they reflected a wider concern within the Conservative Party. Outside the Cabinet, Harry Crookshank, the Minister for Mines, who had been unhappy for some time about Chamberlain's equivocation on the subject of fighting alongside France, had decided, so he told Eden on 24 September, to resign.[53] Halifax's 'change of front' had, indeed, been timely; he had helped prevent a major split in the Cabinet and had done something that would help meet the sensibilities of the dissenters without.

Whilst Halifax was trying to maintain one version of 'national unity', Churchill was trying to create another version of the same. Although he had originally been snubbed by Labour and cut by Eden's acolytes, Churchill remained active in pursuit of an ally. The group he summoned to his flat in

Morpeth Mansions on 22 September revealed how small a band he could muster: Lords Cecil, Lloyd, Horne, Lytton and Wolmer were joined by only three MPs, Nicolson, the Liberal Archie Sinclair and Brendan Bracken; and even this small group of odds and sods preferred to wait for news from Godesberg before forming a 'focus' with Winston. Waving his whisky and soda, 'rather blurry, rather bemused in a way, but dominant and in fact reasonable,' Churchill remained sure that Chamberlain would bring allies to his side.[54]

Eden's position was more delicate. His passivity since resigning had led some of his admirers to fear that he was 'losing a great deal of ground'[55] and, although he did not share that view, the crisis offered an opportunity which he could not afford to neglect. But, unlike Churchill, he was not beyond the political pale, and he acted with caution: a judiciously critical speech in his constituency on 23 September, conversations with disgruntled Conservatives (no caballing with Labour) and well-timed interventions with Halifax – these were Eden's methods.[56] Like others, he looked forward to the creation of a 'real National Government'[57] (in which, naturally, he would play a leading part), but that happy event waited upon the vagaries of Hitler and the French.

News of Chamberlain's defeatist attitude after Godesberg stimulated his opponents. Whilst Wilson was on his way to Germany, Churchill was finding allies – if only in the form of the 'December Club' led by his old comrade Louis Spears. After hearing from Halifax and Chamberlain on 26 September that Wilson's mission was not one of surrender, Churchill went back to his flat where Spears' friends, along with Amery and his own followers, had gathered. There was a good deal of support for the idea of a 'coalition Government' and, after hearing Churchill's news, it was decided that if 'Chamberlain rats again we shall form a united block against him'. In the event of his not 'ratting', they would 'rally behind him'; this did not entail what it might be thought to imply: 'We shall press for a coalition Government and the immediate application of war measures.'[58]

Whether war came or not, the groupuscule intended to 'reverse 1931'; but the betting was now on war. As Amery had put it a few days earlier:

> I cannot help thinking that the French are bound now to take a firm stand, and if so we are in the end bound to follow suit. Otherwise I foresee a terrific row in the House and probably the break up of the Government.[59]

Already reliant on the French, who were hardly a popular cause in the Conservative Party, Churchill and company now decided 'we must get in touch with Russia'.[60] Boothby, who had recently spoken to Litvinov at Geneva, was certain that the 'Russians will give full support',[61] and there was a generally enthusiastic welcome for the idea of sending Churchill round to remind Halifax of Russia's importance. Only Amery seemed to recall that it was within the ranks of the Conservative Party that any new Government would have to find support, and he refused to sign any letter to Halifax concerning Russia, protesting that 'it would only put off too many of our people'.[62]

It is hardly surprising that it was only Amery who thought of this consideration; he was virtually the only real 'Party' man in the room: Churchill, Spears and Ned Grigg were all former Liberals; Archie Sinclair and Robert Bernays still were Liberals (of variegated forms); Lord Cecil had thought of becoming a Liberal, had resigned from Baldwin's Cabinet in 1927 and was most commonly associated with the League of Nations, which Lytton was also heavily involved in; Boothby, Richard Law and Macmillan belonged to the liberal wing of the Conservative Party and the latter had actually resigned the Whip over the Abyssinian crisis; as for Lords Horne and Lloyd, the former had been a close associate of Lloyd George and the latter was such a stern, unbending Tory that he regarded hardly anyone left of himself and Sir Henry Page-Croft as true Conservatives; Bracken and Lindemann were Churchill acolytes: it was no wonder that poor Amery thought it a 'queer collection'. It was certainly an alternative version of 'national unity', but an exceedingly odd one which was unlikely to appeal to solid members of the Conservative Party; not even Amery wanted to be associated too closely with it. But what Amery noted about Russia might also prove to be true of the group itself: 'once war is declared they will only too readily welcome help from the Devil himself'.[63]

But anyone who, taking pity on an exhausted-looking Prime Minister, imagined that he was on his way out, would have been very far from the truth. He might, on his own testimony, look 'pompous, insufferably slow in "diction" and unspeakably repellant in "person" ',[64] but he was as tough as the bird which his corvine features brought to mind. Halifax's change of front in Cabinet on the 25th had come as a great blow, but he moved with the punch. The meeting with the French Ministers and Gamelin on the morning of the 26th went well.[65] Before it began Chamberlain told them that Britain would stand by France, an assurance which, when repeated to the Cabinet, nipped in the bud Stanley's intention of resigning and brought Cooper to withdraw his offer to go; Cooper did say, however, that he was willing to step down if, after talks with the Opposition, Chamberlain needed his post in order to help form a new coalition. Nothing, however, was further from the Prime Minister's intentions.[66]

The new 'tough' line which was foreshadowed by these developments, and explained to Labour and to Churchill that afternoon, was publicly proclaimed in a communiqué issued later by the Foreign Office; Halifax was surprised when he learned that the Prime Minister was not pleased.[67] His bewilderment reveals that the two men were still not 'together'.

Historians are apt to write in generalisations, indeed seem happy to talk about 'public opinion' and the 'Cabinet's view', but Jeeves had more of the root of the matter in him when he explained to his young master that one must 'study the psychology of the individual'. Chamberlain, like most people, fancied himself a good judge of character. Hitler was not a man whom he could like, but he was one who 'had certain standards'; his mind was 'narrow' and 'violently pre-judiced', but 'he would not deliberately deceive a man whom he trusted and with whom he had been in negotiation'. Chamberlain was sure that he had won Hitler's 'respect', and it had been for that reason that, upon reflection, he had been willing to accept the Godesberg terms as he was sure that, in Hitler's mind, there was no difference between them and Berchtesgaden. Hitler had said that after the Sudetenland he 'had no more territorial ambitions in Europe' and that, if the crisis could be solved peacefully, 'it might be a turning-point in Anglo-German relations'. This was what Chamberlain wanted to hear. It was his own objective and it would be, in his opinion, 'a great tragedy if we lost this opportunity of reaching an understanding with Germany on all points of difference between the two countries'. He was determined to use the 'influence' which he now had with Hitler 'to put an end to the horrible nightmare of the present armament race. That seemed to him the big thing in the present issue.'[68]

Chamberlain's carefully crafted letter was designed to play to this point, letting the Führer know that he could have what had been agreed to at Berchtesgaden provided he negotiated; if he did not, then he would be choosing war.[69] The oral message which Wilson was to deliver if Hitler rejected this plea underlined the danger of war.[70] But it was necessary to bear in mind that they were 'dealing with an individual of a peculiar temperament',[71] and the issuing of a communiqué by the Foreign Office before the speech which Hitler was to deliver that evening might well make him decide to dig in his heels.

Chamberlain need not have worried. Wilson had a 'very violent hour' with Hitler and found him in a greatly excited state, 'determined to make a great passionate speech tonight'. Although he was willing, as Chamberlain had asked, to meet a Czech representative, it was only on condition that the Czechs accepted the Godesberg terms. Wilson had decided against delivering the verbal warning.[72]

Although Hitler's speech that evening was a violent diatribe against the Czechs with some vitriolic abuse of Beneš, it did make flattering references to Chamberlain's efforts to preserve peace. It was, therefore, 'more in sorrow than in anger' that Wilson delivered Chamberlain's warning on the morning of 27 September, whilst assuring Hitler that, whether he trusted the Czechs or not, Britain and France would ensure that they carried out their promises.[73]

Hitler replied that he did not intend to attack France and that, if France and Britain attacked Germany, it would be the fault of the Czechs.[74] It seemed as though only the Czechs could now save peace, but at the cost of recasting the map of Central Europe and accepting humiliation; the exercise in cartography had been agreed to, but the extra demands seemed too much to swallow.

Light After Darkness?

It is easier to criticise Chamberlain's policy as one of weakness and folly compounded than to examine it in detail; but it is only through this last method that it can be understood. Even as events seemed to be 'driving us to the edge of the abyss with a horrifying certainty and rapidity',[1] Chamberlain's position was recognisably a development of that which he had adopted back in March. Then, as now, his objective was to remove an obstacle in the way of good Anglo-German relations and to put an end to the arms race. He was 'a man of peace to the depths of my soul' and regarded the prospect of war as a 'nightmare'.[2] Events had carried him beyond his original intentions and the process of negotiating had led to a position that would have been unimaginable in March, but the Czechs and the French had been led by the same forces down the same road; and Chamberlain had not lost sight of what was, for him, the 'great issue' – an Anglo-German entente.

Nor was it necessarily the case that war would be the catharsis that Churchill and others seemed to imagine. That it might 'end civilisation'[3] was a widespread assumption, but there was an even stronger probability that it would not help the Czechs. For all Daladier's talk about drawing the German army away from Czechoslovakia, there was, in fact, no plan that would have achieved this; it was accepted in both Britain and France that the best that could be hoped for was a reconstruction of Czechoslovakia after Germany had been defeated. The participation of Russia in a war was, despite the fond hopes of Churchill and Boothby, doubtful, but it was beyond doubt that she would want a voice in any cartographic exercises after that war; this was a point ignored by Churchill in 1938 and one which he continued, with decreasing success, to try to ignore between 1940 and 1944: for him the war was everything, but others took a more long-sighted view. With Russia an uncertain quantity and Poland and Hungary being bought off with promises of bits of Czechoslovakia,[4] the prospects of a successful Anglo-French intervention in Central Europe were not bright.

The gloomy conclusions prompted by diplomacy and geography were re-inforced by military considerations. Unlike Churchill, Chamberlain had knowl-edge both of what passed for the French war-plan and of the latest report of the British Chiefs of Staff.[5] After a 'squib offensive (to bring us in)', the French plan was to wait behind the Maginot Line until the British had expanded their army and the economic blockade began to bite; this was not a strategy which promised speedy relief to the Czechs (as the Poles were to discover a year later). There were plans to march into Libya – but these presupposed that Italy would enter the war and, as the British Chiefs of Staff report emphasised, such a development would be exceedingly unfavourable to the Allies. The Chiefs were adamant that there was nothing that either Power could do to 'prevent Germany from overrunning Bohemia and inflicting a decisive defeat on Czechoslovakia'. Britain was still a year away from the time when her rearmament programme would be substantially complete; the omens for war were not good.

Historians can, of course, point out that the Chiefs of Staff ignored the 'fundamental grand-strategical questions' of the effect on the balance of power of the cession of the Sudetenland and of whether it would have been better to fight Germany then rather than later;[6] they can also point to German fears that a war would have been a close-run thing.[7] However, apart from pointing up the hardly remarkable fact that all generals feel anxiety at actually using their armies, the 'grand-strategical argument' assumes war as inevitable and an Allied victory as highly probable; Chamberlain shared neither assumption for the reasons outlined above. It also assumes that Chamberlain should have ignored his Chiefs of Staff in the same way that Hitler ignored his; had he done so and had Britain lost the ensuing war, no doubt historians of a similar cast of mind would have blamed the Prime Minister for disregarding professional advice.

'Wobbling' under the strain, Chamberlain was inclined to listen to Wilson's counsel of 'capitulation' and advise the Czechs to close with the Godesberg terms to avoid invasion.[8] But Halifax, who had already sent off telegrams to Prague which indicated that Britain could not advise acceptance of those terms,[9] had come up with a modified version of the Anglo-French plan agreed after Berchtesgaden. Chamberlain decided to let the Cabinet choose which course to take.

His mood was sombre. That afternoon, with no reply from Hitler to Wilson's communication, Chamberlain decided to mobilise the Fleet. In his broadcast that evening he sounded close to despair. It was 'horrible, fantastic, incredible' that 'we should be digging ditches and trying on gas masks here because of a quarrel in a far-away country between people of whom we know nothing'.[10]

Chamberlain has been much criticised for this phrase and, indeed, the whole tone of the speech was attacked at Cabinet that night by Duff Cooper. But it was the authentic voice of its author and expressed the feelings of many ordinary people, such as the shopkeeper who said: 'Me, fight for Czechoslovakia? Why should I? I should lose my business to begin with.'[11]

The same tone was apparent when the Prime Minister addressed his colleagues at 9.30 p.m. Influenced by Henderson's frantic telegrams warning that unless the Czechs were advised to accept, Britain would be abandoning them to the 'fate of Abyssinia', and by reports of bad Czech morale and lack of support from the Dominions, Chamberlain was unwilling to provoke a war over the method of transferring Czech territory when the principle had already been conceded. Ministers had before them the draft of a telegram which advised the Czechs to accept Hitler's terms.[12]

This return to the situation which had been rejected after Godesberg was challenged by Cooper before the 'yes men' of the Cabinet had a chance to intervene.[13] He countered Chamberlain's dolorous recital by mentioning every piece of cheerful news he could think of: Roosevelt had sent a telegram, so had Getulio Vargas (the President of Brazil); pessimism from Frank Mason-MacFarlane, the Military Attaché in Berlin, was only to be expected – and other reports were more favourable; as for the Dominions, well, they did not really matter; what was important was that to advise the Czechs as Chamberlain wanted would be 'one of the basest betrayals in history'. It might mean 'the end of the Government'; it would certainly mean the end of Cooper's connection with it. Pointed questions from Stanley underlined the fact that the Cabinet was really being asked to go back to the decision which they had refused on 24 September.

It was the man who had prevented Chamberlain getting his way then who did so again – and for the same reason. Halifax was well aware of feeling in the Party and had already sent advice to Prague, which Chamberlain now wanted to revoke; he would have, he said, 'great difficulty' in accepting the draft telegram. But the Foreign Secretary was able to provide Chamberlain with a golden bridge across which to conduct an orderly retreat. They had, Halifax said, agreed to concert any further action with the French and this they should now do. Sensing the mood of his colleagues, Chamberlain, in the face of 'powerful and perhaps convincing reasons against the adoption of his suggestion', gave way gracefully. Halifax's compromise plan, which would have given Hitler some areas of the Sudetenland by 1 October and others after consultation and agreement by 31 October, stood as the last offer.[14]

Whilst the Cabinet was sitting, Chamberlain received Hitler's reply to Wilson's communication. Once he had had time to read it the hopes which he had expressed in his broadcast, that there was still a chance of a 'peaceful solution', revived.[15] The Führer said that he would not move his troops beyond those areas (marked red on his map) which corresponded with what the Czechs had been willing to concede after Berchtesgaden; the other regions he claimed (coloured green) could be the subject of a plebiscite; he also offered to join in an international guarantee of Czechoslovakia. It was the first sign of any retreat by Hitler from his position at Godesberg and Chamberlain was willing to make a 'last desperate snatch at the last tuft of grass on the very verge of the precipice'.[16]

On the following morning Chamberlain despatched a last appeal: 'I feel certain you can get all essentials without war and without delay.'[17] He had already sought, the previous afternoon, to enlist Mussolini's support for his policy; this was now followed up with a request for Il Duce to add his voice to this final plea.[18]

Whilst Chamberlain waited to see if his Italian policy would pay any dividend, the prospects if it did not appeared dire. Phipps, who had reported a stiffening in the French attitude in the aftermath of Godesberg,[19] now repeated what he had said on the 24th: France was a divided nation and the 'only whole party that favours war now are the Communists'.[20] From Henderson came an anguished message that it was 'tragic' that

> the British public cannot understand that there is no possibility of peace in Central Europe until the Czechs (and the Slovaks) are reduced to a Czech State, governing Czechs but not *Sudetendeutsche*, Poles, Hungarians, etc. That is the basic fact. Hard though it may be on the Czechs, it is harder for all Europe to suffer permanently for the mistake of Versailles.[21]

He pleaded that, with the issue still hanging in the balance, nothing should be said in the Commons that afternoon which might upset German sensibilities.[22]

When the Commons assembled that afternoon to hear Chamberlain's statement, 'the general feeling was . . . that war was inevitable within the next few days'.[23] Amery was 'by no means an optimist about the outcome' of a war for which Britain was 'unprepared', but hoped that 'the same national character that has got us into this mess, will see us through to the end'.[24] Some of the wilder 'young men', including Macmillan, had been all for 'an immediate pogrom to get rid of Neville and make Winston Prime Minister before the House met'; quite how they proposed to achieve this was unclear, but Amery 'poured cold water' on their fantasies.[25]

When Chamberlain arrived, it was to cheers from 'all parts of the House';[26] his 'chronological statement of events' was listened to in 'dead silence', and as he approached recent events the tension rose.[27] When he had been speaking for nearly an hour, he had come almost up to date. Mussolini's appeal had, he reported, resulted in Hitler agreeing to postpone mobilisation for twenty-four hours. Then there was a disturbance along the front bench as two pieces of paper, brought in by Cadogan,[28] were passed along. They reached Simon, who interrupted Chamberlain as he was approaching his peroration by tugging at his coat. Channon, who was sitting nearby, heard Chamberlain ask: 'Shall I tell them?' and Simon whisper, 'Yes.'[29] The Prime Minister announced that Hitler had agreed to meet himself, Mussolini and Daladier at Munich on the morrow. The Government's supporters rose and cheered frantically and they were joined, after Attlee's approval, by the Opposition, who looked 'a little foolish'.[30] It was, indeed, a 'piece of drama that no work of fiction ever surpassed'.[31] Churchill could only mutter: 'You were very lucky.'[32]

Churchill's lack of grace was as natural as Chamberlain's ungracious response to it. Just as the 'anti-Italians', like Eden, looked 'foolish' and 'discomforted',[33] so too did those like Churchill who had prophesied war. For Chamberlain it was not only a tremendous (but unplanned) coup de theâtre, it was a vindication of his policy towards Mussolini and of his patient hammering away at Hitler; of course it might yet all fail, but in his heart Chamberlain did not believe that it would, not now, not after such efforts and so many hopes.[34] But it had come not as 'luck' but as the result of hard work.

'Discomforted' was just the word to describe the attitude of Chamberlain's opponents. Amery, ever the realist, was relieved at the removal of the prospect of imminent war (as were so many others), but he realised that whatever happened at Munich, the Czechs would pay the price; was it, he wondered, 'best for us ... to accept German hegemony and preoccupation with Central Europe'.[35] This mixture of 'physical relief' and moral anxiety was a common reaction.[36] Churchill was convinced that Chamberlain intended to 'rat' again and wanted his new-found allies to join him in sending a telegram to the Prime Minister, 'saying that if he imposed further onerous terms on the Czechs, we shall fight him in the House'; but Eden had too much sense to appear to be conducting a vendetta, and Attlee did not think that the Labour Party would like to sign any such document.[37] But Churchill's fear was shared not only by men like Harvey,[38] but also by the Czechs themselves, who begged that Chamberlain should not let Hitler impose worse conditions upon them.[39]

The qualified acceptance which the Czechs gave to Halifax's compromise plan worried its author, and he warned them that they ought to do nothing to make Chamberlain's task more difficult and that they should give him 'a wide discretion'.[40] In the event, Chamberlain took that discretion and, comparing what was agreed at Munich with the Godesberg ultimatum, did not do too badly

– although his plea that the Czechs should be allowed to participate in the conference was rejected.[41]

At Heston on the morning of 29 September Chamberlain said that he hoped, 'like Hotspur in *Henry IV part I*', to 'pluck from this nettle danger, this flower, safety'. He was uneasily aware that all that the Führer had agreed to was to postpone mobilisation for a day and thought, upon his arrival at Munich, that 'the storm signals were out'; it was with 'instant relief' that he greeted the

FOUR'S COMPANY
All together: 'Well, before we go on, here's to Self-sacrifice!'
The Munich Agreement, 12 October, 1938.

'moderate and reasonable attitude' which Hitler adopted when the conference began half an hour after noon.[42]

It was one of the most disorganised conferences in diplomatic history, a 'hugger-mugger affair'[43] with no trace of Germanic efficiency, and for most of the last five hours 'chaos ruled'.[44] Proceedings began at 12.30 p.m. and did not finish until 2 a.m. on 30 September, by the end of which period Chamberlain was, although very tired, greatly relieved. In stark contrast to Godesberg, Hitler made concessions. The German proposals (put forward by Mussolini) for 'evacuation and occupation' surprised Chamberlain by 'their moderation' and by the 'degree of latitude which they left to the International Commission'. As Cadogan was to comment when he saw the final agreement: '*far* better than I expected'.[45]

The Munich Agreement was, on paper, a considerable improvement on the Godesberg terms (as even Duff Cooper admitted) and bore a marked resemblance to the Anglo-French plan formulated after Berchtesgaden.[46] Instead of a German occupation of all the 'red' (German majority) areas on Hitler's map by 1 October, there would be a phased occupation of four of those areas by 10 October; there would be an International Commission to lay down conditions governing the occupation and evacuation and to supervise plebiscites. Much would, of course, depend upon the spirit in which Germany carried out her obligations but, given Hitler's surprising climb-down, there seemed reasons for confidence that he was not hell-bent on war.

In the face of Hitler's retreat, it would have been a negation of all Chamberlain's beliefs for him to have resorted to the war which so many of his later critics would have welcomed at this point. Now the opportunity had finally come to do something to improve Anglo-German relations. At about 1 a.m., whilst they were waiting for the draftsmen to complete the final agreed text, Chamberlain asked Hitler whether 'he would care to see me for another talk'.[47] A meeting was duly arranged.

William Strang, the assistant Under-Secretary at the Foreign Office who was accompanying the Prime Minister, found any attempt to catch up on his sleep disrupted by a message from his master asking him to 'draft a short statement on the future of Anglo-German relations'. This he proceeded to do in the intervals of dressing and breakfasting. Chamberlain inserted into it a reference to the Anglo-German Naval Agreement of 1935 which, as he told Strang who wondered if this was something to be proud of, was 'the type of agreement which we should now try to reach with Germany'; indeed, at the meeting the Prime Minister raised the question of limitation of bombing aircraft. Strang asked whether Daladier should be told, but Chamberlain had no intention of involving the French.[48]

Chamberlain showed the document to his Parliamentary Private Secretary, Alec Dunglass (later Lord Home), at breakfast. Its three short paragraphs stated that both Prime Minister and Führer recognised that 'the question of Anglo-German relations is of the first importance for the two countries and for Europe' and went on, after referring to the Naval Agreement as 'symbolic of the desire of our two peoples never to go to war with one another again', to express a joint resolve to consult over the removal of other 'possible sources of difference'.[49] Describing this passage in his memoirs, Lord Home has Chamberlain use one of the arguments later used by those who defended his actions: 'If Hitler signed it and kept the bargain, well and good . . . if he broke it, he would demonstrate to all the world that he was totally cynical and untrustworthy,' which would have its value in 'mobilising public opinion against him, especially in America'.[50]

At the Führer's private flat the two men discussed disarmament and the affairs of South-East Europe (where Chamberlain denied any intention of trying to encircle Germany), and then Chamberlain got on to the reason he had gone there. He produced the declaration and asked if Hitler would sign it. As his interpreter translated it, 'Hitler frequently ejaculated Ja! Ja! and at the end he said Yes I will certainly sign it. When shall we do it?' Chamberlain said ' "Now", and we went at once to the writing table and put our signatures to the two copies which I had brought with me.' Thus was the famous 'piece of paper' signed.[51]

Upon arrival back at Heston Chamberlain flourished the paper and read its contents to an elated audience. The streets on the way to Buckingham Palace were lined with 'people of every class, shouting themselves hoarse'. Downing Street was almost impassable. Inside No. 10 someone with a sense of history suggested that Chamberlain should repeat from the balcony the words Disraeli had used sixty years previously when he too had returned from Germany with 'Peace with Honour'. Dunglass heard the Prime Minister coldly disdain such a piece of theatricality. Yet, a few minutes later, Chamberlain stood on the balcony and, to the wildly cheering multitude below said: 'My good friends, this is the second time in our history that there has come from Germany to Downing Street peace with honour. I believe it is peace for our time.'[52] Seldom have two sentences so blasted a reputation.

It seems likely that the words were hardly out of his mouth before Chamberlain regretted them. His first reaction to the suggestion: 'I don't do that sort of thing',[53] was much more in keeping with his character, and within the week he was explaining the remarks away (to a somewhat surprised House)[54] as the product of 'a moment of some emotion, after a long and exhausting day'.[55] That he regarded Munich as providing an opening for better Anglo-German relations was the most that he believed. As he told his sister Hilda, when he refused to bask in the praise lavished upon him: 'It seems to assume so much. We have avoided the greatest catastrophe . . . [but cannot] put all thoughts of war out of our minds and settle down to make the world a better place.'[56] For a while Chamberlain was the most popular man in the world, and gifts poured into Downing Street, matched in profusion (if not value) by tens of thousands of letters of gratitude; in Bucharest a picture was painted of him, holding 'this flower safety', crushing 'this nettle danger' underfoot.[57] The Czechs had neither cause nor spirit for joining in the universal rejoicing. Poland and Hungary were swift in demanding their share of the spoils and, despite British appeals to the Poles to desist, the Czechs yielded at once;[58] as Newton commented: 'Czech spirit seems indeed somewhat broken.'[59] This was not surprising; having been 'the spoilt child of the Allies and of Geneva',[60] Czechoslovakia now felt herself abandoned. A 'shattered' Jan Masaryk summed it up: 'Your people have finished us – let me down. You advised us to mobilise; then you told us to give up our defences – and now we cannot defend ourselves against any brigand.'[61]

Those taking the view that everything depended upon how the Germans carried out their part of the agreement found ample cause for pessimism. Roger Makins, one of the most promising young men in the Foreign Office, served on the International Commission set up by the Munich Agreement and gave a chastening account of its proceedings to Rab Butler:

> We started off with an attempt to draw a frontier in committee with a good deal of shouting and banging of the table, but negotiation, even in such spiritual atmosphere, is not the Nazis' strong suit, and the Ambassadors were soon presented with a twelve-hour ultimatum, to which they had no choice but to agree. After the Germans had obtained all (and more) to which in the most generous assumption they were entitled, plebiscites became both unnecessary and dangerous, and would not have been of much help to the Czechs.[62]

This had not stopped the Germans from suggesting that there might be plebiscites in areas where they might benefit. But this had produced an outraged protest from Henderson, who said that Hitler had promised that any rectifications of the frontier after occupation would be made in Czecho-slovakia's favour:

> If the Chancellor now went back on all these assurances [the] Prime Minister's confidence in his good faith would be completely destroyed, there would be no possibility of any talk of an Anglo-German understanding and I personally would do my utmost to be relieved of a mission which had become utterly distasteful to me.[63]

There were no plebiscites, but, in Makins' graphic phrase: 'The Commission . . . was able to do little more than watch the constriction of the rabbit by the boa . . . Czechoslovakia will in future be little more than a German colony'; but this, he concluded, 'was implicit in the Munich Agreement'.[64] It was, perhaps, fortunate that Chamberlain had to face his parliamentary critics before the Commission finished its labours in late November.

An exhausted Chamberlain, who had retired to Chequers after reporting to the Cabinet, regarded the prospect of having to take part in four days of debate with loathing; but he was without neither weapons nor arguments – and his opponents were in a dilemma.

'Morbid Anatomy'

Macaulay advised those who wished 'to be well-acquainted with the morbid anatomy of governments' to study the history of Spain in the seventeenth century;[1] some modern historians would advise those who wish 'to know how great states may be made feeble and wretched' to study the history of modern Britain.[2] The impression that it was a mixture of naiveté, aristocracy and the public-school spirit which led to the 'collapse of British power' was further strengthened by the defence offered by Chamberlain's apologists for his policy. One of the last to deploy the 'classic Chamberlain defence' was Rab Butler in his memoirs. The lines along which he proceeded were familiar ones: Munich was a regrettable necessity, but it did gain an extra year in which to rearm and it did, by proving beyond peradventure what a nasty piece of work Hitler was, ensure that the Empire entered the war united. This defence has been subject to a good deal of criticism, and recent commentators have shown how inconsistent Butler's arguments were with the attitude he held at the time.[3] This is not surprising, for the apologia was a political artefact constructed after the event and it obscures the assumptions which underlay Chamberlain's foreign policy.

The arguments deployed by Henderson, that Germany was attempting to redress the grievances of Versailles, and that there could be no peace until the cartographic exercise was complete, were accepted by the architects of British foreign policy.[4] Cadogan thought it was 'no use Halifax wringing his hands and making pretty speeches deploring the use of force' when 'every German will tell you that from 1918 to 1932 the rule of force was in operation against them'.[5] There was even a certain grim satisfaction amongst those who prided themselves upon their 'realism' at having to retreat from the untenable position adopted at Versailles of 'policing Europe'. It was simply not possible for Britain to 'protect our own interests all over the world and at the same time claim a preponderant voice in the ordering of affairs in Continental Europe'. The best thing for Britain to do now, Cadogan argued, was to 'cut our losses in Central Europe'.[6]

Amery, who was no friend of the Munich Agreement, was perceptive enough to see that its 'real justification' lay in the liquidation of an untenable French position in Eastern Europe.[7] As Halifax told Phipps in November, one of the 'chief difficulties of the past has been the unreal position which France was occupying in Central and Eastern Europe'.[8] This position was the result of the circumstances of 1919, and those who wanted to uphold it, even at the cost of war, were simply ignoring the march of history for, in Butler's words: 'This is a period in which the peace settlement is being revised.'[9] The Government's objective was to ensure that this was done by peaceful means.

This 'insular' school of Conservative thought on foreign policy saw a need to limit British commitments and make 'our foreign policy and our strength more nearly coincide'.[10] This meant accepting 'German predominance in Central Europe', but as Halifax had 'always felt' that this was 'inevitable' once Germany had 'recovered her normal strength', and as Cadogan did not see that it damaged essential British interests,[11] this was something to be accepted in the spirit of 'what can't be cured must be endured'.[12] There were, of course, those who argued that Munich had opened a 'free way' for 'all the German designs of *Mittel Europa* nursed by the Kaiser'. But when Maisky put just those arguments to Halifax in October, he was met with the reply that his doctrine meant having a 'war with Germany every fifteen or twenty years to prevent worse things happening'. That was not something which the 'insular' school could accept.[13] Moreover if, as Butler believed, German policy was: 'Infiltrate East. Bluster West', then why should Britain risk war just to save Russia.[14]

This was not defeatism. Rearmament was, everyone agreed, essential, but although a 'vitally necessary first step', it was 'not a policy'.[15] The 'greatest lesson' of the crisis was, in Halifax's view, the 'unwisdom of having a foreign policy with insufficient armed strength'. Defence policy had to relate to foreign policy, and Chamberlain had for some years tried to ensure that it did so. German expansion in Eastern Europe was a 'normal and natural thing', but Western Europe was a different matter. Whatever 'painful readjustments' had to be made in the east to accommodate the rise of German power, it was vital that Britain and France 'uphold *their* predominance' there by 'the maintenance of such armed strength as would render any attack upon them hazardous'; similarly, their respective positions in the Mediterranean and the Near East had to be 'firmly maintain[ed]'.[16]

This, then, was the policy which evolved from the underlying attitudes of Chamberlain, Halifax and Butler to foreign policy, modified as they were by the experience of Munich. But the crisis had other effects. It intensified that 'return to Party politics' which Chamberlain's accession to the premiership had brought;[17] it invested a great deal of the Prime Minister's prestige in the success of his foreign policy; and it created a climate in which German intentions were now eagerly scrutinised – by Chamberlain's supporters looking for reasons for optimism, and by his opponents for signs to justify their pessimism.

The warmth of the public reception which he received contrasted painfully for Chamberlain with the attitude of the House: 'the whole world seemed to be full of my praises' whilst the Commons seemed full of critics who poured out a 'ceaseless stream of vituperation'.[18] When the Commons debate on the Munich Agreement opened on 3 October, the first speech came from the latest addition to the ranks of the public critics, for, in Butler's words: 'Duff's veins have stood out and he has been very rude and now he has gone.'[19] Unable to stomach what the Prime Minister had done, although unable to suggest any other path he could have taken, the former First Lord's speech was a brilliant restatement of the 'balance of power', 'cosmopolitan' school of thought.[20]

Forcefully though Cooper's arguments were expressed, they seemed, to those who thought like Chamberlain, redolent of one 'reared in Edwardian politics'; they failed to take into account 'the facts of life'.[21] Of more significance was the fact that his had been the only resignation. Oliver Stanley had talked about resigning, but had not done so, and Harry Crookshank had resigned, only to rescind his letter under pressure from Chamberlain and the Whips.[22] But the crisis, and the debate which followed, revealed an uneasiness which could only be assuaged by the positive developments in Anglo-German relations which Chamberlain's agreement with Hitler promised.

The Prime Minister's immediate political problems were as nothing compared to those of his opponents. Their difficulty can be seen from Amery's dilemma when, due to address an audience in his Birmingham constituency on the evening of 30 September, he was told firmly by his wife that the city was 'delirious with enthusiasm and gratitude to Neville, and that it was quite hopeless to address a critical speech to my Clifton Road audience'.[23] Criticism in the House was one thing, but those who wished to attack the man who had saved peace in *foro publico* had to gather themselves quietly, in conventicles, lest they be discovered and roasted slowly before their constituency committees.

Naturally enough, covert criticism, made in the Club or the private residence, was not what the great dissentient who dwelt in Morpeth Mansions wanted. Incandescent with rage on 'Munich eve', he declared (at a meeting of 'The Other Club') that, 'at the next general election he would speak on every socialist platform in the country against the Government'.[24] This act of self-sacrifice, however, did not only not commend him to fellow Conservatives, but was, alas, declined by Mr Attlee. When he tried to gather support for a 'vehement letter of protest' against 'the betrayal' of the Czechs, Attlee and Eden politely declined to be drawn, as did Amery; no letter was sent.[25]

The dissidents were now, potentially, in deep trouble if Chamberlain chose to 'cash in' on his success by holding a general election. It was this prospect which prevented Churchill from being, as it were, returned to store; but those who dwelt in the cave of Adullam were fewer in number and more sullen than ever.

Churchill, casting around for any odd combination which offered safety, sent out Macmillan as an envoy to Dalton and Labour.[26] The parallel that came most readily to men's minds was the 1918 election, when Lloyd George's friends had been given 'the coupon' as a sign of grace; fearing to be served with the same coin, Churchill sought to find a common platform based on 'collective security' and 'national unity and strength'. Macmillan's naive protest: 'That is not our jargon', was met with the cry of the buccaneer at bay: 'It is a jargon we may all have to learn.'[27]

Not everyone, however, was in Churchill's desperate straits. When Amery attended a meeting of Churchill's 'queer mixed group' on 3 October, there was a discussion on what they should do if Chamberlain called an election and 'ostracised those of us who did not support' him in the debate; there were few takers for Churchill's suggestion of 'forming a definite group' to oppose Chamberlain.[28] Indeed, the dissentients had a problem even deciding what to do at the end of the debate on Munich. Churchill pugnaciously wished to vote against the Government, scorning Amery's cautious advice that they should abstain: 'Which indicated disapproval of the particular policy but not a general hostility to the Government';[29] nevertheless, when the moment of truth came, the great rebel meekly abstained. Perhaps he was convinced by Amery's argument that, even if it was a 'weak line', it was 'one that can be defended in one's constituency'.[30]

This fear of local Conservative associations was not unfounded. Although Chamberlain did not call an election, local associations did call their members to account. Amery feared that he would have trouble and was disturbed that Jim Thomas and Anthony Crossley, both 'Edenites', were being called to account for their actions.[31] Although Eden himself was untroubled, his acolytes came under great pressure. Cranborne, whose South Dorset seat had been held by a Cecil since time immemorial, wrote to his uncle, Lord Cecil, on 16 October:

> I am in great trouble with my local Blimps, but have extracted from them, after a very long wrangle, a free hand to say what I like about the Government's foreign policy. They think, all the same, that I am (a) a socialist, (b) a war-monger and (c) a poison-pen about the P.M.[32]

Richard Law, who made one of the best and bitterest speeches during the Munich debate, wrote to tell Emrys Evan to 'give your boneheads hell'[33] and was inclined to blame everything on the women:

> If women didn't have the vote there wouldn't be any Women's Conservative Associations. They're the villains of the piece. How foolish our fathers were to suppose that women would ennoble and sanctify politics. The brutes, untouched as they are by any but the most crudely material considerations, they have brought nothing but degradation and dishonour to politics. A phenomenon like Neville Chamberlain would have been inconceivable before 1918.[34]

Harold Nicolson, who was inclined to agree with this misogynous outburst, noted that 'historians of our decline will say that we were done the moment we gave women the vote'.[35] Duff Cooper, by contrast, found that most women opposed Chamberlain;[36] perhaps they knew different women.

All this misogyny was slightly unfair on two maiden ladies in Hampshire, who were adjured by their brother to leave their MP, Viscount Wolmer, alone; for, as Chamberlain wrote to his sisters, he belonged to those who 'hadn't voted against us and were troubled in their minds' but who, if left alone, 'would come home and bring their tails behind them'.[37] Nevertheless, poor Wolmer had his problems, and when he voted with the Government on Churchill's attempt to get a Ministry of Supply, Chamberlain guessed 'he would not have done so at all if he had not had a shaking up from his Committee'.[38] Nor did the one rebel who resigned from the Cabinet escape censure; Duff Cooper was, in effect, put on probation by his executive committee in what was the safest Conservative seat in the country.[39]

The finale of the debate on Munich exposed the deep divisions within the ranks of the dissidents. Eden and Amery were so impressed by Chamberlain's final speech that they decided that they could, in all conscience, vote for him, but decided to abstain out of deference to those who had followed them thus far![40] It is doubtful whether this show of vacillation 'rattled' the Cabinet as much as one authority, following Nicolson's somewhat biased account, has claimed.[41]

Chamberlain had, however, given a pledge that there would be no immediate election. His opponents later claimed that this abstinence was more or less enforced as the result of a powerful speech from Sidney Herbert, a respected backbencher who was an old friend of Cooper's (although on less cordial terms with at least one member of the Eden conventicle).[42] But this canard is incapable of disproof as there is no evidence that Chamberlain was planning to hold an election. The prospect of a general election had been in his mind earlier in the year, and before Whitsun he had asked Conservative Central Office to produce details of a 'propaganda' campaign which could be put across to the electorate 'starting after the summer recess, and continuing until the general election'.[43]

At the same time, however, it was necessary to take steps to ensure that Britain and France maintained their predominance in Western Europe, the Mediterranean and the Near East. The rearmament programme was thus stepped up, with particular emphasis being placed upon the production of heavy bombers. Anglo-French talks were held in late November, in which the French were chivvied about their air strength and, in turn, pressed the British to increase the size of their army. But, as this ran counter to Chamberlain's 'limited liability' strategy and British foreign policy did not envisage a large-scale commitment to a European land war, Chamberlain declined to be drawn in that direction.[44]

The economic overtures which Chamberlain had made to Hitler at Munich were also followed up in the form of conversations about reductions in tariffs and the possibility of freer trade in the Balkans.[45] However, events in the two months after Munich were barren of fruitful results. The atrocious persecution of the Jews on the infamous *Kristallnacht* in early November meant that 'our policy of appeasement must for the time being be put on the shelf'.[46] As Halifax told the Foreign Policy Committee on 14 November: 'No useful purpose would be served by a resumption at the present time of the contemplated Anglo-German conversations.'[47]

There were those, like Butler, who remained optimistic, but the failure of Munich to produce positive results created problems for the Government even as it created opportunities for its opponents.

Where Chamberlain had considered the idea of an election as a way of solving his political problems, only to dismiss it as inopportune, Halifax's thoughts after Munich ran along different lines: it was entirely characteristic that Chamberlain should have thought of fighting his way out of trouble whilst his Foreign Secretary should have sought to broaden the appeal of the Government by inviting Eden to return to the fold. Eden's careful attitude during the Munich debate was a sign which Halifax did not ignore, and, after a conversation with him on 11 October, he had written to Chamberlain urging him that 'this is the psychological moment' for endeavouring to get 'national unity', adding that 'if it is not taken, it may be a long time before another recurs'.[48] Hoare added his voice to those urging that Eden should be brought into the Government.[49]

Chamberlain found the advice uncongenial. He had suffered enough opposition from within the Cabinet over Munich, and what he wanted was 'more support for my policy', not reinforcements for the weaker brethren. Moreover, he suspected that Eden's 'agreement' with his policy stopped short at the

LA BELLE FRANCE!
'Why, one hardly needs an umbrella this time, Neville.'
Chamberlain and Halifax and a sunny outlook for Anglo-French relations,
23 November 1938.

rearmament strand; the former Foreign Secretary did not agree with talking to dictators and would be no use in implementing the 'conciliation part'.[50] Cheers for Eden from Labour and the Sinclairites during a debate on the Ministry of Supply in early November made it 'plain beyond a peradventure' that 'the difference between him and me is fundamental'.[51] Butler forecast that there would be a 'broadening of the Government sometime before the election next year', but confessed that he did not know 'how it will come about'.[52]

Whoever was added to the Government, it was clear that Churchill would not be amongst them. His 'conspiracy' with Masaryk during the crisis was known to Chamberlain; Churchill's 'doings and sayings ... demonstrated for the nth time how completely Winston can deceive himself when he wants to', as well as 'how utterly credulous a foreigner can be when he is told the thing he wants to hear. In this case ... that "Chamberlain's fall is imminent".'[53] The Prime Minister was not inclined to forget Churchill's antics.

During the Munich debate Churchill had criticised the Government's proposal to adjourn the House until November, calling it 'derogatory to Parliament' and declaring that the country wanted the House to be in continuous session during a national emergency. This met with 'tittering laughter' from government benches. When Chamberlain said that it was up to the Speaker to decide whether to reconvene the House, Churchill implied that everyone knew that such a decision rested with the Government. Chamberlain said that this was 'unworthy', adding that to suggest that the Government was unaware of the gravity of the crisis was a 'repetition of tittle tattle'.[54] Churchill responded with 'a ridiculously pompous note of protest',[55] only to receive a cutting rejoinder:

> I am sorry if you think my remarks were offensive, but I think that you are singularly sensitive for a man who so constantly attacks others.
>
> I considered your remarks highly offensive to me and to those with whom I have been working.
>
> I had not regarded these remarks, wounding as they were, as requiring a breach of personal relations, but you cannot expect me to allow you to do all the hitting and never hit back.[56]

Chamberlain's determination to carry on with his own course, unencumbered with Edens, Churchills or Coopers, was amply demonstrated by the reconstruction of the Cabinet he carried out in late October.

Chamberlain's main problem was that whilst he saw the need for an accretion of strength, he could 'not see it among any of the younger men'. The idea, assiduously fostered by some of those concerned, that this was because all the talented men were in the cave of Adullam, will not withstand examination.[57] Crossley, Emrys Evans, Gunston and Richard Law were all to lose their seats in 1945 without ever reaching Cabinet rank and never returned; Ronald Cartland was killed in 1940; of the remainder, Boothby, for all his later fame as a 'personality' and television performer, was one reason why Churchill was excluded from 'Edenite ranks';[58] and Cooper, whose interest in his own political career was already on the wane, went on to become a distinguished Ambassador in Paris. Only Eden, Cranborne and the then obscure Macmillan had substantial political careers before them.

This might, of course, suggest that the Conservative Party was even shorter of talent than Chamberlain realised, but the reasoning behind the changes reflected a commitment to his own idea of what constituted a National Government. Only Hailsham, one of his oldest political friends, was asked to step down; he had been frail since suffering a stroke, but the news of his retirement was (courteously) withheld until after his son's election at Oxford.[59] His place as Lord President of the Council was taken by Runciman, who, at sixty-eight, was two years older and who had first entered Parliament as a Liberal in 1899 and had been retired by Chamberlain in May 1937. The 'National' label was further retouched by the addition to the Cabinet of the former Governor of Bengal, Sir John Anderson, as Lord Privy Seal, and by adding the Dominions to MacDonald's responsibilities as Colonial Secretary. Only one Conservative received promotion, and that was the fifty-eight-year-old Lord Stanhope, who replaced Cooper at the Admiralty. With two peers and two non-Conservatives promoted, it was as well that another of Chamberlain's selections declined the honour; Lord Samuel might have been a 'nasty smack' at 'Master Archie [Sinclair]', but the appointment of another sixty-eight-year-old Liberal peer would have done little for Conservative morale.

The reconstruction was an extraordinarily insensitive one, giving heart to the Government's critics and none to most of its supporters. Had appeasement begun to pay dividends then the mutterings of discontent would have died away, but as it did not, they persisted, coming to the surface in December with reports in the *Evening Standard* of an 'Under-Secretaries' Revolt'.

As the author of these rumours was Churchill's son, Randolph, at least one of the Ministers mentioned as a target of the 'revolt', Hore-Belisha, assumed there was nothing to it, only to be disabused when he spoke to his own Under-Secretary, Lord Strathcona and Mount Royal.[60] The leading 'rebel', Robert Hudson, Secretary of the Department of Overseas Trade, told Chamberlain on 8 December that although he and his friends supported 'appeasement', they 'and many people in the country thought that certain members of his Government were not contributing as fast as we should like to see to the essential corollary of appeasement, namely rearmament'.[61] That a junior Minister should 'actually . . . intimate that unless I got rid of at least two and preferably four of my colleagues he and a number of younger Ministers would have to reconsider their position', astonished Chamberlain.[62] That Hudson, like other complainants, stressed their complete support for him whilst criticising his appointments increased his dissatisfaction and his desire for an election.

Hudson's complaints came at the end of 'an exceptionally depressing week'. 'Venomous' attacks on British policy by the German press, Hitler's 'failure to make the slightest gesture of friendliness' and Mussolini's attacks on the democracies, gave comfort only to Chamberlain's opponents.[63] Added to these difficulties were problems with the farmers over the Government's proposals to introduce legislation dealing with milk production, at a time when rural constituencies were already rife with discontent over poor prices for wheat and barley. There was, once more, talk of an early election, but Butler's view that 'there will not be one' was quite correct.[64] In the circumstances Chamberlain thought: 'it doesn't look as if there were anything to do but go on and bear it though that may presently prove to be impossible'.[65] But with anti-Munich candidates reducing the Conservative majority at Oxford and actually taking Bridgwater on 17 November, the omens were not good.

These things brought on a sharp attack of self-pity: 'Sometimes I feel that I wish democracy at the devil and I often wonder what Prime Minister had to go through such an ordeal as I.' With Hoare, Simon, de la Warr, Elliot and Shakespeare Morrison all variously named along with Runciman and Winterton as excess baggage, Chamberlain lamented that whereas Baldwin had 'had me to help him', there was 'no one who stands to me in the same relation and consequently I have to bear my troubles alone'.[66] This was to ignore the temperamental difference between himself and Baldwin; where the latter needed a capable deputy to do all the business he could not be bothered to do, a deputy to Chamberlain would, himself, have had nothing to do. But if the Prime Minister was lamenting that the 'material' available to him for any reshuffle was 'meagre in the extreme', some of his opponents were writing in the same vein about their own ranks.

Perhaps the most marked feature of the post-Munich period was the uncertainty on both sides of the political divide on foreign policy: if Chamberlain could not be certain that the dictators would play up in the way he wanted, the same was true, mutatis mutandis, for his opponents. Hopes nourished by the wilder Eden acolytes such as Harvey that he would 'break away from the party and lead a crusade in the country'[67] soon withered in this climate. The most that he was willing to do was to form something approximating to a 'group'.

This may seem a shockingly imprecise term to use, but when Harold Nicolson attended a meeting in early November at which the 'group' was constituted, it was decided that: 'We should not advertise ourselves as a group or even call ourselves a group. We should merely meet together from time to time, exchange views and organise ourselves for a revolt if needed.' But from whence would this 'revolt' come if not from the 'group' that would not call itself a 'group'? It is not by such rosewater methods that a Government with a large majority is brought low; but then these men were 'all good Tories and sensible'. Nicolson told his wife not to worry, for he was keeping respectable political company and steering clear of those like Churchill who gave the impression of 'being more bitter than determined, and more out for a fight than for reform'.[68]

Churchill was certainly 'out for a fight', and if he was 'bitter' it was at the way the other dissidents treated him. In the debate on a Sinclairite motion for the creation of a Ministry of Supply on 17 November, Churchill appealed for fifty Conservatives to join him in the 'Aye' lobby; Macmillan and Bracken turned up. To make it worse, in response to a criticism he had levelled at Chamberlain, Cooper had defended the Prime Minister. Churchill was bitterly resentful of this, and when Cooper wrote to explain that he could hardly be expected to share severe criticisms of an administration of which he had so recently been a member, Churchill responded that their 'small band of friends' had to 'stick together', adding that 'some of my friends' had wondered whether there was something more behind Cooper's words: 'the desire to isolate me as much as possible from the other Conservatives who disagree with the Government'.[69]

It was perhaps such fears that drove Churchill into surreptitious contacts with Liberals in his own constituency. There was unrest in Epping and, although he was able to come to a modus vivendi with the local Party branches, there was, as a senior local figure noted, 'undoubtedly a serious split in their ranks'.[70] Far from pressurising local groups to get rid of Churchill, the Party organisation was actually trying to pour oil on troubled waters – the last thing they wanted was yet another by-election. Churchill's action in December in supporting the Duchess of Atholl, who had resigned her seat to fight on the issue of Chamberlain's foreign policy, further strained local loyalties – but she did lose the election – and Churchill had not supported the Independent candidate at Oxford, Lindsay, against a Conservative, pro-Munich candidate; he was careful not to go too far in his opposition.[71] Even so, he found allies a scarce commodity.

When his own son-in-law, Sandys, was thinking of forming a 'nucleus' of 'abstentionists' in October and November, he was inclined to agree with Nicolson that association with Churchill would 'kill them'[72] – and sought, instead, to get Amery to lead it.[73] The sad fact was that, much though Churchill might resent it and deny it, a charge made by Chamberlain in the House on 17 November went home because it corresponded with the thoughts of so many: 'If I were asked whether judgement is the first of my Rt Hon. friend's many admirable qualities I should have to ask the House of Commons not to press the point.'[74] As Amery gloomily reflected after a talk with Attlee in October: 'there is no real leadership in him . . . As for our own volcanoes they are all extinct and I see no minor peaks that suggest the possibility of hidden fire.'[75]

Lack of cohesion among his opponents was, however, scant comfort for a Prime Minister who was still waiting to see some results from his foreign policy, which would justify it and which would then clear the way to an election.

The Persistence of Appeasement

'The Prime Minister sometimes reminds me of the Stuart Kings – he is clear and upright but inelastic'; there is much to recommend Butler's view of Chamberlain's character.[1] The adulation of which he had been the recipient had not gone to his head, but it had done a great deal to convince him that his foreign policy was the correct one. It was this which governed his reluctance to broaden the basis of his Cabinet, as he was 'not prepared for the sake of what must be a sham unity, to take as partners men who would sooner or later wreck the policy with which I am identified'.[2] It irritated him that people were still 'talking and thinking as though Munich had made war more instead of less imminent', and one of his reasons for not yielding (despite the urgings of Halifax) to cries for a Ministry of Supply or for conscription was a desire to get 'back to the view that though there are gaps to fill up we need not believe that we have got to make huge additions to the programme now being put into operation'.[3]

On 26 October the Cabinet had set up a Committee headed by Inskip to consider proposals for extending the scope of the defence programmes and accelerating current production.[4] Schemes for expansion created considerable anxiety at the Treasury. Sir John Simon pointed out that they were proposing to increase expenditure at a time when 'the yield of revenue is sagging with the declining activity of the country as a whole'; he doubted whether the Air Ministry's programme could be 'financed beyond 1938–40 without the gravest danger to the country's stability'.[5] The increases were, of course, designed to reinforce current defence policy: the air force received top priority, with an increase in heavy bombers for offensive operations and more spending on defence against aerial warfare; the navy came next; and, despite pleas from the French and (ironically in view of Hudson's attacks) Hore-Belisha, the army remained confined to its role as a field rather than an expeditionary force.[6]

Chamberlain still looked to diplomacy to relieve pressure on arms spending, hoping that his contacts with the dictators might 'enable me to talk to these ruffians'. This would permit a 'restoration of confidence', which would then 'allow us to stop arming and get back to the work of making the world a better place'.[7] There was, therefore, little to be gained from going through the administrative upheavals which the creation of a Ministry of Supply demanded because, with any luck, by the time it was established 'we might find that the need was slowing off'.[8] There remained, of course, the danger that the 'suspicious' dictators, provoked by 'opponents of my policy here' and stimulated by 'bad advisers', would slip 'back into the old rut'.[9]

These fears were borne out by the anti-Jewish atrocities of November, which 'horrified' Chamberlain, and by reports of Hitler's intentions. It seemed to the Prime Minister as though there was 'some fatality about Anglo-German relations which invariably blocks efforts to improve them'.[10] Information from secret sources indicated that Hitler had no desire to follow up the Munich contacts and, indeed, that he regarded the agreement with great distaste. In a speech to journalists on 10 November, he spoke with great harshness about the British and of his determination to expand German domination in Eastern Europe.[11] When the Foreign Policy Committee of the Cabinet considered this and other reports on 14 November, Halifax drew the conclusion that further progress towards diplomatic appeasement was impossible at the moment and that their priority should be 'the correction of the false impression that we were decadent, spineless and could with little impunity be kicked about'.[12] These reports were followed up in late November by rumours that Hitler was determined to go to war if there was any attempt to prevent German expansion, and that he regarded Britain as his chief enemy.[13]

These reports were taken a good deal more seriously by Halifax than they were by the Prime Minister, who pointed out that they were, in fact, less precise than the sort of information which they had been getting during the summer from men like von Kleist. German behaviour towards Czechoslovakia, her patent ambitions in Memelland and Danzig, her behaviour towards the Jews, all conspired to reinforce the impression created in Halifax's mind by the September crisis. He told Dirksen on 14 December that he had been 'a good deal disappointed by the deterioration in the situation since Munich' and that a recent speech by de la Warr was 'by no means' incorrect in describing British opinion as 'coming to feel that it was not possible to reach agreement with the German Government, which seemed to us to make no response'.[14]

Given the lack of opportunity to pursue diplomatic initiatives on one front, Chamberlain had decided after 14 November that the 'only line of advance (beyond rearmament) is through Musso'.[15] The long-postponed Anglo-Italian

Agreement had finally come into operation on 2 November after Mussolini had agreed to withdraw ten thousand troops from Abyssinia.[16] Chamberlain's proposal to follow this up with a visit to Rome was accepted by the Italians, but a series of anti-French demonstrations in Italy, accompanied by criticisms of British policy, drove Chamberlain to exclaim, 'What fools these dictators are!'[17] Cadogan wrote to the Ambassador in Rome, Lord Perth, on 12 December asking him to warn his hosts that there was a danger that the visit would be called off if such activities were not curtailed; with a touch of the irritated pessimism that was beginning to creep into Chamberlain's tone at this time, he commented that: 'a section of opinion in this country holds that it is impossible to get on terms with the "Dictators". The latter certainly seem to do their best to justify this point of view.'[18]

Until the September crisis relations between Prime Minister and Foreign Secretary had proceeded smoothly, but then it had become apparent that Chamberlain's 'major objective' of bringing British policy 'back to saner and more realistic grounds' was not at all times and in all places compatible with Halifax's 'main objective' of preserving 'national unity'.[19]

Halifax's advocacy of broadening the Cabinet and setting up a Register for National Service were the first outward signs of the fact that the gap which had opened up in the aftermath of Godesberg was widening. This was partly the result of something which became increasingly apparent to others over the next few months: that Halifax's emergence as an independent political force gave him a confidence to express views which dissented from those of the Prime Minister.[20] At the Foreign Policy Committee meeting on 14 November he had taken the rumours of intended German attacks more seriously than had Chamberlain. Then, just before Christmas, the two men had a 'slight tiff', which was a sign of the way the wind was blowing.[21]

That 'insensitivity' in personal matters, which had created problems in Eden's day, had not vanished from Chamberlain's style of leadership with his departure. He was inclined to use Sir Horace Wilson as a source of advice on foreign policy and to have speeches on the subject prepared at 10 Downing Street. On 13 December he consulted Cadogan about an address which he was going to give at the Foreign Press Association. Horrified at its 'weakness', Cadogan told Halifax about the speech and asked that they should try to get the text stiffened up. But when Halifax saw Chamberlain, he was told that the speech had already been printed and distributed. The almost inexhaustibly patient Halifax shrugged the incident off, but both Cadogan and Harvey were, for once, in agreement in calling it a 'bad speech'.[22]

One reason why Chamberlain's remarks now seemed 'weak' was that the trickle of secret information arriving at the Foreign Office was turning into a flood – and however the auguries were divined, it began to seem that 1939 would be a crucial year. The rumours of November, coming from Carl Goerdeler, an opponent of the Nazi regime who had contacts in military circles,[23] had spoken of Hitler's hostility towards Britain but had confirmed Foreign Office suspicions that German expansionism was aimed eastwards, but only two days after the fuss over Chamberlain's speech, there came fresh information – this time that London was to be bombed in the near future.[24] The man carrying this dramatic news, Ivone Kirkpatrick, had just returned from being Henderson's deputy in Berlin, and his source assured him that his news came from the German War Office. As MI5 had picked up similar rumours, there appeared to be legitimate cause for alarm.

Chamberlain remained sceptical, but the rumours could scarcely be disregarded. The Committee of Imperial Defence decided to tighten up on defences against aerial attack, and all Departments were ordered to have their war-plans ready for the end of March. The 'tiff' with Halifax was also mended when, a few days later, Chamberlain asked for, and used, a Foreign Office draft in his next speech. Its firmer tone, and the fact that he used the Foreign Office text, inspired Harvey with the thought that 'the old man seems definitely to have given up hope of Germany';[25] this, however, was decidedly premature.

The rumours of war, particularly the prospect of a westward advance, were certainly depressing and, combined with the 'Under-Secretaries' Revolt', unrest in the agricultural constituencies and criticism from his opponents, gave Chamberlain a gloomy Christmas; but his spirit was resilient and his pessimism less deep-rooted than Halifax's, who was beginning to succumb to the atmosphere of the Foreign Office. When the former *Morning Post* editor, 'Taffy' Gwynne, suggested to him that he should, in effect, adopt Churchill's policy, he retorted indignantly that he was not ready to do that; as he told his sisters: 'Fortunately my nature is, as Lloyd George says, extremely "obstinate" and I refuse to change.' It was a mark of the perception which he now had of Halifax that he went on to write that he could see 'plainly that my successor would soon be off the rails'.[26]

The visit which he and Halifax paid to Rome was crucial from this point of view. For Chamberlain it provided an opportunity to build on a relationship which, although it had cost him a Foreign Secretary, had also brought the bonus of Mussolini's intervention in September. Cadogan warned him that Italian policy would, as ever, continue to vacillate, seeking always to choose the stronger Power, and that it was, therefore, important to dispel any impression of weakness or decadence.[27] Chamberlain might, perhaps, have been a little depressed had he been able to hear Mussolini's private comment that he and

Halifax were 'not made of the same stuff as the Francis Drakes and the other magnificent adventurers who created the Empire. These are . . . the tired sons of a long line of rich men and they will lose their Empire';[28] but he did not hear them. Instead, he heard the spontaneous enthusiasm of the Italian people for the man who had saved Europe from war, and the pacific assurances of a Mussolini who liked to talk big but still played safe.

The 'truly wonderful' visit enabled Chamberlain, in his own eyes, to achieve 'all I expected to achieve and more'; and it had 'definitely strengthened' the channels of peace.[29] Mussolini had expressed his desire for peace and for a reduction of the arms race – both music to Chamberlain's sorely tried ears; and, on the 'delicate' subject of the rumours of German intentions, had assured the Prime Minister that it was 'out of the question' that she would attack in the west. For his part, Chamberlain had made it clear that any 'aggressive action' taken under the impression that the democracies would not fight would be taken over a misapprehension.[30] His mood upon his return to England was more optimistic than it had been for some time.

It needed to be, for during his absence there had been fresh rumours about malign German intentions. Gladwyn Jebb summarised their tenor in a report written on 19 January for the Foreign Policy Committee: 'All our sources are at one in declaring that [Hitler] . . . is barely sane, consumed by an insensate hatred of this country, and capable of ordering an immediate aerial attack on any European country and of having this command instantly obeyed.'[31] This time the information indicated that Holland and/or Belgium were in danger. At the Foreign Policy Committee meeting on 23 January which considered these reports, Halifax again took a more gloomy view of them than some of his colleagues, but the Cabinet concurred with the view taken at the Foreign Policy Committee that it was impossible to ignore the reports. It was decided to ask President Roosevelt to speak out before a speech which Hitler was due to give on 30 January, and the Chiefs of Staff were asked to consider whether an attack upon Holland constituted a casus belli for Britain.[32]

Not everyone was inclined to take Halifax's view of the deluge of reports which had inundated the Foreign Office since early November. As the Secretary of State for India, Lord Zetland, commented to the Viceroy, Lord Linlithgow, in late January:

> Much of the information is of an alarmist character and the Foreign Office have recently taken a somewhat pessimistic view of the prospects for the next few weeks. It has, however, sometimes occurred to me that behind all this flood of information . . . there is a deliberate intention, namely, to create among the public here, where alarmist rumours have had wide circulation, a feeling of nervousness and apprehension, the purpose of which would be to

make us amenable to any future threat of force in which it might indulge in connection with his demand for the return of German colonies.[33]

This was a line of thought with which Chamberlain had some sympathy, as his remarks at the Foreign Policy Committee meeting showed. After all, not only were the reports mutually contradictory, but they were also from sources which, as had been shown in the past, were less than reliable.

Thus, although the reports were passed on to America,[34] and the Cabinet was inclined to treat an attack on Holland as a casus belli, Chamberlain deprecated any announcement of this. The decision necessarily entailed staff talks with the French and, if possible, with the Belgians and the Dutch.[35] There was no dissent from the Cabinet when the matter was discussed on 1 February, although it was recognised that such a step was 'almost tantamount to an alliance'. But Chamberlain resisted Halifax's attempt to press for the Staff talks to cover not merely an invasion of Holland but also the wider subject of a general war in the west; this, he maintained, was unnecessary. On the one hand his speech to the Foreign Press Association had made it plain that Britain's obligations to France were 'founded on identity of interests', and, on the other, if the current Franco-Italian tension led to war, Britain might want to stay out in order to avert the possibility of Germany entering it on Italy's side.[36] He did, however, make it clear in the House on 6 February that any threat to France's 'vital interests' would 'evoke the immediate co-operation of Great Britain'.[37] Cadogan hoped that this would mark 'a turning-point', whilst an astonished Nicolson regarded it as a 'complete negation of his appeasement policy'.[38] Both were premature in their expectations.

Chamberlain was not in a headlong flight from 'appeasement', which led directly to the guarantee to Poland and thence to the Second World War. Nothing in his policy envisaged allowing the Germans to advance westwards, or allowing them to menace the peace of Europe: 'Our motto is not defiance, and, mark my words, it is not, either, deference. It is defence.'[39] The gestures towards Anglo-French solidarity were necessary parts of this policy and, far from feeling doubtful about success, by early February the Prime Minister was feeling distinctly optimistic.

Writing to his sisters on 4 February he confessed that he was 'beginning to feel at last that we are getting on top of the dictators . . . They missed (or rather Hitler missed) the bus last September, and once you have done that in international affairs it is difficult to reproduce the situation.' The fact that rearmament had progressed to a state where 'they could not make nearly such a mess of us now as they could have done, while we could make much more of a mess of them,' and that public opinion would not now accept any German claims that Britain was treating them 'roughly and unfairly', meant that the scales were tilting in favour of peace, as did Germany's bad economic condition and the threat, however vague, of American intervention foreshadowed in Roosevelt's recent speech. These things allowed Chamberlain to take the 'firmer' line which his critics praised without, apparently, being able to appreciate the connection between 'diplomacy and strategic strength'. He was convinced that his policy was succeeding.[40]

Those who imagined that 'old brolly' (as Channon called him)[41] was changing his policy were apt to attribute it to the influence exercised by Halifax.[42] He had kept his lines with Eden open and had even, on 9 February, delivered an address to The Focus, at which he spoke 'simply and sincerely' and 'much more strongly' than any other Minister had done, at least in the view of the usually sceptical Amery.[43] The speech he made to the Parliamentary Foreign Affairs Committee on 16 February 'made an admirable impression on the Edenites',[44] impressed everyone with his 'charm, sincerity and high ideals', and left Channon wondering whether he was 'saint turned worldling, or worldling become saint'.[45] He certainly remained an advocate of improving the Government's position by inviting Eden back.

The Prime Minister, however, refused to entertain the idea, being more impressed with Eden's predicament as he tried, on the one hand, to convince the Government of his loyalty and, on the other, to satisfy the expectations of his friends: 'In short Our Anthony is in a dilemma from which he would very much like me to extract him.' But as he knew that he could not do that without 'sacrificing my policy', Eden would have to wait and, preferably, 'proclaim his repentence'.[46]

The 'optimistic view of the situation', which Chamberlain continued to take, received powerful reinforcement with Henderson's return to Berlin in mid-February. His long absence was the result of a malignant growth in the mouth, and the painful operation which he had undergone in London had left him physically under par, but determined to go back and see out his mission. Conversations with Ribbentrop and Goering gave him very different impressions from those produced in the Foreign Office by the reports of dissident Germans: 'My definite impression', he telegraphed on 18 February, 'is that Herr Hitler does not contemplate any adventures at the moment and that all stories and rumours to the contrary are completely without real foundation.'[47] Vansittart was quick to accuse Henderson of not 'being in touch with reality'.[48] He thought that Henderson's 'illusionist stuff' was another attempt 'on the high road to leading us up the garden path again'.[49] Given the ease with which Vansittart swallowed rumours from sources which, as Cadogan admitted, were unverifiable,[50] because they fitted with his prejudices, it was rather unfair of him to criticise Henderson for doing something similar.

One man who was impressed by the reports was the Prime Minister. Although contacts on the high diplomatic and political fronts between Britain and Germany had been badly affected by the events of November, discussions on economic matters had been quietly proceeding. In December the Federation of British Industries and its German counterpart had announced the opening of discussions to improve trade between their two countries, and the Board of Trade and the Colonial Office had been exploring tariff concessions and negotiating a coal cartel, the last of which came into force at the end of January. In his speech on 30 January Hitler had admitted that the German economy needed to export more, and he had said that the colonial concessions which he sought need not lead to war.[51] Cadogan's hopes that relief at Hitler's speech would not 'lead to a surge of optimism' were not realised as there was even a 'Hitler rally' on the Stock Market.[52] Although the economic talks did not go as smoothly as Chamberlain might have hoped, the invitation to Oliver Stanley to visit Berlin for further conversations was encouraging.[53] Even more so were the reports of a talk given by the Duke of Saxe-Coburg on 15 February.

The Duke, a grandson of Queen Victoria, a fanatical Nazi and an old Etonian contemporary of Henderson's,[54] was Chairman of the Anglo-German Society in Berlin. In his speech, he referred to the progress made in Anglo-German economic negotiations and expressed the hope that it would continue; it would, he said, be 'important for the whole world if our two peoples could co-operate in full confidence with one another'. Henderson thought that these sentiments had been expressed with the 'personal approval of Herr Hitler himself'. To Chamberlain this seemed to come 'closer to that response for which I have been asking than anything I have seen yet'. He proposed, he told Henderson on 19 February, to 'make some sympathetic allusion' in this sense in his next speech, and went on, in a veritable paean of optimism, to descant upon the prospects which this, and the ending of the Spanish Civil War, might be opening up. If Franco-Italian relations could be smoothed over, then they could, through Mussolini's good offices, 'begin to talk about disarmament'; and if that went well, 'we might begin to think of colonial discussions'.[55]

Being sceptical about the reports which the Foreign Office put such store by, Chamberlain had been anxious to 'endeavour to dispel the atmosphere of gloom' which press coverage had spread, and a speech by Hoare towards the end of January began the 'counter campaign', as Zetland called it.[56] Butler, whose views 'were those of the Prime Minister rather than those of Halifax',[57] had certainly never 'fully accepted' the stories of 'the horrors Hitler might do' and shared this optimism, as did Lord Dunglass and Wilson.[58] His chief at the Foreign Office did not.

Indeed, so little did Halifax take this view that he took the unprecedented step of writing to Henderson on 20 February to tell him that he thought the Prime Minister's prognostications were 'generally rather optimistic'.[59] Harvey found his master 'almost unrecognisable from the Halifax of a year ago', but his new 'boldness' naturally led to rumours that he and Chamberlain no longer saw 'eye to eye'.[60] Another sign of what, by March, had been true for some time came when Halifax discovered that an optimistic briefing from Chamberlain lay behind a spate of cheerful articles in the press, which were very far from expressing his own view of events.[61] This was capped on 10 March with a speech from Hoare foreseeing a 'golden age'.[62]

Conscious that 'we are getting near to a critical point where the whole future direction of European politics will be decided', Chamberlain wanted to create a climate of feeling in which Hitler would be capable of 'approaching us without the danger of a snub'.[63] Hoare's speech, like his own press briefing, had been part of his 'counter campaign' to dispel the gloom created by the rumours of the last few months. Halifax felt obliged to register his strongest protest yet, not merely because Downing Street had by-passed the Foreign Office, but because of his growing unease with the Prime Minister's views. He thought that the Germans would be encouraged to think that the British were 'feeling the strain', whilst the French might be discouraged into thinking that Chamberlain was about to spring something like a Runciman mission on their disputes with Italy.[64]

Already news from Czechoslovakia was making Halifax uneasy. On the day he wrote his letter to Chamberlain, 10 March, the Czechs dismissed the Slovak Premier, Tiso, who promptly appealed to Hitler. On 14 March the Slovaks announced their independence and German troops crossed the frontier; the following day President Hacha, under duress, placed Bohemia and Moravia under German 'protection'. 'No balder, bolder departure from the written bond has ever been committed in history,' recorded a stupefied Channon: 'It is a great day for the Socialists and the Edenites. The PM must be discouraged and horrified.'[65] Chamberlain was both.

Since Godesberg Prime Minister and Foreign Secretary had begun to drift apart in the degree of optimism each was disposed to attach to the possibility of building upon the Anglo-German Agreement signed at Munich. Halifax, who talked to Cadogan, Harvey, Vansittart and Eden, as well as the Prime Minister, was more inclined than his leader to place weight upon the flood of rumours; now it seemed that his pessimism had been justified.

The End of Appeasement?

'Nothing seems any good; it seems as if nobody will listen to or believe me'; thus, Cassandra-like, did Vansittart lament after the German occupation of Prague.[1] But although the great man may have fancied a likeness between himself and that daughter of Priam whose fate it was to prophesy truly and yet to be ignored, there was an even more marked resemblance between 'Van' and the boy who cried wolf.

British intelligence gathering was neither as good as Britain's enemies believed nor as bad as later detractors (including Churchill) made out;[2] its chief defect was that whilst information flowed in in copious quantities, no means of evaluating its reliability existed.[3] Each of the Service Departments had its own intelligence service, added to which were the government-controlled Secret Intelligence Service (SIS) and the Industrial Intelligence Committee (IIC) under Major Desmond Morton; on top of this came the information gathered by Vansittart's various sources, including Colvin and Lord Lloyd. What Vansittart's lament neglected to say was that although some of the stuff which had been passed to him had been accurate (at least up to a point), much of it had been, not to put too fine a point on it, dross of a high order.

Part of the problem with evaluating intelligence reports stemmed from their point of origin. Vansittart's information came from anti-Nazi elements inside Germany, who were very anxious to impress upon the British Government the need to fight Hitler; as Professor Watt has commented: 'much of the misinformation was spread deliberately by elements seeking to manipulate the British Government'.[4] This was particularly true of the spate of rumours which had marked late 1938 and early 1939. It was, perhaps, merely fortuitous that these 'scare stories' had all concerned German attacks westwards, thus arousing in Halifax and others anxieties that earlier fables about German designs on the

Ukraine had failed to raise – but a better explanation than mere chance is on offer.

'Vansittart's Germanophobes', as Inskip called them,[5] included members of the anti-Hitler elements in the German General Staff. Their attempt to persuade the British that Hitler was determined to go to war over Czechoslovakia had been frustrated in 1938 by Chamberlain's dramatic seizure of the initiative; having failed to get action by telling the truth about Hitler's designs, it seems, in Watt's trenchant words, 'a reasonable supposition that [they] . . . decided to doctor the reports so as to trick the British at their most sensitive spot' – the fear of a surprise attack on London.[6] They also challenged the confidence of Butler's definition of German policy as being 'Bluff West. Infiltrate East'. By making it appear that Britain was herself in the firing line, they stimulated the Staff talks with the French, which were enormously to increase the pressure on Chamberlain to commit himself to a full-scale continental war.

Chamberlain's refusal to take all the various warnings thrust at him is, then, not quite as culpable as it might appear. It may be true (to quote the title of the American edition of Colvin's book) that there are 'None so Blind' as those who will not see, but it is also true that there are none so credulous as those who are told what they want to hear. The problem facing Chamberlain as the stories of the occupation of Prague filtered in on 15 March was that the climate of opinion, soured as it was by the 'scaremongers', was not one which lent itself easily to a dispassionate analysis of German intentions, even if the means of making such an evaluation had existed – which they did not.

It is tempting to see the road from Prague as leading straight to war, via the abandonment of appeasement, but the story is more interesting if the temptations of hindsight (and the legends of the defeated) are resisted. Chamberlain's initial reaction was certainly one of profound disappointment, but the guarantees to Romania, Greece and Poland arose not out of any conviction that his previous policy had been wrong, but rather out of the political and diplomatic situation created by Hitler's actions coming, as they did, on top of the prolonged season of rumour. Indeed, it might be said that those who had concocted the stories which Halifax and others had swallowed, succeeded in their basic aim of twisting British policy towards a position in which war became a probability rather than a possibility.

Chamberlain's initial public comments, made in the Commons on 15 March, suggested disappointment rather than despair. His later claim, that they were made at a time when he was not in possession of the full facts and had been 'misunderstood', is more revealing about his response to the reaction to his remarks than it is about his state of mind on 15 March.[7] Whilst there was regret

THE IDES OF MARCH
John Bull: 'Thank goodness that's over!'
15 March 1939.

at Germany's action, there was neither retreat nor surrender. Chamberlain stressed, as the Cabinet had that morning, that the occasion was not one in which Britain had any legal obligations to the 'disintegrated' Czechoslovak state. The only action he announced was the cancellation of the Hudson-Stanley visit to Berlin. Refusing to indulge in accusations of bad faith, Chamberlain said that he did not believe 'that anything of the kind which has now taken place was contemplated by any of the signatories of the Munich Agreement at the time of its signature'. Admitting that it was a 'terrible shock to confidence' to find Hitler occupying territory to which Germany had no racial claim, he nevertheless declared that:

> Though one may have to suffer checks and disappointments from time to time, the object which we have in mind is of too great significance to the happiness of mankind for us lightly to give it up or set it on one side.[8]

This, thought Cadogan, was 'Fatal!'[9]

Contrary to some assertions, there was, in fact, a good deal of support on the Conservative benches for Chamberlain's remarks, even if they did appear insipid and inadequate to his opponents. His real problem came from the change that had taken place in Halifax's perceptions of the German problem.[10] All the evidence available to SIS suggested that Germany had few troops in the west and was massing them eastwards; it, therefore, seemed 'clear, that from the purely military point of view, Germany may be preparing for a drive through Hungary, in concert with Bulgaria, accompanied by defensive action only in the west'.[11] In other words, 'Infiltrate East. Bluster West' still applied. Both he and Simon resisted any clamour for a further extension of British commitments in Eastern Europe as placing control of her destiny in the hands of others;[12] but it soon became difficult to hold this line.

Writing to the Viceroy on 20 March, Zetland commented that, 'the full significance of what Hitler did . . . was not grasped immediately; but forty-eight hours' reflection brought home both to the Government and to the public generally the real meaning . . .'[13] This, however, begs more questions than it answers and attributes to cerebration what is more properly due to skilfully deployed political persuasion.

Hitler's action had caught Chamberlain on the crest of a wave of confidence. His optimistic remarks to the press were not 'for copy' only, but rather the reflection of a belief that, 'Like Chatham, "I know that I can save this country and I do not believe that anyone else can."' The 'prodigal sons', as he called Churchill, Cooper, Eden and company, were 'fairly besieging the parental door', and God was in his heaven and all was, if not right with the world, then in a fair way to getting there in a year or two.[14] Now the winds of change had shifted. The Conservative dissidents followed Eden's 'softly softly' tactics and did nothing so vulgar as to crow,[15] but the discontent was there in the lobbies of the Commons all the same, and the scent was taken by the sensitive political antennae of the Foreign Secretary, who 'binged up' the Prime Minister.[16]

Halifax's political position was now immensely strong. Where the instantly discredited prophet of the 'golden age', Hoare, retired to bed with influenza and diminished political credibility to contemplate resignation,[17] Halifax reaped the rewards of the cautious. Although his speech in the Lords on the 15th had been redolent of what his biographer called 'the old language of appeasement', this reflected a last commitment to Chamberlain's views rather than any settled conviction. In private he was firm with the German Ambassador, anxious to bring Eden and possibly even Churchill into the Government, and 'asserted himself' with the Prime Minister.[18]

The result was heard on 17 March in Birmingham, when Chamberlain, instead of delivering a homily on domestic politics at a long-standing speaking engagement, chose to speak to the nation on foreign policy. It was a performance of great skill, which began with a warning that the quietness of his previous statement should not be mistaken for an absence of strong feeling, continued with a defence of his foreign policy and then moved on to the attack. The plight of the Jews and the Austrians was deplored and the inconsistencies of Hitler's statements about having no more territorial claims and wanting racial purity were contrasted with his recent actions: 'Is this the end of an old adventure, or the beginning of a new?' Was it, he asked, 'a step in the direction of an attempt to dominate the world by force'? He declined to give any answer to these questions, but announced that he was conferring with the Commonwealth, France and others who knew that 'we are not disinterested in what goes on in South-Eastern Europe'. The peroration, playing upon the sacrifices he had already made which proved his sincerity as a man of peace, concluded upon a characteristic note:

> While I am not prepared to engage this country by new unspecified commitments, operating under conditions which cannot now be foreseen, yet no greater mistake could be made than to suppose that, because it believes war to have been a senseless and cruel thing, this nation has so lost its fibre that it will not take part to the utmost of its power in resisting such a challenge if it were ever made.[19]

As an exercise in rallying public and parliamentary opinion, the speech was a success,[20] but, as the American Ambassador told Halifax, it did 'definitely carry a corroboration that we should resist further German aggression'.[21] However, whilst affronted at Hitler's actions and deeply mistrustful of his previous assurances, it is by no means certain that Chamberlain intended to go this far. But even as the Foreign Office looked round for a policy, there was yet another of those wild rumours which had already so usefully soured the atmosphere.

On 16 March the Romanian Minister in London, Vergil Tilea, had informed Sir Orme Sargent that, according to his information, Germany intended to absorb Hungary as a prelude to an attack on his own country; was there, he wondered, any possibility of the British supplying the Romanians with armaments? Sargent, whose frame of mind was not far removed from that of Vansittart's, replied that as this raised momentous questions, there could be no immediate answer.[22] The following afternoon Tilea was back, this time with an even more dramatic story.

For some weeks the Germans and Romanians had been negotiating over the terms of an economic agreement; now, according to Tilea, the Germans had asked for a complete monopoly over Romanian exports and made other demands, in return for which they would guarantee her frontiers; these demands had, he said, amounted to an ultimatum.[23] Telegrams were despatched post-haste to Ankara, Athens and Belgrade asking what the respective Governments would be prepared to do in the way of helping the Romanians.[24] It is a sign of how rattled the Foreign Office was by recent events, as well as how susceptible it was to scaremongering, that, after receiving a telegram from Sir Rex Hoare in Bucharest which called Tilea's story 'utterly improbable',[25] another circular had to be sent out asking for action on the earlier one to be suspended.[26]

But by this time the damage had been done. The rumour had been circulated round Europe and men's minds had been drawn towards South-East Europe at a time when, in Henderson's words, the critics of Munich had been given 'a handle'.[27] Just to keep the pot stirring, news had also been received from Phipps in Paris that a 'completely reliable source' (odd how few sources seem to have been anything else) reported that Hitler's 'personal wish' was to 'make war on Great Britain before June or July'; it seemed, however, that a 'clear and certain warning' (such as withdrawing ambassadors) would stimulate the army, who were 'still doubtful about Hitler', to resist his wishes.[28]

It was all good *Boys' Own Paper* stuff. No one appears to have asked how it was that Hitler who, so reliable sources had had it, was going to advance into the Ukraine in January, or was it Holland, was now going, having occupied Prague, to move against Hungary, Romania and Britain all in the next few months. So tense was the atmosphere created by the blow to the hopes raised after Munich that any rumour, however incredible or fantastic, had not only a hearing, but men who were prepared to swear that they had it from someone who had it from someone close to someone who was close to someone who was close to Hitler's entourage.

By the time the Cabinet met on the morning of 18 March, Tilea's story had been substantially discredited, but that did not stop Halifax from thinking that there would be 'an advantage' in considering what they would have done had it been true. No one inquired what this 'advantage' was, which was just as well since, apart from relieving the tension of doing nothing, it is rather hard to pinpoint.

Sir John Anderson confirmed in portentous manner what was already perfectly plain; a quick reference to the Chiefs of Staff produced the news that

German domination of Romania would be bad for Britain, but that without the help of Powers like Russia and Poland, there was not a lot that could be done. He did suggest that, failing these Powers, a permutation of Greece, Turkey and Yugoslavia might be of some use; wisely he did not specify what use – they were, after all, discussing hypotheses.

What did emerge was further evidence of the division of views between Prime Minister and Foreign Secretary. Halifax, who now regarded the 'real issue' as being 'Germany's attempt to obtain world domination', was prepared to equate Romania and Holland as being of equal interest from Britain's point of view. Chamberlain, on the other hand, although convinced that Hitler's attitude 'made it impossible to negotiate on the old basis with the Nazi regime', did not rule out 'negotiations with the German people'. He was not prepared to talk about guaranteeing Romania against German attacks, but rather in fashioning a deterrent. Regarding his own speech as a 'challenge' to Germany 'on the issue of whether or not' she intended to 'dominate Europe by force', he was still not convinced, unlike Halifax, that she would take up this challenge. What he wanted to do was to discover whether 'we could obtain sufficient assurances from other countries to justify us in a public pronouncement that we should resist further acts of aggression on the part of Germany'.

Accordingly, telegrams were sent out asking the Russians, Poles, Yugoslavs. Turks, Greeks and Romanians whether they would 'join us in resisting any act of German aggression aimed at obtaining domination in South-East Europe'.[29] Chamberlain had never envisaged letting Germany dominate Europe by force, and he had, until now, been unconvinced that this was Hitler's aim; now he was doubtful and it was necessary to find a way of deterring Germany that would not, of itself, lead to the war he still hoped to avoid.

The bellicose tone of the Cabinet contrasts markedly with the downcast mood of the previous September and is not to be explained purely by reference to indignation at Prague. The latest Chiefs of Staff appreciation of the strategic situation, prepared in February, had had some encouraging news; it had also had the usual gloomy stuff when it came to measuring the relative strength of armed forces, but the fact that it was taking into account other things, like morale and latent economic strength, gave heart to those who saw Germany as fragile in both areas. The time, it seemed, was propitious, given British rearmament, for a little firmness.[30]

Chamberlain and Halifax, along with Simon, Stanley, Wilson and Cadogan, met on Sunday morning to consider the terms of the telegram to be despatched. But by this time replies had been received to the circular despatched after Tilea's démarche; these suggested that the reply to the question which the Cabinet wished to pose would be 'What will *you* do first?' Chamberlain, foreseeing this, had come armed with a fresh suggestion: France, Poland and Russia should be asked whether they would be willing to join in a declaration that, in the event of any more untoward changes in the cartography of Europe, they would consult together about what action to take.[31]

This project was sold to the Cabinet the following day, 20 March.[32] Halifax met head-on any objection that a proposal to 'consult' was 'not a very heroic decision': firstly, it was action which could be taken immediately; secondly, such a declaration of 'solidarity' would have 'an immense political influence'; and, finally, it would take time to decide exactly what action should be taken in any of the various circumstances which might arise. This last point was of particular importance given Hitler's modus operandi, which seemed to be to encourage states to disintegrate from within. The formula accepted by the Cabinet met Chamberlain's two (rather contradictory) desires: to avoid 'specific commitments', yet to provide a deterrent. If Germany showed signs 'that she intended to proceed with her march for world domination', she would be faced with the prospect of a two-front war, a war waged 'not in order to save a particular victim, but in order to pull down the bully', as Chamberlain put it.

For the Prime Minister this was a 'bold step', which 'involved a considerable advance on any action which we had previously taken'. Although it embodied no binding commitment, it carried the 'definite implication' that 'consultation' would be succeeded 'by action'. For Corbin, the French Ambassador, who was shown a draft of the telegram embodying Cadogan's proposals, it was a cause for 'horror'. Convinced that there was '*some* force' in this, Cadogan obtained Chamberlain's agreement to 'touch up' the circular to contain a commitment to consult 'about joint resistance' to action which threatened the independence of any European state.[33] Roger Makins' description of it as 'amateur collective security' was an apt one.[34]

Even though he had agreed to the revised formula, it would be a mistake to conclude that the differences between Foreign Secretary and Prime Minister were now at an end. Under the pressure of events since Munich, Cadogan now thought that they had 'reached the crossroads',[36] an opinion shared for the same reasons by Halifax. Indeed, when he saw Count Raczynski, the Polish Ambassador, on the morning of 21 March, he told him that the British would be inclined to treat any German threat to Danzig as 'a grave question which was of concern to all'; an attitude emphasised when he saw Bonnet later the same day. It was, he told the Frenchman, 'essential to stop German aggression wherever it might start'. Bonnet, who was delighted to find the English speaking in such firm tones, agreed, emphasising the vital importance of Poland.[37]

Chamberlain's attitude was somewhat different. He placed more hope on the threat of a two-front war deterring Germany from any future action of an aggressive kind,[38] and thought that the declaration would not 'constitute a guarantee of the existing frontiers and . . . the status quo'; Germany's claims in Memelland and Danzig were, in his eyes, not necessarily ones which would invoke Great Power consultations. Hoping that an announcement by the Four Powers would be deterrent enough in itself, Chamberlain also wanted to enlist Mussolini into the good fight by getting him to try to 'put the brake' on Hitler.[39]

Here too there were differences between Foreign Secretary and Prime Minister. The objections which the former had made to the proposal in Cabinet were amplified by Cadogan when he saw what the Prime Minister proposed to say: 'the whole effect is to lead Mussolini to suppose that our intention is to bring about another Munich meeting'. But Foreign Office attempts to turn the letter into a warning to Mussolini to behave himself were rejected by Chamberlain, who called Cadogan's draft 'a monument of clumsiness', and went ahead with his own version which was designed 'to make Mussolini see that if Hitler goes on as he has begun it will mean war and induce him to warn his partner'.[40]

It was the hopes he placed in Mussolini which partly account for Chamberlain's attitude towards Russia. Historians have been quick to cite his self-confessed 'most profound distrust' of Russia as though it was something odd.[41] Certainly to those who were thinking in terms of a military solution it was, as the discussion at the Foreign Policy Committee on 27 March was to show, but these were not the terms in which Chamberlain was thinking; he was still convinced that a purely diplomatic combination would deter Hitler – and to this a Soviet connection was death. When he spoke with Bonnet and Daladier on 22 March, he feared that Polish mistrust of the Soviets might kill the projected four-Power declaration. The French Foreign Minister thought that Polish participation was more important than Russian and, when Chamberlain queried his reasoning, Bonnet replied that 'Romanians remembered more than one Russian invasion, and some of the upper class preferred Hitler to Stalin'.[42]

There was, of course, in Chamberlain's attitude a visceral distaste for an unpleasant dictatorship, but there was also a disbelief in the offensive capabilities of the recently purged Red Army and a mistrust of Russian diplomacy.[43] Stalin's response to the British circular was a case in point. He had welcomed it, but was willing to sign only after France and Poland.[44] The distrust which the Poles habitually showed to their communist neighbour was to kill the projected declaration. By 24 March it was clear that the Poles were not willing, publicly, to side with Russia against Germany. Given the mistrustful attitude of Romania and other Balkan states towards the Soviets, it seemed that a diplomatic bloc could only be constructed at the price of their extrusion. By 25 March the Foreign Office had reached the conclusion that this must be done.[45]

Chamberlain, who as early as 18 March had thought that 'Poland was very likely the key to the situation' and that 'our communication to Poland should probably be to go somewhat further than . . . to other countries', found nothing to cavil at in this.[46] On 24 March Count Raczynski had proposed a 'confidential bilateral understanding' between his country and Britain, which would have the effect of giving Poland security without risking German claims of encirclement.[47] The Foreign Office meeting on 25 March had looked favourably on this idea, as did Chamberlain the following day, and it came before the Foreign Policy Committee on the 27th with their imprimatur.[48] But again, Halifax's motives were not Chamberlain's.

The Foreign Office now seem to have accepted that a war was as inevitable as anything in human affairs could be; the concern was to ensure that it was fought on favourable conditions. Great significance was attached not only to earlier Chiefs of Staff reports about weaknesses in Germany's morale and her economy, but also to reports from Mason-MacFarlane in Berlin that 'the situation *at the moment and for the next* few months is very distinctly more unfavourable to Germany than it is likely to be in the course of the next decade'.[49] Chamberlain, who 'never accept[ed] the view that war was inevitable', was quite willing to indulge in the building of diplomatic combinations, but assumed that there would be room for manœuvre and concessions in places like the Polish corridor, where Germany had justified claims.[50]

The Foreign Policy Committee was a good deal less impressed by the plan emanating from the Foreign Office. Ironically, in view of his reputation as a fascist sympathiser, it was Sir Samuel Hoare who was the most astringent critic of the decision to exclude Russia, which would, he said, 'be regarded in many quarters as a considerable defeat for our policy'. But Halifax's insistence on the importance of Poland and of her mistrust of the Soviets, provided a catch-all answer. Halifax's remarks at the Foreign Policy Committee made plain how far he was now willing to go. Admitting that there was 'probably no way in which France or ourselves could prevent Poland and Romania from being overrun', he still thought that if he had to choose between 'doing nothing, or entering into a devastating war', he would prefer the latter as the lesser evil. The Foreign Policy Committee agreed to go ahead with the plan as submitted. But this did not envisage a unilateral guarantee: Poland was to be expected to reciprocate. The Gadarene rush towards a unilateral guarantee was precipitated, as so much of recent British policy had been, not by considered thought, but by a 'war scare'.

Chamberlain did not feel that he had changed his policy, which remained, as he told de Valera on 25 March, 'the securing of peace by the removal of reasonable causes of war, whilst pursuing a policy of rearmament'. He hoped that giving assurances to states like Poland and Romania would encourage them to resist Hitler's demands – and that it would deter him from making any demands.[51] But if they failed to stand up for themselves, Chamberlain did not intend to play Don Quixote: 'Our ultimatum would mean war and I would never be responsible for presenting it.'[52]

He went along with Halifax's suggestions because they provided the only alternative to his own brainchild of a four-Power declaration. No longer able to 'feel safe with Hitler', Chamberlain was a prey to the rumour-mongers. Hore-Belisha's assertion on 21 March, at the state banquet for President Lebrun, that Germany was massing her troops in the west, compounded with stories of attacks on Lithuania and air raids on London, caused Chamberlain acute anxiety. Logic told him that not all the stories could be true, but dealing with a 'fanatic' made for uncertainty, and precautions were taken against air and submarine attacks.[53]

The proposals for reciprocal guarantees to Poland and Romania were, in this climate, unanimously agreed to by the Cabinet on 29 March, but Halifax made it clear that the negotiations might take 'a long time'. His worries that the Poles might not like a reciprocal obligation went relatively unnoticed; after all, the Polish Foreign Minister, Colonel Beck, was due in London at the end of the week, and there was time enough to spare.[54] Yet, at a moment's notice, Ministers found themselves summoned to an emergency Cabinet the following morning and presented with a proposal to extend a unilateral guarantee to Poland.

Halifax's unhappiness at the prospect of anything hindering the forging of a Polish connection was brought sharply into focus later on the afternoon of 29 March, when Cadogan brought to his attention the story which had just been given to him by Colvin. The recently expelled *News Chronicle* journalist had long been a source of Vansittart's, and he now brought the dramatic news that Germany had 'everything ready' for a 'swoop on Poland', which was to be followed by similar action against the Baltic republics after which, with a Russian alliance in his pocket, Hitler would turn his attention to the British Empire.[55] Colvin was duly wheeled over to Downing Street to tell his story. He was then, and remained, under the impression that his tale had a dramatic impact on British policy; in fact, he was merely used by Halifax to impress upon the Prime Minister and his colleagues the need for firm action.

Other information to the same effect as Colvin's was already known to the Foreign Office, which, in its current crusading mood, was inclined to give it greater credence than rumours suggesting that Hitler wanted to negotiate with Poland.[56] As Butler wrote in his diary shortly after Easter: 'Halifax is determined to set up a force to counter Germany and . . . is going ahead single-mindedly.'[57] In the face of this Chamberlain conceded the necessity for firm action, but insisted on putting the matter to the Cabinet.

Halifax told his colleagues that the main concern was that Hitler should not outflank them on Poland before negotiations had been concluded. A declaration of support for Poland might perhaps prevent him putting his plan into action, thus helping 'discredit' him in 'Army circles'; and it would also 'educate' German public opinion to the likelihood that Hitler's policy would end in a two-front war. The possibility that all this might lead the fabled 'opposition' to Hitler to remove him was waved about, not as a probability, or even much of a possibility, just as a source of courage. To those who replied that such a declaration was to give Beck what he wanted, Halifax reassured them that this was 'an interim measure only' designed 'to meet what was apprehended to be an immediate threat'.[58]

There was very little here for any critic to get hold of once the 'interim' nature of the guarantee was mentioned; moreover, as Zetland put it, there was 'now little disposition in any quarter to dissent from the view that in light of the bloodless victories which Germany had achieved', nothing 'short of a definite warning that force would be met by force' was likely to stop her. With a 'feeling almost of relief', Ministers departed having agreed to Halifax's plan.[59]

At the Foreign Policy Committee that afternoon, Halifax admitted that if France or Poland raised any objections to the guarantee, its publication would have to be postponed, but he advised his colleagues against waiting for confirmation of the rumours of an imminent German attack on Poland. Since the information available to the Chiefs of Staff made them doubt that any such thing was about to happen, this was wise of Halifax.[60]

The stage was now set. Attempts by the Opposition parties to get Chamberlain to include some reference to Russia in his statement to the House were met with the response that 'the present arrangement was only intended to cover the interim period'. He did, however, postpone the timing of the statement to give the Cabinet another chance to look at the terms of the announcement. The Prime Minister told Ministers that the terms of the statement had been modified 'so as to make it relate more directly to the interim period'.[61]

At 2.52 p.m. Chamberlain rose in his place on the front bench, looking, according to Nicolson, 'gaunt and ill'.[62] He announced that if, during the period when 'consultations' were proceeding, there should be any 'action which clearly threatened Polish independence' and which the Poles 'considered it vital to resist', they would have the support of the British Government.[63] In his own mind he had left himself enough flexibility to allow further changes in frontiers, and had left in British hands the decision as to whether Polish independence was threatened.[64] Labour's Arthur Henderson was nearer the point when he said that the consequences of what the Prime Minister had said would make it 'as momentous a statement as has been made in this House for a quarter of a century'.[65] That this was so was, however, more the work of Viscount Halifax and the Foreign Office than it was of Chamberlain.

Facilis Descensus Averni

If, as Virgil would have it, the way down to hell is easy, then the first step had been taken. Chamberlain had stressed the 'interim' nature of the guarantee in the House and had done so in full awareness of the latest Chiefs of Staff reports, which indicated that there was little possibility of an imminent German attack on Poland.[1] The guarantee was, therefore, in his eyes a gesture. It was also necessary to prevent Poland from falling into Germany's orbit if Hitler was to be threatened with the prospect of a war on two fronts.[2] The Prime Minister's attitude had changed, but he had not abandoned his policy. Rather, he had given up, for the moment, hope of 'constructive' appeasement and was, instead, engaging in what might be called 'negative appeasement'; negotiation had given way to a desire merely to avoid war.[3]

For a while this was compatible with Halifax's desire to take a moral stand; not that Chamberlain was well-placed to resist his call for a harder line. Halifax's position was an immensely strong one. On the one hand reports from Mason-MacFarlane in Berlin and from the Chiefs of Staff indicated that the next few months were ones in which Britain could afford to challenge Hitler: German morale was low; there was mistrust of Hitler in 'Army circles'; and a challenge might just, in itself, be enough to unseat the dictator.[4] Not too much hope was invested in this prospect, but it did contribute to a greater willingness to declare that a 'devastating war' was preferable to another 'bloodless victory' by Germany. On the other hand was the effect of events in Prague upon public and parliamentary opinion.

Although Chamberlain's anodyne statement on 15 March had been well-enough received on Conservative benches, the undoubted effect of Hitler's violation of the Munich Agreement upon popular opinion was not one which Halifax was inclined to ignore – especially as it matched so readily his own feelings. That broadening of the Government towards which the Foreign

Secretary still looked for political salvation could only, realistically, be accomplished after Chamberlain's policy had been modified in the eyes of the dissentients; the guarantee to Poland had achieved this feat. Halifax was not short of advice that an 'all Party Government . . . under your leadership . . . would be acceptable to all', but he was not a disloyal man; and, in any event, he was well able to bring pressure upon the Prime Minister.[5] The tabling by the 'Eden group' of a motion calling for a 'truly National Government' was interpreted by Chamberlain as an attempt to drive a wedge between himself and Halifax, something about which he was bound to be sensitive as he could hardly afford to lose another Foreign Secretary.[6]

The Prime Minister was between a rock and a hard place, with little prospect of extrication. An election was impossible at that moment, and to leave it until 1940, which was the latest it could be, was to invite Baldwin's fate in 1929. Later in 1939 was a possibility, but that would leave him at Hitler's mercy if a crisis arose. A tough stand was, therefore, both politically necessary and diplomatically advisable. But Chamberlain had no more decided to go to war than he had decided to bring Churchill into his administration. What had happened however, was that both possibilities were now present in his mind; but as long as it looked as though war could be avoided, he would leave Churchill out to avoid antagonising the dictators: 'the fact is that the nearer we get to war the more his chances improve and vice versa'.[7]

There were signs of a conciliatory attitude from the other side too. The odd hot-head like Macmillan might write to *The Times* demanding a 'National Government on the broadest possible basis',[8] and criticise Eden for being 'too soft and gentlemanlike', whilst shouting for the 'boneheaded' Chamberlain's removal,[9] but both Churchill and Eden knew that the Conservative Party would not wear that. At a meeting of the 1922 Committee on 21 March, Churchill remained quiet whilst others, urging the need for conscription, criticised the Government – 'in some ways v. much of a politician,' noted Amery.[10] He was also careful, in the debate following the announcement of the Polish guarantee, to praise the Government's Russian policy (which was much criticised) as 'well-conceived'.[11] As fresh crises arose in early April he kept in close touch with Chamberlain and Halifax[12] and let his 'strong desire' to enter the Government be known to the Prime Minister.[13]

Eden, who was quick to deny that his motion for a National Government on 29 March had been critical of the Prime Minister, was similarly cautious.[14] With Halifax, Stanley and, it was said, Hoare, all pressing for his inclusion in the Government, Eden, who was 'itching to be back at work again', saw no reason to abandon the 'gentlemanlike' approach just as it appeared likely to pay a dividend.[15] During the heated debate on 13 April occasioned by the Italian occupation of Albania, his was the one speech which cheered the depressed Premier, who responded with a kind note.[16]

If the Prime Minister was not yet willing to heed the siren voices, he was at least prepared to be a little nicer to his enemies. He had seen the Labour leaders on 30 March to give them advance warning of the guarantee, and afterwards, at Archie Sinclair's request, had agreed to see Lloyd George. His hope that, by so doing, he would deflect the criticisms of his old antagonist was quickly dashed, but he did gain some emotional satisfaction: 'I looked at his red face and white hair [and] all my bitterness seemed to pass away for I despised him and felt myself the better man.'[17]

The old Adullamite's main line of criticism was that, without Russian assistance, the guarantee was 'an irresponsible game of chance' which was likely to turn out badly.[18] But Chamberlain's own feeling that Russia was a 'very unreliable friend with very little capacity for active assistance' was reinforced by Colonel Beck during his visit to London on 3 April. Whilst willing to reciprocate the British guarantee, he would in no wise get Poland involved with the Soviets.[19]

Beck's reluctance is perfectly understandable. He was still trying to balance between his two great neighbours and regarded the British guarantee as useful leverage in negotiations with Germany.[20] This provided Chamberlain's justification, and as Halifax, despite the clamour from the Opposition (official and unofficial), shared the Prime Minister's views, Russia remained on the periphery of British foreign policy.

Any hope that this might encourage Mussolini to loosen his links with the Axis was discouraged by his lukewarm response to Chamberlain's letter of 20 March, and finally dashed by the events of Good Friday.[21] On 7 April Italian troops invaded Albania, and King Zog and the glamorous Queen Geraldine fled with their two-day-old son and whatever wealth they could carry. Cadogan concluded that the invasion 'proves Musso a gangster as Czecho proved Hitler, and we must set up a barrier with Greece and Turkey'.[22]

This feeling, which was, it transpired, shared by Halifax and by the French, led to demands, supported by Churchill and others, for firm action. Chamberlain, who viewed the whole business less tragically, wished that Mussolini had accomplished his business 'to make it look like an agreed arrangement'. He was not unwilling to be soothed by the noises coming from Rome, but the incident did whittle away 'such faith as I ever had in the assurances of dictators'.[23] However, the events of the next few days drove him to condemn Mussolini as 'a sneak and a cad'; but as he was also describing Attlee as a 'cowardly cur', it will be apparent that he was somewhat out of temper.[24] Nor was it surprising that he should have been so.

In the first place he had had to deal with demands from within the Cabinet for 'interim' guarantees for Greece and Turkey, which grew in volume after the 10th when the Greeks expressed themselves alarmed at Mussolini's intentions.[25] From outside came Churchill's incessant telephone calls and letters prophesying that Greece would, if not guaranteed, slip into the Axis camp.[26] Chamberlain was, as he showed at the Foreign Policy Committee on 10 April, reluctant to take any dramatic action against the Italians, who were, after all, now withdrawing their troops from Spain, but the demand from Halifax, Hoare and Stanley was almost irresistible.[27] Once news came on the 13th that the French were going to guarantee not only Greece but also Romania, Chamberlain found himself 'bounced' into a position even beyond that occupied by Halifax; but, fearful that French morale would collapse if not supported, he found himself dragged along with the tide. Having guaranteed Poland, how could he now deny the same thing to other threatened nations?[28]

Having yielded to the demands for a debate, Chamberlain at least had something to offer the House on 13 April, but his attempt to defuse Labour criticism by giving Attlee (in confidence) details of what he was planning before the debate were ineffective; and Churchill, whom he had also sent for 'in the hope of keeping the House as united as possible', spoke critically and with 'an acid undertone'. This, Chamberlain later discovered, was because he had imagined that he had been sent for to be offered the post of Minister of Supply and had, therefore, 'been smarting under a sense of disappointment only kept in check by his unwillingness to do anything' which would prevent an offer being made. Feeling 'very dispirited and very lonely', he was uncomforted by Margesson's assurances that his standing was unaffected. The incessant personal attacks, accompanied by the moves which he had allowed himself to be pushed into, left him at a low ebb – so low that he was even tempted to take Churchill into the Cabinet.[29] The 'gaunt and ill' look, which Nicolson had noted in the Prime Minister's countenance as he rose to announce the Polish guarantee, led to rumours that he was 'already failing' and that he 'cannot last out physically much longer'.[30]

But Chamberlain was a resilient man. He usually managed to encourage himself to 'sail happily on the surface' of events, knowing that too much contemplation of the awesome fact that his was the word which might decide the fate 'not only of this generation, but of the British Empire itself,' only made him 'miserable'.[31] As the clouds lifted over the following weeks, so did the despair. This was helped by the efforts of Butler who, resentful at the way Halifax had kept him out of the decisions on Poland and Romania, and seeing that the Foreign Secretary was 'veering away' from the Prime Minister, increasingly aligned himself with Chamberlain.[32] He turned up at the House on 13 April to

give him 'moral support', and passed on reports from the Duke of Buccleuch
and others which indicated that Hitler was astonished at British actions and
harboured no evil designs.[33] Although unconvinced, Chamberlain thought that
this probably signified that the Führer realised 'that he has now touched the
limit and has decided to put the best face on it';[34] and the tone of Hitler's
speeches seemed to support this qualified optimism. Every week that passed
without war, he wrote to his sisters at the end of April, 'makes war more
unlikely'; whilst expecting further crises, he could not 'see Hitler starting a
world war for Danzig'.[35]

Chamberlain's reviving optimism as the storm clouds thinned was seen by his
opponents as '"appeasement" raising its ugly head again',[36] but those (both
contemporaries and historians) who talk about the Government's policy being
'recast fundamentally' and appeasement 'abandoned' are accurate in their
judgments only as far as they refer to Halifax and the Foreign Office.[37]
Vansittart may have been incredulous that Chamberlain, Wilson and Henderson were 'still where they were' on foreign policy in early May,[38] and later
commentators might see this 'renewed interest in "appeasement"' as something requiring censure,[39] but the argument here pursued is that there had been
no simple abandonment of appeasement.

Prague had, for a season, forced Chamberlain to emphasise the negative part
of his policy and to add to its usual manifestation, rearmament, the concept of a
diplomatic front in Eastern Europe. But he had never seen the guarantees as
ruling out either further negotiation – when the time should be right – or
frontier revision in Germany's favour – provided she behaved herself; still less
did he see himself as being bound to go to war when Poland wanted on an issue
chosen by the Poles:[40] 'It is we who will judge whether their independence is
threatened or not.'[41] His policy was still 'a balanced one'.[42]

This is more than could have been said for those who criticised him for
wanting to sell the Poles down the river and who accused him of mere
anti-Soviet prejudice for his tardiness in concluding a pact with the Russians.
Chamberlain's mistrust of Russia was hardly ill-placed. The Soviet regime was,
whatever Labour supporters deluded themselves into thinking, a tyranny quite
as odious as Hitler's, and to doubt whether 'she has the same aims and objects
that we have or any sympathy with democracy as such',[43] was merely to show a
clear-eyed realism about Stalin. Moreover, as talks with the Poles, Romanians,
Greeks and Turks showed, the Soviets were 'thoroughly mistrusted by everyone except our fatuous opposition'.[44]

In his talks with Chamberlain in early April, Beck had stressed that it would
be 'dangerous to bring Russia into any discussions',[45] a message driven home by
the British Ambassador in Warsaw[46] and by the Romanian Foreign Minister,

Grigore Gafencu, during conversations in London on 23 and 24 April.[47] It was all very well for Dalton loftily to disregard Gafencu's opinion of the Soviets, but he had no responsibility for British diplomacy; those who had were more circumspect.[48] Aware of the advantages of a Soviet connection, Chamberlain still thought that to obtain it at the price of losing Poland and Romania would be to wreck his policy of building a diplomatic deterrent and would replace it with a policy of military encirclement, which would, as Halifax remarked in Cabinet on 17 May, make war 'more likely'.[49] Nor, pace the starry-eyed optimism of Churchill and Dalton, was it obvious that Stalin was willing to plunge Russia into a terrible war merely to extirpate fascism.

The mainsprings of Russian policy are obscure and likely to remain so, but Stalin, as a good Marxist, was quite willing to believe that Western imperialists were behaving as they should and were trying to divert German expansion eastwards. He expressed this fear, along with some indication of his thinking, in a speech to the Party on 10 March; not, it is true, without obscurity, for Marxist jargon does not easily lend itself to the purposes for which clarity of diction is employed, but anyone who chose to regard it as a blank cheque for the Western Powers was showing a faith that was, indeed, blind.[50] It would not have been a bad idea had Chamberlain been behaving as Maisky and Marxism prescribed, but he was not doing so and it is a nice irony that Chamberlain's opponents, by feeding Maisky (and, through him, Stalin) with their own suspicions, may well have scuppered their own policy. In proclaiming his desire for peace, Stalin implied that, provided no one attacked Russia, he was willing to let well alone. His own faith in the offensive capabilities of the Red Army seems to have matched the much-criticised views held by the British Chiefs of Staff.[51]

Chamberlain hoped to gain Russian aid without putting off the Poles and Romanians by asking them for a unilateral declaration of support for any of their neighbours who were attacked,[52] but the Russian terms, delivered on 18 April, revealed that they wanted much more.[53] They proposed an Anglo-French-Russian pact of mutual assistance, an offer of tripartite assistance to 'Eastern European States between the Baltic and Black Seas and bordering the USSR', and the swift consummation of such an agreement. They also wanted a British statement that the Polish guarantee was directed solely against Germany and, as if that would not have given Colonel Beck palpitations enough, wished to amend the current Polish-Romanian Treaty to ensure that it was not 'directed against the USSR'; as it had been concluded in 1921 in response to the Russian threat, this too was unlikely to go down well. In addition, there was to be no negotiation of a separate peace treaty, the simultaneous conclusion of a military convention and negotiations with Turkey. Cadogan's description of the terms as 'mischievous' was confirmed by Kennard's comments that they would destroy any chance of Anglo-Polish co-operation.[54] Chamberlain's verdict that they would be 'fatal to any hope of combining Balkan Powers to resist German aggression', was not merely anti-Soviet prejudice.[55]

Regard for the susceptibilities of the states Britain had guaranteed, suspicion of Soviet motives and military capabilities, and the fear that a Russian alliance 'would make war inevitable', led the Cabinet on 3 May to accept that they should respond by asking the Soviets to reconsider the idea of making a unilateral declaration along the lines previously suggested.[56] As long as Prime Minister and Foreign Secretary maintained a united front, this would remain British policy.

If the Government's response on 6 May, a reiteration of the proposal for a unilateral Soviet declaration,[57] was not the manifestation of crude anti-communism which its opponents alleged, then nor were its warnings to Colonel Beck the simple repetition of a desire to serve the Poles as the Czechs had been the previous year.[58]

During his conversations with the British in early April Beck had been, to say the least of it, disingenuous about the state of his negotiations with the Germans. On 26 March Ribbentrop had put forward a series of proposals, which included the return of Danzig to the Reich, a rail/road link across the Polish Corridor, and Polish adhesion to the anti-Comintern pact. Beck was no more willing to accept this last suggestion than he was to countenance joining the British in a Soviet alliance — he wanted to balance between his two neighbours.[59] Nothing had been said about these things to the British, who only learnt of them in late April. Anxious about rumours that the guarantee was making the Poles intransigent in their negotiations, and that Hitler intended to act against Danzig in the near future,[60] the Foreign Office sent Beck a message on 17 April which, whilst emphasising that they stood by the guarantee, tried to indicate the need for flexibility.[61]

There was great anxiety in 'hawkish' circles lest the warning should be interpreted by Beck as the prelude to another Munich;[62] these susceptibilities remained unimpaired by the revelation on 23 April of Beck's duplicity. The Colonel's response to the rumours of war was insouciant and, in assuring his allies of his willingness to negotiate, he revealed, for the first time, something of the history of recent German-Polish relations. The revelation of Hitler's terms and the Polish rejection of them caused even the mild Halifax to comment that Beck had been 'somewhat less than frank'.[63] By early May, when they had 'succeeded in worming out' of the Poles the facts of the situation, it was plain that Beck had shown a 'remarkable disinclination to tell the truth'.[64] Henderson's comment that had the terms been known, the guarantee would have 'seemed a still more undesirable and risky departure from normal British policy',[65] was not so much a reassertion of appeasement, as an acknowledgment that they had all been sold a pup by Colonel Beck.

At the Cabinet on 3 May when the response to the Soviet terms was discussed, Halifax expressed his anxiety about getting into a situation where 'the issues of peace and war depended solely on the judgement of the Polish Government'.[66] Chamberlain had already made plain his dissatisfaction with a BBC report which gave the impression that this was the case,[67] and it was decided to send a telegram to Warsaw expressing 'confidence that Poland would not lightly reject an equitable settlement' merely because of the British guarantee.[68]

Chamberlain's policy of constructing a diplomatic deterrent which would preserve peace was under threat from three directions. First was the risk that negotiating with the Soviets would drive away the Poles and Romanians; second was the fear that the guarantees, by making the Poles intransigent, would lead to a war over Danzig; and third came the possibility, foreseen by Hoare in early April, that the Germans would cry 'encirclement' and launch a preventative war.[69] There was no easy answer to the question of how to meet these challenges, but there was a feeling in the Prime Minister's entourage by the end of April that the reaction to Prague had been overdone; a feeling intensified by the revelation of Beck's duplicity.

Under pressure from the French and from the Minister of War, Hore-Belisha, Chamberlain had, on 26 April, announced the introduction of conscription. He had not done this very willingly as it was bound to exacerbate relations with Germany.[70] It was partly in an effort to alleviate the worst effects of this that Henderson was sent back to Berlin on 23 April.[71] The Vansittart elements within the Foreign Office regarded this as a harbinger of appeasement, and when, in early May, a letter appeared in *The Times* from Lord Rushcliffe arguing that the guarantees to Poland were not unconditional, and it became apparent that 'No. 10 [was] . . . talking appeasement again', it seemed to Harvey and others that the appeasers were up to their old tricks.[72]

The revelation of Polish duplicity had little effect upon those who believed that war was inevitable;[73] having swallowed the Russian camel, it was hardly likely that Churchill and company would strain at the Polish gnat. But amongst those who refused to accept the inevitability of war (and, therefore, refused to pursue a policy which would make it inevitable) there remained considerable anxiety over the prospect of getting dragged into war over Danzig. Moreover, it was by no means evident to some of the Prime Minister's entourage that the sky was dark enough to warrant the drastic step of a Soviet alliance.

Gafencu, who had been to Berlin before coming to London, had emphasised that he 'did not think Herr Hitler wanted war', but rather to have Britain's 'friendship . . . but on a basis of equality'.[74] These were sentiments which were echoed by other recent visitors to Berlin. Butler was inclined to give these some credence.[75] Hitler's speech in the Reichstag on 28 April seemed to give further encouragement to this line of thought. Given the way in which Hitler had used the occasion to tear up the Polish-German Treaty of 1934 and to denounce the Anglo-German Naval Agreement of 1935, Chamberlain's optimism was a cautious one, but he thought it indicated that Hitler knew he had gone as far as he could go, and he could not see him starting a 'world war for Danzig'.[76] Channon and Dunglass thought that a constructive response might be to press the Poles to make concessions on Danzig.[77] Butler, whom the Prime Minister now regarded as his sole, if 'not very influential, ally',[78] pressed Halifax on the issue, not without effect as the warning telegram of 3 May shows.

Cadogan, who picked up through a 'telephone intercept' that 'No. 10 [was] . . . talking appeasement again', quizzed Wilson on the matter, only to receive a denial,[79] but the differences between Downing Street and the Foreign Office were to intensify as pressure grew to settle terms with the Soviets. To Channon the project was 'the pet scheme of the leftish clique in the FO',[80] but Halifax, having found it abhorrent on 3 May, gradually came round to the notion that it had to be swallowed.

In part this was the inevitable consequence of his belief that Hitler had to be stopped and a moral stand taken, which left him with few arguments to counter those of Eden and Harvey that Russia was essential to this cause. Halifax disliked the Bolsheviks, but, just as he had been willing to apply realpolitik to dealing with the Nazis in 1937 and 1938, now it was Stalin who reaped the benefit. The replacement of Litvinov by Molotov at the Commissariat of Foreign Affairs in early May seemed an ominous sign and, coming as it did 'when negotiations have from the Soviet view been held up for some two weeks', there were those who worried that it signified the abandonment of Litvinov's policy of 'collective security'.[81] But such fear only made men like Harvey more anxious to close with the Soviets.

Nor was it merely Eden and his officials who pushed Halifax in this direction. The French, who had let the Russians know of their favourable attitude towards a tripartite pact to supplement their existing alliance, were also powerful advocates against the Foreign Secretary's conscientious scruples.[82] Initial Russian responses suggested to Halifax that it might yet be possible to secure from the Soviets a unilateral declaration of support, but the hopes that he so boldly expressed to the Cabinet on 10 May proved to be false.[83] The Russian reply on 15 May insisted upon a tripartite pact.[84] The prospect of a complete breakdown in negotiations concentrated Halifax's mind. At a meeting of the Foreign Policy Committee on 16 May the Chiefs of Staff had come down in favour of the alliance, and Halifax, whilst acknowledging in Cabinet the following day that the Russian proposal was a 'wide departure from our previous plan' which would make war 'more likely', was less hostile than before.[85] By 20 May he had come round to the view that 'we had gone so far that the little more would not make much difference in its effect on Hitler'; but Chamberlain still held that it 'would finally tip the balance over to war'.[86]

So deeply unhappy was Chamberlain at the way in which the wind had set that he told Cadogan that he would rather resign than sign an alliance with the Soviets.[87] He could not rid himself of the feeling that Stalin's chief concern was 'to see the "capitalist" powers tear each other apart whilst they stay out themselves'.[88] But as Molotov made it clear to Halifax in Geneva that the alternative to negotiating on Soviet terms was to break off negotiations – and the Foreign Office was only too well aware of rumours of a possible Russo-German agreement[89] – and the Poles and Romanians dropped their objections, Chamberlain found himself with little cover left.[90]

Harvey suspected Chamberlain and Wilson of not wanting the Soviet alliance 'because appeasement would be dead after all',[91] but Chamberlain's own words express better the reason for his reluctance even in the face of overwhelming pressure: 'the alliance would definitely be a lining up of opposing blocs and an association which would make any negotiation or discussion with the totalitarians difficult if not impossible'.[92]

But with the French, most of the Cabinet, the Foreign Secretary and a substantial proportion of the Commons all pressing for a Soviet alliance, Chamberlain had to yield. A face-saving formula was found before the Cabinet on 24 May. It was proposed that Article XVI of the League should provide the cover under which Russia would come to the aid of the Western Powers if attacked.[93] As this would, in Chamberlain's phrase, 'catch all the mugwumps' and 'give . . . a temporary character' to the Soviet connection, it provided a suitable cover under which Chamberlain could retreat.

With the great decision made, Chamberlain recovered his equanimity. Although 'still in the danger zone', he thought Hitler had 'missed the bus last September', but could see no prospect of détente 'as long as the Jews obstinately go on refusing to shoot Hitler'.[94] Virgil was correct.

'Die for Danzig?'

'Die for Danzig?', the 'French peasant has no desire to die for the Poldèves,' wrote Marcel Déat in *L'œuvre* in early May.[1] This echoed Sir Oswald Mosley's, 'Who the heck cares for Beck?', and, as both men were fascists, such remarks have been dismissed without much attention being paid to them. This not only unjustly neglects Mosley's sensible ideas on foreign policy, but also evades the awkward question – why die for Danzig?[2]

When the question of a guarantee to Poland was raised in Cabinet on 20 March, Chamberlain had stressed that it did not mean that 'existing frontiers' and the 'status quo' were to be maintained 'indefinitely', and when someone had asked whether 'German aggression against Danzig and Memel' would invoke the guarantee, the reply was that 'the test must be whether the action proposed was such as to constitute a threat to the security and political independence of Poland'.[3] Chamberlain had always been clear, both in his own mind and in Cabinet, that it was the British who were to be the judges of what constituted a threat to Polish independence.[4] Whether it would be possible to ensure that this happened was another matter, and the telegrams despatched to Warsaw on 17 April and 3 May were eloquent witnesses to the anxiety which Chamberlain felt.

Henderson had no doubt that the German case 'on the immediate issue' of Danzig was 'very far from being either unjustifiable or immoral'. The division of Germany by the Polish Corridor had been a major German grievance and one of the main mistakes of Versailles. Henderson was 'appalled' at the thought of Danzig being even the ostensible cause of war and even more so at 'our fate being in the hands of the Poles', who, whilst 'heroic', were 'foolhardy' and, as Beck's recent behaviour showed, hardly trustworthy.[5] He thought there could 'be no permanent peace in Europe until Danzig has reverted to Germany'.[6]

Kennard, the British Ambassador in Warsaw, rejected Henderson's allegations that one of the effects of the British guarantee had been to make the

Poles intransigent towards the German offers. Fully admitting that 'Danzig is in itself a bad wicket on which to make a stand' and that 'in normal circumstances it might be wiser for Poland to reconcile herself to the fact that she cannot indefinitely maintain her position there', Kennard saw it as representing a stand upon the principle that Germany could not use violent methods to obtain her diplomatic desiderata.[7]

Henderson was aware of this argument; indeed, he informed Cadogan on 14 May that he had told his hosts that if war resulted from 'unilateral action as regards Danzig' it would not be over the city itself, but rather on a 'matter of principle' – namely 'the necessity of resistance to the German method . . . of making brute force the sole arbiter in international affairs'.[8] But, thinking as he did that the Poles would have done well to accept Hitler's terms, he found it hard to see 'how we are going to find a satisfactory issue out of our present eastern obligations'.[9]

A proposal from the Holy Father, Pius XII, to hold a conference to discuss questions threatening 'a conflagration' foundered upon the Pope's refusal to consider dealing with Stalin and the British fear that it would look like 'another "Munich" conference'.[10] The shadow of last September also hung over any attempts to influence the Poles in their negotiations with the Germans; Kirkpatrick thought that any attempt to 'press them to be conciliatory' would lead them to 'think that we are preparing another Munich at their expense, with utterly disastrous results', whilst Makins' remark that 'it would be better to let the Poles play their own hand in this question' enunciated the Foreign Office view with precision.[11] According to this line of thought 'another "Munich"' had to be avoided at all costs – even if it meant, in effect, leaving the decision on war or peace to Colonel Beck.

This was not the policy which Chamberlain had thought he was im- plementing at the end of March, and it was one with which Halifax showed himself intermittently unhappy. Given the volatile situation in Danzig, he wanted to be kept aware of Polish policy, but received little save obfuscation from Beck. When, on 10 May, he asked what the Poles would do if the Danzig senate voted for union with the Reich, warning that it was important that they should 'take no step which will give Germany an excuse for putting her in the wrong with world opinion',[12] Beck replied that he did not think the senate would take such action; if it did, he would 'react in an energetic manner' and, of course, would keep the British informed.[13] 'Have we', minuted a plaintive Foreign Secretary, 'got an undertaking from Beck to consult us before taking action that might lead to war?'[14]

The answer to Halifax's question reveals the pass to which his own desire to take a 'moral stand' had brought British policy. At the end of March Britain had given an interim guarantee to Poland pending conclusion of an agreement; this was supplemented in mid-April by guarantees to Romania and Greece and the opening of negotiations with Turkey. All this was part of Chamberlain's policy of constructing a diplomatic barrier to German expansion in the east. The distrust felt by these countries for Russia had been one of three reasons for not getting too closely involved with the Soviets; Chamberlain's own distrust of their motives and his fear that an alliance would be seen by Germany as part of a policy of military encirclement, being the other two. Under pressure from the French, the Foreign Office part of the Cabinet and the House of Commons, Chamberlain had agreed to enter into negotiations for an alliance. At the same time, thanks again to pressure from the same sources, the guarantee to Poland had been converted into something approximating to Bonnet's comment to the press in early May: 'it was for Poland to decide freely herself whether, and at what points, her vital interests were affected; and that she could rely, if necessary, on the full support of France and Great Britain'.[15]

Chamberlain's problems were now formidable: on the one hand was the danger of allowing either the Poles or the Germans to assume that a 'blank cheque' had been issued to the former; but on the other lay that of arousing suspicions that another 'Munich' was in prospect; the one thing worse than a deterrent which did not deter was one which provoked the other side to war by arousing fears of encirclement. Then there was the problem of the Russian alliance; for all that the Cabinet, the Labour Party and the Adullamites favoured it, Chamberlain saw that it might disrupt his peace front by frightening off Poland and Romania. Trying to formulate a policy which would satisfy those who assumed war was inevitable whilst leaving the door open for peace was an impossible task; what is remarkable is not Chamberlain's failure, but his persistence. It was all very well for Lloyd George to attack him and praise the dictators for their efficiency, but, as Chamberlain remarked in late May, 'they have no press and no opposition to contend with'.[16]

Firm speeches by himself and Halifax on 8 June, which, nevertheless, did not close the door on improvements in Anglo-German relations, epitomised Chamberlain's policy.[17] He no longer had the slightest faith in Hitler or his word, but he was prepared to believe that the threat of a real war might drive the Führer to be more reasonable; then, as he told an unofficial emissary from Goering on 6 June, it was for Hitler to make the first move.[18] Chamberlain still wanted a 'permanent peace between this country and Germany', but that would require a settlement of the colonial problem – and he knew that to raise that in the current climate would mean that 'I should be swept out of office without a moment's delay'.[19]

Munich cast a long shadow, and although Halifax's speech had only mentioned the prospect of better relations with Germany, it was enough to bring Churchill out of the woodwork, alarm the Poles[20] and require a further statement on 12 June emphasising that the guarantee to Poland still stood.[21] But where Churchill saw Danzig as the swiftest way to the war which he had long foretold,[22] Chamberlain was apt to regard it as a problem which could, if Hitler was willing, be solved. Danzig was bound to remain a 'danger spot', but if the policy of the 'menacing silence' worked, then the guarantee need not lead to war; this remained Chamberlain's policy into August.[23]

From this point of view the Soviet alliance was not the panacea its proponents alleged; nor was it the simple matter they imagined. Most of Russia's neighbours disliked the idea of being guaranteed by her,[24] and the prospect of an Anglo-Soviet alliance destroying his 'peace front' by driving Poland and Romania away was regarded with dismay by Chamberlain.[25] The attitude of the Soviets towards the negotiations did nothing to make the Prime Minister more enamoured of the idea of entering into an alliance with them. Rumours of increasing German-Soviet contacts were played down by the British Ambassador in Moscow, Sir William Seeds,[26] but an ominous silence from Berlin on the subject of the Bolshevik menace, and a speech from Molotov on 31 May which denied any contradiction between negotiating with Britain and France and opening trade talks with Germany and Italy, cast doubts on this. Molotov's conduct of the negotiations did nothing to suggest he was hurrying to conclude an alliance.[27]

The Soviet connection was, of course, the great banner under whose device Adullamites consorted with the Labour Party and advocates of a 'Popular Front' such as Sir Stafford Cripps; their willingness to blame lack of progress in the Anglo-Soviet talks on Chamberlain was a useful card in Molotov's hand. Suggestions that Eden or Churchill might go to Moscow in early June to speed up negotiations were turned down by Chamberlain, who saw them as a first step towards the duo joining the Cabinet and 'perhaps later on the substitution of a more amenable Prime Minister'.[28] His response to a great 'bring back Churchill' campaign at the beginning of July was a firm refusal to do so. He was unimpressed by claims that it would convince Hitler that 'we mean business'; he wanted to impress Hitler with Britain's resolve, not convince him that a preventative war was about to be launched.[29]

Chamberlain's refusal to be pushed by Halifax into widening his Cabinet was matched by a refusal to panic over fresh 'war scares'. Reports from Warsaw at the end of June that 'rumours . . . were gaining considerable ground' that the Anglo-French guarantee would not be implemented,[30] were swiftly followed by panicky messages from Paris that Hitler was about to act against Danzig.[31] Bonnet warned the Germans on 1 July that any such attempt would lead to war,[32] but neither the French nor the 'hawkish' element in the Foreign Office succeeded in eliciting such a response from Chamberlain. He felt that the speech which Halifax had delivered at Chatham House on 29 June had sufficiently emphasised British firmness[33] and, whilst allowing the press to highlight the rumours,[34] he confined himself to a speech on 10 July reaffirming the guarantee. This, it seemed, was enough to allay eighty per cent of the suspicions raised in Warsaw.[35]

The 'hawks' in the Foreign Office, whilst approving the 'menacing silence',

THE CALCULATING BEAR
Halifax and Ribbentrop try to coax the Bear,
12 July 1939.

did not see how it could succeed with Henderson back in Berlin. Vansittart dismissed him as 'pro-German' and 'anti-Polish',[36] and Harvey described his 'streams' of telegrams and letters as 'hysterical'.[37] But Henderson's language to the Germans remained firm, and reminders that the German case over Danzig was not unreasonable were echoed by Chamberlain's own belief that, 'if the dictators would have a modicum of patience', a 'way could be found of meeting German claims while safeguarding Poland's independence and economic security'.[38]

Beck's cool reaction to the 'scare' at the beginning of July was reassuring to Chamberlain,[39] and a visit to Warsaw by General Ironside in mid-July seemed to confirm that the 'blank cheque' would be drawn only in the direst emergency.[40] By this time there seemed to be abundant evidence that 'Hitler may have been influenced by recent signs of British determination',[41] in which case, if the Poles did act cautiously and welcomed any constructive German approach on Danzig, war could well be avoided. There were, it was true, rumours that August would be 'the danger period',[42] but there always were rumours. Provided Hitler did not try to solve the Danzig question in the near future, war need not break out.[43]

This lull in the tension which had existed since March coincided with a growing impatience on Chamberlain's part with the Soviets. Strang, writing on 20 July, described the negotiations as 'a humilating experience' in which 'time after time we have taken up a position and a week later we have abandoned it'; and all the while 'we have had the feeling that Molotov was convinced from the beginning that we should be forced to abandon it'.[44] Having accepted practically all the Soviet conditions by the beginning of July, the British and French found themselves pressed for further concessions.[45] Even though they had conceded that Russia would not guarantee Holland and Switzerland, and that the Baltic republics should, despite their own unwillingness, be included in any guarantee, the Allies had not gone far enough:[46] the Soviets wanted a guarantee against 'indirect aggression', which they wished to define in such a way that they would be able to attack, say, Latvia, if she attempted to improve her relations with Germany; they also wanted a military convention signed simultaneously with the diplomatic alliance.[47] Further concessions were made on the last point, but the first one was something which the British refused to concede.[48]

This deadlock did not worry Chamberlain unduly, for agreement on such terms would be bound to damage relations with Poland and Romania.[49] But, if the 'menacing silence' appeared to be working, the question, posed by Henderson in late May, of what positive steps could be taken to improve Anglo-German relations, still remained to be answered.[50]

Having concluded by early July that Hitler had been 'intimidated' by Britain's 'display of force',[51] Henderson suggested to Halifax on 9 July the lineaments of a 'constructive effort for peace' which might be made once the Russian negotiations had ended.[52] Although Halifax was not inclined to take up immediately the suggestion of direct talks with Hitler, he, and Chamberlain, were in agreement that, having established their position publicly, 'the less said the better'. Chamberlain asked Ministers to be 'as economical in their references to foreign affairs as the state of public opinion here would permit'.[53] Halifax was inclined, like Chamberlain, to think that although the Danzig question ought not 'to be incapable of solution under favourable conditions', those 'conditions do not in fact prevail at this moment and that we have to work for their recreation';[54] others were more optimistic.

Butler had never liked the Polish guarantee. He disliked the idea of an alliance with the Soviets even more, and took the view that by 'gratuitously planting ourselves in Eastern Europe', the British had enabled Stalin to keep his options open.[55] He was anxious to move British policy from the 'negative state' of the 'menacing silence' towards the 'constructive purchasing of peace' and, as early as 12 June, had rehearsed for Halifax's benefits the 'forward moves' that he considered might be made: these included diplomatic steps, such as weaning Italy and Spain away from Hitler, but also economic ones such as 'reasonable adjustments' in areas such as trade and colonial policies.[56] He kept Halifax supplied with information which supported Henderson's line that Hitler was unlikely to risk his life's work on the throw of the dice of war, unless he felt encircled, and argued that 'we still have a task to do to persuade Hitler we are not preparing for aggression or a preventative war'. Butler wanted to 'go cannily' – counselling caution to Colonel Beck and looking for opportunities to build upon the positive references to Germany in Halifax's Chatham House speech.[57] But the furore which followed the public airing of similar ideas in mid-July illustrated the formidable opposition which any 'forward moves' in Germany's direction would arouse.

The day after Butler's suggestions to Halifax, 18 July, Wilson had a conversation with Goering's assistant, Dr Wohltat, in which he had emphasised British willingness to co-operate with Germany once she had created suitable conditions; but he was careful not to commit the Prime Minister to any initiatives[58] – which was more than could be said for Wohltat's next British contact, Robert Hudson. Since his unsuccessful attempt to persuade Chamberlain to remove Hore-Belisha in December, Hudson had suffered the disappointment of seeing the trade mission which he was supposed to have taken to Berlin cancelled by the events of March. By the end of June he was thoroughly dissatisfied with the state of British policy and critical of Chamberlain; writing to Churchill, he urged him to combine with Halifax to 'cut the Gordian knot' by securing the creation of a 'War Government'.[59] In conversation with Wohltat on 20 July he took the opportunity to revive, on his own initiative, some of the ideas that had informed British thinking on trade talks earlier in the year, and even floated the possibility of a British loan to Germany in return for disarmament.[60]

When Henderson had suggested at the end of May that some 'economic help' might be given to Germany, the Foreign Office reaction had been sharp: 'let us stop talking nonsense about economic help. The Germans have evolved a system which, by ignoring economic rules, is leading to economic deterioration and perhaps disaster. Whether we would or not we *can't* help.'[61] Henderson's ideas had remained confined to Whitehall, but Hudson's did not – and the 'menacing silence' was broken.

On 22 July the *News Chronicle* reported a 'new and very sensational attempt' at appeasement and, in the face of other reports, Hudson granted an 'exclusive interview' to the *Daily Express* on 24 July explaining, as the headline had it: 'I Planned the Peace Loan to Germany.'[62] The story coincided with reports from Berlin of the advice which the British had been giving the Poles to behave cautiously over Danzig and gave Chamberlain's opponents the perfect opportunity to say: 'There, I told you so. He means to sell out the Poles.' This, as Chamberlain told his sisters on 23 July, 'makes it impossible for me to enter into conversations with the Germans on any subject'.[63]

Chamberlain's annoyance with Hudson was moderated only by the accumulating evidence that 'Hitler has concluded that we mean business and that the time is not ripe for a major war'. The British rearmament effort was nearing its peak, and although the Allied forces would not be numerous enough to 'win a smashing victory', that was not Chamberlain's objective:

> What you want are defensive forces sufficiently strong to make it impossible for the other side to win except at such a cost as to make it not worthwile. That is what we are doing and though at present German feeling is it is not worth while *yet*, they will presently come to realise that it never *will* be worth while. Then we can talk.[64]

Hudson's gaffe had shown the dangers of talking *in foro publico*, but there were 'other and discreeter channels by which contact can be maintained'. Chamberlain was well aware that his critics thought it would be a 'frightful thing to come to any agreement with Germany without first having given her a thorough thrashing to larn her to be a toad'; this was not his view.[65]

Two intermediaries offered themselves as 'discreeter channels', but although both Axel Wenner-Gren and Birger Dahlerus stressed British determination to their patron, Goering, neither man brought an Anglo-German entente much closer.[66] A more promising source was the press baron, Lord Kemsley, who saw

Hitler in late July and told him that he would 'never understand England unless you think of Neville Chamberlain as our Führer'. Hitler expressed his contempt for the subject of the Hudson-Wohltat talks – 'Germany was not after money' – but did suggest that Britain and Germany might each put their 'demands on paper, and that this might lead to a discussion'; he also mentioned that he would want Germany's colonies and the cancellation of the Treaty of Versailles.[67]

Chamberlain saw Kemsley on 31 July and later, after consultation with Halifax and Wilson, decided to follow up this approach – making it clear that 'we regarded the suggestion as indicating a German initiative'.[68] 'His' letter, which Kemsley passed on to the Reich press chief, Otto Dietrich, asked Hitler for a statement of exactly what it was he wanted. Dietrich doubted whether Hitler had suggested that both sides should 'put down' their desiderata, but promised to pass the letter on to the Führer.[69]

Meanwhile, Butler's efforts bore some fruit. Through his friend Lord Brocket, Butler arranged to see Theodor Kordt of the German Embassy on 2 August. Kordt wanted to know whether 'we [would] recognise a German lebensraum in Eastern Europe if they indicated some quietude by some concrete act', and whether the Germans were to regard the conversations with Wohltat as 'meaning anything'.[70] Chamberlain thought that they ought to follow this up by Wilson seeing Kordt, but, to no one's great surprise, it was the Ambassador himself, Dirksen, who turned up on Wilson's doorstep the following morning.[71]

It is perhaps evidence of the desire of the German emissaries to cover themselves against allegations of having gone too far, as well as of a wish to convince the Führer that negotiations should be opened with Chamberlain, that both Wohltat and Dirksen should have represented Wilson, in their official records, as having presented them with a detailed programme of items to be discussed.[72] Wilson's own accounts make it clear that he stuck to Chamberlain's line that any fresh negotiations were entirely dependent upon the 'pre-restoration of the confidence that had been shattered in March' and that some announcement 'on a grand scale' by Hitler was necessary. Chamberlain's view was that 'the wise course would be to keep the movement alive if the Germans wished that to be the case', and he suggested that they might draw up a 'hypothetical agenda' for use in such circumstances.[73]

The Prime Minister was careful to keep these contacts secret, and, somewhat against his will, he kept his lines to Moscow open. On 25 July the Government decided to concede the Soviet demand for immediate military conversations and, on 5 August, a military mission, headed by Admiral Sir Reginald Plunkett-Ernle-Erle Drax, left for Moscow.[74] Chamberlain's reservations about the Russians were, it transpired, as accurate as his convictions about Hitler's state of mind were wrong.

Throughout the period of the Anglo-French-Soviet negotiations there had been rumours of German-Soviet talks.[75] On 4 July Henderson told Cadogan that he felt 'intuitively that the Germans are getting at Stalin',[76] and on 22 July the Soviets announced that 'negotiations with regard to trade and credit' had been renewed with Germany.[77] The Germans had not been blind to the possible implications of Litvinov's dismissal in early May, and on 18 May Ribbentrop had authorised his Ambassador in Moscow to suggest that economic talks might be opened. This Molotov had welcomed, but his suggestion that 'political bases' must be established showed Hitler that his guesses had been correct: the Soviets were on offer to the highest bidder.[78] Given the fact that the Western Powers could never offer Stalin what Hitler could – that is carte blanche in the Baltic republics; and given that, thanks to 'sources' in the Foreign Office, the Germans were aware of the full details of the British atittude, it was an unequal struggle.

Suggestions that the stories of the Hudson-Wohltat talks convinced Stalin to press ahead with economic talks with Germany will not hold water.[79] The Soviets had already communicated their agreement to Germany on 18 July,[80] and, in any case, Stalin was aware that Hitler had decided to settle the Polish question by force – and that his timetable set the end of August as the last date by which he could hope to start a successful war.[81] The Russian dictator was thus in a position to ensure that the wicked capitalist powers did not direct Hitler in his way by promising the Führer territorial concessions which the Western Allies could not. As Butler had feared, the Polish guarantee had given the Russians room for manœuvre – and they had seized it adroitly. As on previous occasions Chamberlain's critics queered their own pitch, as suggestions like Lloyd George's that the 'Chamberlain clique' was aiming at an agreement with the Germans[82] could only help strengthen the arguments inside the Kremlin for a deal with Hitler.

It was precisely such suspicions that, once Parliament was in recess, Chamberlain would 'do another Munich' which prompted Churchill to support an Opposition motion that Parliament should reconvene on 21 August; he could not, he said in the debate on 2 August, trust the Prime Minister's judgment.[83] Chamberlain could not resist the obvious '*tu quoque*' retort, as Churchill's lack of judgment had been notorious in the Commons for thirty-odd years; this annoyed Churchill 'so much that he actually went out of his way to associate himself with Sinclair's fatuous and imbecile proposition that if Parliament had met earlier last September we could have ... saved the independence of Czecho-Slovakia'.[84]

The Adullamites had been as divided as ever upon how to react to the opposition motion. Churchill's hard line met with no favour in Eden's eyes.[85]

This had come as little surprise to the increasingly disillusioned Nicolson, who had already concluded that 'Anthony does not wish to defy the Tory party and is in fact missing every boat with exquisite elegance'.[86] But Chamberlain's reaction to his opponents in what, Hitler permitting, looked increasingly like the election year, was such as to make Eden's moderation understandable. He was quite prepared to envisage the loss of Conservative seats at Odiham and King's Norton if it meant that 'disloyal members of the team' such as Wolmer and Ronald Cartland were removed from the House;[87] indeed, so much did he resent Cartland's personal attack on him in the debate on 2 August that he decided to take steps to 'stimulate local opposition' to him.[88] If the summer passed, as Chamberlain hoped, with a few alarums and excursions and no wars, there would be an election in the autumn.

The prospect of a general election posed problems for those who had opposed Chamberlain's foreign policy. Eden encapsulated the dilemma he and his friends faced in a letter to Jim Thomas on 12 August: they could hardly stand under Chamberlain's banner but 'what then should our attitude be?' They could 'form a group of our own', 'stand as independent Conservatives', or they could, perhaps, 'seek to create a new Party' – although the question of 'what should our relations be with Winston' would need answering by then.[89] Churchill, convinced that the problem would not arise because war would come first, took himself off to see the Maginot Line.

At the last meeting of the Cabinet before the recess Halifax had 'nothing of importance to report' regarding Danzig. Indeed, he reminded his colleagues that, although it was often stated that 'we were committed to fight for Danzig', the 'true position' was that 'Danzig, of itself, should not be regarded as providing a casus belli'; it was only 'if a threat to Polish independence arose from Danzig' that 'this country would clearly become involved'.[90] If the 'menacing silence' had worked, then the prospect held out by the Kemsley initiative might yet lead to peace; but if Hitler tried force at Danzig, 'it will mean starting the European war'.[91]

Chamberlain's War

When Chamberlain made the Polish guarantee in March, he did not see it as leading inevitably to war; indeed, he saw it as the first step towards constructing a deterrent. By the end of July he believed that he had constructed a 'peace front' which might well deter the Führer, and while a Russian alliance would be a useful addition to this, it was not essential. During August the deterrent was weighed in the balance and, in order that it should not be found totally wanting, it proved necessary to declare war. But, if Chamberlain lost faith in Hitler's unwillingness to hazard all on the chance of war, he did not abandon hope that, once the Polish campaign was over, there would be no more war, that in the face of a stalemate in the west, the Germans would either suffer economic collapse or a sudden accession of common sense: not until May 1940 did the Prime Minister abandon his faith that the deterrent power of defence would spare Europe the horrors of the war which he had striven so hard to avoid.

With the Commons in recess, the Prime Minister did not let prophecies of an August crisis prevent him from going off to the wilds of Scotland to enjoy the salmon fishing. By 13 August he had been at Lairg for almost a week 'without my being called back', but he did not anticipate that he would be granted another week's leisure.[1] Nor was he. Two days later he received an anxious letter from Halifax describing the crisis that seemed to be breaking in Danzig,[2] and on 19 August he received an urgent letter summoning him to London.[3] The time of trial had come.

On 4 August the Poles had delivered a stern warning to the Danzig senate about the consequences of its reported decision to refuse to recognise Polish customs officers and to open the border with East Prussia, but a denial of any such intention seemed to bring the crisis to an end.[4] But Beck's triumph provoked Hitler to action. His failure to crack the nerves of the Poles in the way he had the previous year with the Czechs he put down to what he saw as unwarranted British interference, and he now determined to tighten the screw; he could not believe, despite the 'menacing silence', that when faced with the prospect of war the British would die for Danzig.[5] On 10 August the Poles were handed a note of protest from Berlin about their 'ultimatum' to the Danzig senate and warned that any deterioration in Polish-German relations which resulted would be their responsibility.[6]

Beck's response was a firm rejection of any German right to interfere – and a request to Halifax for the conclusion of the long-postponed Anglo-Polish alliance and a 'preventative démarche' by Britain and France in Berlin. Halifax was not enamoured of the indefinite extension of British commitments to Poland and thought that 'we must (however we do it!) make it plain that our guarantee was not a blank cheque'; a suitable warning was sent to Warsaw on 12 August.[7] Cadogan, who did not think it was the moment to make a 'preventative démarche' in Berlin, preferred to await the outcome of the talk which Hitler was to have with Carl Burckhardt, the League's Commissioner in Danzig, on 11 August.[8] It was the results of this conversation which prompted Halifax's letter on 14 August to Chamberlain.

Hitler's attitude towards the Poles had been highly belligerent and, when confronted by Burckhardt with the prospect of this leading to general war, Hitler's response had been: 'So be it. If I have to wage war, I would rather do it today than tomorrow.' He wanted, he said, 'a free hand in the East', but expressed a willingness to 'conclude a definitive pact' with the English with whom he wanted 'to live in peace'; he was, he said, willing to talk 'with an Englishman who knows German' as a way of avoiding the 'catastrophe' which loomed.[9] The idea interested Halifax, but, as he told Chamberlain, 'apart from the difficulty of finding the individual, I find it a bit difficult to imagine what he would say'; if Hitler 'really wants to annex land in the East on which he can settle Germans and grow wheat, I confess I don't see any way of accommodating him'. 'Things', Halifax warned, 'do not look too good and a good deal of talk is going on about very early action being taken. It may so turn out but we have, of course, heard it before.'[10]

The British were now in a delicate situation. The Polish request for an alliance was, as it had been since March, on ice pending the conclusion of a pact with the Soviets that had still not been concluded. But even before the arrival of the military mission on 11 August there had been signs that might have been taken for omens. On 3 August Molotov had, at a time when he was considering coming to a deal with Hitler that would destroy the Baltic states' independence, chosen to take offence at Butler's remarks in the Commons a few days earlier that the question of the independence of the Baltic states was the one obstacle in the way of an alliance.[11] Seeds, who had seen this as a 'major set-back', was

THE OLD SEA-DOG
'Any telegram for me?'
Opinion turns to Churchill, 12 July 1939.

appalled when it transpired that Drax's instructions were to 'go slowly' until the political aspects of the negotiations were complete, and he argued strongly against this line.[12]

Even as the Foreign Office debated and agreed to Seeds' request, they were being outflanked. On 14 August the German Ambassador in Moscow was told to prepare the way for a visit to Russia by Ribbentrop; a Nazi-Soviet pact was essential for Hitler if Chamberlain's bluff was to be called.[13] On 15 August Seeds was authorised to proceed as swiftly as possible towards the conclusion of an agreement, but Molotov, with the Germans almost in his pocket, insisted that any Anglo-Soviet deal must involve Poland and Romania opening their borders to the Red Army. To this Beck steadfastly refused to agree.[14]

From Berlin Henderson, who still doubted whether Hitler intended to go to war, reported on 16 August that German military preparations were being 'stepped up'. It was, he told Halifax, 'just like last year, everything is ready for all eventualities'; he was 'hoping for the best whilst expecting the worst'.[15] Vansittart's sources told him that 'the worst' was primed for 25–28 August, but whilst thinking that he was 'the first casualty' of the 'war of nerves', Cadogan summoned Halifax to London and drafted a letter for the Prime Minister.[16]

Cadogan felt that although the rumours of imminent German action might or might not be true, there would be some merit in making one final attempt to convince Hitler that any move against Danzig would result in war.[17] Henderson had suggested that Chamberlain might either send a letter, or an emissary such as General Ironside, to see the Führer; the Prime Minister was firmly in favour of the former. But even as Cadogan, Halifax, Chamberlain and Wilson were working on it, news came through on 22 August that a Nazi-Soviet pact had been signed.[18] The letter was despatched that evening after being approved by the Cabinet. Its intention was to prevent a repetition of what was alleged to have been Sir Edward Grey's mistake in 1914, leaving Germany in ignorance of Britain's intention to fight.[19] But as Hitler had just avoided the Kaiser's mistake of risking a war on two fronts, it was doubtful how much effect it would have.

The British Government was caught totally by surprise. Although there had been persistent rumours of Soviet-German contacts, no one had supposed they would have such a result.[20] Any embarrassment which Churchill and Lloyd George may have felt at the actions of 'the Bear' was redirected as anger at Chamberlain for giving a guarantee to Poland without first obtaining Soviet help.[21] Whatever view was taken, it seemed that Henderson was right to say that 'with the Russian pact in his hand the initiative is now Hitler's'.[22]

The Führer was, accordingly, in an uncompromising mood when he saw Henderson on 23 August, and his response to Chamberlain's letter showed that he was ready for a general war. The British Ambassador, convinced that his mission had ended in failure, thought that, short of the Poles agreeing to negotiate, there was nothing that could be done:[23] '*Intimidation*', he told Halifax on 24 August, 'will not deter him and it is useless to think it will.'[24]

But Chamberlain shared neither Henderson's fears nor his view that they could not 'leave the Poles in the lurch, tho' we have, I fear, led them up the garden path'.[25] The Prime Minister's speech to the Commons on 24 August emphasised what Henderson had told Hitler the previous day – Britain did not want war, but she would stand by Poland.[26] Although MPs approved of his statement, the Adullamites remained suspicious of Chamberlain's intentions, whilst Channon thought that most of his colleagues were 'secretly' hoping that 'the Poles will climb down',[27] and, like Butler and Henderson, saw this as the only way of avoiding war.[28]

The 'worst trial' for the Prime Minister came the following lunchtime when he heard that Hitler had sent for Henderson to see him at 1.30 p.m. Was this the ultimatum that would lead to war? As the hours crawled by this appeared unlikely, and a telephone call to Berlin elicited the news that Hitler had put forward a 'proposal which we might think was an attempt to drive a wedge between us and Poland'; Henderson was flying back to London for consultation. By the time both the Ambassador's telegrams reporting his conversation with Hitler had been decyphered it was after midnight and Chamberlain, who had refused to 'sit up' for them, had gone 'to bed and to sleep!'[29]

The despatches which awaited him after breakfast on 26 August hardly indicated that Hitler was going to launch an assault on Danzig later that day. The Führer had certainly intended to do this when he saw Henderson on 23 August, but since then Chamberlain's firm stand and Mussolini's vacillations had combined to make him change his mind.[30] Hitler's message was certainly well-calculated to appeal both to those who partook of the Henderson/Channon view of Poland, as well as to those who regarded the Polish guarantee as 'a grave tactical blunder and a betrayal of national interests'.[31] Declaring that 'the German-Polish problem must be solved', he also professed his desire for 'an Anglo-German understanding' in which he would guarantee the British Empire in return for colonial and other concessions.[32]

If Hitler had hoped to provoke a debate between those who took the Henderson/Channon line on Poland, and those who did not, he was successful. Harvey thought it was 'the most impudent document that I have ever seen', a view endorsed by Cadogan, whose draft reply was 'an exercise in brutality'.[33] But Halifax was less dismissive, as was Butler, who deplored the Foreign Office 'inhibition' against putting any pressure on the Poles to come to terms with Germany,[34] and regarded the only 'alternative to war' as 'a German-British agreement including Colonies AND a reasonable Polish settlement'; he contemplated without distaste the prospect of any attempt to 'secure a Danzig agreement' ending up as a 'final revision of the Versailles Treaty with the aid of Mussolini'.[35]

When Cadogan went round to Downing Street on the morning of 26 August, he found that Halifax was unwilling to use his draft, preferring instead the version which Wilson and Butler drew up after lunch whilst he sat with the Prime Minister and the Foreign Secretary on a bench in the garden.[37] Harvey, who thought both men were 'working like beavers' for a Polish 'Munich',[38] described the product of their collaboration as 'very flabby',[39] a view endorsed by Cadogan, who relied upon the Cabinet to stiffen it up.[40]

Both Chamberlain and Halifax were alive to the danger that Hitler was trying to split Britain and Poland, but since the two countries had signed an alliance on the 25th, they could discount it on that score. The fact that the Führer had made the proposals at all rather than attacking Poland on 26 August, as all the rumours had said he would, seemed in itself significant and, when combined with fresh overtures from Goering via Dahlerus, indicated, at the least, that Hitler 'had not quite made up his mind'.[41]

The process of drafting a reply to Hitler's suggestions turned out to be a long one. When the Cabinet met on the evening of 26 August, Ministers fulfilled Cadogan's hopes by damning the Butler/Wilson draft as 'somewhat too deferential' and as treating Hitler's suggestions 'with somewhat too much respect'. But at the same time as wanting to take a 'firm' line, Ministers also wanted to be 'moderate' and to explore the possibilities of Poland being able to open bilateral talks with Germany on the 'minorities question'.[42] The final draft was not ready until 28 August, but the delay was not without purpose.

It was clear from both the Ambassador in Rome, Sir Percy Loraine, and Henderson that the Nazi-Soviet pact had disrupted the Rome–Berlin axis.[43] News from Goerdeler suggested that the German army was not ready for war, and the impression that Hitler 'has cold feet' was furthered by the constant messages from Dahlerus.[44] In these circumstances, as even Churchill recognised,[45] there was everything to be said for 'playing it long' and giving time for 'world opinion to show itself and to isolate the man or nation that would destroy the peace'. Chamberlain hoped that when Hitler realised that the pact with Russia had not, in fact, destroyed the 'peace front', but rather lost him Italian and Japanese support, he would draw back from the brink.[46]

In this atmosphere there was clearly no point in either hurrying or in appearing to 'wobble' oneself. Britain's determination to stand by Poland was emphasised to Dahlerus as was her desire to see Polish-German negotiations open;[47] the latter point was supported by Mussolini,[48] and both of them were highlighted in the British reply to Hitler's proposals which were taken to Berlin by Henderson on 28 August. The question of Anglo-German relations was, Hitler was told, separate from Polish-German relations, and progress in them depended upon a peaceful settlement of the latter.[49]

Although the terms of the final British reply indicated that neither retreat nor surrender was in prospect, rumours of the Butler/Wilson draft aroused the 'witch-finding' instincts of Chamberlain's opponents. Churchill telephoned the Polish Ambassador, only to be told that Beck was satisfied with 'the support he was receiving', and Vansittart assured Bracken that 'our note to Hitler was everything that could be desired'.[50] Beck was willing to open negotiations,[51] and as Henderson told the Führer when he saw him on the night he arrived back in Berlin, 'he had to choose between friendship with England which we offered him and excessive demands on Poland which would put an end to all hope of British friendship'.[52]

Henderson, who successfully elicited from Hitler that his minimum demands were the return of Danzig, the Corridor and parts of Silesia, was 'not unhopeful' that when he had had time to consider the British reply and the request that he should open discussions with the Poles, his 'answer may not be too unreasonable'; if that was so, 'we shall have to be no less firm with the Poles'.[53] Even Vansittart had to admit that Henderson had carried out his task admirably – though he cavilled at his mentioning the prospect of an Anglo-German alliance.[54] In fact, had it not been for Cadogan, Chamberlain would have been willing to have offered Hitler a 'non-aggression pact';[55] the reappearance of the idea was unwelcome, and Henderson was warned not to repeat it.[56]

Halifax was not, as he assured both Harvey and Kirkpatrick on 27 August, planning to 'rat on the Poles'. One purpose of the British guarantee had been to prevent Hitler from browbeating the Poles as he had the Austrians and Czechs. Halifax's plan was to 'get into negotiation and then be very stiff' – 'and then Hitler would be beat'.[57] The information passed by Dahlerus from Goering seemed to give some hope that this strategy might succeed, but when Hitler saw Henderson on the evening of 29 August the dictator was 'far less reasonable' than on the previous day. During a 'stormy' interview, Hitler declared that he could 'not sacrifice Germany's vital interests' for British friendship. Although willing to talk to the Poles, he did not think that negotiations would succeed.[58]

Henderson responded to Hitler's outbursts with 'a dose of his own medicine'. It was not 'the duty of a British representative to shout', but on this occasion, when Hitler raved that the British did not care about all the poor Germans being killed in Danzig, Henderson 'fairly let him have it'. This was not merely to 'satisfy a long-felt want', but also in the hope that it would have a 'salutary' effect.[59]

The gloom which reigned in Whitehall, when the first accounts of the interview came in gave way to a more optimistic attitude as Hitler's terms were decyphered and it became clear that they were not as bad as had been thought.[60] The Germans were willing to open talks with the Poles and accepted Britain's 'good offices in securing the despatch to Berlin of a Polish Emissary with full powers', and they disclaimed 'any intention of touching Poland's vital interests or questioning the existence of an independent Polish State'.[61] When the Cabinet met on the morning of 30 August it was felt that, although Hitler's attitude was deplorable, his terms did not preclude further efforts to save peace. But the one thing Chamberlain would not accept was the demand for an immediate despatch of a 'Polish Emissary' to Berlin – that savoured too much of the 'old technique'.[62]

The latest information from Dahlerus suggested that rumours about Germany's economic problems hindering her military effort might be justified, and that Hitler might be willing to accept a plebiscite at Danzig and a reasonable method of negotiation.[63] Certainly, given Polish fears of being treated like the Czechs, this last was a major consideration.[64] The British reply, which was handed to Ribbentrop at midnight on 30 August by Henderson, emphasised these points and asked for both sides to refrain from any provocative actions whilst proposals were formulated.[65] But when the British Ambassador suggested that Germany should negotiate in a more normal manner with Poland, Ribbentrop's reply was to produce 'a lengthy document which he read out in German aloud at top speed'. Henderson asked for the text of these proposals, only to be told that, as the Germans had heard nothing from the Poles, 'it was now too late'.[66]

Had it not been for 'the seriousness of the situation' Henderson would have walked out; as it was, he now regarded the situation as 'nearly hopeless'. But he could still hardly bring himself to abandon the attempt to avoid war, and pointed out in a letter to Halifax on 31 August that the German proposals, as far as he understood them, did not actually threaten Poland's independence.[67] At 2 a.m. he put this view to Lipski, the Polish Ambassador,[68] and, after a short sleep, he spent the rest of the day trying to get him to start negotiations,[69] even urging Halifax to put pressure upon Beck.[70] But the Poles would have none of it: 'It would be fatal for M. Beck or a Polish representative to come to Berlin. We must for Heaven's sake stand firm and show a united front and Poland if deserted by her allies was prepared to fight and die alone. This German offer was a trap.'[71]

The British had no intention of 'deserting' the Poles. Ciano's efforts to mediate, first by suggesting that if the Poles would concede Danzig, Mussolini would convene a conference on the other outstanding questions, and then asking if the British and French Governments would agree to a conference on 5 September to revise the Versailles settlement, foundered on the rock of

British determination not to be seen to be putting undue pressure on the Poles.[72] Beck was the beneficiary of Beneš' calvary. When Lipski did see Ribbentrop just after 1 o'clock on 31 August, he reported that he was willing to negotiate, but had brought no proposals with him. When he tried to telephone the news to Warsaw, he discovered that his telephone lines had been cut.[73]

Neither Chamberlain nor Beck actually possessed a copy of Hitler's 'sixteen points', but late that night they were able to pick them up on German radio, which claimed that the Poles had had two days in which to consider them.[74] Halifax sent a telegram advising Beck to get hold of the sixteen points through Lipski.[75] Shortly before 5 a.m. on 1 September the German army crossed the Polish frontier, which saved Beck's response to Halifax from sounding churlish.

Halifax saw the Polish Ambassador, Count Raczynski, at 10.30 a.m. and, in reply to his statement that the German action 'was a plain case as provided for by the treaty', said that 'I had no doubt on the facts as he had reported them that we should take the same view'.[76] Certainly, when a weary and disappointed Chamberlain opened the Cabinet meeting an hour later, 'under the gravest possible condition', he assumed that the 'event against which we had fought so long and so earnestly had come upon us'; but with 'clear' consciences there could 'be no possible question now where our duty lay'.[77] But there were 'three complications' to an outright declaration of war: the efforts of Goering, via Dahlerus, to localise the war with Poland; Mussolini's attempts to secure a re-run of Munich; and the 'French anxiety to postpone the actual declaration as long as possible until they could evacuate their women and children and mobilise their armies'.[78]

Dalherus rang the Foreign Office from Berlin whilst the Cabinet was still in session and said that the Führer still wanted to discuss matters. The news was passed on to Halifax, who had just secured the agreement of his colleagues to the terms of a stern warning to Hitler, and no one was in any mood to compromise. It was agreed that their reply should be 'stiff and should stress the fact that the only way in which a world war could be stopped would be if the German troops left Polish territory and hostilities were suspended'; no hope was to be held out that 'we should act as mediators between Germany and Poland'.[79]

The Chiefs of Staff thought that Britain ought to deliver an ultimatum which expired at midnight, but that brought up the question of concerting action with the French who, in order to avoid the appearance of being 'dragged into war by us', wanted to make their declaration first. Halifax thought that the two countries should act together and the Cabinet agreed. This was to cause Chamberlain great problems, for by the afternoon Bonnet had telephoned to say that the French could neither declare war nor sanction an ultimatum until after Parliament had met on the morrow.[80]

Thus, when Chamberlain spoke to the Commons that evening, he was unable to announce either that an ultimatum was being delivered or that war would be declared.[81] The Prime Minister's obvious 'moral agony', as he reminded MPs that 'eighteen months ago in this House I prayed that the responsibility might not fall upon me to ask this country to accept the awful arbitrament of war', won him 'deep sympathy', but the lack of action to suit the words of the rest of the speech aroused bewilderment amongst Adullamites and others.[82] This was stilled somewhat by the news that Churchill had been invited to join the Cabinet, but suspicions of another 'Munich' remained – and were fanned into flames by the events of the morrow.

Chamberlain's position was a difficult one, but any expectations he may have had that the French would make it easier for him next time he faced the House were disappointed by Bonnet's insistence on 2 September that any ultimatum must have a two-day time-limit. The reasons for this became apparent to Halifax when Ciano telephoned him just before he was due to go to the Lords. The Italians had secured Hitler's assent to the idea of holding a conference, and Bonnet had, it seemed, gone along with the idea – 'rather too far', Cadogan suspected. Halifax expressed interest, but stressed that the Germans would have to withdraw from Poland. As Ciano did not think that the Germans would agree to this, his proposal was, in effect, a non-starter.[83]

But the fact that Hitler was prepared to listen to the idea of a conference, provided the Anglo-French note was not an ultimatum, meant that it was necessary to stop the statements which were due to be made in both Houses that afternoon. Halifax postponed his own appearance and then went with Harvey to stop Sir John Simon from delivering Chamberlain's statement.[84] Given his reputation as an arch-appeaser, no more inappropriate person than Simon could have been found to announce to the House that 'the Prime Minister will be coming down . . . later in the sitting'. In the long wait that followed, rumours of all descriptions circulated, but the most persistent concerned Mussolini's attempt at mediation and Bonnet's 'unsatisfactory' attitude.[85] Speculation mounted when, towards 4.30 p.m., there was a '*sauve qui peut* from the Front Bench' as its occupants left the Chamber; 'the House at once sensed something was afoot'.[86]

After stopping Simon's statement Halifax had gone to see Chamberlain at No. 10, where he telephoned Bonnet. The Frenchman said he had 'hedged' with Ciano; on the first of his questions, whether the Anglo-French note delivered in Berlin the previous day was an ultimatum, he had 'replied in the affirmative'; but he had equivocated on the subject of whether the Germans could have until noon on 3 September to answer it. Chamberlain thought that Ciano's proposals were important enough to summon an emergency Cabinet – hence the unseemly scramble from the front bench. By the time Ministers assembled at 4.30, Chamberlain and Halifax had reached some tentative conclusions.[87]

After outlining the reasons for calling the Cabinet, Halifax told his colleagues that they proposed to make a statement in the Commons to the effect that Henderson's message had not been an ultimatum and that the Germans could have until noon on the morrow to answer it; but 'the primary condition for any conference would be that German troops should first withdraw from Polish soil'. Although the last point met with universal assent – thus, in effect, negating Ciano's initiative since he thought it unlikely that the Germans would agree to it – there was fierce argument over the proposal to postpone the time-limit. Hoare warned about the possible effect on public opinion, Kingsley Wood about the effects of delay upon the Poles, and their protests were taken up by Hore-Belisha, Oliver Stanley, Malcolm MacDonald, Leslie Burgin and Walter Elliot; the arrival in the middle of the meeting of a message from the Poles requesting 'the immediate fulfilment of British obligations' added weight both to their case and their anger.

The Cabinet agreed to let Chamberlain and Halifax draft a statement. Further telephone calls to Paris produced more arguments from Bonnet in favour of delay, but finally a joint Anglo-French statement was agreed upon.[88] By the time Chamberlain rose to make his statement at 7.45 p.m. the lobbies were alive with rumours that the French were 'ratting'.[89] If Channon, Butler and Dunglass were hugging themselves with thoughts that 'peace might again be saved, as by a miracle, by Italian intervention', the Adullamites were in a deeply suspicious mood. Chamberlain's statement unleashed 'all the resentment' which his opponents had been storing up for so long and precipitated a major crisis.[90]

According to Amery, the announcement that Britain and France were still considering what time-limit to attach to their note to Hitler when the Poles had been under attack for two days 'staggered' the House. When Arthur Greenwood rose from the Opposition benches, Amery 'could not help . . . shouting to him to "Speak for England"'.[91] His restrained yet effective criticism of the delay brought Chamberlain to his feet again to explain the need to keep in step with the French, but his statement that he did not think the French were weakening merely created further doubts.

Writing to his sisters on 10 September, Chamberlain described what happened next as 'a sort of mutiny' 'got up' by 'a certain number of my colleagues . . . who always behave badly when there is any trouble'.[92] After the session Simon had found himself the focus of Cabinet discontent: at a meeting held in his room, disgruntled Ministers declared 'a strike'.[93] Impressed by the vehemence of feeling expressed, Simon reported their opinions to the Prime Minister, adding that he shared them. Faced with this revolt on top of what had just occurred in the Commons, Chamberlain had no option but to agree to see the disgruntled Ministers.

They came in 'looking very sullen'. For all their protest that Chamberlain's statement had been different from what had been agreed at Cabinet, it had not, in fact, been so. But Chamberlain did not make that point, perhaps realising that what they were really protesting about was that the warnings which had been given earlier about 'public opinion' had proved correct. He explained to them the problems which the French attitude was causing, and afterwards Simon delivered a letter to him stating that 'our view was that in no circumstances should the expiry of the ultimatum go beyond 12 noon tomorrow' – and that even this was only a concession to allow the French to come into line. Chamberlain asked Simon to see him at Downing Street at 10 o'clock and let him put his view to the French Ambassador, Corbin. Whilst Simon did so, Chamberlain rang Daladier to tell him that if the French insisted upon further delays, 'it would be impossible for the Government to hold the situation here'.[94] Another Cabinet was summoned for 11.30.

Chamberlain explained to his disgruntled and suspicious colleagues that, after prolonged argument with Daladier and Bonnet, the Frenchmen had been told that unless they agreed to an ultimatum being delivered the following morning and expiring at noon, the British would have to go ahead alone. This defused the tension, and discussion focused around the harmless topic of exactly when the British ultimatum should be delivered; it was finally agreed that Henderson should present it at 9 a.m., and that if Hitler had not replied by 11 o'clock that he was willing to withdraw his troops from Poland, war would be declared.[95]

One 'Minister' who was present at none of these meetings was Churchill. Disgruntled at having heard nothing from Chamberlain during the day, he was urged by an angry Boothby to 'break him and take his place'. But Churchill was too canny for that, and preferred to write a restrained letter asking the Prime Minister to 'let me know how we stand, both publicly and privately' before the House reconvened at noon on 3 September.[96]

Ministers left Downing Street in the middle of a torrential thunderstorm. Channon, 'broken-hearted' at the disappearance of the last hope, 'begged David Margesson to do something', only to receive the reply, 'It must be War, Chips old boy. There's no other way out.'[97] The scenes in the Commons and the reaction of the Cabinet to them had convinced the Chief Whip, and his words proved accurate.

When Cadogan arrived at Downing Street on the morning of 3 September with Halifax, there had been no reply to the British ultimatum. At 11.15 the Prime Minister spoke to the nation. 'You can imagine', he said in a voice which conveyed the agony he was suffering more than any words could, 'what a bitter blow it is to me that all my long struggle to win peace has failed.' At noon he went to the Commons. He read the British ultimatum and, after announcing that there had been no reply to it, he said 'consequently, this country is at war with Germany'. This then was where it all ended: 'everything that I have worked for, everything that I have believed in during my public life has crashed into ruins'.[98]

The Prime Minister was speaking no more than the truth.

Epilogue

'Good, but not the speech of a war leader,' was Amery's verdict on Chamberlain's speech. He thought Churchill would be Prime Minister by the end of the year; if it took slightly longer, then Amery had at least the dubious consolation of being right on the first point.[1] Indeed, Chamberlain would have agreed with him, for almost the only crumb of comfort he found in the whole 'nightmare' was to reflect that although he had been 'indispensable' before war broke out because 'no one else could carry out my policy', the position had now changed: 'Half a dozen people could take my place.' Until the time came to make peace, he did not 'see that I have any particular part to play'.[2]

The prospect of all the human suffering that war would bring horrified Chamberlain, and the war he sought to wage differed but little from the policy he had attempted to pursue before 3 September. He could not bring himself to believe that the war would last very long, and he did not look for a 'military victory – I very much doubt the feasibility of that' – but rather for a 'collapse of the German home front'. In other words, it was necessary to continue to remain firm until the Germans saw the obvious – that in modern war the defensive side had the advantage.[3] Upon this hope rested all the strategy of the Chamberlain Government.

'Time', Chamberlain believed, 'is with us.'[4] 'Hold on tight, keep up the economic pressure, push on with munitions production and military preparations with the utmost energy', but 'take no offensive unless Hitler begins it', was Chamberlain's recipe for victory.[5] The longer Hitler took to make his offensive in the west, the less chance he would have of pulling it off. In the meantime, it was necessary to guard against 'peace offensives', which were much 'the most effective way' of Hitler achieving his objectives.[6]

The Foreign Office was, naturally, suspicious of any of Hitler's 'peace offers'. Apart from the nature of any such proposals, the 'deepest point of difficulty', as Halifax put it in late September, was 'what assurance anyone can possibly have that any undertakings accepted would be observed'.[7] Chamberlain himself was slightly more encouraging, but his sine qua non was that 'Hitler himself shall play no part in the proposed new order'. In return for this, and for a restoration of frontiers and disarmament, Chamberlain was prepared to agree to 'economic assistance for Germany, to no demands for reparations, and to Colonial discussions'.[8]

There were still moments when his despair broke out: 'How I hate and loathe this war. I was never meant to be a War Minister';[9] but for the most part he took what comfort there was in the fact that his diagnosis of the course of the war seemed to be turning out correctly.[10]

Chamberlain's main problem in Cabinet was with the one colleague who did not share his assumptions about the course of the war – Churchill. Although, on a personal level, his relations with the former chief Adullamite were good, Churchill's incessant talk at Cabinets and his habit of writing interminably long letters which, Chamberlain correctly suspected, were 'for quotation in the Book that he will write hereafter', created a certain amount of tension.[11] This was exacerbated by a bellicose broadcast given by Churchill in November, which Butler thought 'beyond words vulgar'[12] and which the Prime Minister considered had done 'incalculable harm' in alienating neutral powers. But he continued to pay the 'heavy price' which Churchill's inclusion in the Cabinet exacted.[13]

The price was higher than Chamberlain could have anticipated. Churchill's war was not Chamberlain's; he wanted action, not a long wait. But when the action came in April it was disastrous, and the Narvik campaign proved the prelude to the parliamentary revolt which broke the Prime Minister's hold on power. But, as that revolt coincided with Hitler's offensive in the west and the start of a war that was bound to be different from the one Chamberlain had planned for, there was a seemliness in his departure. As he recognised:

> I could not have made any radical reconstruction of my Government because there was not sufficient new material in my Party and moreover in the more active phase of the war I feel that Winston is the right man for the head in view of his experience and study of war.[14]

The suddenness of his fall from power, as well as the manner of it, were 'very painful' for such a proud man, but Chamberlain, unlike Asquith in the last war, stayed on to help the new Prime Minister.[15] Indeed, his help was essential. Chamberlain remained leader of the Conservative Party and thus of the largest element in the National Coalition, and many Conservatives, who had abstained in the crucial vote on 8 May, took the view on reflection that they had perhaps been rather harsh on their leader.[16] Churchill needed Chamberlain's help and he got it – but not for long.

Apart from the odd crippling attack of gout, Chamberlain's health had stood up to the strain of the last year of his premiership remarkably well – particularly for a man in his seventies. Indeed, writing to his sisters in February 1940 he commented that he could not 'help reflecting how much more easily I carry it [the strain of office] than Father did when he was several years younger than I'.[17] But, after the great fall of May, he began to feel tired, and by July was writing that, 'I have lost my spring and my spirits'; with no 'country pursuits' any more, and the gnawing problem of how the war was to be won, the pleasure went out of life.[18] This proved the preliminary sign of the cancer that was to kill him.

On 26 July Chamberlain informed the Prime Minister of his condition and of the fact that he might need to resign if a second operation was necessary. Churchill, gracious in such situations, and also conscious of how much he needed Chamberlain, told him to take as much time off as he liked – but to remain in the Cabinet.[19] But the operations were not, and could not be, a success. By early September Chamberlain was mentally adjusting himself to the 'life of an invalid'[20] and, on 22 September, he wrote to Churchill offering him his resignation.[21] Churchill accepted it on 29 September and offered him the Garter the following day;[22] but he preferred to 'die plain "Mr Chamberlain" like my father before me'.[23] On 9 November he did just that.

Chamberlain had feared that history, written by those who had replaced him, might judge him harshly, and he was correct.[24] But not even the edifice erected by Churchill could survive unscathed that opening of the records which, Chamberlain hoped, would explain his policy. The 'Guilty Men' syndrome has run its course, and Chamberlain's reputation stands better now than it has ever done – and the flood of books which will mark the fiftieth anniversary of 1939 will revive it still more. The venom of his opponents pursued him long, but his was the only policy which offered any hope of avoiding war – and of saving both lives and the British Empire. Butler wrote of Chamberlain: 'I looked upon him as the last leader of the organisation in the State which I joined very late in its life, but which had been responsible for so much of England's greatness.'[25] Under his successor the 'greatness' would be lost – and the Party was never the same again – but that is another story.

NOTES

Place of publication is London unless otherwise stated.

Prologue

1. Neville Chamberlain MSS, Birmingham University Library, NC 2/24A, Chamberlain's diary, 4 October 1940.

Chapter 1

1. *Loc. cit.*, Neville Chamberlain's correspondence with his sisters, NC 18/1/1006, Neville to Hilda Chamberlain, 30 May 1937.
2. K. Feiling, *Neville Chamberlain* (1946), remains the best single-volume biography; D. Dilks, *Neville Chamberlain vol. I* (Cambridge, 1984), takes the story up to 1929 in more detail.
3. Liverpool City Library, Papers of the seventeenth Earl of Derby, 920.DER.(17) 33, Derby to Churchill, 28 May 1937.
4. R. R. James (ed.), *Chips: The Diaries of Sir Henry Channon* (1967), p. 130.
5. M. Gilbert, *Winston S. Churchill, vol. V* (1976) (henceforth cited as *Churchill V*); J. Charmley, *Lord Lloyd and the Decline of the British Empire* (1987), pp. 170–200; C. Bridge, *Holding on to the Empire* (1986), all deal with the India episode.
6. NC 18/1/1009, Neville to Hilda Chamberlain, 26 June 1937.
7. NC 18/1/1012, Neville to Hilda Chamberlain, 18 July 1937.
8. N. H. Gibbs, *Grand Strategy, vol. I* (1976), pp. 440–50; B. Bond, *British Military Policy between the Two World Wars* (1980), ch. 8; R. Shay, *British Rearmament in the 1930s* (Princeton, 1977), ch. 2; J. Charmley, *Duff Cooper* (1986), pp. 85–91.
9. Feiling, p. 296; NC 2/23A, Chamberlain diary, 17 June 1936.
10. Sir N. Henderson, *Failure of a Mission* (1940), p. 17.
11. *Ibid.*, pp. 19–20.
12. 920.DER.(17) 33, Derby to Chamberlain, 10 June; Chamberlain to Derby, 16 June.
13. L. B. Namier, *Diplomatic Prelude 1938–1939* (1948), p. 218.
14. I. G. Colvin, *Vansittart in Office* (1965), p. 210.
15. The Earl of Avon, *Facing the Dictators* (1962), p. 511.
16. W. N. Medlicott *et al.* (eds), *Documents on British Foreign Policy, Second Series, vol. XIX* (henceforth cited as DBFP) (1982), no. 53, p. 105, fn. 31.
17. Colvin, pp. 18–19.
18. *Ibid.*, p. 348.
19. Avon, p. 242.
20. G. Gooch and H. Temperley (eds), *British Documents on the Origins of the War, 1898–1914, vol. III* (1930), Appendix I.
21. *Ibid.*, p. 426.
22. DBFP XIX, no. 53, Henderson's memo, 10 May, p. 104, fn. 27.
23. *Ibid.*, no. 16, Henderson to Eden, 5 July 1937.
24. *Ibid.*, p. 32.

25. *Ibid.*, p. 37, Vansittart minute, 22 July.
26. *Ibid.*, no. 53, Henderson to Sargent, 20 July.
27. Sir Charles Petrie, *The Life and Letters of Sir Austen Chamberlain, vol. II* (1940), p. 259.
28. Henderson, p. 13.
29. Avon, pp. 509–10; Colvin, p. 146. My copy of Colvin, which was owned by a former diplomat, Nigel Law, bears the following annotation in the margin against the claim that Vansittart selected Henderson: 'Eden told me that he, Eden, was responsible. N.L.'
30. J. Harvey (ed.), *The Diplomatic Diaries of Oliver Harvey 1937–40* (henceforth cited as *Harvey diary*) (1970), p. 41.
31. DBFP XIX, no. 295, Eden to Henderson, 6 November 1937.
32. *Ibid.*, no. 301, Henderson to Eden, 8 November.
33. *Ibid.*, no. 319, note by Mr Strang for Halifax, 13 November.
34. *Ibid.*, no. 246, Eric Parker to Halifax, 13 October; no. 272, Sargent minute, 27 October.
35. NC 18/1/1025, Neville to Hilda Chamberlain, 24 October 1937.
36. *Ibid.*; Avon, p. 509.
37. J. A. Cross, *Sir Samuel Hoare* (1977); D. Carlton, *Anthony Eden* (1981); R. R. James, *Anthony Eden* (1987); and A. R. Peters, *Anthony Eden at the Foreign Office 1931–8* (1986), all contain good accounts of these events.
38. James, ch. 1 for Eden's paternity.
39. Avon, p. 445.
40. *Harvey diary*, 26 March 1937, pp. 33–4.
41. *Ibid.*, 11 November 1937, p. 59.
42. DBFP XIX, no. 273, Eden minute of conversation with Halifax, 27 October; no. 283, Chamberlain's minutes on Henderson to Eden, 2 November.
43. *Ibid.*, no. 310, Cranborne minute of conversation with Chamberlain, 10 November.

44. Avon, pp. 511–12.
45. NC 18/1/1027, Neville to Hilda Chamberlain, 6 November.
46. NC 18/1/1028, Neville to Ida Chamberlain, 14 November.
47. NC 18/1/1030, Neville to Ida Chamberlain, 26 November.
48. DBFP XIX, no. 258, p. 423, fn. 6.

Chapter 2

1. A Gentleman with a Duster (pseud. for H. Begbie), *The Conservative Mind* (1924), pp. 47–8.
2. The Earl of Birkenhead, *Halifax* (1965), ch. 1.
3. J. Campbell, *F. E. Smith, First Earl of Birkenhead* (1983), p. 744.
4. Birkenhead, p. 124.
5. *Ibid.*, p. 131.
6. *Conservative Mind*, p. 51.
7. A. J. P. Taylor, *Beaverbrook* (1972), pp. 270, 327.
8. Public Record Office, Kew (henceforth cited as PRO), Halifax Papers, FO 800/328 Hal/38/38, Halifax to Sir Roger Lumley, 21 March 1938.
9. Cambridge University Library, Baldwin Papers, vol. 103, fo. 27, Irwin to Baldwin, 23 April 1929.
10. V. Lawford, 'Three Ministers', *The Cornhill*, winter 1956/7, pp. 73–4.
11. Taylor, p. 329.
12. Birkenhead, p. 349.
13. H. H. E. Craster, *Speeches on Foreign Policy by Viscount Halifax* (henceforth cited as *Halifax speeches*) (1940), pp. 37, 39.
14. *Ibid.*, p. 48.
15. DBFP XIX, no. 336, Halifax's account of his visit, p. 547.
16. Birkenhead, p. 366, Henderson letter, 4 November.
17. *Ibid.*, p. 366, Halifax letter, 9 November.
18. DBFP XIX, no. 336, Halifax's account, p. 541.
19. Birkenhead, p. 368.
20. DBFP XIX, no. 336, p. 543.
21. Birkenhead, p. 372.
22. Avon, p. 515.
23. DBFP XIX, no. 336, p. 545; Birkenhead, p. 370.

24. *Ibid.*, p. 546.
25. *Ibid.*, p. 547.
26. *Ibid.*, p. 549.
27. DBFP XIX, Annex to no. 346, p. 572 foll.
28. *Ibid.*, no. 349; NC 18/1/1030, Neville to Ida Chamberlain, 26 November.
29. DBFP XIX, no. 348, Eden memo, 26 November 1937.

Chapter 3
1. Avon, p. 323; DBFP XV (1976), no. 460, Eden memo, 17 January 1936; Peters, p. 171.
2. DBFP XV, Annex IV (b), pp. 769–91.
3. DBFP XVI, (1977), no. 272, Cabinet minutes, 25 April 1936, pp. 357–8; Peters, pp. 189–93.
4. Peters, p. 195.
5. Churchill College, Vansittart MSS. VNST 1/14, memo, 21 May 1936.
6. Avon, p. 445.
7. K. Middlemas, *The Diplomacy of Illusion* (1972), p. 45.
8. NC 2/23A, Chamberlain diary, 2 August 1935.
9. M. Gilbert, *Winston S. Churchill, vol. V, companion volume III* (henceforth cited as *Churchill c.v. III*) (1982), pp. 287–8.
10. W. S. Churchill, *The Second World War, vol. I, The Gathering Storm* (1975, collected edn), pp. 136–7; K. Middlemas and J. Barnes, *Baldwin* (1969), pp. 969–73; S. Roskill, *Hankey, vol. III* (1974), p. 237.
11. Gibbs, p. 125, quoting Chamberlain to his sisters, 28 July 1934.
12. *Ibid.*, p. 447, quoting Chamberlain to his sisters, 9 February 1936.
13. *Ibid.*, p. 258.
14. NC 2/23A, Chamberlain diary, 27 April 1936.
15. Middlemas, p. 53, quoting Chamberlain to his sisters, 13 April 1937.
16. NC 18/1/1010, Neville to Ida Chamberlain, 4 July 1937.
17. DBFP XIX, no. 15, minutes of CID meeting, 5 July, p. 22 foll.

18. *Ibid.*, no. 65, Chamberlain to Mussolini, 27 July 1937.
19. *Ibid.*, Appendix I, Chamberlain diary, 28 February. See Peters, pp. 283–4; Carlton, p. 108; James, p. 178.
20. DBFP XIX, no. 69, fn. 1.
21. *Harvey diary*, Harvey to Eden, 25 July, pp. 411–15.
22. NC 18/1/1014, Neville to Hilda Chamberlain, 1 August 1937.
23. DBFP XIX, nos 80, 81, Grandi/Chamberlain conversation, Mussolini to Chamberlain, 31 July.
24. PRO, Avon Papers, FO 954/13A, It/37/23, Chamberlain to Halifax, 7 August 1937.
25. NC 18/1/1015, Neville to Ida Chamberlain, 8 August.
26. NC 18/1/1018, Neville to Hilda Chamberlain, 29 August.
27. Avon, pp. 454–5; FO 954/13A, It/37/27, Eden to Halifax, 11 August 1937.
28. DBFP XIX, no. 144, Cabinet minutes, 8 September.
29. NC 18/1/1020, Neville to Hilda Chamberlain, 12 September 1937.
30. Avon, p. 471.
31. NC 18/1/1020, Neville to Hilda Chamberlain, 12 September 1937.
32. *Harvey diary*, 22 September, p. 47.
33. *Ibid.*, p. 48.
34. Lawford, p. 83.
35. *Harvey diary*, 15 October, pp. 50–51.
36. Avon, pp. 447–8.
37. K. Rose, *The Later Cecils* (1975).
38. He had reached this conclusion a decade later, see: British Library, Emrys Evans MSS. Add. Mss. 58240, fo. 192, Cranborne to Emrys Evans, 9 January 1947.
39. *Harvey diary*, 3 November, p. 56.
40. *Ibid.*, p. 416.
41. Avon, p. 493.
42. *Ibid.*
43. G. Peden, *British Rearmament and the Treasury 1932–9* (Edinburgh, 1979), p. 87 foll.; Gibbs, ch. 8.
44. NC 18/1/1003, Neville to Hilda Chamberlain, 25 April 1937.
45. Gibbs, p. 275 foll.

46. DBFP XIX, no. 316, p. 501 foll., COS report.
47. *Ibid.*, no. 348, Eden memo, 26 November 1937.
48. Avon, pp. 512–13; FO 954/10A Ger/37/51, Eden to Chamberlain, 16 November 1937.
49. *Harvey diary*, 17 November, p. 61.

Chapter 4
1. DBFP XIX, no. 354, Anglo-French conversations, 29, 30 November 1937.
2. *Ibid.*, p. 602.
3. *Ibid.*, p. 612.
4. *Harvey diary*, 5 December, pp. 62–3.
5. DBFP XIX, no. 459, Eden to Chamberlain, 1 January 1938.
6. L. W. Fuchser, *Neville Chamberlain and Appeasement* (New York, 1982), ch. 4.
7. NC 18/1/1028, Neville to Ida Chamberlain, 14 November 1937.
8. NC 18/1/1024, 1031, Neville to Ida Chamberlain, 16 October, 12 December 1937.
9. NC 7/11/29/19, Fisher to Chamberlain, 15 September 1936; see also G. Peden, 'Sir Warren Fisher and British Rearmament against Germany', *English Historical Review*, 1979, p. 42.
10. *Harvey diary*, 7 December, p. 63; Peters, pp. 306–7.
11. NC 18/1/1031, Neville to Ida Chamberlain, 12 December 1937.
12. NC 18/1/1012, Neville to Hilda Chamberlain, 18 July 1937.
13. Taylor, pp. 327, 384, 386.
14. NC 2/23A, Chamberlain diary, 15 March 1937.
15. Patrick Donner, *Crusade* (1984), p. 210.
16. Taylor, p. 322.
17. NC 18/1, Chamberlain to Hilda Chamberlain, 22 May 1935.
18. NC 2/23A, Chamberlain diary, January 1934.
19. Peden, pp. 17–18.
20. Churchill College, Lloyd MSS., GLLD 5/5, Lloyd to David Lloyd, 25 March 1936.

21. R. V. F. Heuston, *Lives of the Lord Chancellors* (1964), pp. 580–88.
22. Roskill, p. 207.
23. Feiling, pp. 314–15.
24. DBFP XIX, no. 401, Cabinet meeting, 22 December 1937.
25. *Ibid.*, no. 394, Eden to Henderson, 17 December; no. 409, Eden memo, 1 January.
26. *Harvey diary*, 19–23 December, p. 65.
27. DBFP XIX, no. 410, Eden to Chamberlain, 1 January 1938.
28. *Ibid.*, Appendix I, Chamberlain diary, 19 February 1938, p. 1139.
29. *Ibid.*, no. 415, Chamberlain to Eden, 7 January.
30. *Harvey diary*, 1–13 January 1938, p. 67.
31. DBFP XIX, no. 418, Eden to Chamberlain, 9 January.
32. NC 18/1/1026, Neville to Ida Chamberlain, 30 October 1937.
33. D. Dilks (ed.), *The Diaries of Sir Alexander Cadogan 1938–1945* (henceforth cited as *Cadogan diary*) (1971), p. 30.
34. NC 18/1023, Neville to Hilda Chamberlain, 9 October 1937.
35. Feiling, p. 325.
36. NC 18/1/1032, Neville to Hilda Chamberlain, 17 December 1937.
37. *Harvey diary*, 19–23 December, p. 65.
38. *Ibid.*
39. *Ibid.*, 1–13 January 1938, p. 66.
40. DBFP XXI (1985), nos 438, 441, 464.
41. *Ibid.*, no. 471, p. 638 quoting Chamberlain MSS.
42. *Ibid.*, no. 480, p. 647, Chamberlain minute, 11 January 1938.

Chapter 5
1. DBFP XIX, nos 421–4, Lindsay to Chamberlain, 13 January.
2. Churchill, pp. 158, 160.
3. DBFP XIX, Appendix 1, p. 1140, Chamberlain diary, 19 February 1938.

4. *Cadogan diary*, 13 January, p. 36.

5. DBFP XIX, no. 434, Cadogan to Eden, 13 January.

6. *Ibid.*, nos 421–4, Lindsay to Foreign Office, 11, 12 January.

7. *Harvey diary*, note to Eden, pp. 69–70.

8. *Ibid.*, 15 January, p. 70.

9. DBFP XIX, p. 1160, Chamberlain diary, 19 February 1938.

10. *Harvey diary*, 15 January, p. 70.

11. Avon, pp. 553–4.

12. *Cadogan diary*, 16 January, p. 38; *Harvey diary*, 16 January, p. 71.

13. DBFP XIX, no. 445, Eden to Chamberlain, 17 January.

14. FO 954/29, US/38/3, Eden note, 17 January.

15. DBFP XIX, no. 446, Lindsay to Eden, 18 January.

16. FO 954/29, US/38/11, Lindsay to Eden, 7 February.

17. Feiling, pp. 322–4.

18. FO 954/29, US/38/11, Lindsay to Eden, 7 February.

19. Feiling, pp. 322–4.

20. Avon, pp. 558–9.

21. DBFP XIX, no. 449, Eden note, 18 January.

22. Avon, p. 560.

23. *Ibid.*, p. 563.

24. James, p. 191.

25. DBFP XIX, Appendix I, Chamberlain diary, 19 February.

26. Carlton, pp. 122–3; *Harvey diary*, 20 January, p. 76.

27. *Harvey diary*, ibid.

28. C. A. MacDonald, *The United States, Britain and Appeasement 1936–9* (1981), ch. 5; D. Reynolds, *The Creation of the Anglo-American Alliance 1937–41* (1981), p. 16 foll.; R. Ovendale, *Appeasement and the English-Speaking World* (Cardiff, 1975), ch. 4.

29. DBFP XIX, Appendix I, Chamberlain diary, 19 February.

30. NC 18/1/1037, Neville to Hilda Chamberlain, 30 January 1938.

31. DBFP XIX, no. 465, 21st meeting of the Foreign Policy Committee, 24 January.

32. *Ibid.*, no. 468, Foreign Office to Henderson, 25 January.

33. DBFP XIX, no. 469, Eden memo, 25 January.

34. *Ibid.*, p. 804, fn. 3, Vansittart, 28 January.

35. *Ibid.*, p. 810, fn. 17, Wilson to Chamberlain, 23 January.

36. DBFP XIX, no. 471, Henderson to Foreign Office, 26 January.

37. DBFP XIX, Appendix I, Chamberlain diary, 19 February, p. 1140; the letters are at NC 1/17/5–8.

38. NC 1/20/1/182, Neville to Mary Endicott Chamberlain, 6 February.

39. Avon, p. 570; *Harvey diary*, 31 January, pp. 80–81.

40. NC 18/1/1037, Neville to Hilda Chamberlain, 30 January.

41. NC 1/17/9, Neville to Ivy Chamberlain, 3 March.

42. Avon, pp. 567–8, 572; *Harvey diary*, 6 February, pp. 83–4.

43. *Cadogan diary*, 4 February, p. 44.

44. Avon, pp. 573–4.

45. DBFP XIX, no. 522, fn. 4, Cabinet meeting, 16 February.

46. *Ibid.*, Appendix I, Chamberlain diary, 19 February.

47. *Ibid.*

48. *Cadogan diary*, 17 February, p. 49.

49. FO 954/13A, It/38/10, Eden to Chamberlain, 18 February.

50. DBFP XIX, Appendix I, Chamberlain diary, 19 February.

51. *Cadogan diary*, 17 February, pp. 48–9.

52. *Harvey diary*, Appendix J, pp. 419–21.

53. M. Muggeridge (ed.), *Ciano's Diplomatic Papers* (1948), pp. 161–2.

54. *Ibid.*, p. 165.

55. R. R. James (ed.), *Memoirs of a Conservative* (1969), p. 272.

56. DBFP XIX, Appendix I, Chamberlain diary, 19 February; Lord Templewood, *Nine Troubled Years* (1954), p. 278.

57. Accounts of the interview can be found at: DBFP XIX, no. 573, and Appendix I, Chamberlain diary, 19 February: Avon, Appendix C,

pp. 616–18; and Muggeridge, pp. 164–8.

58. Avon, p. 582.
59. Muggeridge, pp. 182–3.
60. Avon, p. 585.
61. *Harvey diary*, 18 February, p. 93.
62. Duff Cooper diary, 19 February 1938.
63. Avon, p. 591; *Harvey diary*, 19 February, p. 95; *Cadogan diary*, 19 February, p. 51.
64. NC 2/24A, Chamberlain diary, *c.* 27 February.
65. NC 2/24A; *Harvey diary*, 20 February, p. 97; Cooper diary, 20 February; Avon, pp. 590–96.
66. NC 18/1/1040, Neville to Hilda Chamberlain, 27 February.
67. NC 1/17/9, Neville to Ivy Chamberlain, 3 March.
68. FO 800/328, Hal/38/38, Halifax to Sir Roger Lumley, 21 March 1938.
69. NC 18/1/1040, Neville to Hilda Chamberlain, 27 February.

Chapter 6
1. *Churchill c.v. III*, p. 914.
2. *Ibid.*, p. 916, Cazalet to Baldwin.
3. NC 18/1/1001, Neville to Hilda Chamberlain, 10 April 1937.
4. Dilks, *Chamberlain*, p. 195.
5. *Ibid.*, p. 327.
6. NC 18/1/1133A, Neville to Ida Chamberlain, 3 December 1939.
7. Dilks, p. 441.
8. *Ibid.*, p. 499.
9. *Ibid.*, p. 449.
10. Charmley, *Lloyd*, pp. 167–94; S. Ball, *Baldwin and the Conservative Party* (1988), ch. 6; Lord Beaverbrook, *Men and Power* (1956), pp. xxiii.
11. NC 18/1/1058, Neville to Ida Chamberlain, 4 July 1938.
12. N. Nicolson (ed.), *Diaries and Letters of Harold Nicolson, vol. I, 1930–39* (henceforth cited as *Nicolson diary*) (1966), p. 328.
13. *Ibid.*, p. 324.
14. Avon, p. 597.
15. *Ibid.*, pp. 599–600; *Nicolson diary*, pp. 324–5; Carlton, pp. 132–3.

16. Carlton, p. 133.
17. N. Thompson, *The Anti-Appeasers* (1971), p. 2.
18. Emrys Evans MSS., Add. Mss. 56247, fos 22–3, Evans to Leo Amery, 1 July 1954.
19. *Churchill c.v. III*, pp. 160–62.
20. *Ibid.*, p. 401, WSC to RSC, 13 November 1936.
21. *Ibid.*, p. 162.
22. D. Irving, *Churchill's War* (Australia, 1987), pp. 59–60.
23. *Churchill c.v. III*, p. 296.
24. *Ibid.*, p. 363.
25. D. Dutton, *Austen Chamberlain* (1985), p. 307.
26. *Churchill c.v. III*, p. 401.
27. Thompson, p. 130.
28. *The Times* obituary, 18 July 1986.
29. *Churchill c.v. III*, p. 483.
30. R. Boothby, *I Fight to Live* (1947), p. 141.
31. e.g. NC 7/11/31/31, Boothby to Chamberlain, 17 May 1938.
32. N. Mosley, *Rules of the Game* (1982), p. 152.
33. Taylor, p. 336.
34. *Churchill c.v. III*, pp. 15, 245–6, 1079.
35. *Ibid.*, p. 483.
36. C. E. Lysaght, *Brendan Bracken* (1979), p. 68.
37. *Ibid.*
38. *Ibid.*, p. 154, speech in May 1938.
39. *Churchill c.v. III*, p. 990, WSC to Lord Derby, 12 April 1938.
40. *Ibid.*, pp. 774 foll.
41. R. S. Churchill, *The Rise and Fall of Sir Anthony Eden* (1959), p. 154; *Nicolson diary*, p. 334.
42. India Office Record Library (IORL), Brabourne Papers, EUR. MSS. F.97/22B, Butler to Brabourne, 23 February 1938.
43. *Nicolson diary*, 11 April 1938, p. 334.
44. John Ramsden, *The Age of Balfour and Baldwin* (1978), p. 366.
45. Carlton, pp. 134–6.
46. *Churchill c.v. III*, pp. 1037, 1043.
47. B. Pimlott, *The Diaries of Hugh Dalton* (henceforth cited as *Dalton diary*) (1987), p. 227.

48. *Nicolson diary*, 11 May 1938, p. 339.
49. *Ibid.*, 9 November 1938, p. 377.
50. Add. Mss. 58247, Evans to Amery, 1 July 1954.
51. Add. Mss. 58238, Law to Evans, 30 December 1939.
52. *Dalton diary*, 7 April 1938, p. 225.
53. NC 18/1/1046, Neville to Hilda Chamberlain, 9 April 1938.

Chapter 7
1. IORL, EUR. MSS. F.97/22B, Butler to Brabourne, 9 March 1938, fo. 80.
2. *Ibid.*, Butler to Brabourne, 9 March 1938, fos 79–80.
3. *Churchill c.v. III*, p. 939.
4. IORL, EUR. MSS. F.97/22B, Butler to Brabourne, 23 February, fo. 88.
5. FO 800/328, Hal/38/38, Halifax to Lumley, 21 March 1938.
6. Birkenhead, p. 380.
7. FO 800/328, Hal/38/101, draft letter from Halifax to Mrs Lindsay, November 1938.
8. R. A. Butler, *The Art of the Possible* (1971), p. 27.
9. R. A. Butler, *The Art of Memory* (1982), p. 38; Butler MSS., RAB G.10/28, character sketch by Rab.
10. Butler, *Art of Memory*, p. 46.
11. IORL, EUR. MSS. F.97/22B, Butler to Brabourne, 9 March 1938, fo. 81.
12. NC 1/17/9, Neville to Ivy Chamberlain, 3 March 1938.
13. DBFP XIX, no. 573.
14. NC 2/24A, Chamberlain diary 19 February.
15. DBFP XIX, nos 609, 610.
16. DBFP I (1949), no. 8.
17. NC 18/1/1041, Neville to Hilda Chamberlain, 13 March 1938.
18. *Cadogan diary*, 16 March, p. 62; *Harvey diary*, 15 March, pp. 115, 118; James, *Eden*, pp. 206–7.
19. R. J. Minney, *The Private Papers of Hore-Belisha* (1960), p. 106.
20. NC 18/1/1042, Neville to Ida Chamberlain, 20 March.

21. RAB G.9/5–7, Beaumont to Butler, 16 March, Butler to Beaumont, 18 March.
22. Winston Churchill, *Arms and the Covenant* (1975, collected edn), p. 451.
23. C. Barnett, *The Collapse of British Power* (1972), pp. 474, 505, 509–13; T. Taylor, *Munich* (1979), pp. 629–33; W. Murray, *The Change in the European Balance of Power, 1938–9* (Princeton, 1984), p. 159.
24. NC 18/1/1043, Neville to Hilda Chamberlain, 27 March 1938; see also *Cadogan diary*, 14 March 1938, p. 62.
25. NC 18/1/1042, Neville to Ida Chamberlain, 20 March 1938.
26. Taylor, pp. 621–5.
27. DBFP I, no. 86, 15 March.
28. Taylor, pp. 662–6.
29. Barnett, Taylor and Murray, *locs. cit.*, argue the contrary.
30. IORL, MSS. EUR. F.97/22B, Butler to Brabourne, 12 October 1938, fos 27–8.
31. RAB G.9/13, Butler to Ian Black, 21 April 1938.
32. FO 800/328, Hal/38/38, Halifax to Lumley, 21 March 1938.
33. *Harvey diary*, 16, 19 March, pp. 125–9.
34. PRO. Cabinet Committee on Foreign Policy, Cab. 27/623, FP(36) 26, 18 March.
35. NC 18/1/1043, Neville to Ida Chamberlain, 20 March 1938.
36. *The Times*, 19 March 1938.
37. Cab. 27/623, FP(36) 26, 18 March.
38. Cab. 27/623, FP(36) 27, 21 March.
39. PRO, Cabinet minutes, Cab. 23/93, 15(38), 22 March.
40. Cooper diary.
41. DBFP I, pp. 95–7; *Halifax speeches*, pp. 131–8.
42. NC 18/1/1043, Neville to Hilda Chamberlain, 27 March 1938.
43. *Halifax speeches*, p. 142.
44. IORL, MSS. EUR. F.97/22B, Butler to Brabourne, 31 May 1938, fo. 48.

Chapter 8

1. Barnett, p. 514.
2. Fuchser, pp. 116–17.
3. Murray, pp. 162, 408.
4. A. Bryant (ed.), *In Search of Peace* (1938), p. 177.
5. G. Weinberg, *The Foreign Policy of Hitler's Germany, vol. II* (Carolina, 1980), p. 329.
6. PRO, Foreign Office General Correspondence, FO 371/21132, R8248/188/12; Weinberg, pp. 329–31.
7. FO 371/21674, C1866/132/18, Cadogan memo, 17 March; DBFP I, no. 140, Newton to Halifax, 12 April.
8. Cab. 23/92, meeting of 14 March.
9. Peden, ch. 3, esp. pp. 65, 88–9; W. N. Medlicott, *Britain and Germany* (1969), p. 32.
10. Weinberg, pp. 81, 341–3, 360.
11. DBFP I; no. 148, Chilston to Halifax, 19 April, pp. 161–5; see also no. 151.
12. Weinberg, pp. 4, 206–7, 323.
13. Murray, pp. 174–6.
14. Chamberlain, p. 171.
15. Not 17th as in DBFP I, p. 623, and Murray, p. 167 (though on p. 409 he gets the date correct); FO 800/313, Henderson to Halifax, 7 April 1938.
16. FO 800/269, 22 April; *Cadogan diary*, p. 70.
17. DBFP I, no. 121, pp. 108–12; quotation from p. 625, Henderson to Halifax, 13 April 1938.
18. FO 800/269, Halifax to Henderson, 19 March 1938.
19. DBFP I, no. 138, Halifax to Newton, 11 April; no. 152, Henderson to Halifax, 20 April.
20. NC 18/1/1042, Neville to Ida Chamberlain, 20 March.
21. *Cadogan diary*, pp. 68–9.
22. Templewood, pp. 294–5; DBFP I, no. 122.
23. DBFP I, nos 122, 123, 129, 133, 138, 143, 144, 150, 154, 155.
24. *Ibid.*, no. 164, p. 217.
25. *Ibid.*, p. 218.
26. *Ibid.*, p. 220.
27. *Ibid.*, p. 221.
28. Weinberg, pp. 341–2, 362–3.
29. DBFP I, no. 164; *Harvey diary*, pp. 133–4, which although it is dated 28 April, must have been at least partly written after 29 April.
30. NC 18/1/1049, Neville to Ida Chamberlain, 1 May.
31. DBFP I, pp. 626–7, Henderson to Halifax, 3 May; S. Newman, *March 1939* (Oxford, 1976), chs 3 and 4; G. Schmidt, *The Politics and Economics of Appeasement* (1986 edn), pp. 95–118, 146–58.
32. DBFP I, no. 166; *Harvey diary*, 2 May, pp. 134–5.
33. DBFP I, nos 176, 180, 181, 193, 197.
34. *Ibid.*, pp. 627–8, Halifax to Henderson, 12 May; nos 220, 262, 277; *Harvey diary*, 21 May, p. 142.
35. *Ibid.*, no. 180, Halifax to Henderson, 5 May.
36. *Ibid.*, nos 193, 198, 203.
37. *Cadogan diary*, 11 May, p. 75.
38. DBFP I, no. 203, p. 282.
39. NC 18/1/1050, Neville to Hilda Chamberlain, 8 May.
40. NC 18/1/1051, Neville to Ida Chamberlain, 13 May.
41. *Ibid.*, 1054, to Ida, 28 May.
42. *Ibid.*, 1050, to Hilda, 8 May.
43. *Harvey diary*, 22 April, 19 May, pp. 128, 140–41; *Cadogan diary*, 7 May, p. 75.
44. IORL, EUR. MSS. F.97/22B, Butler to Brabourne, 24 April, fos 53–4.
45. C. Coote, *Companion of Honour* (1965), p. 157.
46. *Harvey diary*, 22 April, p. 128.
47. NC 18/1/1051, Neville to Ida Chamberlain, 13 May; J. A. Cross, *Lord Swinton* (1982), pp. 212–15.
48. NC 18/1/1051, Neville to Ida Chamberlain, 13 May.
49. *Nicolson diary*, 17 May, p. 341.
50. Coote, p. 157.
51. NC 18/1/1050, Neville to Hilda Chamberlain, 8 May.
52. DBFP I, no. 237.
53. *Ibid.*, nos 244, 245.

54. *Cadogan diary*, 21 May, p. 79.
55. DBFP I, no. 249; cf. *Documents on German Foreign Policy, series D. vol. II* (henceforth cited as DGFP II) (1950), no. 184, pp. 311–13.
56. NC 18/1/1053, Neville to Hilda Chamberlain, 22 May.
57. DBFP I, nos 249, 254; DGFP II, nos 184, 186.
58. *Harvey diary*, 21 May, p. 143.
59. NC 18/1/1053, Neville to Hilda Chamberlain, 22 May.
60. *Cadogan diary*, 21 May, p. 79.
61. Cab. 24(38), 18 May; see also *Harvey diary*, 21 May, p. 142.
62. DBFP I, nos 264, 349.
63. Cab. 23/93, Cab. (38)25, 22 May; *Cadogan diary*, 22 May, p. 79; Cooper diary, 22 May.
64. DGFP II, no. 189, has Henderson using this phrase, which he does not in BD I, no. 273.
65. DBFP I, no. 271, Halifax to Phipps, 22 May.
66. *Ibid.*, nos 293, 295, 296, 297, 305, 313.
67. *Ibid.*, nos 323–4; no. 347, fn. 1, p. 401; no. 349, pp. 406–9.
68. *Ibid.*, no. 347, FO to Phipps, pp. 401–2.
69. *Ibid.*, no. 208, Henderson to Halifax, 12 May.
70. *Ibid.*, no. 218, Henderson to Halifax, 14 May.
71. *Ibid.*, pp. 628–9, Henderson to Halifax, 19 May.
72. *Ibid.*, no. 313, Henderson to Halifax, 25 May.
73. NC 18/1/1053, Neville to Hilda Chamberlain, 22 May.
74. *Ibid.*, 1054, to Ida, 28 May.
75. *Ibid.*

Chapter 9
1. IORL, EUR. MSS. F.97/22B, Butler to Brabourne, 31 May 1938.
2. Churchill College, Margesson Mss. MRGN 1/4, Margesson to Baldwin, 4 March 1941.
3. Butler Mss. RAB G.10/29.
4. NC 18/1/1046, Neville to Hilda Chamberlain, 9 April 1938.
5. NC 18/1/1029, Neville to Hilda Chamberlain, 21 November 1937.
6. IORL, EUR. MSS. F.97/22B, Butler to Brabourne, 8 July 1938.
7. MRGN 1/5, 'Candid portrait of Neville Chamberlain'.
8. Feiling, pp. 350–51; also NC 18/1/1041, Neville to Hilda Chamberlain, 13 March 1938, and 18/1/1056, Neville to Ida Chamberlain, 28 May 1938.
9. RAB G.11/185, Anne Chamberlain to Butler, 7 January 1941.
10. *Halifax speeches*, pp. 154–5.
11. *Ibid.*, pp. 178–9.
12. *Nicolson diary*, 12 May 1938, p. 340.
13. Taylor, p. 653.
14. DBFP II, no. 380, FO to Strang, 7 June.
15. *Ibid.*, p. 629, Henderson to Halifax, 19 May.
16. *Ibid.*, p. 627, Henderson to Halifax, 3 May.
17. *Churchill c.v. III*, p. 1101.
18. Cab. 24/277, CP(38)127, 24 May.
19. Murray, p. 170; Newman, p. 39 and *passim*.
20. Cab. 27/623, FP(36)30.
21. *Harvey diary*, 5 June 1938, p. 145.
22. NC 18/1/1054, Neville to Ida Chamberlain, 28 May 1938.
23. DBFP II, esp. nos 329, 330, 345, 346, and after ch. 5, esp. no. 353.
24. *Ibid.*, nos 281, 284, 349 (esp. fn. 1, pp. 410–11), 359.
25. *Ibid.*, no. 421, Halifax to Phipps, 17 June.
26. *Ibid.*, no. 347, FO to Phipps, 30 May.
27. *Ibid.*, no. 432, FO to Newton, 22 June.
28. *Ibid.*, nos 398, 420, FO to Phipps, 11 and 17 June; for the Czechs see nos 345–6, 382, 389, 396, 399, 416, 432.
29. *Ibid.*, no. 405, Henderson to FO.
30. *Ibid.*, no. 403, Newton to Halifax, 13 June.
31. *Ibid.*, no. 485, Halifax to Henderson, 15 June.
32. DBFP II, pp. 501–65 *passim*.
33. *Ibid.*, nos 444, 446.
34. *Churchill c.v. III*, p. 1112.

35. DBFP II, no. 521, Newton to FO, 20 July.
36. *Ibid.*, no. 525, Newton to Halifax, 21 July.
37. FO 800/309, H/VI/24, Wilson to Halifax, 22 June.
38. *Ibid.*, H/VI/29, Halifax to Runciman, 1 July.
39. DBFP II, no. 556, letter 28 July.
40. *Harvey diary*, 11–16 July, pp. 161–2.
41. *Ibid.*, 18 July, p. 163; *Cadogan diary*, 18 July, p. 87.
42. The endlessly entertaining *All Souls and Appeasement* by A. L. Rowse (1961) is the *locus classicus* of this view.
43. Bryant, pp. 255–6.
44. DBFP II, no. 574, 3 August.
45. NC 18/1/1059, Neville to Hilda Chamberlain, 9 July.
46. *Churchill V*, pp. 951–3.
47. Prem. 1/283, Simon to Chamberlain, 14 July.
48. NC 18/1/1058, Neville to Ida Chamberlain, 4 July.
49. FO 800/328, Hal/38/59, Butler to Halifax, 30 July 1938.
50. FO 800/314, H/XV/58, Henderson to Halifax, 3 August.
51. DBFP II, no. 551, Henderson to Halifax, 26 July.
52. FO 800/268, Henderson Mss., fo. 220, to High Commissioner Bruce, 25 May 1937.
53. FO 800/270, fo. 59, Henderson Mss. note, undated but probably early May 1939.
54. DBFP II, no. 587, Halifax to Henderson, 5 August.
55. R. Macleod & D. Kelly (eds), *The Ironside Diaries 1937–40* (henceforth cited as *Ironside diary*) (1962), 12 August, p. 58.
56. *Harvey diary*, 6 September, p. 167; DBFP II, no. 587.
57. FO 800/314, H/XV/61, Henderson to Halifax, 6 August.
58. DBFP II, no. 587.
59. FO 800/309, H/VI/39, Henderson to Halifax, 17 August.
60. FO 800/314, H/XV/64, Sargent minute, 12 August.

61. DBFP II, no. 587.
62. FO 800/309, H/VI/39 Halifax marginalia.
63. *Ibid.*, Henderson to Halifax, 17 August.
64. J. Barnes & D. Nicholson (eds), *The Empire at Bay: The Leo Amery Diaries 1929–45* (henceforth cited as *Amery diary*) (1988), p. 508, 26 July 1938.
65. FO 800/304–308 contain the voluminous papers of the mission.
66. DBFP II, no. 644, Runciman to Halifax, 18 August.
67. *Ibid.*, Appendix II, pp. 656–7.
68. *Ibid.*, no. 686, Runciman to Halifax, 25 August.
69. Prem. 1/265, fo. 194, Wilson to Chamberlain, 25 August.
70. FO 800/314, H/XV/62, Vansittart minute, 10 August; Colvin, pp. 217–31; *Cadogan diary*, pp. 92–3.
71. Charmley, *Lloyd*, pp. 210–17; see also V. L. Ramsden-Atherton, *Lord Lloyd, the British Council and Foreign Policy 1937–41* (University of East Anglia unpublished thesis, 1988) *passim*; Lloyd Mss., Churchill College, GLLD 19/9, contains many letters from Colvin. See also Colvin, pp. 217–27; DBFP II, Appendix IV, p. 683.
72. DBFP II, Appendix IV, pp. 683–6, 687–8; *Churchill c.v. III*, pp. 1119–20.
73. *Ibid.*, pp. 686–7, Chamberlain to Halifax, 19 August.
74. Prem. 1/330, fo. 12, Butler to Wilson, 2 August.
75. FO 800/314, H/XV/68, Henderson to Halifax, 22 August. The version in DBFP II, no. 665, has been slightly edited.
76. DBFP II, nos 662, 666, Henderson to Halifax, 22 August.
77. *Ibid.*, no. 608, Halifax to Henderson, 11 August.
78. DBFP II, nos 558, 562–4, 573, 592, 594, 614, 620.
79. Prem. 1/330, fos 5–8.
80. Prem. 1/265, fos 194–8, Wilson to Chamberlain, 25 August.
81. *Ibid.*, nos 706, 707, 710, 29 August.
82. Cab. 24/94, 36(38).

Chapter 10

1. Cab. 23/94, 36(38), 30 August, from which all the quotations are taken; *Harvey diary*, 6 September, p. 169.
2. NC 18/1/1066, Neville to Ida Chamberlain, 3 September.
3. Prem. 1/266A, fo. 363, memo, 30 August.
4. DBFP II, no. 736, 738, Henderson to Halifax, 1 September.
5. *Ibid.*, no. 746, Newton to Halifax, 2 September.
6. *Ibid.*, nos 727, 735, Halifax to Newton, 31 August, 2 September; nos 736, 738, 757 from Henderson, 1 and 4 September.
7. Birkenhead, p. 391.
8. *Dalton diary*, 5 September, p. 236.
9. K. Young, *The Diaries of Sir R. Bruce-Lockhart vol. I, 1915–38* (henceforth cited as *Lockhart diary*) (1973), 16 August, p. 392.
10. *Nicolson diary*, 31 August.
11. FO 800/309, H/VI/48, minute, 29(?) August.
12. *Churchill c.v. III*, pp. 1130–31, 1137; *Nicolson diary*, 22, 26 August, pp. 356–8; *Dalton diary*, 5 September, pp. 236–7.
13. *Dalton diary, ibid.*
14. DBFP II, no. 708, 29 August; no. 761, 4 September.
15. *Nicolson diary*, 26 August, p. 358.
16. *Lockhart diary*, 16 August, p. 392.
17. The Earl of Avon, *The Reckoning* (1965), p. 21.
18. Colvin, Wheeler-Bennett, Namier and Rowse, along with Churchill, Eden and Cooper are the repositories of this view, and very entertaining it is too.
19. NC 18/1/1067, Neville to Hilda Chamberlain, 6 September.
20. FO 800/314, H/XV/82, Chamberlain to Halifax, 6 September.
21. FO 800/314, H/XV/81, Halifax to Henderson, 6 September.
22. *Cadogan diary*, 6–8 September, pp. 94–5; *Harvey diary*, 8 September, pp. 171–2.
23. *Cadogan diary*, 9 September, p.

96; DBFP II, nos 809, 810, 9 September.
24. *Ibid.*, no. 815, Halifax to Henderson, 9 September.
25. NC 18/1/1068, Neville to Ida Chamberlain, 11 September.
26. Templewood, p. 299.
27. Lord Eccles, *By Safe Hand* (1983), pp. 101–2.
28. Henderson, p. 145.
29. DBFP II, no. 767, 4 September.
30. *Ibid.*, no. 770, 4 September.
31. *Ibid.*, no. 771, 4 September.
32. *Ibid.*, no. 772, FO to Cadogan, 4 September.
33. *Ibid.*, no. 793, FO to Cadogan, 6 September.
34. *Ibid.*, no. 691, 25 August; A. Adamthwaite, *France and the Coming of the Second World War* (1977), pp. 201–2.
35. Adamthwaite, p. 177.
36. *Harvey diary*, 19 September, p. 188.
37. DBFP II, no. 729, Halifax to Phipps, 31 August.
38. FO 800/314, H/XV/87, Phipps to Halifax, 10 September.
39. *Ibid.*, H/XV/56, Henderson to Halifax, 18 July 1938.
40. NC 18/1/1068, Neville to Ida Chamberlain, 11 September.
41. DBFP II, pp. 647–8, Henderson to Wilson, 9 September.
42. *Ibid.*, p. 649, Henderson to Wilson, 9 September.
43. NC 18/1/1068, Neville to Ida Chamberlain, 11 September; *Harvey diary*, 10 September, p. 174.
44. *Harvey diary, ibid.*
45. Templewood, pp. 301–2.
46. FO 800/311, H/XIV/278, Halifax to Phipps, 30 March 1938.
47. DBFP, no. 827, Halifax to Henderson, 10 September; NC 18/1/1068.
48. *Ibid.*, no. 830.
49. Cab. 23/95, 37(38).
50. Charmley, *Lloyd*, pp. 218–19; *Harvey diary*, 11, 12 September, pp. 175–6; FO 800/314, H/XV/91, Halifax minute, 11 September.
51. Cab. 23/95, 37(38); *Harvey diary*, 12 September, p. 176, reporting Vansittart's words.

52. Cooper diary, 12 September 1938.
53. *Ibid.*
54. DBFP II, no. 839, 12 September.
55. *Ibid.*, no. 852, Phipps to FO, 13 September.
56. *Ibid.*, no. 855, Phipps to FO, 13 September.
57. Cooper diary, 13 September.
58. DBFP II, no. 862, 13 September; *Cadogan diary*, 13 September, p. 98.
59. Templewood, p. 300.
60. NC 18/1/1069, Neville to Ida Chamberlain, 19 September.
61. Cooper diary, 14 September; Cab. 23/95, 38(38).
62. DBFP II, no. 878, Henderson to FO, 14 September.
63. NC 18/1/1069, Neville to Ida Chamberlain, 19 September.

Chapter 11
1. Chamberlain at Heston upon his return; Movietone Newsreel. See also NC 18/1/1069, Neville to Hilda Chamberlain, 17 September.
2. NC 18/1/1068, Neville to Ida Chamberlain, 11 September.
3. Macaulay's essay on *The Succession in Spain.*
4. FO 800/313, H/XV/15, Henderson to Halifax, 16 March 1938.
5. DBFP II, no. 590, Henderson to Halifax, 6 August 1938; no. 594, Henderson to Halifax, 8 August 1938.
6. DBFP I, no. 166, Halifax to Newton, 2 May 1938, reporting Jan Masaryk.
7. Macaulay's essay on *Burleigh and His Times.*
8. FO 800/328, Hal/38/38, Halifax to Sir Roger Lumley, 21 March 1938.
9. FO 800/313, H/XV/28, Henderson to Halifax, 5 April 1938.
10. Cab. 23/95, 38(38), p. 7.
11. DBFP II, Appendix III.
12. *Ibid.*, Runciman to Beneš, 21 September, p. 676.
13. FO 371/22344, R8044/113/67, for the briefing paper from the Foreign Office; Cab. 23/95, 38(38), for the discussion in Cabinet of the options.

14. Cab. 23/95, 38(38).
15. NC 18/1/1068, Neville to Ida Chamberlain, 11 September.
16. NC 18/1/1069, Neville to Ida Chamberlain, 19 September; Weinberg, p. 431. All quotations come from Chamberlain's letter; other sources for the conversation are in DBFP II, nos 895, 865.
17. Taylor, pp. 740–42.
18. NC 18/1/1069, Neville to Ida Chamberlain, 19 September; DBFP II, no. 897.
19. PRO, Cab. 65/51, WM(45)22.
20. *Harvey diary*, 15 September, p. 180; *Amery diary*, 16 September, p. 509.
21. *Dalton diary*, 17 September, pp. 238–40.
22. *Nicolson diary*, 14 September, p. 360.
23. *Harvey diary*, 17 September, p. 185.
24. *Nicolson diary*, 19 September, pp. 360–61.
25. Cooper diary, 11 September.
26. The account is based on: Cab. 23/95, 39(38); Cooper's diary for 17 September.
27. Lady G. Cecil, *Life of Robert, Marquess of Salisbury*, vol. 2 (1921), p. 171.
28. K. Bourne, *The Foreign Policy of Victorian England* (1970), pp. 389–90.
29. NC 18/1/1068, Neville to Ida Chamberlain, 11 September.
30. *Nicolson diary*, 15 September, p. 360.
31. Adamthwaite, p. 210.
32. DBFP II, no. 822, Phipps to Halifax, 10 September; no. 843, Halifax to Phipps, 12 September; FO 800/311, H/XIV/297, Phipps to Halifax, 14 September.
33. DBFP II, no. 834, Phipps to Halifax, 11 September; no. 842, Halifax to Phipps 12 September.
34. *Ibid.*, no. 855, Phipps to Halifax, 13 September.
35. *Ibid.*, nos 857, 858, Phipps to Halifax, 13 September; Adamthwaite, p. 210.
36. *Harvey diary*, 16 September, p. 182.
37. DBFP II, no. 907, Phipps to Halifax, 17 September.

38. FO 800/311, H/XIV/297, Phipps to Halifax, 14 September.
39. Adamthwaite, p. 177.
40. Cab. 23/95, 39(38), p. 20.
41. *Ibid.*, p. 36.
42. Adamthwaite, p. 215.
43. DBFP II, no. 928, for the British record; Templewood, pp. 305–8, and Weinberg, pp. 439–42, add material from other sources.
44. Weinberg, pp. 440–41.
45. *Cadogan diary*, 18 September, p. 100.
46. Weinberg, p. 422; Chamberlain does not mention any such conversation in his letters, and neither Hoare, Cadogan nor Harvey refer to it.
47. Cab. 23/95, 40(38), p. 4.
48. *Cadogan diary*, 19 September, p. 101.
49. *Amery diary*, 19 September, p. 510.
50. Coote, p. 166.
51. Cooper diary, 19 September.
52. *Ibid.*; Cab. 23/95, 40(38).
53. *Ibid.*; R. J. Minney (ed.), *The Private Papers of Hore-Belisha* (henceforth cited as *Private Papers*) (1960), p. 142.
54. Coote, p. 167; *Dalton diary*, 19, 20 September, pp. 241–2.
55. *Churchill c.v. III*, p. 1165.
56. Coote, p. 168 (20 September).
57. *Harvey diary*, 20 September, p. 189.
58. *The Reckoning*, p. 25.
59. *Nicolson diary*, 20 September, p. 362.
60. *Churchill c.v. III*, p. 1170.
61. Coote, p. 169; Roskill, pp. 381–2.
62. Coote, p. 168 (20 September).
63. DBFP II, no. 961, Newton to Halifax, 19 September; nos 978, 981, Newton to Halifax, 20 September; no. 986, Newton to Halifax, 21 September; no. 991, Halifax to Newton, 21 September; no. 993, Newton to Halifax, 21 September.

Chapter 12

1. Taylor, p. 777; Weinberg, p. 442.
2. *Harvey diary*, 19 September, p. 187; *Lockhart diary*, 19 September, p. 396.
3. *Dalton diary*, 19 September, p. 241.
4. *Ibid.*, 20 September, pp. 242–3.
5. *Churchill c.v. III*, pp. 1171–2.
6. *Ironside diary*, 22 September, p. 62.

7. *Private Papers*, p. 143 (21 September).
8. *Lockhart diary*, 25 September, p. 397.
9. Butler MSS. RABG9/8, Beaumont to Butler, 21 September.
10. *Lockhart diary*, 17 September, p. 396.
11. Taylor, *Beaverbrook*, p. 384.
12. *Cadogan diary*, 21 September, p. 102.
13. Prem. 1/266A, fos 266–7, Cadogan minutes, 20 September.
14. *Ibid.*, Cab. 41(38); also Cooper diary, 21 September.
15. Cooper diary, *ibid.*
16. The account here is based on: DBFP II, no. 1033; Cab. 23/95, 42(38); Cooper diary, 24 September.
17. DBFP II, no. 1048, from Godesberg, 23 September.
18. *Ibid.*, no. 1003.
19. FO 800/309, H/VI/77, Cooper to Halifax; H/VI/79, Stanley to Halifax; both 22 September.
20. *Ibid.*, H/VI/78, Halifax to Cooper, 22 September.
21. Cooper diary, 22 September.
22. DBFP II, no. 1058, Halifax to Chamberlain, 23 September.
23. RAB G10/26, character sketch.
24. DBFP II, nos 1020, 1025, 22 September.
25. *Ibid.*, nos 1030, 1031, to Phipps and Henderson.
26. *Ibid.*, no. 1044, FO to Chamberlain; no. 1043, FO to Butler, 23 September.
27. *Cadogan diary*, 24 September, p. 104; Birkenhead, p. 399.
28. Cooper diary, 24 September.
29. *Private Papers*, p. 145; Cab. 23/95, 42(38).
30. *Harvey diary*, 25 September, p. 157; *Private Papers*, pp. 145–6.
31. Coote, pp. 171–2.
32. Cooper diary, 24 September.
33. *Harvey diary*, 25 September, p. 157.
34. DBFP II, no. 1076, Phipps to FO, 24 September.
35. *Cadogan diary*, 24 September, p. 103.
36. *Ibid.*; Cooper diary, 25 September, from which the quotation is taken. The official record is at Cab. 23/95, 43(38).

37. Birkenhead, p. 400.
38. *Ibid.*, p. 401.
39. Cab. 23/95, 43(38).
40. Templewood, p. 311.
41. Cooper diary, 25 September; *Private Papers*, p. 147.
42. See the account in my *Duff Cooper* for a discussion of this 'resignation'.
43. Templewood, p. 312. The official British account is at DBFP II, no. 1093.
44. DBFP II, no. 1092.
45. Templewood, p. 313; *Cadogan diary*, p. 105.
46. Cooper diary, 25 September.
47. Cab. 23/95, 44(38).
48. Cooper diary, 25 September.
49. M. Cowling, *The Impact of Hitler* (Cambridge, 1975), ch. 8; Thompson, pp. 175–7; *Nicolson diary*, 26 September, pp. 366–7; *Dalton diary*, 24, 25 September, pp. 244–6; *Amery diary*, 23–26 September, pp. 513–17; *Churchill c.v. III*, pp. 1177–80; *The Reckoning*, pp. 26–8.
50. FO 800/309, H/VI/81, Amery to Halifax, 24 September.
51. Irving, pp. 109–10.
52. FO 800/309, H/VI/82, 24 September.
53. *The Reckoning*, p. 27; *Harvey diary*, 17 September, p. 184.
54. *Churchill V*, pp. 977–9.
55. *Nicolson diary*, 19 September, p. 361.
56. *The Reckoning*, pp. 25–7.
57. *Amery diary*, 22 September, p. 512.
58. *Nicolson diary*, 26 September, pp. 366–7.
59. *Amery diary*, p. 485.
60. *Nicolson diary*, 26 September, p. 367.
61. *Ibid.*, p. 366.
62. *Amery diary*, 26 September, p. 517.
63. *Ibid.*
64. NC 18/1/1029, Neville to Hilda Chamberlain, 21 November 1937.
65. DBFP II, no. 1096; Cab. 23/95, 45(38).
66. Cooper diary, 26 September.
67. *Churchill V*, pp. 984–5.
68. Cab. 23/95, 42(38), pp. 11–13.
69. DBFP II, no. 1097.
70. Cab. 23/95, 45(38).

71. DBFP II, no. 1096.
72. *Ibid.*, nos 1115, 1116, 1118.
73. *Ibid.*, no. 1121, FO to Henderson, 27 September.
74. *Ibid.*, nos 1128, 1129.

Chapter 13
1. NC 18/1/1070, Neville to Hilda Chamberlain, 2 October.
2. Bryant, p. 276.
3. DBFP II, no. 1158, Chamberlain to Hitler, 28 September.
4. *Ibid.*, no. 1102, FO to Kennard, 26 September; DBFP III (1949), ch. 1, for fuller details.
5. Adamthwaite, pp. 228–35, and Murray, pp. 209–12, for French plans; Cab. 53/41, COS 765, 14 September, for the Chiefs of Staff.
6. Barnett, p. 537.
7. Murray, pp. 177–84, ch. 7 *passim*.
8. *Cadogan diary*, 27 September, p. 107.
9. DBFP II, no. 1136, FO to Newton, sent at 5.54 p.m.
10. Bryant, pp. 274–6, for text.
11. *The Price of Peace*, Channel 4, 8 September 1988.
12. Cab. 23/95, 46(38).
13. Cooper diary, 27 September.
14. DBFP II, no. 1140, sent 6.45 p.m.
15. DBFP II, no. 1144, for the text.
16. NC 18/1/1070, Neville to Hilda Chamberlain, 2 October.
17. DBFP II, no. 1158, sent 11.30 a.m., 28 September.
18. *Ibid.*, no. 1159.
19. *Ibid.*, nos 1106, 1109, 26 September.
20. *Ibid.*, no. 1160, 28 September.
21. FO 800/309, H/VI/89, Henderson to Halifax, 28 September.
22. DBFP II, no. 1171.
23. Templewood, p. 319.
24. *Amery diary*, 26 September, p. 518.
25. *Ibid.*, 27 September, p. 519.
26. *Channon diary*, 28 September, p. 170; the text of the speech is at Bryant, pp. 279–300.
27. *Nicolson diary*, 28 September, p. 369.
28. *Cadogan diary*, 28 September, p. 109.
29. *Channon diary*, 28 September, p. 171.
30. Cooper diary, 28 September.

31. NC 18/1/1070, Neville to Hilda Chamberlain, 2 October.
32. *Nicolson diary*, 28 September p. 371.
33. *Channon diary*, 28 September, p. 171.
34. NC 18/1/1070, Neville to Hilda Chamberlain, 2 October.
35. *Amery diary*, 28 September, p. 521.
36. *Nicolson diary*, 28 September, p. 371.
37. *Ibid.*, 29 September, p. 372
38. *Harvey diary*, 29 September, p. 201.
39. DBFP II, no. 1194, Newton to Halifax, 28 September.
40. *Ibid.*, nos 1203 (for the qualified acceptance) and 1210 (for Halifax's message).
41. *Ibid.*, no. 1227, Wilson's account of the conference; Cab. 23/95, 47(38), confirms this.
42. NC 18/1/1070, Neville to Hilda Chamberlain, 2 October.
43. W. Strang, *Home and Abroad* (1956), p. 144.
44. DBFP II, no. 1227; Cab. 23/95, 47(38).
45. *Cadogan diary*, 30 September, p. 110.
46. DBFP II, no. 1224, for the British text.
47. NC 18/1/1070, Neville to Hilda Chamberlain, 2 October.
48. Strang, pp. 146–47.
49. DBFP II, no. 1228, for the text.
50. Lord Home, *The Way the Wind Blows* (1976), p. 66.
51. NC 18/1/1070, Neville to Hilda Chamberlain, 2 October.
52. Feiling, p. 381.
53. Home, p. 66.
54. *Amery diary*, 8 October, pp. 528–9.
55. Feiling, pp. 381–2.
56. NC 18/1/1072, Neville to Hilda Chamberlain, 15 October.
57. Olivia Manning, *The Balkan Trilogy* (1981 edn), p. 100.
58. DBFP III, nos 83, 85, 91, 1 October.
59. *Ibid.*, no. 97, Newton to Halifax, 1 October.
60. *Ibid.*, no. 136, Kennard (Warsaw) to Halifax, 5 October.
61. *Lockhart diary*, 4 October, p. 399.
62. RAB G.11/130, 18 October; in the catalogue this was wrongly attributed to Sir Douglas Haking and mis-dated 1940!
63. DBFP III, no. 179, Henderson to Halifax, 11 October.
64. RAB G.11/130, 18 October.

Chapter 14
1. Macaulay's essay on *The Succession in Spain*.
2. Barnett's *The Collapse of British Power* is the *locus classicus* of this argument.
3. Butler's account is in *The Art of the Possible*, ch. 4; P. Cosgrave, *An English Life* (1981), ch. 3; P. Stafford, '... R. A. Butler at the Foreign Office 1938–39', *Historical Journal*, 1985, p. 910. Anthony Howard's *Rab* (1987) is disappointing on this period.
4. See above, ch. 7, and PRO Henderson MSS. FO 800/270, fos 55–9, ms. notes dated '*c.* May 1939'; FO 800/268, fos 220–21, Henderson to Mr Bruce, 25 May 1937, and FO 800/269, fo. 299, ms. note, undated, marked '? end of 1938?' From internal evidence it must be post-March 1939.
5. *Lockhart diary*, 21 October 1938, p. 404.
6. *Cadogan diary*, pp. 117–19; see also D. Lammers, 'From Whitehall after Munich', *Historical Journal*, 1973, pp. 831–52.
7. *Amery diary*, 30 September, p. 523.
8. FO 800/311, H/XIV/314/A, Halifax to Phipps, 1 November 1938; also at DBFP III, no. 285.
9. RAB G.9/120–122, speech to 'The Parlour', 30 November 1938.
10. *Loc. cit.*, Halifax to Phipps, 1 November.
11. *Cadogan diary*, p. 119.
12. FO 800/270, fos 55–9, ms. notes dated '*c.* May 1939'.
13. DBFP III, no. 184, Halifax to Lord Chilston, 11 October 1938.

14. RAB G.9/120–22, speech November 1938.
15. *Cadogan diary*, p. 117.
16. *Loc. cit.*, Halifax to Phipps, 1 November.
17. IORL, EUR. MSS. F.97/22B, Butler to Brabourne, 9 March 1938.
18. NC/18/1/1071, Neville to Ida Chamberlain, 9 October.
19. IORL, EUR. MSS. F.97/22B, Butler to Brabourne, 12 October 1938.
20. Charmley, *Duff Cooper*, pp. 125–7.
21. IORL, EUR. MSS. F.97/22B, Butler to Brabourne, 12 October 1938.
22. NC/18/1/1071, Neville to Ida Chamberlain, 9 October.
23. *Amery diary*, 30 September, p. 523.
24. *Cooper diary*, 29 September.
25. *Amery diary*, 30 September, p. 523; *Nicolson diary*, 30 September, pp. 372–3.
26. *Dalton diary*, p. 247; H. Macmillan, *Winds of Change* (1966), pp. 568–70.
27. Macmillan, p. 569.
28. *Amery diary*, 3 October, p. 524.
29. *Ibid.*, 5 October, p. 526; see also *Nicolson diary*, 5, 6 October, pp. 375–6.
30. *Amery diary*, 5 October, p. 526.
31. *Ibid.*, 11 October, p. 530.
32. British Library (BL), Cecil of Chelwood MSS., ADD. MSS. 51081, fo. 142, 16 October.
33. BL, Emrys Evans MSS., ADD. MSS. 58238, fo. 1, Law to Evans, 15 October.
34. *Ibid.*, fo. 4, Law to Evans, 30 December 1939.
35. *Nicolson diary*, 8 October, p. 376.
36. Duff Cooper, *Old Men Forget* (1953), p. 251.
37. NC 18/1/1071, Neville to Ida Chamberlain, 9 October.
38. NC 18/1/1075, Neville to Hilda Chamberlain, 6 November.
39. Charmley, *Duff Cooper*, p. 132.
40. *Amery diary*, 6 October, pp. 527–8.
41. Thompson, pp. 189–90; *Nicolson diary*, 6 October, p. 376.
42. Macmillan, pp. 570–71; Cooper, p. 251.
43. NC 8/21/7, Joseph Ball to Chamberlain, 1 June 1938.
44. Gibbs, pp. 492–502.
45. Newman, pp. 55–8.
46. IORL, EUR. MSS. F.97/22B, Butler to Brabourne, 19 November 1938.
47. Cab. 27/624, minutes of FPC, 14 November.
48. FO 800/328, Hal/38/38, Halifax to Chamberlain, 11 October.
49. *Churchill c.v. III*, p. 1202, Hoare to Chamberlain, 5 October.
50. NC/18/1/1074, Neville to Hilda Chamberlain, 28 October.
51. NC/18/1/1075, Neville to Hilda Chamberlain, 6 November.
52. IORL, EUR. MSS. F.97/22B, Butler to Brabourne, 7 November.
53. NC/18/1/1071, Neville to Ida Chamberlain, 9 October.
54. *Churchill c.v. III*, p. 1204.
55. NC/18/1/1071, Neville to Ida Chamberlain, 9 October.
56. *Churchill c.v. III*, pp. 1204–5, Chamberlain to Churchill, 6 October.
57. *Nicolson diary*, 6 October, pp. 375–6.
58. ADD. MSS. 58247, Emrys Evans to Amery, 1 July 1954.
59. NC/18/1/1074, Neville to Ida Chamberlain, 22 October.
60. *Private Papers*, pp. 161–2.
61. Churchill College, Halifax MSS. A.4.410.22, Hudson to Halifax, 12 December 1938.
62. NC 18/1/1079, Neville to Hilda Chamberlain, 11 December.
63. NC 18/1/1080, Neville to Ida Chamberlain, 17 December.
64. IORL, EUR. MSS. F.97/22B, Butler to Brabourne, 14 December.
65. NC 18/1/1080, Neville to Ida Chamberlain, 17 December.
66. *Ibid.*
67. *Harvey diary*, 10, 11, 13 October, pp. 211–13.
68. *Nicolson diary*, 9 November, pp. 377–8.
69. *Churchill c.v. III*, pp. 1281–4, 19 and 22 November.

70. *Ibid.*, p. 1240, Sir H. Worsley to Ramsay Muir, 26 October.
71. *Ibid.*, pp. 1239, 1291, 1308–9.
72. *Ibid.*, p. 1244; Nicolson ms. diaries, Balliol College, Oxford, 27 October.
73. *Amery diary*, 29 November, p. 537.
74. *Churchill c.v. III*, p. 1280.
75. *Amery diary*, 21 October, p. 532.

Chapter 15
1. IORL, EUR. MSS. F.97/22B, Butler to Brabourne, 14 December 1938.
2. NC/18/1/1072, Neville to Hilda Chamberlain, 15 October 1938.
3. NC/18/1/1074, Neville to Ida Chamberlain, 22 October 1938.
4. Gibbs, pp. 296–301.
5. *Ibid.*, p. 297.
6. *Ibid.*, chs 9, 12 and 14.
7. NC/1/20/1/186, Neville to Mary Endicott Chamberlain, 5 November 1938.
8. NC/18/1/1074, Neville to Ida Chamberlain, 22 October 1938.
9. NC/1/20/1/186, Neville to Mary Endicott Chamberlain, 5 November 1938.
10. NC 18/1/1076, Neville to Ida Chamberlain, 13 November 1938.
11. Weinberg, pp. 515–16; W. K. Wark, *The Ultimate Enemy* (1985 edn), p. 113.
12. Cab. 27/627, FP(36) 32nd mtg, 14 November. Barnett (p. 550) gives the reference Cab. 27/624, as does Newman (p. 71); Wark (p. 113) Cab. 27/622; only Dilks, in *Cadogan diary*, p. 125, gives the correct reference.
13. *Cadogan diary*, pp. 126–7.
14. DBFP III, no. 432, Halifax to Berlin, 15 December.
15. *Cadogan diary*, 14 November, p. 125.
16. DBFP III, ch. 6.
17. NC/1/18/1078, Neville to Ida Chamberlain, 4 December.
18. Prem. 1/327, fo. 70, Cadogan to Perth, 12 December.
19. IORL, EUR. MSS. F97/22B, Butler to Brabourne, 14 December 1938.

20. On this phenomenon see *Harvey diary*, 17 February, p. 255; *Amery diary*, 9 February, p. 542; and *Channon diary*, 16 February, p. 184.
21. IORL, EUR. MSS. F.97/22B, Butler to Brabourne, 14 December.
22. *Ibid.*; see also *Cadogan diary*, 13 December, pp. 227–8; and *Harvey diary*, 13 December, pp. 129–30.
23. S. Aster, *1939: The Making of the Second World War* (1973), pp. 39–40 for Goerdeler.
24. *Ibid.*, pp. 43–4; *Cadogan diary*, pp. 130–31.
25. *Harvey diary*, 25 December, p. 229; 17 December, pp. 228–9, for the speech.
26. NC/18/1/1081, Neville to Ida Chamberlain, 8 January.
27. *Cadogan diary*, p. 134; DBFP III, no. 485, from Perth.
28. *Cadogan diary*, pp. 136–7.
29. NC/18/1/1082, Neville to Hilda Chamberlain, 15 January.
30. DBFP III, no. 500, for records of the meetings.
31. *Cadogan diary*, p. 139, quoting Jebb's minute in Cab. 27/627, FPC (36) 74; see also Aster, pp. 46–8.
32. Cab. 27/624 for the FPC; Cab. 23/97, 2(39) for the Cabinet.
33. IORL, Zetland MSS., EUR. MSS. D.609/11, Zetland to Linlithgow, 29 January 1939.
34. DBFP IV (1952), no. 5, to Washington, 24 January 1939.
35. *Ibid.*, nos 40, 81, FO to Phipps, 28 January, 3 February; Aster, pp. 48–9.
36. Cab. 23/97, 3(39), 1 February.
37. *Cadogan diary*, p. 147.
38. *Nicolson diary*, 7 February, p. 390.
39. Feiling, p. 394.
40. NC/18/1/1084, Neville to Hilda Chamberlain, 5 February 1939.
41. *Channon diary*, 15 January 1939, p. 184.
42. *Harvey diary*, pp. 253–4, letter to Halifax, 14 February.
43. *Amery diary*, 9 February, p. 542.
44. *Harvey diary*, 17 February, p. 255.
45. *Channon diary*, 16 February, p. 184.

46. NC/18/1/1085, Neville to Ida Chamberlain, 12 February.
47. DBFP IV, no. 118, Henderson to FO, 18 February; FO minutes on it are in FO 371/22965, C2139/15/18.
48. Aster, p. 55.
49. FO 800/315, H/XV/124, Vansittart minute, 17 February 1939.
50. *Cadogan diary*, p. 158.
51. Newman, pp. 79–80, for all this.
52. *Cadogan diary*, 30, 31 January, pp. 145–6.
53. Newman, pp. 80–84.
54. R. Griffiths, *Fellow-Travellers of the Right* (1980), pp. 229, 281.
55. DBFP IV, Appendix I, iii; also FO 800/315, H/XV/126, Chamberlain to Henderson, 19 February.
56. IORL, Zetland MSS., EUR. MSS. D.609/11, Zetland to Linlithgow, 29 January 1939.
57. *Harvey diary*, 29 January, p. 249.
58. RAB G.10/79–85, Butler to Brabourne, 17 February.
59. DBFP IV, Appendix I, iv, Halifax to Henderson, 20 February.
60. *Harvey diary*, 10 March, p. 261.
61. *Cadogan diary*, 10 March, p. 155; Feiling, pp. 396–7.
62. Templewood, p. 328.
63. NC 18/1/1085, Neville to Ida Chamberlain, 12 February.
64. Feiling, p. 397.
65. *Channon diary*, 15 March, pp. 185–6.

Chapter 16
1. Colvin, p. 296.
2. *Ibid.*, p. 293; *Cadogan diary*, p. 158.
3. *Cadogan diary*, p. 158. What follows is based upon the accounts given in: D. Dilks (ed.), *Retreat From Power, vol. I 1906–1939* (1981), pp. 139–69; E. May (ed.), *Knowing One's Enemies* (Princeton, 1986 edn), pp. 237–70; and M. Bentley & J. Stevenson (eds), *High and Low Politics in Modern Britain* (Oxford, 1983), pp. 214–54.
4. Bentley & Stevenson, p. 253.
5. Churchill College, Inskip Diary, 28 January 1938.

6. May, p. 226; see also Watt's essay in May (ed.), p. 248.
7. NC 18/1/1091, Neville to Ida Chamberlain, 26 March.
8. Hansard, 345 HC Deb. 5s., cols 435–40; Thompson, pp. 201–2; Newman, pp. 100–3.
9. *Cadogan diary*, 15 March, p. 157.
10. Thompson, pp. 202–5, leans too heavily on Nicolson.
11. FO 371/22958, C3565/13/18, minute by Jebb, 18 March.
12. Hansard, 345 HC Deb. 5s., col. 557, for Simon; Cab. 23/98, 15 March 1939.
13. IORL, Zetland MSS., EUR. MSS. D.609/11, Zetland to Linlithgow, 21 March 1939, p. 72.
14. NC 18/1/1089, Neville to Ida Chamberlain, 12 March 1939.
15. *Nicolson diary*, 17 March, p. 393; *Amery diary*, 16 March, pp. 548–9.
16. Birkenhead, p. 432; *Harvey diary*, 18 March, p. 263; *Cadogan diary*, 16 March, p. 157.
17. Templewood, p. 329.
18. Birkenhead, p. 432.
19. CMD. 6106, *Documents concerning ... the outbreak of hostilities ...* (henceforth cited as Blue Book) (1939), document no. 9.
20. *Channon diary*, 17 March, p. 186; Newman, p. 105; NC 18/1/1090, Neville to Hilda Chamberlain, 19 March 1939; IORL, Zetland MSS., EUR. MSS. D.609/11, Zetland to Linlithgow, 21 March 1939, p. 73.
21. DBFP IV, no. 416, Halifax to Lindsay, 18 March.
22. *Ibid.*, no. 298, Sargent minute, 16 March.
23. *Ibid.*, no. 395, Halifax to Hoare (Bucharest), 17 March.
24. *Ibid.*, no. 390 (circular), 17 March.
25. *Ibid.*, no. 399, Hoare to Halifax, 18 March.
26. *Ibid.*, no. 422, 19 March.
27. *Ibid.*, Appendix I, viii, Henderson to Halifax, 15 March.
28. *Ibid.*, Appendix I, ix, Phipps to Halifax, 17 March.

29. Cab. 23/98, 12(39), 18 March.
30. Gibbs, p. 657 foll.; Wark, pp. 212–14.
31. *Cadogan diary*, 19 March, p. 161; NC 18/1/1190, Neville to Hilda Chamberlain, 19 March; IORL, Zetland MSS., EUR. MSS. D.609/11, Zetland to Linlithgow, 21 March.
32. Cab. 23/98, 13(39), 20 March.
33. *Cadogan diary*, 20 March, p. 161.
34. *Harvey diary*, 21 March, p. 266.
35. *Cadogan diary*, 20 March, p. 161.
36. *Ibid.*
37. DBFP IV, no. 471, Halifax to Kennard, 21 March; no. 458, record of Halifax/Bonnet conversations 21 March.
38. NC 18/1/1190, Neville to Hilda Chamberlain, 19 March; 18/1/1091, Neville to Ida Chamberlain, 26 March.
39. Cab. 23/98, 13(39), 20 March.
40. Prem. 1/327, fo. 22 foll., Wilson memo, 21 March; *Cadogan diary*, 20 March, pp. 162–3; DBFP IV, no. 448.
41. Newman, pp. 138–45; Aster, p. 89.
42. DBFP IV, no. 484.
43. NC 18/1/1091, Neville to Ida Chamberlain, 26 March.
44. DBFP IV, no. 490, from Moscow, 22 March.
45. Prem. 1/321, memo by Cadogan and Strang, 26 March; *Cadogan diary*, 26 March, p. 163.
46. Cab. 23/98, 12(39), 18 March.
47. DBFP IV, no. 518, FO to Kennard, 24 March.
48. Cab. 27/624, FPC minutes, 27 March.
49. FO 371/22958, C3954/13/18, n.d. memo; Wark, p. 118, and *Cadogan diary*, 26 March, pp. 163–4, for its influence.
50. NC 18/1/1190, Neville to Hilda Chamberlain, 19 March; Prem. 1/321, Chamberlain minute, 26 March.
51. FO 800/310, H/XI/191, memo, 27 March, of Chamberlain/de Valera meeting, 25 March.

52. NC 18/1/1091, Neville to Ida Chamberlain, 26 March.
53. *Ibid.*
54. Cab. 23/98, 15(39), 29 March.
55. NC/18/1/1092, Neville to Hilda Chamberlain, 2 April; Colvin, pp. 303–5.
56. The rumours are summarised in FO 371/22971, C6143/15/18, minute by F. K. Roberts and Jebb, 24 April.
57. Butler, *The Art of the Possible*, p. 77.
58. Cab. 23/98, 16(39), 30 March.
59. IORL, Zetland MSS., EUR. MSS. D.609/11, Zetland to Linlithgow, 4 April 1939.
60. Cab. 27/624, FPC, 30 March.
61. Cab. 23/98, 17(39), 31 March.
62. *Nicolson diary*, 31 March, pp. 393–4.
63. Hansard, 345 HC Deb. 5s., col. 2415.
64. NC 18/1/1092, Neville to Hilda Chamberlain, 2 April.
65. Hansard, 345 HC Deb. 5s., col. 2417.

Chapter 17
1. Cab. 23/98, 16(39), 30 March, Chiefs of Staff report, Annex B.
2. Newman, pp. 170–73, for British fears.
3. NC 18/1/1091, Neville to Ida Chamberlain, 26 March.
4. DBFP IV, Appendix V, Ogilvie-Forbes (Berlin) to Strang, 29 March; Mason-MacFarlane memo, 28 March.
5. *Harvey diary*, 25 March, p. 268.
6. Nicolson ms. diaries, 27, 29 March 1939.
7. NC 18/1/1095, Neville to Ida Chamberlain, 23 April 1939.
8. Macmillan, p. 593.
9. *Nicolson diary*, 11 April, p. 397.
10. *Amery diary*, 21 March, p. 549.
11. Hansard, 345 HC Deb. 5s., col. 2502.
12. *Churchill c.v. III*, pp. 1436–9.
13. NC 18/1/1094, Neville to Hilda Chamberlain, 15 April.
14. NC 18/1/1092, Neville to Hilda Chamberlain, 2 April.

15. *Harvey diary*, 16 April, p. 280.
16. NC 18/1/1094, Neville to Hilda Chamberlain, 15 April.
17. NC 18/1/1092, Neville to Hilda Chamberlain, 2 April.
18. Aster, p. 115; Newman, p. 205.
19. DBFP V, nos 1, 2, records of meetings.
20. Weinberg, pp. 501–3, 559–61; Newman, pp. 157–73.
21. DBFP IV, no. 596, Perth to Halifax, 1 April.
22. *Cadogan diary*, 7 April, p. 170.
23. NC 18/1/1093, Neville to Ida Chamberlain, 9 April.
24. NC 18/1/1094, Neville to Hilda Chamberlain, 15 April.
25. Cab. 23/98, 20(39), 10 April; *Cadogan diary*, 9, 10 April, pp. 171–2.
26. *Churchill c.v. III*, pp. 1436–9.
27. Cab. 27/624, FPC (36)41, 10 April.
28. Adamthwaite, pp. 308–10; *Cadogan diary*, 12, 13 April, p. 173.
29. NC 18/1/1094, Neville to Hilda Chamberlain, 15 April.
30. *Nicolson diary*, 31 March, p. 393; *Harvey diary*, 16 April, p. 280.
31. NC 18/1/1092, Neville to Hilda Chamberlain, 2 April.
32. *Channon diary*, 5, 13 April, pp. 192–3.
33. RAB G.10/3–4, Buccleuch to Butler, 24 April.
34. NC 18/1/1095, Neville to Ida Chamberlain, 23 April.
35. NC 18/1/1096, Neville to Hilda Chamberlain, 29 April.
36. *Harvey diary*, 3 May, p. 286.
37. Murray, p. 286; *Dalton diary*, p. 258; Gibbs, ch. 18; Aster, pp. 69–71, all make the judgments. *Harvey diary*, March and April 1939, and *Nicolson diary*, March and April, make similar assumptions.
38. *Dalton diary*, 8 May, p. 262.
39. Stafford, '... R. A. Butler ...' p. 915.
40. Cab. 23/98, 16, 17(39), 30, 31 March.
41. NC 18/1/1092, Neville to Hilda Chamberlain, 2 April.
42. FO 800/270, fos 82–3, Wilson to Henderson, 12 May 1939.
43. NC 18/1/1096, Neville to Hilda Chamberlain, 29 April.
44. *Ibid.*
45. DBFP V, nos 1 and 2.
46. *Ibid.*, nos 204 (to Halifax), 213 (to Cadogan), 18 April.
47. *Ibid.*, nos. 278, 279, 285.
48. *Dalton diary*, 23 April, pp. 260–63.
49. Cab. 23/99, 28(39), 17 May.
50. DBFP IV, no. 452, Seeds (Moscow) to Halifax, 20 March.
51. Weinberg, p. 550, whose excellent account these paragraphs generally follow.
52. Cab. 23/98, 20(39), 13 April.
53. DBFP V, no. 201, Seeds to Halifax, 18 April.
54. DBFP V, no. 204, Kennard to Halifax, 18 April.
55. NC 18/1/1096, Neville to Hilda Chamberlain, 29 April.
56. Cab. 23/99, 26(39), 3 May.
57. DBFP V, nos 397, 401, Halifax to Seeds, 6 May.
58. *Dalton diary*, 23 April, pp. 260–63.
59. Weinberg, pp. 498–502, 527–8, 536–9, for Polish-German relations.
60. DBFP V, no. 163, from Berlin, 14 April; no. 237, from Warsaw, 20 April.
61. DBFP V, no. 197, from Halifax, 17 April.
62. FO 371/23017, C5349/54/18, Sargent minute, 17 April.
63. DBFP V, no. 274, Kennard to Halifax, 23 April; no. 268 from Berlin, 23 April (for Halifax's comment); no. 326, Strang minute, 1 May.
64. *Ibid.*, no. 361, Mr Speaight's minute, 3 May.
65. FO 800/270, fo. 72, Henderson to Wilson, 9 May.
66. Cab. 23/99, 26(39), 3 May.
67. *Cadogan diary*, 2 May, p. 178.
68. DBFP V, no. 346, Halifax to Kennard, 3 May.
69. NC 7/11/32/129, Hoare to Chamberlain, 2 April.

70. Gibbs, pp. 491–502; *Private Papers,* ch. 21.
71. Henderson, pp. 220–21.
72. *Harvey diary,* pp. 431–5, has Rush-cliffe's letter and Harvey to Halifax, 3 May.
73. DBFP V, no. 268, from Berlin, minutes by Makins, 23 April.
74. DBFP V, no. 278, conversations, 24 April, p. 303.
75. RAB G.10/3–4, Buccleuch to Butler, 24 April.
76. NC 18/1/1096, Neville to Hilda Chamberlain, 29 April.
77. *Channon diary,* 1 May, p. 195.
78. NC 18/1/1101, Neville to Hilda Chamberlain, 28 May.
79. *Cadogan diary,* 3 May, p. 178.
80. *Channon diary,* 15 May, p. 199.
81. DBFP V, no. 359, Seeds to Halifax, 5 May.
82. DBFP V, no. 446, Phipps to Halifax, 10 May; no. 528, Strang minute, 16 May; no 531, Corbin to Halifax, 16 May; Adamthwaite, pp. 310–11.
83. DBFP V, no. 433, Halifax to Seeds, 9 May; Cab. 23/99, 27(39), 10 May.
84. DBFP V, no. 520, Seeds to Halifax, 15 May.
85. Cab. 23/99, 29(39), 17 May.
86. *Harvey diary,* 20 May, p. 290; DBFP V, no. 576, Halifax to Cadogan, 21 May.
87. *Cadogan diary,* 20 May, p. 182.
88. NC 18/1/1100, Neville to Ida Chamberlain, 21 May.
89. DBFP V, no. 413, Henderson to Halifax, 8 May, and minutes; *Harvey diary,* 20 May, p. 290.
90. DBFP V, no. 586, Kennard to Cadogan, 22 May; no. 589, Foreign Office memo on negotiations, 22 May.
91. *Harvey diary,* 20 May, p. 291.
92. NC/18/1/1101, Neville to Hilda Chamberlain, 28 May.
93. Cab. 23/99, 30(39), 24 May.
94. NC/18/1/1101, Neville to Hilda Chamberlain 28 May.

Chapter 18
1. DBFP V, no. 360, Phipps to Halifax 4 May.
2. Sir Oswald Mosley, *My Life* (1968), ch. 20; R. Skidelsky, *Oswald Mosley* (1975), ch. 23.
3. Cab. 23/98, 13(30), 20 March.
4. See ch. 18.
5. DBFP V, no. 364, Henderson to Halifax, 4 May.
6. FO 800/270, fo. 102, Henderson to Wilson, 24 May.
7. DBFP V, no. 340, Kennard to Cadogan, 2 May.
8. PRO, Cadogan MSS., FO 800/294, C2/39/12, Henderson to Cadogan, 14 May.
9. DBFP V, no. 364, Henderson to Halifax, 4 May.
10. DBFP V, no. 362 (4 May); no. 385, Halifax to Osborne (Vatican), 5 May; *Harvey diary,* 4–7 May, pp. 287–8.
11. FO 371/23017, C5469/54/18, Kirkpatrick minute, 19 April; Makins minute, 20 April.
12. DBFP V, no. 442, Halifax to Kennard, 10 May.
13. *Ibid.,* no. 459, Kennard to Halifax, 10 May.
14. FO 371/23018, C6910/54/18, Halifax minute, 10 May.
15. DBFP V, no. 384, Phipps to Halifax, 5 May.
16. NC 18/1/1100, Neville to Ida Chamberlain, 21 May.
17. *Halifax speeches,* pp. 270–80.
18. DBFP VI, Appendix III (i), conversation between Wenner-Gren and Chamberlain, 6 June; Prem. 1/304, Chamberlain to Lord Francis Scott, 12 June.
19. DBFP VI, *ibid.*
20. *Churchill c.v. III,* pp. 1516–17.
21. *Halifax speeches,* pp. 280–81.
22. *Churchill c.v. III,* pp. 1569–70, Churchill to Rothermere, 19 July.
23. NC 18/1/1107, Neville to Hilda Chamberlain, 15 July.
24. For examples see DBFP VI, nos 243, 278, 5, 8 July (Finland), and nos 256, 294, 6, 11 July (Estonia).

25. NC 18/1/1100, Neville to Ida Chamberlain, 21 May.
26. DBFP VI, no. 681, Seeds to Halifax, 1 June.
27. DBFP V, nos 648, 657, 665, 670, 681, 27–30 May, 1 June, Seeds to Halifax; Weinberg, pp. 569–75, is a better informed and more balanced account than the pro-Soviet effusions of A. J. P. Taylor in *The Origins of the Second World War* (1961), pp. 228–48, and the similarly tinged account in Aster, ch. 6.
28. NC 18/1/1102, Neville to Ida Chamberlain, 10 June.
29. NC 18/1/1106, Neville to Ida Chamberlain, 8 July.
30. DBFP VI, no. 163, Kennard to Halifax, 28 June.
31. *Ibid.*, no. 186, Phipps to Halifax, 30 June.
32. *Ibid.*, no. 209, Kennard to Halifax, 1 July.
33. *Ibid.*, no. 222, Halifax to Norton (Warsaw), 3 July.
34. *Ibid.*, no. 257, Cadogan to Norton (Warsaw), 6 July.
35. *Ibid.*, no. 309, Norton to Cadogan, 12 July.
36. FO 371/23018, C7096/54/18, Vansittart minute, 20 May.
37. *Harvey diary*, 3 May, p. 286.
38. NC 18/1/1107, Neville to Hilda Chamberlain, 15 July.
39. DBFP VI, no. 209, Norton to Halifax, 1 July.
40. *Ibid.*, nos 341, 347, 361 from Warsaw, 18, 20 July.
41. *Ibid.*, no. 372, memo by F. K. Roberts, 20 July.
42. DBFP VI, Appendix 1 (x), Henderson to Halifax, 12 July; no. 319, Halifax to Henderson, 13 July.
43. NC 18/1/1107, Neville to Hilda Chamberlain, 15 July.
44. DBFP VI, no. 376, Strang to Sargent, 20 July.
45. Cab. 27/625, FP (36) 56th mtg, 4 July.
46. DBFP VI, nos 225, 226, Seeds to Halifax, 4 July.

47. *Ibid.*, no. 285, Seeds to Halifax, 10 July.
48. *Ibid.*, nos 298, 300, 305, Halifax to Seeds, 12 July; nos 378, 379, Halifax to Seeds, 21 July.
49. NC 18/1/1107, Neville to Hilda Chamberlain, 15 July.
50. DBFP V, nos 658, 659, Henderson to Halifax, 28 May; no. 664, Henderson to Kirkpatrick, 29 May; no. 671, Henderson to Halifax, 30 May; no. 727, Henderson to Cadogan, 6 June; DBFP VI, no. 9, Henderson to Halifax, 9 June; no. 108, Henderson to Cadogan, 20 June; no. 118, Henderson to Halifax, 21 June, and the letters to Halifax contained in Appendix I.
51. FO 800/316, H/XV/221, Henderson to Halifax, 11 July.
52. DBFP VI, Appendix I (ix), Henderson to Halifax, 9 July.
53. DBFP VI, no. 319, Halifax to Henderson, 13 July.
54. DBFP VI, no. 395, Halifax to Henderson, 21 July.
55. RAB G.10/28, 'Character sketch' by Rab, n.d. but *c.* August 1939.
56. FO 800/315, H/XV/177, Butler to Halifax, 13 June.
57. FO 800/316, H/XV/236, Butler to Halifax, 17 July.
58. DBFP VI, no. 354, Wilson memo, 19 July.
59. *Churchill c.v. III*, pp. 1538–40.
60. DBFP VI, no. 370, Hudson's memo, 20 July.
61. FO 800/315, H/XV/170, Ashton-Gwatkin minute, 7 June, on H/XV/168, Henderson to Halifax, 28 May.
62. Aster, pp. 246–9, for an excellent account.
63. NC 18/1/1108, Neville to Ida Chamberlain, 23 July.
64. *Ibid.*
65. NC 18/1/1110, Neville to Hilda Chamberlain, 30 July.
66. DBFP VI, Appendix III, for Wenner-Gren; Appendix IV, for Dahlerus; see also no. 463, Halifax minute, 25 July.

67. Prem. 1/332, record of Kemsley/ Hitler conversation, 27 July.
68. *Ibid.*, Wilson memo, 1 August.
69. *Ibid.*, note of conversation with Dietrich, 3 August.
70. Prem. 1/330, fo. 12, Butler to Wilson, 2 August.
71. *Ibid.*, fos 3–7, Wilson memo, 3 August.
72. Aster, pp. 245–8, 256–8.
73. Prem. 1/330, fo. 1, Wilson note, 4 August.
74. Aster, pp. 290–300.
75. DBFP V, no. 413, Henderson to Halifax, 8 May; no. 574, Cadogan to Halifax, 21 May; *Harvey diary*, 20 May, p. 291; NC/18/1/1100, Neville to Ida Chamberlain, 21 May 1939.
76. FO 800/294, C2/39/23, Henderson to Cadogan, 4 July.
77. DBFP VI, no. 399, Seeds to Halifax, 22 July.
78. Weinberg, pp. 571–4.
79. J. W. Wheeler-Bennet, *Munich* (1948), p. 406.
80. Weinberg, p. 605.
81. *Ibid.*, p. 604.
82. Aster, p. 288; *Nicolson diary*, 20 July, pp. 406–7.
83. *Churchill c.v. III*, pp. 1581–3.
84. NC 18/1/1111, Neville to Ida Chamberlain, 5 August.
85. *Nicolson diary*, Nicolson to V. Sackville-West, 2 August, p. 407.
86. *Ibid.*, 18 July, p. 406.
87. NC 18/1/1108, Neville to Ida Chamberlain, 23 July.
88. NC 18/1/1111, Neville to Ida Chamberlain, 5 August.
89. *The Reckoning*, pp. 57–8.
90. Cab. 23/100, 40(39), 2 August.
91. NC 18/1/1107, Neville to Hilda Chamberlain, 15 July.

Chapter 19
1. NC 18/1/1112, Neville to Hilda Chamberlain, 13 August.
2. Prem. 1/331A, fos 179–81, Halifax to Chamberlain, 14 August.
3. NC 18/1/1114, Neville to Ida Chamberlain, 19 August.

4. DBFP VI, nos 542, 543, Shepherd (Danzig) to Halifax, 4 August; nos 545 (to Shepherd), 549 (to Norton) from Halifax, 4 August; nos 558 (from Kennard), 566 (from Shepherd), 5 August.
5. Hitler's letters of 23 August (Blue Book, no. 60), 25 August (Blue Book, no. 68), bear out this interpretation. Weinberg, pp. 557–60, 579–84, 610–22.
6. DBFP VI, no. 611, Kennard to Halifax, 10 August.
7. FO 371/23025, C11185/4/18, Halifax minute, 10 August, telegram to Kennard, 10 August (also at DBFP VI, no. 610), and 12 August (DBFP VI, no. 635).
8. *Cadogan diary*, 11 August, p. 194; DBFP VI, no. 645, Halifax to Kennard, 12 August.
9. DBFP VI, no. 695, Makins minute, 14 August.
10. Prem. 1/331A, fos 179–81, Halifax to Chamberlain, 14 August.
11. DBFP VI, nos 512, 525, Seeds to FO, 2, 3 August.
12. *Ibid.*, no. 647, Seeds to FO, 13 August.
13. Weinberg, p. 607; Aster, p. 307.
14. Aster, pp. 304–7; *Cadogan diary*, p. 196.
15. FO 800/316, H/XV/259, Henderson to Halifax, 16 August.
16. *Cadogan diary*, 18, 19 August, pp. 196–7.
17. *Cadogan diary*, pp. 197–9, for full text of Halifax to Chamberlain, 19 August.
18. *Cadogan diary*, 22 August, pp. 199–200.
19. Blue Book; no. 56, Chamberlain to Hitler, 22 August; drafts are to be found in Prem. 1/331A.
20. D. Dilks, 'Appeasement and Intelligence', in Dilks (ed.), *Retreat from Power* (1981), pp. 164–6, for the best account.
21. *Churchill c.v. III*, p. 1597.
22. FO 800/316, H/XV/268, Henderson to Halifax, 24 August.

23. Blue Book, nos 57, 58, Henderson to Halifax, 24 August.
24. FO 800/316, H/XV/268, Henderson to Halifax, 24 August.
25. *Ibid.*, H/XV/267, Henderson to Halifax, 22 August.
26. Blue Book, no. 64.
27. *Channon diary*, 24 August, p. 209.
28. FO 800/316, H/XV/267, 268, Henderson to Halifax, 22, 24 August; RAB G.10/110–112, memo by Butler, 'September 1939'.
29. NC 18/1/1115, Neville to Hilda Chamberlain, 27 August.
30. Weinberg, pp. 629–40; Aster, pp. 335–7.
31. FO 800/316, H/XV/269, Lord Tavistock to Halifax, 24 August.
32. Blue Book, no. 68, Henderson to Halifax, 25 August.
33. *Harvey diary*, 25 August, p. 309; *Cadogan diary*, 25 August, p. 201.
34. RAB G.10/111, 'September 1939', note by Rab.
35. RAB G.10/94–5, 'Position of British policy', note by Rab, *c.* 25/6 August.
36. *Cadogan diary*, 25, 26 August, pp. 201–2.
37. RAB G.10/112, 'September 1939'; *Cadogan diary*, 26 August, p. 202.
38. *Harvey diary*, 27 August, p. 307.
39. *Ibid.*, 26 August, p. 306.
40. *Cadogan diary*, 26 August, p. 202.
41. Cab. 23/100, 43(39), 26 August.
42. *Ibid.*
43. FO 800/319, H/XIX/57, Loraine to Halifax, 22 August; FO 800/316, H/XV/270, Henderson to Halifax, 25 August.
44. *Cadogan diary*, 27, 28 August, pp. 202–3.
45. *Churchill c.v. III*, p. 1600, unsent letter to Chamberlain, 30 August.
46. NC 18/1/1115, Neville to Hilda Chamberlain, 27 August.
47. *Cadogan diary*, pp. 202–3.
48. Cab. 23/100, 44(39), 27 August.
49. Cab. 23/100, 45(39), 28 August; Blue Book, no. 74.
50. Cooper diary, 29 August 1939.
51. *Cadogan diary*, 28 August, p. 203.
52. Blue Book, no. 75, Henderson to Halifax, 28 August.
53. FO 800/316, H/XV/271, Henderson to Halifax, 29 August.
54. DBFP VII, no. 455, Henderson to Halifax, 29 August, Vansittart minute.
55. *Cadogan diary*, 28 August, p. 203.
56. DBFP VII, no. 545, Halifax to Henderson, 30 August.
57. *Harvey diary*, 27, 29 August, pp. 308, 309.
58. Blue Book, no. 80, Henderson to Halifax, 29 August.
59. FO 800/316, H/XV/272, Henderson to Halifax, 30 August.
60. *Cadogan diary*, 29 August, p. 204.
61. Blue Book, no. 78, Hitler's reply, 29 August.
62. Cab. 23/100, 46(39), 30 August.
63. *Cadogan diary*, 30 August, pp. 204–5; *Harvey diary*, 30 August, p. 310.
64. Blue Book, no. 84, Kennard to Halifax, 30 August; no. 88, Halifax to Henderson, 30 August.
65. *Ibid.*, no. 89, British reply, 30 August.
66. *Ibid.*, no. 90, Henderson to Halifax, 30 August.
67. FO 800/316, H/XV/275, Henderson to Halifax, 31 August.
68. Henderson, p. 273.
69. *Ibid.*, pp. 273–4.
70. DBFP VII, no. 587, Henderson to Halifax, 31 August.
71. Aster, p. 362; Henderson, p. 274.
72. *Cadogan diary*, 31 August, pp. 205–6; *Harvey diary*, 31 August, pp. 310–11.
73. Aster, p. 365; Blue Book, no. 104.
74. *Cadogan diary*, 31 August, p. 206.
75. DBFP VII, no. 356, Halifax to Kennard, 1 September.
76. DBFP VII, no. 689, Halifax to Kennard, 1 September.
77. Cab. 23/100, 47(39), 1 September.
78. NC 18/1/1116, Neville to Ida Chamberlain, 10 September.
79. Cab. 23/100, 47(39), 1 September; *Cadogan diary*, 1 September, p. 211.
80. Cab. 100/23, 48(39), 2 September; *Harvey diary*, 1 September, p. 312.

81. Blue Book, no. 105, Chamberlain's statement.
82. *Amery diary*, 1 September, p. 570; *Nicolson diary*, 1 September, pp. 416–18.
83. Cab. 23/100, 48(39), 2 September; *Cadogan diary*, 2 September, p. 212.
84. *Harvey diary*, 2 September, pp. 313–14; R. A. C. Parker, 'The British Government and the Coming of War with Germany, 1939', pp. 5–7, in M. R. D. Foot (ed.), *War and Society* (1973).
85. *Nicolson diary*, 2 September, p. 418.
86. *Channon diary*, 2 September, p. 212.
87. Cab. 23/100, 48(39), 2 September.
88. *Harvey diary*, 2 September, p. 314; *Channon diary*, 2 September, p. 212.
89. RAB G.10/111, notes on 'September 1939'.
90. *Channon diary*, 2 September, p. 213.
91. *Amery diary*, 2 September, p. 570. I have no wish to enter the tiresome argument over whether it was in fact Bob Boothby who said this, as *Nicolson diary*, p. 419, records, except to say I would not hang a cat on the combined testimony of Nicolson and Boothby.
92. NC 18/1/1116, Neville to Ida Chamberlain, 10 September.
93. Simon diary, cited in Parker, pp. 11–12; Sir Reginald Dorman-Smith called it a 'strike', *Churchill c.v. III*, pp. 1607–8.
94. Parker, pp. 11–13, citing Inskip and Simon diaries.
95. Cab. 23/100, 49(39), 2 September.
96. *Churchill c.v. III*, pp. 1603–6.
97. *Channon diary*, 2 September, p. 214.
98. Hansard, HC Deb. 5s., cols 291–2, 3 September.

Epilogue
1. *Amery diary*, 3 September, p. 571.
2. NC 18/1/1116, Neville to Ida Chamberlain, 10 September.
3. *Ibid.*
4. NC 18/1/1121, Neville to Hilda Chamberlain, 17 September.
5. NC 18/1/1124, Neville to Ida Chamberlain, 8 October.
6. NC 18/1/1126, Neville to Ida Chamberlain, 22 October.
7. FO 800/317, H/XV/295, Halifax to Lord Noel-Buxton, 27 September 1939.
8. John Colville, *The Fringes of Power* (1985), 29 October 1939, p. 45.
9. NC 18/1/1125, Neville to Hilda Chamberlain, 15 October.
10. NC 18/1/1126, 1129, Neville to Ida Chamberlain, 22 October, 5 November 1939.
11. NC 18/1/1121, Neville to Hilda Chamberlain, 17 September.
12. Colville, 13 November, p. 51.
13. NC 18/1/1140, Neville to Ida Chamberlain, 27 January 1940.
14. NC 1/23/80, Neville to Dorothy Lloyd, 18 May 1940.
15. NC 18/1/1155, Neville to Ida Chamberlain, 11 May 1940.
16. Churchill College, Croft MSS. CRFT 1/7, Croft to Chamberlain, 12 May; Baldwin MSS. vol. 174, fos 273–7, Davidson to Baldwin, 12, 14 May; *Channon diary*, 13 May, p. 252.
17. NC 18/1/1144, Neville to Hilda Chamberlain, 25 February 1940.
18. NC 18/1/1165, Neville to Hilda Chamberlain, 14 July.
19. NC 2/24A, Chamberlain diary, 26 July.
20. *Ibid.*, 9 September.
21. NC 7/9/97, Chamberlain to Churchill, 22 September.
22. NC 7/9/99, 101, Churchill to Chamberlain, 29, 30 September.
23. NC 7/9/102, Chamberlain to Churchill, 1 October.
24. NC 18/1/1158, Neville to Ida Chamberlain, 25 May 1940.
25. RAB G.11/180, Butler to Annie Chamberlain, 22 December 1940.

BIBLIOGRAPHY

1. Manuscript Sources
Public Record Office, Kew

a) *Foreign Office*
FO 371 Foreign Office, General Correspondence
FO 800 Private Papers Series:
Sir Alexander Cadogan
Lord Cranborne
Lord Halifax
Sir Nevile Henderson
Sir Orme Sargent
FO 954 Avon Papers
FO 434 Confidential Print, S.E. Europe
FO 1011 Papers of Sir Percy Loraine

b) *Prime Minister's Papers*
Prem. 1 Neville Chamberlain
Prem. 3 Winston Churchill

c) *Cabinet Office Papers*
Cab. 2 Committee of Imperial Defence
Cab. 21 Registered Files
Cab. 23 Cabinet Meetings, Minutes
Cab. 24 Cabinet Meetings, Memoranda
Cab. 27 Cabinet Committee on Foreign Policy
Cab. 53 Chiefs of Staff Committee
Cab. 55 Joint Planning, Sub-Committee
Cab. 63 Hankey Papers

d) *Treasury*
T.160 Finance Files
T.161 Supply Files
T.188 Leith-Ross Papers

2. Private Papers
Leo Amery Diaries, courtesy of the Rt Hon. Julian Amery MP

Baldwin Papers, Cambridge University Library
Beaverbrook Papers, House of Lords Record Office
R. A. Butler Papers, Trinity College, Cambridge
Lord Brabourne Papers, India Office Record Library
Cadogan Papers, Churchill College
Lord Cecil of Chelwood, British Library
Neville Chamberlain, Birmingham University Library (courtesy of Dr B. Z. Benedikz)
Duff Cooper Papers, Churchill College
P. Emrys Evans, British Library
17th Earl of Derby, Liverpool City Library
Halifax Papers, Churchill College
Sir H. Knatchbull-Hugessen, Churchill College
Linlithgow Papers, India Office Records Library
Lloyd of Dolobran, Churchill College
Lord Margesson Papers, Churchill College
Sir H. Page-Croft, Churchill College
Sir E. Phipps, Churchill College
Sir L. Spears, Churchill College
Sir R. Storrs, Pembroke College, Cambridge
Sir W. Strang, Churchill College
Templewood Papers, Cambridge University Library
Sir R. Vansittart, Churchill College
Zetland Papers, India Office Record Library

3. Published Primary Sources
Place of publication is London unless otherwise stated.

Documents on British Foreign Policy, 1919–1939, E. L. Woodward (ed.) *et al.*:
Second Series, vols XVIII, XIX (1984–5)
Third Series, vols I–VII (1946–54)
Documents on German Foreign Policy:
Series D, vols V–VIII (1953–5)
Parliamentary Debates, House of Commons, Fifth Series
A Bryant (ed.), *In Search of Peace* (1938)
H. E. Craster (ed.), *Speeches on Foreign Policy by Viscount Halifax* (1940)
M. Gilbert (ed.), *Winston S. Churchill, vol. V, companion vol. III* (1982)

4. Published Diaries/Memoirs
Duchess of Atholl, *Working Partnership* (1958)
The Earl of Avon, *Facing the Dictators* (1962)
The Reckoning (1965)
J. Barnes & D. Nicholson (eds), *The Empire at Bay: The Leo Amery Diaries 1929–45* (1988)
R. Boothby, *I Fight to Live* (1947)
Recollections of a Rebel (1978)
R. A. Butler, *The Art of the Possible* (1971)
The Art of Memory (1982)
W. S. Churchill, *The Second World War, vol. I, The Gathering Storm* (1975, collected edn)
Arms and the Covenant (1975, collected edn)
Sir John Colville, *The Fringes of Power* (1985)
A. Duff Cooper, *Old Men Forget* (1953)
H. Dalton, *The Fateful Years* (1957)
D. Dilks (ed.), *The Diaries of Sir Alexander Cadogan, 1938–45* (1971)
Lord Eccles, *By Safe Hand: Letters of Sybil & David Eccles 1939–42* (1983)
T. Evans (ed.), *The Killearn Diaries* (1972)
P. J. Grigg, *Prejudice and Judgement* (1948)
Earl of Halifax, *Fulness of Days* (1957)
J. Harvey (ed.), *The Diplomatic Diaries of Oliver Harvey, 1937–40* (1970)
Sir N. Henderson, *Failure of a Mission* (1940)

Lord Home, *The Way the Wind Blows* (1976)
R. R. James (ed.), *Chips: The Diaries of Sir Henry Channon* (1967)
Memoirs of a Conservative (1969)
Sir I. Kirkpatrick, *The Inner Circle* (1959)
V. Lawford, *Bound for Diplomacy* (1963)
R. Macleod & D. Kelly (eds), *The Ironside Diaries 1937–40* (1962)
H. Macmillan, *Winds of Change* (1966)
R. J. Minney (ed.), *The Private Papers of Hore-Belisha* (1960)
M. Muggeridge (ed.), *Ciano's Diplomatic Papers* (1948)
N. Nicolson (ed.), *Harold Nicolson: Diaries and Letters, vol. I 1930–39* (1966)
Sir H. Page-Croft, *My Life of Strife* (1948)
B. Pimlott. (ed.), *The Political Diary of Hugh Dalton* (1986)
N. Rose (ed.), *Baffy: The Diaries of Blanche Dugdale 1936–47* (1973)
Sir W. Selby, *Diplomatic Twilight* (1953)
Lord Simon, *Retrospect* (1953)
Sir W. Strang, *Home and Abroad* (1956)
Lord Templewood, *Nine Troubled Years* (1954)
Sir R. Vansittart, *The Mist Procession* (1958)
K. Young (ed.), *The Diaries of Sir R. Bruce Lockhart, vol. I, 1915–38* (1973)

5. Secondary Sources
This includes only works which were found to be most useful.

a) *Biographies*
C. F. Adam, *Life of Lord Lloyd* (1948)
D. Carlton, *Anthony Eden* (1981)
J. Charmley, *Duff Cooper: The Authorised Biography* (1986)
Lord Lloyd and the Decline of the British Empire (1987)
R. S. Churchill, *The Rise and Fall of Sir Anthony Eden* (1959)
I. G. Colvin, *Vansittart in Office* (1965)
C. Coote, *A Companion of Honour* (1963)
P. Cosgrave, *An English Life: R. A. Butler* (1981)
J. A. Cross, *Sir Samuel Hoare* (1977)
Lord Swinton (1982)

D. Dilks, *Neville Chamberlain, vol. I* (1984)

D. Dutton, *Austen Chamberlain* (1985)

K. Feiling, *Neville Chamberlain* (1946)

M. Gilbert, *Winston S. Churchill, vol. V* (1976)

R. V. F. Heuston, *Lives of the Lord Chancellors* (1964)

A. Horne, *Harold Macmillan, vol. I* (1988)

A. Howard, *Rab: The Life of R. A. Butler* (1987)

R. R. James, *Churchill: A Study in Failure* (1970)
Anthony Eden (1987)

C. E. Lysaght, *Brendan Bracken* (1979)

W. Manchester, *The Caged Lion: Winston Spencer Churchill 1932–40* (1988)

N. Mosley, *Rules of the Game* (1982)
Beyond the Pale: Sir Oswald Mosley 1933–80 (1983)

A. R. Peters, *Anthony Eden at the Foreign Office 1931–8* (Aldershot, 1986)

B. Pimlott, *Hugh Dalton* (1985)

N. Rose, *Vansittart: Portrait of a Diplomat* (1978)

S. Roskill, *Hankey, vol. III* (1974)

R. Skidelsky, *Oswald Mosley* (1975)

A. J. P. Taylor, *Beaverbrook* (1972)

G. Waterfield, *Professional Diplomat: Sir Percy Loraine* (1980)

b) *General Works*

A. Adamthwaite, *France and the Coming of the Second World War* (1977)

S. Aster, *1939: The Making of the Second World War* (1973)

S. Ball, *Baldwin and the Conservative Party* (1988)

C. Barnett, *The Collapse of British Power* (1972)

M. Beaumont, *The Origins of the Second World War* (1978)

P. M. H. Bell, *The Origins of the Second World War in Europe* (1986)

B. Bond, *British Military Policy between the Two World Wars* (1980)

C. Bridge, *Holding on to the Empire* (1986)

M. Cowling, *The Impact of Hitler* (Cambridge, 1975)

D. Dilks (ed.), *Retreat from Power, vol. I, 1906–1939* (1981)

D. Dilks & C. Andrew (eds), *The Missing Dimension: Governments and Intelligence Communities in the Twentieth Century* (1984)

R. Douglas, *1938: In the Year of Munich* (1977)
The Advent of War (1978)

J. T. Emmerson, *The Rhineland Crisis* (1977)

L. W. Fuchser, *Neville Chamberlain and Appeasement* (New York, 1982)

F. R. Gannon, *The British Press and Germany 1936–9* (1971)

N. H. Gibbs, *Grand Strategy, vol. I* (1976)

M. Gilbert, *The Roots of Appeasement* (1966)

R. Griffiths, *Fellow-Travellers of the Right* (1980)

P. Haggie, *Britannia at Bay: The Defence of the British Empire Against Japan 1931–41* (1981)

J. Haslam, *The Soviet Union and the Struggle for Collective Security* (New York, 1984)

M. G. Hitchens, *Germany, Russia and the Balkans: Prelude to the Nazi-Soviet Non-Aggression Pact* (1983)

R. F. Holland, *Britain and the Commonwealth Alliance 1918–39* (1981)

M. Howard, *The Continental Commitment* (1972)
War and the Liberal Conscience (Oxford, 1981)

D. Irving (ed.), *Breach of Security* (1968)
Churchill's War (Australia, 1987)

D. E. Kaiser, *Economic Diplomacy and the Origins of the Second World War* (Princeton, 1977)

P. M. Kennedy, *The Realities Behind Diplomacy* (1980)

P. Kyba, *Covenants without Swords: Public Opinion and British Defence Policy* (Ontario, 1983)

R. Langhorne (ed.), *Diplomacy and Intelligence during the Second World War* (Cambridge, 1985)

W. R. Louis (ed.), *The Origins of the Second World War: A. J. P. Taylor and his Critics* (1971)

C. A. MacDonald, *The United States, Britain and Appeasement 1936–9* (1981)

D. Mack Smith, *Mussolini's Roman Empire* (1976)

G. Martel (ed.), *The Origins of the Second World War Reconsidered* (1986)

E. May (ed.), *Knowing One's Enemies* (Princeton, 1986)

W. N. Medlicott, *Britain and Germany* (1969)

K. Middlemas, *The Diplomacy of Illusion: The British Government and Germany 1937–9* (1972)

W. J. Mommsen & L. Ketternaker (eds), *The Fascist Challenge and the Policy of Appeasement* (1984)

W. Murray, *The Change in the European Balance of Power, 1938–9* (Princeton, 1984)

L. B. Namier, *Diplomatic Prelude 1938–1939* (1948)
In the Nazi Era (1952)

S. Newman, *March 1939: The British Guarantee to Poland* (Oxford, 1976)

R. Ovendale, *Appeasement and the English-Speaking World* (Cardiff, 1975)

G. Peden, *British Rearmament and the Treasury 1932–9* (Edinburgh, 1979)

L. R. Pratt, *East of Malta, West of Suez: Britain's Mediterranean Crisis 1936–9* (Cambridge, 1975)

D. Reynolds, *The Creation of the Anglo-American Alliance 1937–41* (1981)

K. Robbins, *Munich 1938* (1968)

E. M. Robertson (ed.), *The Origins of the Second World War* (1971)

W. R. Rock, *British Appeasement in the 1930s* (New York, 1977)

S. Roskill, *British Naval Policy between the Wars*, 2 vols (1968, 1976)

A. L. Rowse, *All Souls and Appeasement* (1961)

G. Schmidt, *The Politics and Economics of Appeasement* (1986 edn)

R. Shay, *British Rearmament in the 1930s* (Princeton, 1977)

A. J. P. Taylor, *The Origins of the Second World War* (1961)

T. Taylor, *Munich: The Price of Peace* (1979)

N. Thompson, *The Anti-Appeasers: Conservative Opposition to Appeasement in the 1930s* (1971)

C. Thorne, *The Approach of War* (1967)

N. Waites (ed.), *Troubled Neighbours: Franco-British Relations in the Twentieth Century* (1971)

W. K. Wark, *The Ultimate Enemy* (1985)

D. C. Watt, *Personalities and Policies* (1965)
Too Serious a Business (1975)

G. Weinberg, *The Foreign Policy of Hitler's Germany*, 2 vols (Carolina, 1970, 1980)

J. W. Wheeler-Bennett, *Munich: Prologue to Tragedy* (1948)

c) Articles

A. Adamthwaite, 'War Origins Again', *Journal of Modern History*, 1984
'The British Government and the Media 1937–8', *Journal of Contemporary History*, 1983

H. Aulach, 'Britain and the Sudeten Issue 1938', *Journal of Contemporary History*, 1983

D. Carlton, 'Against the Grain – In Defence of Appeasement', *Policy Review*, 1980

F. A. Coghlan, 'Armaments, Economic Policy and Appeasement ... 1931–37', *History*, 1972

J. P. Dunbabin, 'British Rearmament in the 1930s', *Historical Journal*, 1975

A. L. Goldman, 'Two views of Germany: Henderson vs Vansittart', *British Journal of International Studies*, 1980

J. Haslam, 'The Soviet Union and the Czech Crisis 1938', *Journal of Contemporary History*, 1979

A. Hillgruber, 'England's Place in Hitler's Plans for World Domination', *Journal of Contemporary History*, 1974

P. M. Kennedy, 'Idealists and Realists: British Views of Germany 1864–1939', *Transactions of the Royal Historical Society*, 1975
'The Tradition of Appeasement in British Foreign Policy 1864–1939', *British Journal of International Studies*, 1976
'Strategy vs Finance in Twentieth Century Britain', *International History Review*, 1981
'Appeasement and British Defence

Policy', *British Journal of International Studies*, 1978

D. Lammers, 'From Whitehall after Munich', *Historical Journal*, 1973

V. Lawford, 'Three Ministers', *The Cornhill*, winter, 1956/7

D. B. Lungu, 'The European Crisis of March – April 1939: The Roumanian Dimension', *International History Review*, 1983

C. A. MacDonald, 'Britain, France and the April Crisis of 1939', *European Studies Review*, 1972

'Economic Appeasement and the German Moderates', *Past and Present*, 1972

R. Manne, 'The British Decision for Alliance with Russia, May 1939', *Journal of Contemporary History*, 1974

'The Foreign Office and the Failure of the Anglo-Russian Rapprochement', *Journal of Contemporary History*, 1981

R. J. Overy, 'Hitler's War and the German Economy: A Reinterpretation', *Economic History Review*, 1982

R. A. C. Parker, 'The British Government and the Coming of War with Germany in 1939', in M. R. D. Foot (ed.), *War and Society* (1973)

'British Rearmament 1936–39', *English Historical Review*, 1981

G. Peden, 'The Burden of Imperial Defence and the Continental Commitment Reconsidered', *Historical Journal*, 1984

'A Matter of Timing: The Economic Background to British Foreign Policy, 1937–39', *History*, 1984

'Sir Warren Fisher and British Rearmament against Germany', *English Historical Review*, 1979

A. J. Prazmowska, 'War over Danzig?', *Historical Journal*, 1983

P. W. Schroeder, 'Munich and the British Tradition', *Historical Journal*, 1976

P. Stafford, 'The Chamberlain-Halifax Visit to Rome: A Reappraisal', *English Historical Review*, 1983

'... R. A. Butler at the Foreign Office 1938–39', *Historical Journal*, 1985

S. G. Walker, 'Solving the Appeasement Puzzle', *British Journal of International Studies*, 1980

D. C. Watt, 'Appeasement: The Rise of a Revisionist School?', *Political Quarterly*, 1965

6. Theses

V. L. Ramsden-Atherton, *Lord Lloyd, the British Council and Foreign Policy 1937–41*, PhD, University of East Anglia, 1988

M. J. Rooke, *The British Government's Relations with the States of South-Eastern Europe, 1934–6*, PhD, London, 1980

G. van Kessel, *The British Reaction to German Economic Expansion in South-Eastern Europe, 1936–9*, PhD, London, 1972

Amery, Leopold (1873–1955) Born in British India. Fellow of All Souls, Oxford. Journalist on *The Times*. Conservative MP for Sparkbrook, Birmingham, 1911–45. Cabinet Offices: Admiralty, 1922–4; Colonies, 1924–9; Dominions, 1925–9; India and Burma, 1940–45. It was said of him that had his speeches been half an hour shorter and his stature half a foot taller he could have been Prime Minister.

Baldwin, Stanley (1st Earl) (1867–1947) Educated Harrow and Trinity, Cambridge (where he got a Third). Conservative MP, 1906–37. Leader of his Party, 1923–37. Cabinet Offices: Exchequer, 1922–3; Prime Minister, 1923–4, 1924–9, 1935–7; Lord President, 1931–5. According to Curzon, he was 'a man of the utmost insignificance', but ended up an earl, Prime Minister and Knight of the Garter.

Beneš, Eduard (1884–1948) Czechoslovak representative at Paris Peace Conference, 1919; Foreign Minister, 1918–35; President, 1935–8; President of Government-in-Exile, 1941–5. Namier said of him that he 'tried to survive by being reasonable (and plausible) in an age when reason had ceased to count'.

Bonnet, Georges (1889–1973) French politician. Cabinet rank in various Governments after 1926; Minister of Foreign Affairs, 1938–9; Minister of Justice, 1939–40. In favour of 'peace at any price' in September 1938.

Boothby, Sir Robert (Lord Boothby) (1900–86) Educated Eton and Magdalen, Oxford. Scots Conservative MP for East Aberdeenshire, 1924–58; PPS to Churchill, 1926–9. Junior Office: Food, 1940–41; forced to resign. Brilliant, opinionated and in love with Dorothy Macmillan.

Bracken, Brendan (1st and last Viscount) (1901–58) Conservative MP, 1924–45, 1950–51; PPS to Churchill, 1940–41. Cabinet Offices: Information, 1941–5; Admiralty, 1945. Self-made businessman and 'man of mystery'; rumoured to be Churchill's illegitimate son, but despite red hair and lack of judgment was, in fact, only his 'faithful chela'.

Butler, Richard Austen (Rab) (Lord Butler) (1902–82) Born in India. Educated Marlborough and Pembroke, Cambridge. Fellow of Corpus Christi. Conservative MP for Saffron Walden, 1926–65; Master of Trinity thereafter. Junior Offices: India, 1932–7; Labour, 1937–8; Foreign Office, 1938–41. Cabinet Offices: Education, 1941–5; Labour, 1945; Exchequer, 1951–5; and many high offices until 1964. Twice failed to become Prime Minister – the best Prime Minister we never had, so to speak. Feline, intelligent, Chamberlainite, but insufficiently aristocratic for Chips Channon (q.v.), despite marrying into Courtauld wealth.

Cadogan, Sir Alexander (1884–1968) Educated Eton and Balliol, Oxford. Diplomatic Service, 1908; Minister in Peking, 1932–6; Permanent Under-Secretary, 1938–45. Replaced Vansittart and thought by Chamberlain to be a steadying influence upon Eden.

Chamberlain, Neville (1869–1940) Educated Rugby and Mason College, Birmingham. Groomed for business by his father, Joseph. Failed sisal grower in West Indies, 1890–96; successful local businessman and politician thereafter; unsuccessful foray into national politics, 1916–17, as Minister of National Service. Conservative MP, 1918–40. Started late but rose rapidly. Cabinet Offices: Postmaster-General, 1922; Health, 1923; Exchequer, 1923–4; Health, 1924–9; Exchequer, 1931–7; Prime Minister, 1937–40; Lord President, 1940. As he preferred to die 'Plain Mr Chamberlain', like his father, he refused an earldom and the Garter.

Chamberlain Ida (1870–1942) and Hilda (b. 1871) Sisters of Neville, half-sisters of Austen. Settled in Hampshire as maiden ladies. Corresponded regularly with Neville and gave him good advice (which he did not always take).

Channon, Sir Henry ('Chips') (1897–1958) Educated America and Christ Church, Oxford. Married into the Guinness family. Conservaive MP for Southend, 1935–58 (succeeded in the seat by his son Paul); PPS to Rab Butler, 1938–41. Socialite and diarist.

Churchill, Sir Winston Leonard Spencer (1874–1965) Professional soldier, turned journalist, turned MP. Entered Parliament, 1900. Cabinet Offices: Board of Trade, 1908–10; Home Secretary, 1910–11; Admiralty, 1911–15; Duchy of Lancaster, 1915; Munitions, 1917–18; War and Air, 1918–21; Colonial Office, 1921–2; Exchequer, 1924–9; Admiralty, 1939–40; Prime Minister, 1940–45, 1951–5. Order of Merit, KG, but declined an earldom and dukedom. Winner of Nobel Prize for Literature, tireless self-publicist and writer; secular canonisation after 1940.

Ciano, Count Galeazzo (1903–44) Mussolini's son-in-law. Italian Foreign Minister, 1936–43; Ambassador to the Vatican, 1943. Executed, 1944.

Cooper, Sir (Alfred) Duff (1st Viscount Norwich) (1890–1954) Educated Eton and New College, Oxford. Diplomat, 1913–24. Conservative MP, 1924–9, 1931–45. Junior Office, 1926–35. Cabinet Offices: War, 1935–7; Admiralty, 1937–8; Information, 1940–41; Duchy of Lancaster, 1941–3. Ambassador to the French, 1943–7. Resigned over Munich. Famous for being married to Lady Diana Manners, having a ferocious temper, and being brilliant but bone-idle.

Corbin, (André) Charles (1881–1970) French Ambassador: Madrid, 1929–31; Brussels, 1931–3; London, 1933–40.

Cranborne, Viscount (5th Marquess of Salisbury (1893–1972) Conservative MP for South Dorset, 1929–41. Eden's Under-Secretary, 1935–8. Cabinet Offices: Paymaster-General, 1940; Dominions, 1940–42, 1943–5; Lord Privy Seal, 1942–3; Leader of Lords, 1942–5, 1951–7; Lord President of the Council, 1951–7. Known as 'Bobbety'. Close to Eden, who, nevertheless, failed to make him Foreign Secretary in 1955. The most talented Cecil since his grandfather, the third Marquess; much given to threats of resignation.

Daladier, Edouard (1884–1970) French Prime Minister and Minister of War, 1933; Prime Minister and Minister for Foreign Affairs, 1934; Prime Minister and Minister of National Defence, 1938–40; Minister for Foreign Affairs, 1940. The 'Bull of Vaucluse', or, as his many detractors would have it, a bull with snail's horns.

Dalton, Hugh (Lord) (1887–1962) Son of Canon Dalton of Windsor Castle. Educated Eton and King's, Cambridge. Economist, Labour MP, 1924–9, 1929–31, 1935–55. Cabinet Office after 1940. Loud-voiced, unpleasant and of homosexual tendencies.

Dunglass, Lord (14th Earl of Home; Sir Alec Douglas-Home) (b. 1903)

Educated Eton. Unionist MP, 1931–45, 1950–51. PPS to Chamberlain, 1937 –40. Prime Minister, 1963–4.

Eden, (Sir) (Robert) Anthony (1st Earl of Avon) (1897–1977) Educated Eton and Christ Church, Oxford. Conservative MP for Warwick and Leamington, 1923–57. Under-Secretary at Foreign Office, 1931–3. Cabinet Offices: Lord Privy Seal, 1934–5; Minister without Portfolio, 1935; Foreign Secretary, 1935–8; Dominions, 1939–40; War, 1940–41; Foreign Secretary, 1940–45, 1951–5; Prime Minister, 1955–7, resigned after Suez. The 'one strong young figure', according to Churchill; at once the hope and the despair of his friends.

Elliot, Walter (1888–1958) Conservative MP, 1918–23, 1924–45, 1946–58. Cabinet Offices: Agriculture, 1932–6; Scotland, 1936–8; Health, 1938–40. Doctor. Like 'Shakes' Morrison, suffered from having been tipped as 'future Prime Minister'.

Emrys Evans, Paul (1894–1964) Diplomat before 1931. Conservative MP, 1931–45; Chairman Conservative Foreign Policy Committee, 1937–8. Junior Office: 1941–5. Friendly with Eden.

Gamelin, General Maurice (1872–1958) French Commander in Chief, 1938–40.

Goering, Field-Marshal Hermann (1893–46) Nazi chieftain. President of Reichstag, 1932; Air Minister and Commander in Chief German Air Force, 1933–45. Reputed to be a 'moderate', 1937–9. Sentenced to death at Nuremberg, but cheated hangman by suicide.

Grandi, Count Dino (1895–1988) Italian Minister of Foreign Affairs, 1929 –32; Ambassador in London, 1932–9; Minister of Justice, 1939–43. Anglophile, socialite.

Hacha, Dr Emil (1872–1945) President of Czechoslovakia, 1938–9.

Halifax (3rd Viscount, 1st Earl) (Edward Lindley Wood) Fellow of All Souls, Oxford; Master of Foxhounds. Conservative MP, 1910–25. Cabinet Offices: Education, 1922–4; Agriculture, 1924–6; Viceroy, 1926–31; Education, 1932–5; War, 1935; Lord Privy Seal, 1935–7; Lord President, 1937–8; Foreign Secretary, 1938–40. Ambassador in Washington, 1940–46. Tory Grandee whose 'wivvers were quite unwung' by Munich – until afterwards. Friend of Baldwin.

Harvey, Sir Oliver (1st Baron) (1893–1968) Educated Malvern and Trinity, Cambridge. Foreign Office, 1919 onwards. PPS to Eden, 1936–8; to Halifax, 1938–9; to Eden, 1941–3. Ambassador in Paris, 1947–54. Self-consciously 'left of centre' éminence grise to Eden.

Henderson, Sir Nevile Meyrick (1882–1942) Educated Eton. Diplomatic Service from 1905. Ambassador: Belgrade, 1932–5; Buenos Aires, 1935–7; Berlin, 1937–9. Appointed by Eden and Vansittart, who later poured odium upon him. A 'man with a mission'.

Henlein, Konrad (1898–1945) Chairman, Sudeten German party, 1935–8; Gauleiter of Sudetenland, 1939–45. Sentenced to death for war crimes.

Hitler, Adolf (1889–1945) Austrian by birth. Bohemian 'drop-out', evaded Austrian National Service. Served in German Army, 1914–18 (Iron Cross). Political agitator after 1918. Unsuccessful putsch in Munich, 1923. Leader German National Socialist Workers Party. Chancellor, 1933; Führer, 1934–45. Shrewd opportunist and political gambler; anti-Semite and anti-Bolshevist. Committed suicide, 1945.

Hoare, Sir Samuel (Viscount Templewood) (1880–1959) Conservative MP for Chelsea, 1910– 44. Cabinet Offices: Air, 1924–9; India, 1931–5; Foreign Office, 1935; Admiralty, 1936–7; Home Office, 1937

–9; Lord Privy Seal, 1939–40. The one 'Man of Munich' sacked by Churchill in 1940, sent as Ambassador to Franco's Spain, 1940–44. Resigned 1935 over pact with Laval, prompting George V's only known witticism: 'No more coals to Newcastle, no more Hoares to Paris.'

Hore-Belisha, Leslie (1st and last Baron) (1893–1957) Liberal MP for Devonport, 1923–31; National Liberal, 1931–42; National Independent, 1942–5. Junior Offices: 1931–4. Cabinet Offices: Transport, 1934–7; War, 1937–40; National Insurance, 1945. Gave his name to the 'Belisha beacon'; seen as radical reformer at War Office; sacked by Chamberlain in 1940; Halifax advised against his being made Minister of Information because he was Jewish.

Inskip, Sir Thomas Walker Hobart (1st Viscount Caldecote) (1876–1947) Educated Clifton College, Bristol, and King's, Cambridge (Third in Classics). 'Redoubtable rugger player'. Barrister, married daughter of seventh Earl of Glasgow. Ardent Evangelical. Conservative MP, 1918–29, 1931–9. Cabinet Offices: Solicitor-General, 1922–4, 1924–8, 1931–2; Attorney-General, 1928–9, 1932–6; Minister for the Co-ordination of Defence, 1936–9; Dominions, 1939–40; Lord Chancellor, 1940. Successfully led fight against Revised Prayer Book, 1927–8.

Jebb, Sir Gladwyn (Lord Gladwyn) (b. 1900) Private Secretary to Vansittart and Cadogan, 1937–40; Ambassador in Paris, 1954–60.

Kennard, Sir Howard (1878–1955) British Ambassador to Poland, 1935–41.

Kleist-Schenzin, Colonel Ewald von (d. 1945) Leading anti-Nazi. Visited Britain, 1938. Hanged, 1945.

Litvinov, Maxim (1883–1951) Soviet Minister for Foreign Affairs, 1930–39. Married to an Englishwoman. Thought of as 'pro-Western', his replacement by Molotov (q.v.) in 1939 was a bad sign for the future of Anglo-Soviet relations.

Lloyd, Sir George Ambrose (1st Baron) (1879–1941) Educated Eton and Trinity, Cambridge (left without taking degree). Unionist MP, 1910–18, 1924–5. Governor of Bombay, 1918–23; High Commissioner, Egypt, 1925–9, when fell foul of liberal Conservatives, Foreign Office and Labour. Led campaign against India Bill, 1931–5; staunch anti-appeaser thereafter. Stern, unbending tariff reformer, shared Birmingham business background with Neville Chamberlain, whom he admired more than he did Baldwin. Cabinet Offices: Colonies, 1940–41; Leader of the Lords, 1941.

Lloyd George, David (1st Earl) (1863–1945) Liberal MP, 1890–1945. Cabinet Offices: Board of Trade, 1905–8; Chancellor, 1908–15; Munitions, 1915–16; Prime Minister, 1916–22. Leader of Liberal Party, 1926–31. Excluded from office, 1922, 1931, 1935. Sexual activities earned him the nickname 'The Goat'. Detested Chamberlain, who reciprocated. Refused office from Churchill, 1940.

MacDonald, James Ramsay (1866–1937) Labour MP, 1906–18, 1922–31; National Labour, 1931–7. Leader of Labour Party, first Labour Prime Minister, 1924, 1929–31; Prime Minister as head of National Government, 1931–5; Lord President, 1935–7. Refused knighthood and earldom. Increasingly senile after 1933.

MacDonald, Malcolm (1901–81) Son of J. R. MacDonald. Labour MP, 1929–31; National Labour, 1931–5, 1936–45. Cabinet Offices: Dominions, 1935–8, 1938–9; Colonies, 1938–40; Health, 1940–41. High Commissioner Canada, 1941–6. Often mentioned as potential rebel.

Macmillan, (Maurice) Harold (1st Earl of Stockton) (1894–1986) Publisher. Conservative MP for Stockton-on-Tees, 1924–9, 1931–45, 1946

–64. Eccentric, bookish and boring during 1930s. Rebel over economic policy and Abyssinia; close to Churchill in 1938; burnt Chamberlain in effigy on bonfire night, 1938. Prime Minister, 1957–63; elder statesman, 1980s.

Maisky, Ivan (1884–1975) Soviet Ambassador in London, 1932–43. Close contacts with Churchill, Lloyd George, Dalton (q.q.v.). Reported to Stalin their stories about Chamberlain's Germanophilia.

Masaryk, Jan (1886–1948) Son of Tomas Masaryk, founder of Czechoslovakia. Czech Minister in Britain, 1925 –39; Foreign Minister, Government-in-Exile, 1940–45; Foreign Minister, 1948. Died in suspicious circumstances. Bon viveur and Anglophile.

Molotov, Vyacheslav (1890–1988) Soviet Foreign Minister, 1939–49. Negotiated Molotov-Ribbentrop pact, 1939.

Mussolini, Benito (1883–1945) Socialist agitator and journalist, 1904 –15. President, Council of Ministers, 1922–6; Head of Government (Il Duce), 1926–43, when he was deposed; reinstated as head of puppet regime at Salo, by Hitler, 1944. Followed traditional Italian foreign policy of selling his services to highest bidder, 1922–40; thereafter throwing in his lot with Hitler and adding to the ruins for which Italy is famous.

Neurath, Baron Constantin von (1873 –1956) German Foreign Minister, 1932–8, supposed 'moderate'. Later Gauleiter for conquered Czech territories. Jailed at Nuremberg.

Nicolson, Sir Harold (1886–1968) Diplomatist, 1909–29. Journalist until 1935. National Labour MP for West Leicester, 1935–45. Junior Office: 1940 –41. Writer and diarist. Intellectually fastidious; admired Churchill's strength and Eden's youthful idealism.

Phipps, Sir Eric (1875–1945) Diplomatic Service from 1899. Ambassador: Berlin, 1933–7; Paris, 1937–9.

Brother-in-law of Vansittart (q.v.), for whose opinions he had scant respect.

Ribbentrop, Joachim von (1883 –1946) Champagne salesman. Nazi Ambassador in London, 1936–8, when he failed to deliver the entente he had thought was on offer; Foreign Minister, 1938–45. Hanged after Nuremberg.

Roosevelt, Franklin Delano (1882 –1945) American President, 1932–45. Much given to liberal rhetoric in field of foreign policy.

Runciman, Walter (1st Viscount) (1870–1949) Educated Trinity, Cambridge. Liberal MP, 1899–1900, 1901–18, 1924–9, 1929–31; National Liberal, 1931–7. Cabinet Offices: Education, 1908–11; Agriculture, 1911–14; Board of Trade, 1914–16, 1931–7; Lord President, 1938–9. Headed Mission of Inquiry to Czechoslovakia in 1938. Found Beneš procrastinating and the Czechs frustrating.

Sargent, Sir Orme Garton (Moley) (1884–1962) Foreign Office from 1906. Assistant Under-Secretary of State, 1938–9; Permanent Under-Secretary (succeeding Cadogan), 1946–9. Hated foreign travel, never served abroad; anti-appeaser.

Seeds, Sir William (1882–1973) British Ambassador in Moscow, 1939–40.

Simon, Sir John Allsebrook (1st Viscount) (1873–1954) Fellow of All Souls, Oxford. Leading KC, Liberal MP, 1906–18, 1922–31. National Liberal Leader, 1931–40; Lord Chancellor, 1940–45. Cabinet Offices: Foreign Secretary, 1931–5; Home Secretary, 1935–7; Chancellor, 1937–40. Disliked Eden, disliked by Eden and many other for oleaginous manner – known as 'Soapy Simon'; would like to have been liked.

Sinclair, Sir Archibald (1st Viscount Thurso) (1890–1970) Liberal MP, 1931–45. Minister of Air under Churchill. Liberal Leader, 1940–45.

Stalin, Joseph (1879–1953) Communist dictator after 1924. Distrusted Western Powers, fascist Powers, Soviet generals, fellow-revolutionaries and, eventually, everyone. Mass-murderer, who shares with Hitler dubious distinction of having caused the deaths of millions of his fellow-countrymen; ended up on winning side in 1945 and, therefore, extent of crimes only recently exposed.

Stanley, Oliver (1896–1950) Younger son of seventeenth Earl of Derby. Educated Eton and Oxford. Conservative MP for Westmorland, 1924–50. Junior Office: 1931–3. Cabinet Offices: Transport, 1934–5; Labour, 1935–7; Education, 1937–40; War, 1940; Colonies, 1942–5. Often mentioned as potential rebel. Tipped as next Conservative Chancellor, 1945–50. Related by marriage to Cadogan (q.v.).

Strang, Sir William (1st Baron) (1893–1978) Foreign Office from 1919. Head of Central Department (dealing *inter alia* with Germany and Czechoslovakia), 1937–9; Permanent Under-Secretary, 1949–53 (succeeding Sargent). Accompanied Chamberlain to Munich; sent to help Seeds (q.v.) in Moscow during Anglo-Soviet negotiations, 1939.

Thomas, James Purdon Lewes (1st Viscount Cilcennin) (1903–60) Educated Rugby and Oriel, Oxford. Conservative MP, 1931–55. Assistant PS to Baldwin, 1931; PPS to: J. H. Thomas (Dominions Secretary, 1930–5), 1932–5; Eden, 1935–8. Junior Office: Admiralty, 1943–5; Cabinet Office: Admiralty, 1951–6. Fervent 'Edenite'.

Tilea, Viorel Vergil (1896–1972) Romanian Minister, London, 1938–40; founder of Free Romanian Movement, 1940. Anglophile, close links with Lord Lloyd (q.v.).

Vansittart, Sir Robert Gilbert (1st and last Baron) (1881–1957) Educated Eton and Oxford. Entered Diplomatic Service, 1902; PPS to Baldwin and MacDonald (q.q.v.), 1928–30; Permanent Under-Secretary, Foreign Office, 1930–37; refused offer of Paris Embassy, 1936–7; 'kicked upstairs' as Chief Diplomatic Adviser, 1938–40. Germanophobe, Francophile. Diplomatist and dramatist – inclined to melodrama on both fronts. Eden found him overbearing, Chamberlain found him unbearable.

Wilson, Sir Horace John (1882–1972) Educated Bournemouth and London School of Economics. Entered Civil Service, 1900. Chief Industrial Adviser, 1930–39. Seconded to the Treasury, 1935, for duties with Baldwin and Chamberlain; Permanent Head of Civil Service, 1939–42. Supposed by many to be Chamberlain's éminence grise; Butler thought him 'the most powerful man in England'. Real function seems to have been to act as sounding-board for Chamberlain.

INDEX

Amery, Leo, 58; on Runciman, 90; on
  Berchtesgaden, 110; and opposition to
  Chamberlain, 128–30, 136, 137; and
  isolationism, 144; and difficulties of
  opposing Chamberlain after Munich, 145,
  146, 153; convinced by Chamberlain's
  Munich speech, 147; and Churchill, 177,
  210; 'Speak for England', 210; and
  Chamberlain, 210; biography, 243
Anderson, Sir John, 151, 168
Angell, Norman, 55
Atholl, Duchess of, 153
Attlee, Clement, 137, 179; and Churchill,
  145–6; 'a cowardly cur', 178
Austria, German designs on, 14, 18–20;
  Anschluss, 46, 63, 66–7
Avenol, Joseph, 45

Baldwin, Stanley, 3, 35, 53, 59, 60, 152;
  somnolence of, 4, 13, 21, 30, 34; cunning
  of, 12, 35, 63; 'party before country', 23;
  advises Eden to steer clear of Churchill,
  57; possible political resurrection, 78;
  'good old days of', 82, 96; biography, 243
Ball, Sir Joseph, 47
Beaumont, M., 64, 120
Beaverbrook, Lord, 53, 56, 57; unflattering
  view of Halifax, 15, 16; friendly with
  Hoare, 35; view of Simon, 35; isolationism
  of, 120
Beck, Colonel, 173, 174, 192; anti-Soviet,
  180–1, 200; dupes British, 182–3, 186–7,
  191; and Danzig crisis, 197–200, 204–6
Beneš, Eduard: urged to make concessions
  on Sudetenland, 74–6, 84–5;
  procrastinates, 79; and Runciman, 85,
  107; makes concessions and urged to
  make more, 92, 94, 95, 99, 115, 116–19,
  121; abused by Hitler, 131; 'calvary' of,
  205; biography, 240
Bernays, R., 130
Birkenhead, 1st Earl of, 12
Bonnet, Georges: meets Chamberlain and
  Halifax, 76; and crisis over Czechoslovakia:
  sees British as scapegoats, 99–100, 126,
  fears, 113–14, collapse of nerves,
  114–16; Poles more important than

Russia, 171; and Polish crisis, 188–90,
  205–6; and Italian mediation, 206–8;
  biography, 240
Boothby, R.: 'not to be trusted', 54, 55–7;
  and Churchill, 56–7; and opposition to
  Chamberlain, 91, 150; and crisis over
  Czechoslovakia, 93, 128, 130, 133; urges
  Churchill to 'break' Chamberlain, 208;
  biography, 243
Bower, H., 58
Bracken, Brendan: and Churchill, 57–8,
  129, 130, 153, 203; biography, 243
Braun, Eva, 108
Brocket, Lord, 194
Burckhardt, Carl, 198
Burgin, Leslie, 207
Butler, R. A., 57, 120; views on foreign
  policy, 60, 63, 64; character, 62–3; on
  Chamberlain, 82, 154; on Conservative
  Party, 87; on Halifax, 123; on Munich,
  141; defends Chamberlain's foreign
  policy, 143; 'Infiltrate East. Bluster West',
  144, 164; remains optimistic, 148; thinks
  Government will be widened, 149;
  thinks there will be no election, 152; closer
  to Chamberlain than to Halifax, 161,
  179–80, 184; thinks Halifax determined
  to stop Germany, 173–4; dislikes Polish
  guarantee and Russian negotiations, 192,
  195; talks with Kordt, 194; and Baltic
  states, 198; wants to pressurise Poles,
  200–1; draft message to Hitler, 202–3;
  hopes Italian intervention will stop war,
  207; Churchill's 'vulgar' speech, 211;
  biography, 243

Cabinet, Chamberlain's: anti-Czech, 80;
  and the crisis over Czechoslovakia: hears
  Halifax's views, 92–4, told of Plan Z,
  103–4, told of Berchtesgaden, 111–13,
  warned of French perfidy, 114, divisions
  within, 116, places limitations on
  Chamberlain, 120–1, divided over
  Godesberg, 123–4, revolt against
  Godesberg, 124–8, divided after
  Godesberg, 134–5; and the Polish
  guarantee, 168–70, 172–3; and the